Witi Ihimaera's first volume of memoir, *Māori Boy: a memoir of childhood*, won the general non-fiction section of the 2015 Ockham New Zealand Book Awards. He edited, with Tina Makereti, *Black Marks on the White Page* and published the novella *Sleeps Standing/Moetū* (te reo translation by Hēmi Kelly), both in 2017. *Sleeps Standing/Moetū* was the first te reo/English novel published in New Zealand. In 2019, Ihimaera edited, with Whiti Hereaka, *Pūrākau: Māori Myths Retold by Māori Writers*. It was his twelfth edited work of New Zealand and Māori literature, an unparalleled witnessing of a people's literature since they began writing in English. A full list of Ihimaera's publications prior to 2015, and his biography to that year, can be found in *Māori Boy: a memoir of childhood*.

A hard-working writer, Ihimaera premiered his fourth opera, *Flowing Water*, composed by Janet Jennings, at the Hamilton Garden Festival 2018. He was the writer and presenter of *In Foreign Fields* (John Kier, Wena Harawira, Mike Jonathan), a television documentary screened on Māori Television, Easter 2018. It was his "David Attenborough moment", which saw him visiting and filming Commonwealth War Graves during a two-week schedule in Singapore, England, Israel, Tunisia and Turkey (Gallipoli).

Witi Ihimaera was the recipient of a *Chevalier des Arts et Lettres* in advance of Bastille Day in 2017. In the same year he was awarded the Prime Minister's Award for fiction. He was the New Zealand Writer of Honour at the Auckland Writer's Festival, 2018. Since 2015 he has represented New Zealand literature at festivals in Bhutan, India, China, Taiwan, Canada, New Caledonia and England.

He is the patron and a trustee of Kotahi Rau Pukapuka, a foundation committed to publishing a hundred national and international books into Māori.

Native Son

the writer's memoir

WITI IHIMAERA

VINTAGE

For my grandfather

VINTAGE

UK | USA | Canada | Ireland | Australia
India | New Zealand | South Africa | China

Vintage is an imprint of the Penguin Random House group of companies, whose addresses can be found at global.penguinrandomhouse.com.

First published by Penguin Random House New Zealand, 2019

10 9 8 7 6 5 4 3 2 1

Text © Witi Ihimaera, 2019
Photography as credited on page 448

The moral right of the author has been asserted.

All rights reserved. Without limiting the rights under copyright reserved above, no part of this publication may be reproduced, stored in or introduced into a retrieval system, or transmitted, in any form or by any means (electronic, mechanical, photocopying, recording or otherwise), without the prior written permission of both the copyright owner and the above publisher of this book.

Text and cover design by Katrina Duncan © Penguin Random House New Zealand
Cover photograph: Witi Ihimaera collection
Prepress by Image Centre Group
Printed and bound in Australia by Griffin Press, an Accredited ISO AS/NZS 14001 Environmental Management Systems Printer

A catalogue record for this book is available from the National Library of New Zealand.

ISBN 978-0-14377-303-0
eISBN 978-0-14377-304-7

penguin.co.nz

Contents

Prologue 9
Tamaiti
Boy

Part One 33
Whakapapa
Genealogy

Part Two 107
Tōrino
Spiral

Part Three 177
Te Ao Tūroa
The World

Interlude 269
Mana
Inheritance

Part Four 309
Te Ara Auaha
The Creative Way

Part Five 363
Puāwaitanga
Breakthrough

Epilogue 437
Ahau
I Am

Acknowledgements 445

Photo Credits 448

A Glimpse Through the Literary Whakapapa
The mentors, I never forgot you

CHILDHOOD
Teria Pere, Mini & George Tupara, Tilly Tupara, Winiata Smiler, Mafeking Smiler, Mary and Hape Rauna, Hani Smiler, Miss Hossack, Mr Grono, Mrs Cole, Sister Wortley, Brother Murphy, Bulla, Charlie and Blossom Mohi

LITERARY WHAKAPAPA
Julia Keelan and Te Haa o Rūhia Ihimaera Smiler Jnr, Pei Te Hurinui Jones, Bruce Mason, Arthur Jones, Nicholas Zisserman, Noel and Kiriwai Hilliard, Joy Stevenson, Kāterina Mataira, Arapera Blank, Bill Pearson, Barry Mitcalfe, Ian Kidman, Maurice Shadbolt, Robin Dudding, Te Aomamaka Jones and Pax Jones

ACADEMIA
Bruce Biggs, Ranginui Walker, John Rangihau, Bill Parker, Koro Dewes, Judith Binney, Dorothy Crozier, James Bertram

GISBORNE HERALD
Ted Dumbleton, Jack Jones, Percy Muir, May Gillies, Jean Colebrook

POST OFFICE
Fred Leighton, Tom Martindale, Paul Katene

FOREIGN AFFAIRS
Frank Corner, Ken Piddington

THE WIND BENEATH MY WINGS
Ray Richards

AND MY GRANDFATHER
Pera Punahāmoa

Nā reira koutou kua riro ki te Pō, ka maumahara tonu au ki a koutou. Kia rātou, kia koutou, kia tātou, tēnā koutou, tēnā koutou, tēnā koutou katoa.

"... of all the genres, memoir leads us down more unexpected paths than any other. We think we know ourselves, but do we really?"

Fiona Kidman to author,
6 January 2018

PROLOGUE

Tamaiti Boy

To understand my story, you must listen to the myths of my world, the myths that I was told as a child, more potent and real to me than any Greek or Roman legend. They fed my imagination, shaped my perspective and pointed a way forward.

There is also another myth in my life, the one I told myself about myself.

I created it to avoid telling the real story.

Witi Ihimaera

Chapter One

Māori Boy

1.

At the end of 1959, aged fifteen, I sat School Certificate. I required two hundred marks from four subjects to pass, and that's what I managed. One mark less, and my life might have been entirely different.

The pass may have been the minimum, but as my headmaster Jack Allen said to Dad, shaking his hand vigorously as if he didn't quite believe it, "Congratulations, Tom, well done." Not my hand, Dad's.

"You'd think Dad sat the examination," I said to my mother, Julia, as yet another local, queueing up, slapped him on the back.

"Good on you, Tom," he said.

At that time, Te Karaka District High School was a rural school, which, looking back from the present, existed on the faraway edge of the decile, but a pass was a pass no matter how hopeless the hōri or hick the town. Fifth-form School Certificate was as high as you could go as there was no sixth form. Anyway, that would be pushing your luck. Therefore, despite the usual ambitions I had in common with other boys, such as becoming a jet fighter pilot (we did have one in the family, my uncle Baden), my reality was that I would leave school and help Dad on the farm like Keith and David Wright on the landholding next to ours.

To be frank, although I had not taken to agricultural work as to the manner born, I was fond of farming. I don't know why as there was nothing romantic about working the land. Season after season, doing the same repetitive work. Buying the cheapest stock and hoping that cattle grown on sparse grass would bring maximum gain at the annual sales. In summer, mustering the sheep to move from one paddock to the other. Watching cattle dying in times of drought, that was hard to bear.

Or losing lambs even after we'd pulled them out of their mothers. We'd blow into their nostrils to help them breathe the chill air only to feel the slight shiver in their bodies, the sign of impending death.

Then there were the usual chores that my sisters and I had to do before we caught the school bus. We were up at five to light the fire, get the stove going and lay the table for breakfast. My sisters Kararaina, Tāwhi and Viki squabbled over who would take our baby brother Derek from his cradle, change his nappy and feed him. Meanwhile, morning and night, I shared milking, chopping wood, the occasional slaughtering of an animal for its mutton, and other heavier farm duties with my cousins Ivan, Miini, Kiki, Tom and Uenuku (Banana). And when we returned home from school in the afternoons, there were always other jobs to do: fencing, boiling offal for the dogs, daubing maggot-infested sheep with tar or tending the vegetable garden. Sometimes we did the work under instruction from Dad, Uncle and the grizzled old farmhand, Bulla, who had turned up one day looking for work — and stayed. The three men were weaning us from their care, waiting for us to do the tasks whether they did or didn't ask for them to be done.

Constantly balancing profit and loss put paid to any notion that farm life was easy. However, there was something about the physical nature of farming that appealed to me. There was also the ambition of working beside Dad and Uncle Puku to raise Maera Station out of its dire financial situation; all our livelihoods depended on that. Actually, my mother was probably more committed to the farm than we were, and it wasn't a fantasy for her. She loved the life, really loved it, and because she toiled hard on making the farm pay for itself, my sisters and I tried our best to make that a reality for her.

When Dad bought the landholding, nothing had been done to maintain the quality of grass, and even the pasture we already had was being encroached upon by huge swathes of gorse. I dreamt of modernising the farm so that it was the Māori equivalent of the Ponderosa. I pestered Dad and Uncle Puku about topdressing, upgrading the shearing shed and bulldozing a wide access road to the "Other Side" where the stock was; Bulla, sitting on his horse and rolling himself a cigarette, would listen on, amused.

I must have been an irritant to Dad as he already had these ideas himself. Possessing no capital, however, he maintained the farm the hard way with antiquated machinery and — until that bulldozer eventually materialised — shifted the stock along the narrow track and herded the animals one by one across the swing bridge. Sometimes sheep slipped from the track and, if they got jammed on the bridge, I would clamber across their backs to get them flowing again. One misstep and I would be over the sides falling onto the rocks below.

Every summer, our holiday was to go shearing. Had it not been for the extra income shearing brought in, I don't think Mum and Dad could have kept the farm solvent. Do you know the story about the Māori farmer and the Texan farmer? The Texan farmer, in trying to explain the size of his ranch, says, "If I travel from sunup to sundown I still won't have reached the end of my farm." The Māori farmer sympathetically offers, "Yes, I used to have a car like that." The implication was that the Māori farmer had improved his lot but, in our case, we still had that car.

My grandmother Teria may have helped Dad to buy the farm, but the capital we put into it was our capacity to work hard and the equity was our sweat.

2.

My best subject was English — perhaps that was a portent of things to come. But even though I had vowed to write a book about Māori that would be put in front of every school student in New Zealand, English really wouldn't get me anywhere in life, would it? I had to get real, so, following my School Certificate success, I thought I should begin my career as a farmer.

My parents had other ideas. So did my grandfather, Pera Punahāmoa. I became aware of his plans when, the following year, just before I turned sixteen, he started to come up to Maera Station to talk to Mum and Dad. Regularly. To look me over.

Until dogs savaged them to death, Mum had a flock of beautiful Muscovy ducks. My sisters and I, enticing them with breadcrumbs, were trying to show them the way to the new dam that we had built against the prospect of future drought. I learnt then why ducks cock their heads sideways when you try to get their attention; they can't see you when you are leading them from the front. Finally, however, we got the flock to the water and then the trouble was they wouldn't get out. That's when I saw my grandfather's car arriving. Again.

Pera and I had never got on well — I think he tolerated me. I wasn't one of those grandchildren who ran to him crying "Tolo! Tolo!", the affectionate nickname he was known by. Nor had I distinguished myself on the sports field. Instead, I held back rather than rushed forward to him, cocking my head and looking at him with my Anatolian sideways-smile. Maybe I got that smile from our ducks.

I therefore don't blame my grandfather that he had his favourite mokopuna and that I wasn't one of them. After all, I was not, well, heroic. Have you ever come across any instance in mythology where the least masculine and muscled boy is the gladiatorial hero? Nah. Not that I minded, I already had my champion. She was my grandmother Teria and, until she had died four years earlier, I had no need of her consort.

I know this sounds cynical but, following my School Certificate success, Pera must have seen a cloud of flies swarming above my head and, at long last, come to see what the fuss was about.

Noticing Pera and Dad in kōrero I sensed that my future was being deliberated on and, where Grandad was concerned, that would mean only one thing.

A makeover.

Maybe I wouldn't join the sports champions that our family usually bred, but I had shown I had intelligence and perhaps there was a role for me in his favourite portfolio, the Mormon Church. After all, Pera was a Māori Abraham, having a reputation to sustain. He had joined the church in 1937 and since then, with him as our kin chief, our family had become synonymous with Mormonism; the Whaanga and Smith whānau of Nuhaka and the Going family of Northland were others.

Some Māori had achieved extra lustre by sending their children on missions to the United States. Others enticed the young American missionaries to marry their daughters and stay in Aotearoa.

Not only that, but my grandfather held the Melchizedek priesthood, the highest order of spiritual governance in the church. He particularly embraced the notion that Māori were descendants of Laman and were one of the ten tribes of Israel who had dispersed from the Americas when Moroni farewelled them in AD 421 into the Pacific. It was easy for him to switch from being Ringatū to being Mormon, given the Māori–Israelite connection. He believed that the Māori therefore had a legitimate claim to the blessings of the Abrahamic covenant. We also had the duty to share God's favour and divine protection with those nations of the earth who were still in darkness, the remainder of the descendants of Noah. There were now around 20,000 Mormons in New Zealand attempting to build here a Mormon utopia.

Pera was impelled to look the way of his many mokopuna as he had only just completed an assignment in the Labour Mission Project: building a temple and the associated co-educational Church College of New Zealand — CCNZ — on 215 acres at Tuhikaramea, near Hamilton, in the Waikato.

That's where I came in.

From the very beginning of Mormonism in Aotearoa, Latter-day Saint families desired to send their high-school-age children to a church school. In this they were no different to Roman Catholics with daughters for St Mary's or sons for St Andrew's, or Anglicans sending their children to ivy-clad brick buildings that replicated Rugby or Eton. Mormon families were aided in the dream by Matthew Cowley and, more importantly, David O McKay.

In some respects the college (and temple) could be regarded as McKay's vanity project. The great cause of providing for the descendants of the lost iwi of Israel was clearly on his mind. The temple was the first built in the Southern Hemisphere and, floodlit at night, you could see it from miles away. You wouldn't have been the only car driver who asked, "What *is* that thing?" It looked like a celestial wedding cake with phosphorescent icing, piercing the sky.

Both Cowley and McKay had been intimately involved with New Zealand since the 1920s, and McKay was now president of the church. When the Mormon Maori Agricultural College (for boys only) succumbed to the 1931 Napier earthquake, LDS members had pleaded for something to replace it. Seventeen years later, in 1948, McKay had said yes to the new building project but, this time, it was to be a co-ed institution. Given that he was also resident prophet, seer and revelator, who would argue with him?

Central to this story is that the church based its rationale for a college in Polynesia on a somewhat mind-blowing conceit. McKay had looked at the New Zealand education system and decided it wasn't doing the best job for the Māori people, especially Mormon Māori. Only about one Māori student in twenty left school with School Certificate compared with thirty per cent of Pākehā students; fewer Māori stayed on to do two years in the sixth form. Having had a career in education as principal of the church's Weber Stake Academy, McKay knew the church could do better. He equivocated on the vision only once when, despite volunteer labour, building costs began spiralling out of control. But in a visit to New Zealand in 1955, he was persuaded by the fervour of his flock.

"We will not curtail the project," he said. "We will enlarge it."

High schools were built in Tonga and Sāmoa too, and the three schools were administered by a Mormon Pacific Board of Education under Wendell B Mendenhall. The church loved the people of the Pacific, and they loved their church back.

By the time the co-ed institution was dedicated, a small town called Temple View had risen to service the complex. My grandfather was all fired up about some of his grandchildren attending. The field had been tilled, now seeds had to be planted for the harvest. In the college's first two academic years, 1958 and 1959, my cousins Ivan and Cissie joined 342 inaugural students. They were the first and second eldest grandchildren, but by 1960 Ivan had dropped out; I don't know what happened with Cissie.

As the third eldest grandchild I was the next in the queue. Perhaps I would become the family's ring-bearer, but no way was I made of Mormon clay.

When Mum and Dad became Grandad's proxies I could see from their bright eyes that they were hearing angels blowing on trumpets and the Mormon Tabernacle Choir singing hymns of welcome. Wrestling with so many issues, mainly, self-doubt and, even more, self-worth, made me deaf to the clarion calls.

I decided to head Pera off at the pass. I was joined in my effort by my sisters. Living so closely together, we didn't want to foreclose on Dad's dream and Mum's desire to make our lives on the farm.

"I don't care what plans Grandad might be dreaming up for me," I told Dad, "but I'm not going to go to the college." We were dosing sheep at the time. Lift the head, into the sheep's mouth goes the drenching gun, squeeze. "Nor, afterwards, am I going to take a year off as a missionary and proselytise among the pagans. You need me here and this is where I'm staying."

Cross, Dad took the drenching gun from me. "Your uncle Puku and I," he began, "and Bulla, can manage without you."

"I'm not asking you," I answered. "I'm telling you."

But Dad had made up his mind. Imagining the sheep as me. Lifting up my head. Take your medicine, son.

I thought Bulla, the farmhand, might be on my side, but he wasn't. "Maybe you should go out into the world, young fella," he said to me as we were fencing one day.

I've always needed an older male adviser to ask the harder questions that I couldn't ask Dad — or Uncle Puku at the time — about being male and what a man was. You know, the "What's the meaning of life?" kind of questions that plague you when you're transitioning from boyhood to manhood. Some of those questions involved candid pātai about love, sex and male performance and, while Bulla sometimes answered and sometimes didn't, at least he listened.

"You won't get your answers here on the farm," he would say in the end.

I thought I had won until my mother got in on the act. I actually assumed she would want me to stay at Maera Station too. After all, I was her first-born, the only thing she had ever owned, and she never liked to let me go. But I had misread the signs — always an easy thing to do with Mum. When I had seen her simmering I'd assumed that she was dead against the idea — at the time she wasn't Mormon, although she joined later.

But one day I arrived home from school to find her waiting for me, putting my good clothes out for me on my bed. White shirt, tie, coat and trousers — and she had even polished my shoes.

Mum was looking at the walls just above the headboard and along the bed itself, where I had been scribbling with a pencil. Stories, ideas, random thoughts, small illustrations, some pencilled while I was half asleep. "Your father and I painted the walls white to make your room bright," she said. "What are all these marks on it?"

"I dream about things," I answered. "I write them down." Then, "I thought you knew. You're in them."

Mum looked at me in a strange way, disconcerted at the idea of my cocooning myself, as if in the middle of a spider's web. "Get changed," she said. "You're coming into Gisborne with me."

My mother was thirty-eight, a handsome woman with the strong, open looks of her Ngāti Porou ancestry. She had a habit of lifting her face to the light, which threw her high cheekbones into relief and made you aware of her eyes. Sometimes it was as if her face was a mask and there was somebody else looking out at you from behind it.

Whenever Mum said "Get changed", it wasn't a request. You did it. And if the appointment was important, Mum always dressed formally: hat, coat, gloves and stockings with the seams perfectly straight. Today she was in unremitting black as if she was going to a funeral. Driving down from the farm she was very silent.

We arrived in Gisborne and parked the car outside a handsome colonial house in Cobden Street. The residence bespoke the sturdy merchant prosperity that Gisborne's wealth was built on: diamond window panes glinted and flashed in the light, the porch was wide, and dark green shrubs lined the walkway to it. I made my way to the front gate.

"No, not that way," Mum said. Instead, she led me to a back door and rang the bell. The sound echoed away, away, away into the interior of the house. When the door finally opened, a Māori servant was there. Her name was Maria or Mariah; I will call her Maria.

"Mrs Ogilvy is expecting you," Maria smiled.

We were shown through a hallway into a back parlour. There we waited until finally a thin, wan, Pākehā woman arrived.

"Why, hello, Julia, and is this your son?"

I didn't expect what happened next. After all, the mother I had always known was strong and self-confident, always on the front foot, world watch out. Instead, she became somebody else. She sat with knees together, holding her handbag on her lap, and eyes downcast. "Yes, Mrs Ogilvy."

"He's your eldest?"

"Yes, Mrs Ogilvy."

Now, I don't want you to think of Mrs Ogilvy unkindly. After all, she had accepted my mother into her employ when Mum had first come, as a teenage girl, to Gisborne from Uawa to find work. My mother always said she was very happy to work for the family. Throughout the conversation, Mrs Ogilvy addressed questions to my mother and she proffered the answers with a "Yes, Mrs Ogilvy" or a "No, Mrs Ogilvy."

I couldn't understand why Mum had become so subservient. It was almost as if she had disappeared and somebody else who looked like her and talked like her had taken her place. This was not my mother, but some other passive person — and I didn't like it.

And not once did Mrs Ogilvy address a question to me.

The visit didn't last long. There was no doubt who was mistress and who was servant. Had it not been for the large clock ticking in the hallway, I would not have known that we had been there for half an hour. My mother kept diminishing, becoming a koiwi, a person without substance or shadow.

Finally, Mrs Ogilvy said, "Thank you for coming, Julia. Do take the boy to the kitchen where Maria will have some tea and cake for you." She offered Mum an envelope with some money in it. "For achieving his School Certificate," she said.

"I don't take money from people I don't know," I told her.

Mrs Ogilvy paused, only momentarily. "Do with the gift as you see fit," she said to Mum.

Later, following afternoon tea, my mother pressed the envelope on me. I scrunched it up and threw it on the pavement. As we were driving home, I became angry at Mum. I rounded on her and spoke sharply. "Why did you take me to see that lady?" I asked.

What was her reply? "Now you know why I have come to agree with your grandfather," she began. "You must continue your education, son, I don't want you to be a servant to anyone, man or woman, Māori or Pākehā. Your father and I didn't raise you to help us on the farm — thank you for offering, but no thank you."

Not long after that, she began to leave pens scattered around my bedroom. They replaced my pencils and were a reward, I suppose, and an acceptance of what I would do with them. And the web of words I wrote on the walls began to spread throughout the room.

3.

My mother, my grandfather Pera Punahāmoa and, finally, Dad, ambushed me with their ambition.

They put me back on track for what was to become a career in literature although, of course, none of us knew that at the time. And it wasn't a vocation that followed a straight line; rather, the line would eventually turn out to be as crooked as te waewae whakamuri o he kurī. For instance, in the beginning everyone thought my profession lay in the field of classical music.

Some subtle blackmail was also at play. I hadn't quite paid off the piano which my grandmother, Teria, bought for me; my parents and grandfather let me know that if I agreed to carry on my education they would wipe the debt. A clever move that, playing on my indebtedness, and I could see that Grandad thought he had me in his pocket.

"Teria should never have bought that piano for you," he said.

Throughout our relationship the instrument was not a piano at all. Whenever Grandad saw it, he saw an elephant and, if angry with me, he would always bring it up. Ironically, my mother had also, initially, been irritated about the piano. That is, until I clearly showed some adolescent skill in performance and developed a scholarly interest in music which was at odds with my farmboy aspirations. Assuredly my musical talent, rather than literature, was the driving force behind her wanting me to go to the college; I never asked her.

In the end, I caved in. To be frank, I was warming to the idea.

But nothing is ever easy. I didn't know until later that Mum and Dad, already hard-pressed for cash, were paying for my board and tuition at £40 per term. There were also the costs of purchasing the distinctive school uniform — turquoise blue blazer sporting the beehive as emblem for being industrious, and long dark dress uniform trousers — and my school texts. Yet more debt for me to pay back at some point.

Worse, the college required a medical examination as part of its entry procedures.

Dad took me to see Dr Bowker. Everything was going fine as he put stethoscope to my chest, checked my eyesight, asked me to poke out my tongue and tapped my knees. Then he asked me to remove my trousers and underpants.

Such a simple request you might think, but you freeze. And something that has been waiting in the shadows of the surgery blinks, *just to let you know it is there.*

Ssshh, Witi. You don't want anybody to find out what happened to you, do you?

Sweat pops on your brow. And then something frightening rushes across the floor, rising out of the nightmare world of your dreams.

How sweet it was for me to break your arse.

Rearing above you, the memory poises to strike, the jaws widen and you look into the throat of darkness.

"No," I said to Dr Bowker.

My heart was pounding and I could hardly breathe. I pushed him away and he stepped back, surprised. He went to the door and I heard him talk to Dad.

"Would you like to come in to the room, Tom?"

He thought that I was shy and that with Dad there I would feel more comfortable. But it wasn't shyness, I had no problem showing myself. But not to him.

"Perhaps you can ask Witi to remove his clothes."

This was a Passover I would not survive. If Dr Bowker looked at me, inspected me, he might find out what had happened to me four years previously. And even if there weren't any signs physically, my dear father would know — fathers always knew.

"Please, Dad, don't come anywhere near me."

"What's wrong with you?" Dad scolded.

There was no other choice. Grimly, "I'm not going to the college," I said.

I was already heading for the door. I had to get out of there, I would keep my secret.

Dr Bowker stopped me. "It's all right, Witi."

He looked at Dad, concerned, and then they nodded at each other, man to man.

"I will sign the medical certificate, Tom," he said.

Chapter Two

A Trip with My Grandfather

1.

As it happened, Pera Punahāmoa was travelling in his sky-blue Vauxhall to Tuhikaramea.

Why wasn't I surprised? My gaoler was making sure I would be delivered up to my sentencing and my incarceration. It was only to be expected that I should travel to the first term at the college with him.

"You and your granddad can get to know each other better," Dad said helpfully. "He wants to show you off to all the other workers who built the temple and college." Dad added a sweetener. "You can also help with the driving. Pera isn't getting any younger."

My grandfather had been a popular pakeke, elder, among the workers, living with Auntie Mary and her husband Uncle Hape in one of the labourers' huts near the building site; Uncle Danny and my cousin Ivan were there too. As labour missionaries, they were among many from all parts of the country who signed on for two years at the equivalent of a dollar a week, furnished housing and food provided, to make the dream of raising the temple and school come true. The evangelist narrative had similarities to the gathering of Ringatū workers to build the great Ringatū meeting house, Rongopai, in my home valley, Waituhi.

The story had other epic qualities. For instance, Tuhikaramea was an area of unstable peat soil filled with combustive gases. The workers had to manhandle timber and other building materials across the swamp to the site, and some logs — "sacred trees" — came from distant tribal areas. I couldn't help but be inspired by the stories of the "tongues of fire" when gases from the combustible peat shot blue flames into the air.

"We had to dive for cover, eh boys!"

Grandad actually stayed a year longer than his mission required him to do as Hoki Purcell (Katene), a senior construction foreman at the site, valued Pera's qualities as a leader and inspirational mentor. Pera was already possessed of rangatira qualities; his Melchizedek priesthood, combining the dual position of king and priest, glossed him with extra authority.

I should explain. The Old Testament comes from circa 600 BC but Melchizedek was a priest-king who lived around 2000 BC — before Abraham, before even Moses. Thus, in LDS theology the priesthood (it only occurs in Mormonism) existed from the foundation of the world and, no doubt, will be there at world's end. You have to admit that there's something hugely powerful in the idea that generations upon generations of high-ranking Mormon ecclesiastics exist, anticipating all of mankind's catastrophes and ensuring leadership through them.

In my grandfather's case, there was something that the workers at the Tuhikaramea site recognised in him above all other elders — something of the "King of Salem" as Jerusalem was originally called — that marked him out. Hoki Purcell therefore pleaded with Grandad not to leave.

And, of course, the purpose of the temple — gathering the names of the dead for posthumous baptism — was irresistible to Pera. He believed utterly in the collecting of genealogy, specifically in the Pacific region, and the sealing of Mormon generations to each other for time and all eternity. Today, this work is still carried on by family members such as Auntie Alice and, until he died recently, my cousin Tiopira Rauna. The resultant genealogical work has become indispensable for all people wanting to study their family histories, whether they are Mormon or not.

You'll forgive my biblical phrasing but . . .

And so it was that The Patriarch arrived at the farm where He put the one suitcase belonging to the Sacrificial Offering in the back (the college had strict limitations on what you could take and couldn't). Further provisions including The Patriarch's blankets, foodstuffs such as kānga pirau (fermented corn) and kao (dried kūmara), and medical supplies (He had sugar diabetes) were also made ready for the trip. Only then did the Holy Ark begin its sacred journey to the Godly Citadel.

The few boyhood things that were valuable to me and which I

couldn't take — the usual memorabilia of a Māori child, a toy wooden waka, a favourite comic, a kaitaka (spinning top), some sky-blue marbles (a gift from Teria) and other treasures — I buried in a small tin box beside the lemon tree just outside my bedroom window.

Amid much wailing and gnashing of teeth (mine) I said goodbye to Mum and Dad, my three sisters and baby brother Derek.

"Do your best," Mum said.

I had never left "home". At the moment of farewell, the realisation hit me like a fist to the solar plexus and I could have doubled with the pain of it. Even worse, my sisters started to cry out, "Don't go, don't leave us," and that brought me close, but not quite, to tears. There was a great love between us.

Tāwhi inherited my bedroom. By that time my scribblings and pictographs looked like psychotic spiders had been at work. They had woven an indecipherable arachnid web of smudges, blots and stains. Every now and then, a thread would shoot up to the ceiling. Along the web there were clumps of words, as if my unconscious mind had found flies to feast on and wanted to bind them tighter to the web. According to Tāwhi, there were even stories scribbled on the floor under my bed, you can ask her yourself.

I didn't think that Pera would mind my taking the first leg of the driving so hopped behind the steering wheel.

Well, that only lasted until we were out of sight.

2.

Did I forget to tell you that I was to enrol the next day? Pera, however, had other business to do with whakapapa, gathering genealogy.

Any Māori will tell you what that means. Travelling from one keeper of genealogy to the next. Spending time consulting the various family trees, merging your chart's whakapapa with theirs. There's lots of arguing over names and excitement too when various linkages once thought lost are found. All this happens in a painstaking manner, in other words s-l-o-w-l-y, with doubling back and then further cross-checking just in case. But, mauriora, there's great happiness when the genealogies find moments of synchronicity which prove you *are* related.

Don't forget that all this discovery process takes place over centuries.

And it involves very long Māori names that have to be transcribed accurately and by hand.

The consequence is that time flies out the window as you follow the various trails hither and yon, up maunga and down raorao, here, there and everywhere except where you are supposed to be heading.

Well, that's okay if genealogy is your thing, but I was a healthy teenage boy who wasn't particularly tuned to the multilayered complexities of whakapapa. Apart from which Mum and Dad must have known how unenthusiastic I was about spending time with Pera, so, conveniently, they had attacks of amnesia and forgot to mention that there would be . . . delays. They knew I would have insisted on taking the NZR bus if I had known that Grandad would stop off elsewhere on the way, and they would have been right. Not only that, but he drove very slowly, which meant that we could never escape the cloying smell of rotten corn — a delicacy to Pera, but not to me.

What a great start! I spent the first part of the trip to Whakatāne with the window down and looking out of it. Every now and then Pera would complain about the cold air. If I'd had earphones like they do today I would have put them in. I don't recall that I said one word to him except "Yup" or "Nope" whenever he asked a question. I probably shrugged my shoulders otherwise. The whole thing was a pain, but Grandad kept trying his best to make conversation.

I didn't even know we were going to detour from Hamilton until he told me we were sidetracking to visit Uncle Win, who was first assistant at Rangatahi College, Murupara.

"I'm supposed to start at CCNZ tomorrow," I reminded him, articulating the words carefully and with steely precision.

"It talks," he said, or at least the Māori equivalent. And then he turned a deaf ear to my request that we get to Hamilton as soon as possible after the Murupara detour.

He commanded, and I was held to ransom.

3.

From a look at a road map the best "as the crow flies" route from Gisborne would have been from Whakatāne to Murupara via Highway 30 — and then by way of Awakere to Highway 38. From my recollection, however, that was not the way we went. Instead, Pera drove to Rotorua, where he pronounced that we would be sleeping over.

"At a motel?" I asked.

He looked at me as if I were joking — which I was, as long experience had taught me that Māori were like tortoises. They carried their homes with them. Hence the blankets in the back seat and all the boxes of food.

Thank the Lord we arrived when dark was falling because Pera had decided that we would sleep on the side of the street. He found a place in the middle of what passed for Rotorua's suburbia, close to some public conveniences. In full sight of whoever was walking past, he said grace and we had our dinner on our laps: corned beef and cold kūmara and cordial.

When we had finished kai, "I will sleep in the back seat and you will be on the front seat," Grandad said. But he made sure the keys weren't in the ignition.

I suppose he thought I might take the car for a ride. What . . . with him snoring in the back? At least he was kind enough to let me off the leash to go for a walk. "Ten minutes, then you come back."

By the time I returned to the car from looking at the lake he was already dozing.

Rotorua was not exactly the warmest place on the planet, and I froze my balls off. I spent most of the night tossing and turning, trying to go to sleep. Pera didn't know I was still awake whenever he opened a back door to urinate or to inject himself with insulin for his diabetes. I once tried to get out myself, but he said, "Where do you think you're going?"

I was back on a leash, it was after midnight, and he must have thought I was intending to do some nocturnal mischief.

The interior of the windows misted over and the air was smelly, but opening them gave no respite — rotten egg Rotorua was all around. I remember putting a finger on the front window and scrawling something like WHAT AM I *DOING* HERE and I didn't care if Grandad saw it.

At some time in the early morning I watched the sky lighten, a strange orange and blue, probably because of the sulphurous clouds. And then Pera asked, "Are you awake? Good, we shall begin karakia."

We had some breakfast, more of the corn and kūmara washed

down with his watery cordial, and then, before I could take the wheel, Grandad drove on to Murupara. No way had I been able to change his mind and let me do that — I might go over fifty miles per hour.

When we arrived, my beautiful Auntie Margaret welcomed us and said, "Win is still teaching." Pera told her he was a bit tired so she showed him to a bedroom where he could have a moe to get over the trip.

Uncle Win turned up and he was very cross with me. "Why didn't you do the driving?" he asked. "Dad is tuckered out."

I was always in awe of Winiata. If Dad was Zeus in the family pantheon, Uncle Win was Poseidon. A man of enormous intelligence, he had a BA degree and a diploma in social science at a time when Māori with degrees were scarce on the ground. And his rages could cause storms over the ocean, best to avoid them. So I went for a walk around the burg; it was quite impressive, especially the dam.

Maybe I could jump into it.

The next day Grandad told Uncle Win that he wanted to see some elders who were renowned keepers of the whakapapa at Te Whāiti. Uncle Win insisted that I drive, and Grandad assented, but as soon as we were out of sight he said, "Pull over."

"No, Grandfather," I answered. And while he got hot under the collar, well, while I had the wheel *I* was in command.

Five days later . . . after having visited God-knows-who in the Lord-knows-where, we finally returned to Uncle Win's place at Murupara.

"What are you doing keeping your grandfather out all this time?" he asked. "I was just about ready to call the police." His fury kept vaulting over me, belying the velvet sonority of his voice.

This was all my fault? I decided to smoulder in silence, thinking, Grandad, you sure know how to win friends and influence people.

The next morning, hurrah, Pera told Uncle that he had better get me to Hamilton — but he made it sound that I was interfering with his whakapapa work, which didn't go down well with me — or Uncle Win, who growled me again.

But Auntie Margaret gave us some kai, including some bananas, and we resumed our journey.

Oh no, instead of turning towards Hamilton, Pera kept on travelling down Highway 38.

"So where are we going now?" I asked, cross.

"I want to check on something at Te Whāiti and then go on to Minginui," he answered.

This was another thing about Māori. Apart from carrying their own bedding, blankets and food and not taking the direct route to any destination, they also thought they had all the time in the world. And after all, this was about gathering whakapapa, specifically that of my ancestor Ihimaera Te Hanene Ringarore, the Honey Gatherer, so everything else just went on hold.

And so I was traipsed for another three days among the people of Ngāti Whare, trapped in the tribal lands in the western Urewera, and pulled unwillingly after Grandad as he visited their three marae, Murumurunga, Waikotikoti and Waireporepo. The only compensation was the visual splendour of the beautiful Te Whāiti-nui-a-Toi with its stunning Whirinaki Forest.

Perhaps I could escape and go bush.

It must have been a weekend because when we arrived at Te Whāiti the second time there were lots of kids around. As soon as we stopped they crowded around the car, smiling and talking and asking questions in Māori.

"Is this your car?" "Are you the owner?" "Can you take us for a drive?" "Is that your koro with you?"

I'm imagining their questions as I never knew how to speak Māori and could only just understand it. Almost a century had passed since the Native Schools Act of 1867 ruled that the only language to be employed in the education of Māori children was English. The tamariki of Te Whāiti and other isolated rural communities had dodged the bullet.

In my own village of Waituhi, my grandmother Teria and relatives all spoke the reo despite government's wish to deprive them of it as much as it did their land, rights and culture. For a hundred years the language became an underground movement, one of the largest that New Zealand has ever known. But what about those Māori like myself, displaced to cities and towns where the prevailing Pākehā culture held sway? Regardless of the lack of support, Teria assumed that I — we — my generation would *get it*. When we tried to, though, many of us were punished physically for it. Strapped. Caned. Mouth washed out with soap to rid us of the dirty, unsanitary words.

Great way to affirm a language, folks. And the future of the reo appeared to be dire. In 1961, just a year away, the Māori language would be described by JK Hunn in an official report to the Department of Maori Affairs as being "a relic of ancient Maori life".

Yes, some of my generation's elders urged us, "Kōrero Pākehā," and my cousin, Māori academic Haare Williams, told me that as a young boy he was put on display by his iwi for being such a marvellous child. He recited the alphabet and sang a Pākehā song on his marae — and all the iwi applauded this new wonder — except for his own kuia, his elderly grandmother. She walked up to him and placed a hand on his cheek. New sounds were coming out of his mouth and strange words were humming inside him, auē, how they buzzed and stung.

And then she wept at the ways they were altering the āhua — not just the body politic of Māoridom but also the body of the child.

Some of the children at Te Whāiti ran after us as we drove to our destination — Eripitana marae, where Grandad wanted to pay his respects.

Like my own kin of Waituhi who had built Rongopai in honour of Te Kooti, the people of Minginui had similarly built Eripitana for the prophet — but he had never entered Eripitana either. He attended the opening in June 1884 and he refused to go inside. Not because, as in Rongopai's case, the young generation had decorated the meeting house with extraordinary and revolutionary paintings but, rather, here they had carved a figure of a lizard on the central poutokomanawa. And the ngārara had a wide mouth that was turned downward. Seeing the lizard, Te Kooti predicted that Ngāti Whare would lose all their land but, sympathetically, that their marae at least would remain to sustain the people.

Indeed, when finally, in 2013, the Crown came to apologise to Ngāti Whare for land confiscations, they made their apology at the very marae that had survived their depradations.

After making his homage to the marae, Pera drove on and turned down a dirt road, and we came to a small shack with a cowbail beside it, a fowlhouse and a haystack. He got out of the car and went to the gate and waited. Very soon a man and his wife came onto the verandah and shaded their eyes.

Who was this koroua with the scowling boy, standing in front of their place?

Then they recognised Pera and called him across the threshold.

"Do you want to come in?" they asked me in Māori.

"No, I'll stay here," I replied in English.

There's a photograph of Katherine Mansfield when she visited Te Whāiti in 1907. Who knows, she may have talked to some of my relations. Her gaze though was elsewhere and, out of it, she wrote her short story "The Woman at the Store."

As for me, I folded my arms and waited and waited. At lunchtime, an old lady came out to tell me to come in and have some lunch.

"No," I said, "I've got a banana."

She came out at dinner, by which stage I was so angry I could have combusted on the spot, but I had already made a stand and I decided to keep to it.

"Okay," she said, "enjoy the rest of your banana."

When she went inside, I heard laughter and thought Grandfather and whoever else was with him were laughing at me.

Darkness fell and I drifted off to sleep. It must have been early morning, when the mist was still on the ground, that I heard people saying goodbye to each other. The next moment the front door of the car opened and Pera got in. I pretended to be asleep; I was furious with him. He started the car. Thank goodness, we were finally on our way.

"I know you're awake," he said. "All my whakapapa work is for us, grandson, and that includes you. Maybe, one day, some of it will go in."

"In where?" I snarled.

"That stubborn head of yours."

4.

The following day, we arrived at the college. I knew I would be reprimanded for enrolling at least a week late, and I expected that Pera Punahāmoa would explain that the fault wasn't mine. Instead, he stopped the car outside the office and stayed in the driver's seat because he wanted to get down to the workers' village.

"I'm already running behind schedule," he said. "You can enrol yourself."

I'd been doing it all my life at other schools, what else was new?

I'm fully prepared to admit that I am at fault, not my grandfather, for our broken relationship. However, there were times when he made things worse. *He* was the one who was late for a date?

Some of my other cousins speak so warmly of him, and I only wish I had the same experiences of love and attention from him that they did. But I didn't.

Occasionally I saw Grandad when I was visiting Auntie Mary and Uncle Hape, but we never had much to say to each other. The trouble was that I never knew what he *wanted* from me — well, I did, he wanted my respect and devotion, but I had already given that to my grandmother Teria. Maybe, in lieu of that, perhaps all he wanted was for me to ask him for something, and I was just too stupid and proud to do that.

The farewell was awkward. I didn't feel like saying thanks for the ride. I played it cool and insouciant, as if I didn't care.

"See ya, then," I said.

But as he drove away, I was stricken with terror. I wanted to yell, "Tolo! Tolo! Come back." This was the first time I had ever been away from home and I felt I was being abandoned. My grandfather was the last familiar sign of that world, and he was leaving too. I guess I felt for the first time some sense of love for him or, at least, some sense of need.

Without knowing what I was doing, I began to turn around and around . . .

Where was it? Where *was* it?

A tall Māori man was walking by. I took him to be a teacher. He sensed I was in trouble. He came towards me and, grabbing me by the shoulders, stopped me from my constant revolving.

"Boy? Boy!" He shook me roughly.

I stared at him. "Take your hands off me," I said.

Then I asked him, "Where's Mount Hikurangi?"

PART ONE

WHAKAPAPA
GENEALOGY

Chapter Three

The Demigod, Māui

1.

The great folk hero, Māui, stood between the gods and humankind, not quite one and not exactly the other. He was half-human half-god and his mother, Taranga, aborted him. Thinking him dead, she threw him into the sea. The rich caul that surrounded him was soon carried off by the razoring gulls and fish. And maggots were already hatching from his skin when the great Sky Father, Rangi, seeing the dark clouds of blowflies swarming overhead, rescued him.

In boyhood, Māui was raised by Rangi, who gave him special powers. The Sky Father knew the twilight of the gods was coming. The tribes and tribes of humankind — the progeny of Tāne, god of man and forests — had been growing unruly and ambitious for many years. It was only a matter of time before the gods would leave the world to their great creation and ascend by way of a rainbow bridge to the Māori Valhalla, Hawaiki.

Rangi, however, must have had an inkling that this aborted child could be useful. And so he gave Māui a special role as intercessor between gods and man. He also charged Māui with the creative abilities by which he could manufacture the best conditions for humankind's survival.

Māui's first act upon taking leave of his surrogate parent was a very human one.

He yearned to find out who he was and where he came from. Therefore, godly though he was, he set out to find his decidedly ungodly mother, Taranga, and brothers. Only when he had claimed his humanity did he then set out on his appointed task. He tamed the sun so that humankind would have longer days to live in. He also fished up the many islands of the Pacific Ocean, including Aotearoa, so that we would have homes for our children.

Some people say that the South Island of New Zealand is the derelict canoe that Māui voyaged in while doing his great work. Indeed, when you look at photographs taken from space the island does look like a waka, lying on its side, the elaborate fretwork of its prow half sunk in green glittering waves. Clearly, Māui and his brothers, as well as the pantheon of the gods themselves, were beings of a supernatural dimension.

Maybe they were like the extraordinary star jockeys in Ridley Scott's *Prometheus*.

At the southern extremity of Māui's waka is Stewart Island. Called Rakiura today, it was originally known as Te Punga o Te Waka-a-Māui, the canoe's anchor. If you ever go to Rakiura, you might be lucky enough to witness the incredible Aurora Australis as it floods the sky from Antarctica.

And, of course, the North Island is the fish which Māui caught. Legend tells us that Māui's hook snared itself in Hikurangi Mountain, the first place every morning on the earth's surface to see the sun.

Ah, ko Hikurangi. There, and mark.

2.

The physical description of Māui created of him an amalgam, a Māori golem. Standing between two worlds, the DNA of the gods and humankind twisted him into an altogether misshapen form as if the sperm of one, meeting the human egg of the other, didn't quite know what to do. For instance, one of his arms was reputed to be withered. I often wondered what the consequence was for him when he changed into a fish or bird. When he swam or flew, did his weaker wing or fin make him veer to the left?

The name Māui, itself, happens to be akin to the word for left, mauī. In the pre-macron world that I lived in, I think I can be excused for thinking that the demigod was cack-handed. When I was a boy, although my teachers firmly taped my left hand so that I could only grasp my pencil with the right, I took comfort from that fact.

But perhaps it was Māui's eyes which most signalled his joint inheritance. One was human, but some people say the other was created out of greenstone shards.

Critics thought of Māui as a trickster, but that was because they could see only the comedy in what he did, not the grand design. By relegating him to trickster status they were also implying that he was of a lesser order than their own Celtic, Greek or Nordic gods.

The critics missed the point. They should not have scoffed at Māui's antics but, rather, honoured them. All you gods of Valhalla and Olympus, move over and make room on the paepae for Māui. Why? No matter that Māui was mentored by the benevolent Sky Father, he was from the very beginning humankind's splendid champion. Regardless of an unwitting mother who originally rejected him, or brothers who constantly wished to murder him, he took our side. His wit, intelligence and yes, comic approach, were all put to service in making the world a place for humankind to live safely and comfortably in — why else tame the sun or fish up Te Ika-a-Māui, the North Island, for Māori to live in?

What the Sky Father had not anticipated, however, was that his tasks completed, Māui would continue to take the human side — and challenge the gods themselves.

Chapter Four

Song of the Spiral

1.

And so Pera Punahāmoa left me outside the administration building of the Church College, and disappeared down the road in his sky-blue Vauxhall.

I too make a similar leavetaking. I leave my memoir of childhood, *Māori Boy*, behind and turn to *Native Son*, the writer's memoir. It will be about, primarily, three things. First, the making of a writer. Second, the making of myself as a Māori writer. And third, the magnificent accident of the making of *me*.

Therefore I have a smile on my lips because I will no doubt traverse my literary whakapapa in the same infuriating and impossible manner as my grandfather did when he took me unwittingly and unwillingly looking for his histories, whether I wanted to know them or not.

In traversing these life stories, I will likely elide some personal and historical truths, but that is not my intention. Sometimes, I might be inconsistent, but that is not my purpose either. There might also be some misdirection, I shall own up now, but that will be not because I wish to hide something. Rather, sometimes I will prefer to approach the material in a tangential, Māori way rather than in the accustomed Pākehā, linear manner.

And, of course, as mentioned in the previous volume, the Māori journey has always been to go by the spiral. Indeed, Māori have a saying, "Te tōrino haere whakamua, whakamuri — at the same time as the spiral is going forward, it is returning."

The tōrino makes *me* twirl too. I am not "At the still point of the turning world", as poet TS Eliot would have it. Rather, I am the other, second spiral, spinning on the axis — what Māori call the hā, or breath of life — and intertwining with the first. The two spirals take us forward and they take us back. They take us upward and they take us downward. They take us to and they take us from. They also take us *through*, defying all notions of time: they *will* take us, *are* taking us and *have* taken us — and all in the same moment.

The helices represent our human relationship with time and space. And they comprise the double helix, the symbol of origin, the symbol of infinity. Wherever helices spiral they progress memory by courtesy of their double circularities.

But sometimes, memory is wilful, as it is at this moment, and so the spiral takes me eight years onward from the time my grandfather left me at one threshold — don't worry, we'll return — to the other paepae, the other threshold, that was waiting in 1968.

In that year I answered to the imperative command of the spiral.

I began to shapeshift my own life into that of a writer.

2.

In 1968, I had become a young Māori journalist, twenty-four years old, working at Post Office Headquarters, Wellington. I occasionally spent lunchtimes at Whitcombe & Tombs bookshop on Lambton Quay.

On one walk to the bookshop I saw a man with a gaunt white face and flowing hair and beard, running along the gutter. It was the poet James K Baxter, an apocalyptic sight. As he passed by I felt the turbulence, the disturbance he made in the air.

I liked going to Whitcombe's because I could read books for free without paying for them. One of them was *The Maori People in the Nineteen-Sixties*, newly published that year and edited by Erik Schwimmer, a former editor of the Māori magazine *Te Ao Hou*.

At the time, Māori were one of the fastest-growing populations in the world and we were participating in a second "Great Migration" from country to cities. Some experts considered the rural to urban shift to be as profound as the first migration by canoe from Hawaiki to New Zealand. In 1945, seventy-four per cent of the population still lived in rural areas. However, by 1956 the rural population was down to sixty-five per cent, and by 1966 it was thirty-eight per cent. The new waka — the motor vehicle — had proved an effective carrier of the Maori into a new urban future. The same huge shift in other indigenous demographics was happening throughout the world, but the Māori migration could well have been the largest globally.

Physically, Māori began to move into spaces Pākehā thought they had to themselves, and all of a sudden race relations became of unprecedented concern. Politicians, academics and other thinkers presumed they were looking at a contest which could have long-reaching implications.

Would — or could — a new culture be created, or would the consequences be catastrophic to one or to "the Other"?

The question soon revolved not around how the dominant society could change but, rather, how the Māori could fit in. As far as the reo was concerned, there was no room whatsoever. Racist as fuck? Maybe.

The "Māori problem" was therefore on the minds of politicians, academics and other thinkers, and this was what the essayists in *The Maori People in the Nineteen-Sixties* were looking at. Schwimmer himself wrote on the aspirations of contemporary Māori. Bruce Biggs offered an essay on the Māori language past and present. John Forster wrote on the social position of the Māori; John Harre on Māori–Pākehā intermarriage; Pei Te Hurinui Jones on the Māori kings; Hugh Kawharu on urban immigrants; JR McCreary on Māori population growth and urbanisation; Ralph Piddington on emergent development and "Integration"; Ian Prior on health; James E Ritchie on workers; James and his wife Jane Ritchie on children; Erik Schwimmer again on the Māori and government; and, as a postscript, Ernest Beaglehole came up with some conclusions in his essay on the Māori now.

Binary politics became the name of the game, and people talked about the Māori world and the Pākehā world as if Māori were moving from one to another. I took the same view as Dad: that they were both the same, Māori, world; "the city" was still te ao Māori except that more Pākehā were living in it.

Whether the problem was Māori — or Pākehā — we did have a challenge in making headway. This may be difficult for a younger generation living in the new millennium to understand, but my (Māori) generation, the first to live in cities, had been made constantly aware by our grandparents and parents that we had an overarching destination more important than any personal ambition. Our tūpuna's hopes were encapsulated by the inspirational message which Sir Apirana Ngata, one of the greatest of Māoridom's politicians, wrote in an autograph book in 1949:

> "E tipu e rea mo nga ra o tou ao, ko to ringa ki nga rakau a te Pakeha hei ara mo to tinana, ko to ngakau ki nga taonga a o tupuna Maori hei tikitiki mo to mahuna, a ko to wairua ki to Atua nana nei nga mea katoa." Grow up and thrive for the days destined for you, your hand to the tools of the Pākehā to provide physical sustenance, your heart to the treasures of your ancestors as a diadem for your brow, and your soul to God to whom all things belong.

Tā Api's mantra validated our move — *any* move up, down, ahead, through or out — but required nothing less than the instruction to take our culture with us.

In this specific case, let's look a bit longer at the urban context. Most of our elders, apart from a few such as Eruera and Amiria Stirling, stayed behind. Those Māori who came to Auckland and Wellington were a younger population of mainly working-class families with children under the age of fifteen. Almost seventy per cent of our population was young, and most started to live in sub-urban state houses without a marae in sight — and the hyphen is intentional.

Therein lay the crunch. When you had to get a job in a new society, let alone understand the Pākehā rules, establishing your own culture in it became the last thing on your mind.

One essay in editor Schwimmer's book really spoke to me about how *I* personally could bring our culture into the bigger Pākehā space of the world. Written by academic and novelist Bill Pearson, it had been waiting for me all this time — gotcha. Entitled "The Maori and Literature 1938–1965", the essay contained this paragraph:

> In 1960 Bruce Mason predicted the appearance of a Maori novelist of outstanding talent. I like to share this hope, and am confident that Maori writing will be distinct in its passion, its lyricism and unforced celebration of living.

The New Zealand playwright Bruce Mason had been an earlier editor of *Te Ao Hou*. If anybody had any right to predict a Māori novelist, it was him. Throughout his life Mason put Māori characters front and centre on the stage. His play *The Pohutukawa Tree* had been adapted by the BBC for television where it garnered over 20 million viewers.

No Māori novelist yet?

Something slammed me against the wall. Standing in Whitcombe & Tombs, I recalled as a schoolboy coming across an anthology of New Zealand short stories — but no Māori writer, let alone novelist, was in it. One of the stories about Māori was so poisonous I threw the book out the window, and got caned for it.

The hinengaro, the thought, started to spiral.

The kupu, the words, began to create linkages between myself and the world I lived in.

Here I was in the bookshop and I was one of those Māori *now* that were written about in the essays. I was a statistic, representing the urban Māori generation. The other shoppers were all Pākehā, not a brown face in sight: misery.

And two questions came to me: What would I want these people to know about being Māori? What would I want Māori to know about being Māori?

My brain was racing way ahead into the future. I pondered whether I could be the novelist Mason had predicted! Thoughts sprang quickly around the possibility of writing a novel set in the city I lived in that could explore the pathology of the Māori predicament.

But as I kept thinking, I felt I couldn't do that first off. Perhaps starting with a collection of short stories would be better.

And maybe I should start pre-Wellington, in the time *before*.

A place of loss was a good place to begin from.

I would go back to childhood.

I would start at my village, Waituhi, and use my life as the template for telling the story of the Māori people. Maybe, as I got older, my work would mature and follow the experiences I was having as I traversed the thin strand between earth and sky.

Here, in the place that Māori call Te Ao Tūroa.

3.

I had to ask the permission and blessing of my kuia, my kōkā.

Her name was Nani Mini Tupara. In many respects she was like Māui's adoptive parent, Rangi, except she wasn't a god — or man.

Nani Mini was the one who stood in for my paternal grandmother, Teria, after she died in 1955. She was Pera Punahāmoa's younger half-sister. My father Tom was brought up with Mini by his grandmother Hine Te Ariki Pera and, although she was really his auntie, he called her "Sis". I guess, when Teria died, Mini thought, "Well, Tom was brought up with me, I better bring up Witi now."

Mini had always been in my life, but I guess Teria had been the sky goddess grandmother whereas she was more of an earth goddess grandaunt. She must have known that nobody would be able to displace Teria in my affections; Mini wasn't about to try. My grandmother's patrician appearance, the authoritative way she conducted herself and her thrilling voice had imprinted her indelibly into my memory and imagination. Who could compete with that? But Mini's attributes impressed in other ways and, yes, earth goddess grandaunt sounds right. Indeed, you could say Mini was physically typecast, earthy, open and loving, having the look of a Peruvian Indian and being short, compact and strong with eyes burnt black by the sun. Teria looked after the iwi; Mini looked after the land.

How fortunate I was to have two such grandmothers.

I was visiting Waituhi from Wellington, not long after reading the Schwimmer book, when I made my ambition known to Nani Mini. She was in the kitchen making us a kai and I sang out from her sitting room, "I'm going to be a writer, kui. And I'm starting with a collection of short stories."

"Ka pai," Nani answered. "What's your book about?"

"It will be about Waituhi, about us, but don't worry, the book's fiction." Just in case she didn't know what fiction was, I elaborated for her. "It's not history, it's not real. Instead of using real names, I'm changing them all."

"He aha?" she asked. "What do you mean?"

Oh, the uncluttered arrogant mind of the young man. "Instead of calling Waituhi by its real name, I am changing it to Waipuna and . . ."

This was the difficult part. "I have already written a story about you, but in it you are a lady called Miro."

Well! If Nani Mini had been holding a frypan she would have clouted me over the head with it. And, actually, in the first drafts of the story, "A Game of Cards", I always got confused and called my character Mini in some places and Miro in others.

Nani Mini came into the sitting room. She always called a spade a spade, and she let me have it. "Are you ashamed of Waituhi? Are you ashamed of your iwi?"

Ashamed? The question surprised me. What I was trying to figure out was how to shift non-fiction to fiction, a practical question. Shame didn't enter into it.

"No," I answered, "but this is the way Pākehā fiction is done."

"I don't care if that's the way they do it. You're Māori and you're going to have to figure out how Māori fiction is done."

"That's what I have been trying to do. Pākehā fiction describes people and events that are imaginary and, well—"

"I'm not imaginary." Nani stood in the doorway, arms akimbo and, no doubt about it, she was as real as. "You better remember one thing. Whatever you write, whether it's imaginary or not, it still has the one source, Waituhi. Therefore, acknowledge your work's whakapapa."

She went back to the kitchen to finish off our kai.

"And as far as *I'm* concerned, I don't like the name Miro."

In many respects I should have gone ahead and against Nani Mini's wishes, and created Waipuna. Just as William Faulkner had his fictional Yoknapatawpha County, I would have had the Valley of Waipuna.

But that was what Pākehā fiction did. What should Māori fiction do?

I mulled the question over as we were having our kai. I had to find a place *in between*.

"Okay, Nani," I said. "I'll call Waituhi, Waituhi. And while my characters will be make-believe, they'll live in the valley."

"Make-believe now, is it?" Her eyes widened in puzzlement and, I think, horror. How did you add make-believe, let alone imaginary, people to whakapapa?

But this was how the DNA of my stories started to emerge. Ever since, the people of my fiction have been tied to the genealogy of the village — more or less. I broke the rules by fastening fiction to whakapapa, but I didn't do it wilfully. I prayed really hard as I kept on breaking stuff.

My cousin, writer and teacher Arapera Blank, had an explanation why I got away with it.

"You didn't know any better," she said. "While the rest of us were careful about where we were treading, for fear of breaking tapu and being punished for it, you just went ahead and trod in it. You must have had a pure heart."

There may have been another reason for being forgiven by the gods. When I left Nani Mini's house that day she hastened to a tank in which there was water from the Waipaoa River. She dipped her hands in the water and, as I got into the car, she kept *throwing* it at me. Splashing me with protection.

Drenching me in the love of the kuia.

The poet Bill Manhire has written, "Fiction versus non-fiction is English literature's made-up divide." Had I known that in 1968 perhaps I wouldn't have beat up on myself so much.

Even so, joining fiction to whakapapa would never be easy and I made mistakes. But I owe Nani Mini and all the people of Waituhi for spying on them. Although they soon got accustomed to my sneaking up and eavesdropping on them while they were talking, that didn't stop them from looking at me askance and saying, "We better shut up, here comes Witi-Boy Walton".

Above all, Nani Mini's wise counsel prevented me from ending up with a set of fictions centred on a place called Waipuna instead of Waituhi. In Waipuna, Nani Mini would have been called Miro. Even in my "Waituhi" she was still called Miro. This is why I am including here the following version of "A Game of Cards"

So this one's for you, Nan.

4.
A Game of Cards

The train pulled into the station. For a moment there was confusion: a voice blaring over the loudspeaker system, people getting off the train, the bustling and shoving of the crowd on the platform.

Then, there was Te Haa, my dad, waiting for me. We hugged each other, we hadn't seen each other for a long time. But I could tell something was wrong.

"Your Nani Mini," he said. "She's very sick."

When my grandmother Teria died, Nani Mini took over my upbringing. She rolled up her sleeves, said "Right-o, let's get on with making sure he grows up strong", and became the surrogate kuia that I otherwise would never have had. Everybody used to say I was her favourite mokopuna and that she loved me more than her own children who'd grown up and had kids of their own. She lived across the road from Takitimu marae in the old homestead which everybody called The Blue House. I always thought of it as a museum because it held the prized possessions of the whānau — the feather cloaks, greenstone patu and shields and trophies like the ones for the hockey tournaments which Nani Mini, Pera Punahāmoa and other village elders organised for Māori teams from all over the country. As a child I always used to think that Nani Mini was prosperous but she was, instead, thrifty and knew how to conserve her resources. I wondered why she didn't buy a newer, more modern house. But Nani wasn't thinking of moving.

"Anyway," she used to say, "what with all my haddit kids, and their haddit kids and all this haddit whānau being broke all the time and needing money, what have I got left to buy a new house with?"

The truth was that Nani Mini liked her old homestead just as it was and didn't really care about money either.

"Who needs it?" she used to ask. "I've got my family to look after me, I'm not dumb."

Then she would laugh to herself. But it wasn't true, really, because everyone sent their kids to her place for her to look after! Not for too long. She'd ring up their parents and say:

"When are you coming to pick up your hōhā kids! They're wrecking the place."

I used to like going to Nani Mini's with the rest of my cousins. In particular, I looked forward to Saturdays because that's when all the women would take the day off, and turn up to play cards. Nani loved all card games — five hundred, poker, canasta, pontoon, whist, hearts, euchre — you name it, she could play it.

The sitting room would be crowded with the women. There they'd be, dressed in their best clothes, sitting at various tables among the sports trophies and photographs, the carvings and greenstone. In those days, Māori used to be heavy smokers, so the women would all be puffing clouds of smoke, laughing and joking and gossiping about who was pregnant — and relishing all the juicy bits too.

Nani Mini was always at what was called "the top table", reserved for the best players. Both she and Mrs Heta were the unrivalled champions, and when it came to cards Mrs Heta, whose first name was Maka, was both Nani's best friend and worst enemy.

"You ready to be taken down?" Mrs Heta would ask. "Oh, the cards are really talking to me today."

"Is that so, Maka?" Nani Mini would answer. "We'll have to see about that, won't we?"

The women would begin to play cards. No doubt about it: Nani Mini and Mrs Heta were the queens of the game. They also happened, whenever they didn't have the right cards, to be the biggest cheats I ever saw.

Mrs Heta would cough and reach for a hanky while slyly slipping a card she wanted from beneath her dress. You never saw anybody reneging as much as she did in five hundred — and expecting to get away with it! But her greatest asset was her eyes which were big and googly. One eye would look straight ahead while the other swivelled around, having a look at the cards in the hands of the women sitting next to her.

"Eeee! You cheat," Nani would say. "You just keep your eyes to yourself, Maka tiko bum."

Mrs Heta would look at Nani, highly offended. Then she would sniff and say, "You the cheat yourself, Mini Tupara. I saw you sneaking that ace from the bottom of the pack."

"How come you know I got an ace, Maka?" Nani would say. "I know you! You dealt this hand, and you stuck that ace down there for yourself, you cheat! Well, anā! I got it now! So take that!" She would slap down her hand. "Sweet, eh?" she would laugh. "Good? Ka pai?" Sometimes she would do a little hula, making her victory sweeter.

"Eeee, Mini!" Mrs Heta would reply. "Well, I got a good hand too!"

And she would slap *her* hand down and bellow with laughter. "Take that!"

And always they would squabble. I wondered how they ever remained friends. The names they called each other!

Sometimes, I would go to see Nani Mini when she was by herself, playing patience. That was her game whenever there was nobody around to play with her. And still she cheated! I'd watch her hands fumbling across the cards. I'd hear her say, "Oops," as she turned up a jack or queen she needed, and I'd join her laugh of triumph. "See, mokopuna? I'm too good for this game!"

Nani used to try to teach me some of the games, but I wasn't very interested.

"How are you going to do good things for your people if you can't concentrate?" she would ask. "Here I am, counting on you to get a good education so that you can get the rest of our land back and you're just hopeless, he hōhā koe—"

Not only that, but I didn't yell and shout at her like the women did. She liked the bickering.

"Auē," she would sigh. Then she'd look at me, offer words of wisdom that didn't make sense like, "Don't let me down," or "If you can't beat the Pākehā one way remember that all's fair in love — and cards," and deal out the pack in the only game I ever knew how to play.

"Snap!" I would yell as she let me win.

Now, my kuia was sick.

I went to see Nani Mini that afternoon after I'd dropped my suitcase at home. The koroua, Nani George, her long-suffering husband, opened the door. We embraced and he began to weep on my shoulder.

"You talk to her, moko," he said. "She walked out of the hospital yesterday. She should be back there. It's no use me trying to persuade her; she's still as stubborn as, never listened to anything I say. But you—"

"I'll do my best," I answered.

I walked down the hallway and past the sitting room to Nani Mini's bedroom. The room had a strange antiseptic smell. The window was open. Sunlight shone brightly on the big bed in the middle of the room. Underneath the bed was a big chamber pot, yellow with urine.

Nani Mini was lying in bed. Her pillow was flecked with small spots of blood where she had been coughing. She was so old looking. Her eyes were closed, her face was very grey, and her body was so thin, seeming to be all bones. Even when I was a child she must have been old, but I never realised it. She must be over sixty now. In that big bed, she looked like a tiny wrinkled doll.

Then I noticed the lipstick. Hmmm.

"You can wake up now, Nani," I said sarcastically.

She moaned. A long, hoarse sigh grew on her lips. Her eyelids fluttered, and she looked at me with blank eyes . . . and then tears began to roll down her cheeks.

She took me by surprise. "Don't cry, kui," I said. "I'm sorry. I'm here."

But she wouldn't stop. I sat beside her on the bed and she lifted her hands to me. "Haere mai, mokopuna. Haere mai. Mmm. Mmm."

I bent within her arms and we pressed noses. Then she started to shake with mirth and slapped me hard.

"Snap!" she said.

She started to laugh and laugh and I was almost persuaded she was her own self. But I knew she wasn't. Why do people you love grow old so suddenly?

"What a haddit mokopuna you are," she grumbled, sitting up in the bed. "It's only when I'm just about in my grave that you come to see me."

"I couldn't see you last time I was home," I explained. "I was too busy."

"There's no such thing as being too busy to see your kuia," Nani reproved. "Next time, make time. If you don't I'll cut you out of my will. I'll give it all to Willie Jones, what do you think of that?"

"Go right ahead," I answered. "Willie will need all your cash to pay his fines so he doesn't go to jail."

Willie was my cousin. When I was growing up I always thought that I was the only one Nan Mini talked to about getting an education. Ha, it was Willie who told me she talked to everybody, but I was the only one to take her seriously. Nani liked to spread her bets. That way, one of her cards was bound to do the trick.

"Anyhow," I continued, "I heard Maka cleaned you out in your last game of poker."

"Who told you that?" Nani scoffed. "You know, now that she's old she's gone colour blind. Can't tell a heart from a spade."

She gave a big, triumphant grin. She was my Nani again. The Nani I knew.

We talked for a long time. She wanted to know how I was getting on at university in Auckland. I told her I was doing really well with my studies, which was a lie, because I was seriously brainless and all the ambitions she held for me were rapidly going down the drain. She asked if I had a girlfriend so I made up more lies about who I was seeing and how pretty she was.

"You teka," she said. "Who'd want to have you!"

I brought up the subject of her returning to hospital.

"George has been talking to you," she grumbled. "Well, this is why I came home—"

She showed me all her injection needles and pills.

"I didn't like all those strange nurses looking at my bum when they gave me those injections. I was so sick, mokopuna, I couldn't even go to the lav. Better for George to give me my injections. Better for me to wet my own bed and not their hospital bed."

I played the piano for Nani. She loved "Me He Manu Rere" so I played it for her and we had a sing-along. Afterwards, she held my hands tightly in hers as if she didn't want to let me go, and stared deep into my eyes.

"It's always the women who look after the land," she said, "but who will do it after I am gone?"

When I finally left her I told her I would come back in the morning.

That night the koroua, Nani George, rang up. Dad answered the telephone and woke me.

"Your whaea, Nani Mini, she's dying."

We all rushed to Nani Mini's house. It was already crowded with the other Waituhi families: the Tamateas, Smilers, Waitaikis, everybody. All of Nani Mini's mates were crowded close around her bed. Among them was Nani's rival, Mrs Heta. Nani was lying very still. Then she looked up, saw Mrs Heta and whispered to her:

"Maka . . . Maka tiko bum . . . I want a game of cards."

A pack of cards was found. Everyone sprang into action. The old ladies sat on the bed and began to gossip, as usual puffing up clouds of smoke. Nani George suggested a game of poker in the living room, so all the men trooped in there to do some serious gambling. Wherever there was a table — in the kitchen, on the verandah, anywhere, games of cards started up. The kids played snap in the other bedrooms and, as the night progressed, so did the games, the laughter, the aroha. The house overflowed with card players, even onto the lawn outside Nani's window.

Suddenly, there was a commotion from Nani's bedroom. We all looked to see what was happening. The women had been betting on who would win the best of ten games and Nani and Mrs Heta were neck and neck — and Mrs Heta was squabbling with Nani because it was Nani's turn to deal.

"Eee, Mini," Mrs Heta said, "don't think that just because you can shuffle the pack fast I'm not onto your tricks."

"Quit moaning and start playing," Nani answered. "Well?"

"Dealing all the good cards to yourself," Mrs Heta muttered. "You cheat, Mini." And she made her googly eye reach far over to see Nani's hand.

"You think you can see, Maka tiko bum?" Nani coughed. "You think you're going to win this game, eh? Well, eat your heart out and take that!"

She slammed down a full house.

The other women goggled at the cards. Mrs Heta looked at her own hand. She did a swift calculation and yelled:

"Eee! You cheat, Mini! I got two aces already! Only four in the pack. How come you got three aces in your hand?"

Everybody laughed. Nani and Mrs Heta started squabbling as they always did, pointing at each other and saying:

"You the cheat, not me!"

And Nani Mini said:

"I saw you, Maka tiko bum, I saw you sneaking that card from under the blanket."

She began to laugh. Her eyes streamed with tears.

While she was laughing, she died.

Everybody was silent. Then Mrs Heta took the cards from Nani's hands and kissed her:

"You the cheat," she whispered. "Yes, Mini, you the cheat yourself—"

Mā wai rā, e taurima
Te marae i waho nei?

We buried Nani Mini on the hill with the rest of her family. Yes, Nani, now that you are gone, who will look after the marae? During her tangi, Mrs Heta played patience with Nani, spreading the cards across the casket.

Later in the year, Mrs Heta, she died too. She was buried right next to Nani so that they could keep on playing cards.

I bet you they're still squabbling up there.

"Eee! You cheat Mini!"

"You the cheat, Maka tiko bum. You, you the cheat."

Although, in the version above, I have reinstated Nani Mini, the story is still fiction.

And although some people thought I was a favourite mokopuna, she had many favourites. She bought a blue bus to accommodate them all and drove around Waituhi picking them up — her grandchildren and any others she happened to come across. She took them to the morning kids' movies in Gisborne and, afterwards, off they all would go to the beach to have a fish and chips lunch.

In "A Game of Cards", there might not seem to be much resonance in Mini's character and relationships. You can blame the limitations of the Western short story form. It caused me to simplify what you saw of Mini and to compress the story's events. This was made more so because the story was initially written for radio where the reader's voice provided the nuance or layering.

The radiance of the story, for Māori, lies in the symbolism. The Waituhi Valley has within it a meeting house of staggering beauty called Rongopai. The meeting house was built by Ringatū adherents of the Prophet Te Kooti Arikirangi. It is a painted meeting house, and among its many stunning motifs you will find playing cards. For instance, the club signifies the King of Clubs, the sovereign or saviour yet to come. The diamond represents the mauri whenua, the life force of the people and land.

Thus Nani Mini's leadership is expressed through the cards. She is like Hera Ngāpora, the senior wife of King Tāwhiao, who wore a kākahu on which all manner of card games were printed. The garment signified not only Ngāpora's mana but also alluded to global knowledge outside her immediate realm.

I like to think of "A Game of Cards" as being the Queen of Hearts among my work. Ever since it was published, it's been my calling card. And my beloved Nani Mini, well, let's just say she has always been my trump card in the pack.

5.

Pounamu, Pounamu references our most prized jade and hints at the association with Māui.

If you hold up a piece of greenstone to the light, you are looking through the greenstone iris of Māui's glowing eye. What you will see are what Māori call the roimata toroa, small dark flecks floating in suspension, representing tears. Some people think of them as the tears of the albatross, but they are also the tears of Māui.

I like to consider the collection as equivalent to William Blake's *Songs of Innocence* (my second collection, *The New Net Goes Fishing*, was, by contrast, my songs of experience). With its publication I fulfilled the promise I made to myself as a boy at Te Karaka that I would write a book about Māori and it would be put in front of every school student in New Zealand — whether they wanted it or not. Today, the collection remains my most innocent, yes, Blakeian, work bubbling up from the pure spring of childhood remembered.

While some critics winced at the Māori patois, that was how I heard the people at Waituhi speaking.

Pounamu, Pounamu became more than a book. It became the source, the blueprint or, rather, "green print" of all my work. It's my Rosetta Stone, and it goes together with my "Cave Drawings" as I sometimes like to think of them — those scribblings and pictographs of gods, monsters and spiders — that I covered the walls of my bedroom with at the farm on the Whakarau Road. Indeed, *Pounamu, Pounamu* became a potent demotic text. *The Whale Rider*, for instance, had its precursor in the story "The Whale". The character of Simeon in *Bulibasha* comes straight out of "One Summer Morning". And, of course, that first novel of mine, *Tangi*, was modelled structurally, aesthetically, melodically and linguistically on its prototype story "Tangi".

Today I still use *Pounamu, Pounamu* to evolve literary ideas, devices and techniques and to help me move back to the hieratic, the Māori source of my work, the original mauri — or life force — of it.

I was twenty-eight when the book was published, young when you think of how old most authors are when they publish their first books. Although I had every right to kick up my heels, do forgive my ungainly flight.

I got better at it though, in some ways, could never surpass it.

Chapter Five

That Was the Year That Was

1.

You might think my reaction, when Pera Punahāmoa deposited me at the Mormon College in 1960, was homesickness.

On the contrary, throughout my life, whenever I arrive at a new location I always orient myself. I learnt that from Julia, my mother. For her, as it came to be for me, Mount Hikurangi became the centre of my universe. When I give myself up to the centrifugal forces of the double helix I find myself reconnecting to the umbilical and the rich placenta of the mountain. There had once stood Te Rāwheoro, the Great Library of Uawa, whose equivalent lay in Alexandria.

And it is easy to understand why Mount Hikurangi would hold such potency, and become the source of my mythos. How could it not, when it was already a significant location in the universe? Not only was it the first ancestor all Ngāti Porou paid homage to — "Ko Hikurangi te maunga" — it was also the place where Maui's canoe came to rest when he fished up New Zealand.

Every morning, Hikurangi is the first place on the planet to be draped in the dawn. I have always known that if I am ever lost anywhere, even in the inky starlit blackness of space, all I need to do is wait for the rising of the morning sun.

A flash of light, a twinkling in the distance. *Ah, ko Hikurangi.*

2.

In 1960, the next question was, "Where to from here?"

Here was a relative term that did not only apply to *where*, but also to *when.* I hope, therefore, that you won't mind if I look at the question in terms of the history of the times and, in the first instance, give you quick snapshots of the wider geopolitical view.

At the time that I stood at the college's front doorstep, New Zealand's population was 2.4 million and we were approaching the peak of the baby boom, with 65,746 births to come within the year.

1960 marked the beginning of a new frontier. Prime Minister Walter Nash was in power at a time of relative affluence and suburban growth and Joe Kiwi had discovered his voice. Remember the catchphrase Rugby, Racing and Beer? During the first year I was at the college the Federation of Labour took a deputation to Nash in opposition to the exclusion of Māori from the All Blacks team to South Africa. In spite of a 153,000-signature "No Maoris No Tour" petition and one of the largest public protests New Zealand has ever seen, Mr Nash sat on his hands and the tour went ahead. In South Africa, in the first re-match against the Springboks since 1956, the All Blacks suffered their only series defeat.

"Serves them right," we muttered.

By the end of 1960 Mr Nash was out and Kiwi Keith Holyoake was in. He's the one, so it has been reported, who, when asked what his favourite book was, said, "*The Origin of the Species* by Charles Dickens."

The country was a member of the British Commonwealth, and young New Zealanders traditionally regarded the UK as the destination for our OE (overseas experience). However, the Mother Country was making decisions of its own about its international relationships; the door to their market for our wool and butter began to close as they eyed up the EEC as a more compatible partner. Flash forward to 2019, and Brexit looks somewhat ironic, eh.

But we were discovering new personal freedoms. The fuse was lit for the growing habit of getting out and protesting. The sixties were synonymous with protest, for instance, over environmental issues concerning the Manapouri hydro scheme. French atmospheric tests of nuclear weapons were sounding alarms, as did the visit of the American submarine, the USS *Halibut*: was she nuclear-powered or nuclear-armed?

Māori protest also stepped up. As writer Rowley Habib once quipped, "In the 1960s, Māori started to come off the sleeping pills and wake up to what was really happening around us."

Television started broadcasting in 1960 in glorious black and white; only to Auckland, however, and just for three hours to begin with. Although the rest of the country had to wait, all of a sudden world events previously reported after the fact in newspapers or the day after on radio were now coming to us, virtually as they happened, every six o'clock in our sitting rooms. The consequence of television's growing omniscience was that both time and space were diminished. Events happening on the other side of the world were brought closer to *us*. For instance, I can still remember those grainy images of arguing faces: American President Dwight D Eisenhower, and Russian President Nikita Khrushchev, frightening, because they held the world's balance of power.

Eisenhower and Khrushchev presided over the period known as the Cold War, the jockeying for world supremacy that started immediately following the power vacuum at the end of World War II. The Americans led the Western Bloc (the United States, its NATO allies and others) and the Russians led the Eastern Bloc (the Soviet Union and its allies in the Warsaw Pact.) Since 1947 there had been High Anxiety. Outbreaks such as the Greek Civil War, Berlin Blockade, Chinese Civil War, Korean War, the Hungarian Revolution of 1956 and the Suez Crisis blossomed around us. By 1960, at the height of the Cold War, John Kennedy had come to power (and to presidency the following year), but feint and counter-feint kept bringing the world to the brink of another war. Many problems lay under the surface, ready to explode at the slightest spark. We all nervously watched as the fight was brought into our homes on "the box".

Halfway through my first year at college, an American U2 spy plane was shot down over Russia, and in response Khrushchev walked out of the Paris Summit, which had been called to discuss nuclear arms control. Our teachers asked us to pray for peace — would it be world war this time?

Closer to home, the Vietnam War was in its fifth year. It was known by the South Vietnamese as the American War (an echo of the Māori Wars). The US government viewed its involvement in Vietnam as a way to prevent a communist takeover of South Vietnam. It was part of a wider American containment policy with the stated aim of stopping communism's spread. And the Yanks were pressuring their allies under the ANZUS Pact to join them.

The sixties hadn't really started swinging yet, at least not in New Zealand, but The Beatles, The Rolling Stones and The Who were fair set to take over the long domination of the charts by my beloved Black singers.

A Good Keen Man by Barry Crump, his first book, was published in December 1960; Barry would have been pleased at the appearance of the movie adaptation of another of his novels as *Hunt for the Wilderpeople* in 2016. Even better was that the *Weekly News* began to serialise my eventual mentor Noel Hilliard's novel *Maori Girl*. I wrote from the Mormon College to Mum to save every copy of the magazine, which was delivered by rural mail to the farm; she was not to use it for wrapping the rubbish in.

You'll forgive my final entry but I've always had a passion for flying boats. The last commercial passenger "clipper of the skies" landed in Mechanics Bay, Auckland, and the Coral Route — from Auckland to Fiji, Sāmoa, the Cook Islands and Tahiti — was over. In 2012, I made a special trip to visit the long-abandoned refuelling station at Aitutaki.

A shift of the imagination, and one of those stunning craft skimmed the lagoon and, lifting, headed back into the past.

Chapter Six

Alma Mater

1.

Follow me now as I cross the threshold of the Church College of New Zealand.

The man who rescued me was Brother Elkington, and he was a dorm master. Married to Elsie, he was revered and beloved as "Uncle Jim". Tall and austere, he had an idiosyncratic way of talking, misplacing words and saying things around the wrong way, but somehow you got the meaning.

"We get you enrol," he began, "then leave your suitcase to the dorm and tea time just about the bell."

I was still a bit traumatised, but somehow I managed to cope with the overpowering sweetness of the female staff in the office. "Why, welcome Widdee, we've been waiting oh golly ages for you to turn up, we are sooo glad to see yew."

Over the next couple of years I grew acclimatised to this typical American effusiveness from stateside teachers, but disliked it in the locally employed Māori staff. Bedazzled by American ways they flattened their vowels and affected the usual mannerisms like chewing gum and cracking it, crack crack double crack. They had gone to sleep in the night next to an alien pod, like in the movie *Invasion of the Body Snatchers*, and in the morning had become one of *them*.

If I sound belligerent, that's because I was in no mood for intimacy. I was on the brink of walking out and hitchhiking home to Waituhi. But Uncle Jim calmed me down by showing me around the burg.

Other alumni have recorded their arrival at Temple View from Tatapouri, Tikitiki, Taumarunui, Te Hauke or Timaru. Crash landing on another planet in a galaxy far, far away springs to mind, and so does battling through a fierce snowstorm somewhere in the Himalayas and discovering a serene Shangri-la.

In my case, I heard actor Pat Boone singing, as he did in the teen movie *April Love* (1956), about being young and wishing on a star. Boone was the poster boy for Middle America, bright blue eyes and glossy skin and with a smile full of even, gleaming white teeth.

There was nobody at the time more apple pie than Boone. Every wishing star, he promised, shone just for our generation — and there, shining in the rays of *my* star, was my own special destiny. God had decided to lift a middle-class White American campus town from any Midwestern state you care to name — Utah, Montana, Wyoming, Colorado, Kansas or Oklahoma — and fly it over the rainbow to Aotearoa. And here, God — or rather President McKay — had decreed that for His chosen Māori people the American system of education would prevail, not the New Zealand system which was giving them a fail.

Alice may have fallen down a rabbithole; I fell straight through a CinemaScope screen onto a 20th Century Fox movie set. Landing smack bang in the middle of an Americana wonderland I saw across the road Lucy Ricardo at the door of a bungalow saying goodbye to husband Ricky who was on his way to the office. Down at County Hall, Deputy Sheriff Barney Fife was kindly tipping his hat to old Aunt Bee and helping her across the street. Dobie Gillis in jeans, sneakers and Ivy League jumper carried Thalia Menninger's books to school. She was gorgeous and blonde — so was Dobie — and her girlfriends all had braces on their teeth.

Definitely not Te Karaka.

Roll cameras and *action*. What first impressed was the intensity of colour, the heightened reality. The faculty houses were not just white, but *white* white ultrabrite. They comprised a staff compound on one side of a wide boulevard set amid green manicured lawns. A teacher in GI sunglasses drove by in a gleaming *red* red left-hand drive Cadillac with huge spaceship fins. He was Dr Wendell H Wiser (all the American teachers had initials for their middle names); at his bungalow with its acreage of deep-pile lush carpet, senior "stoodints" met to talk about political science. For supper we were served delicious angel cake by Sister Wiser. She could have stepped straight out of a *House & Garden* magazine, immaculate in her apron, not a hair out of place, red lipsticked to perfection and exuding poise and charm. The cake, whipped froth, exploded my tastebuds with sugar.

Second impression was the spatial layout. The campus was also white *white* Kolynos white. It looked as if it had only just come off some celestial drawing board, and it kept the sense of timelessness — functionality and beauty, as well as divinity — to the very end. On the school side of the boulevard across from the administration building were the classrooms, like a stairway down the slope — or up the slope if you preferred imagery that was heaven-bound — again so bright you needed sunglasses on a glaring summer day.

We were a college not a high school. Our motto was *Kia Hanga Mo Tonu Ake — Build Now for Eternity,* and we were, literally, an American institution in New Zealand and equivalent to an American secondary boarding school. If you were a New Zealand third-former enrolling at the college you entered as an American eighth-grader. By tenth grade you could, if you wished, sit the inferior New Zealand School Certificate or, at eleventh grade, the equally minor New Zealand University Entrance. Whether you did or not, when you completed four years' post-primary work you received an American diploma at a ceremony full of gowns and mortarboards, with a parade, pomp and ceremony — "Gaudeamus Igitur" and all that — and prepared for university studies. Not at just any old crummy New Zealand university but, rather, Brigham Young University or the University of Hawai'i.

As I followed after Uncle Jim a bell clanged, change of class. Starry-eyed students came out of the library building. Most of them were Māori or Pacific Islander — at least seventy per cent of the campus were Polynesian, all dreaming of obtaining a scholarship to study in the Land of Uncle Sam. But the Pākehā students were the ones who caught your eye. Mainly the teenage *Brady Bunch* children of the American teachers, their better diets and healthcare — not to mention their being the Anointed of God — had put them on a different evolutionary pathway to the rest of the human species. Tall, clear-eyed and fresh-complexioned, they even walked differently from us.

Whatever their origin, Māori, Pākehā or Other, the students were all versions of the aforementioned Pat Boone and Shirley Jones — his co-star in *April Love*. They couldn't have been more perfect, the ideal mannequin collegiate kids. The girls were all swinging ponytails and cute checkered pinafores and bobby socks. Some of the boys sported crewcuts and turned-up shirt collars; others wore ivy-league polo shirts and penny loafers and asked girls if they could carry their books to the next class.

Not a scowling rebellious Elvis in sight.

I watched some of them sashay and saunter down towards the splendid and soaring David O McKay auditorium. Was I looking at State of the Art? Was I *what*.

The building held an auditorium, a theatre, a gymnasium and a heated indoor Olympic-size pool. The gym's centrepiece was an indoor basketball court with raked seating on all four sides. With those kinds of facilities, no wonder that CCNZ basketball, rugby and swimming teams were already building a formidable reputation in interschool sporting competitions. News items in the papers and on radio regularly detailed school successes at district and national championships.

The swimming pool had floor-to-ceiling windows and the water sparkled like the Koh-i-Noor diamond. My first glimpse through the wide upstairs observation windows onto the pool was of a young man, Simeon Cruse, preparing to dive. I swear Simeon was at the same level as I was. When he saw me he grinned, winked and, romantic and graceful, turned nonchalantly to execute a perfect swan dive into the water.

The college also had a laundry, barbershop and butcher shop. The three girls dorms were situated as far away as possible from the boys dorms for obvious reasons. And Sister Garlick, the stern but loving matron, must have put soporifics in the kai to neutralise the boys' sex urges, as I can't remember any girl getting pregnant.

Campus was home to approximately seven hundred students per year, twenty-two senior faculty members and up to seventy or so supporting staff. On the north side, landscape artists had created an amphitheatre looking over a huge sports ground with track and field, rugby and soccer grounds — no hockey field . . . yet.

2.

The tour over, Brother Elkington took me to "A" dorm, one of three boys dormitories, and showed me my room. Two bunks, beds top and bottom, three beds already taken.

I was still trying to get over the shock of my orientation. If my descriptions are hyperbolic, excuse me, but the unadulterated splendour of the college invited such excess. Damned if I wasn't impressed. Not, however, I hasten to add, cowed.

"When did you last had a wash?" Uncle Jim asked. "You smell like rotten corn. Boy better shower. I come back ten minutes to take go eat."

He left me pondering my fate. Gloomily I surveyed the stalls.

My next orientation happened, uninvited.

Any boy who has been to a boarding school will tell you the first lesson you learn is that there is always an alpha male. How you come through the encounter with him determines your relationships with the rest of the group.

I was showering, shampooing my hair and my eyes were closed. I heard some of the boys arriving back to the dorm. I found out later that they had just finished basketball practice.

All of a sudden, I felt somebody yank me, brutally, out from beneath the water. In the hierarchy of any college boarding school, the sports jock always gets the priority. "You're finished, bud."

I'm trying to recapture the breathtaking stupidity of a sixteen-year-old boy. You can blame the mood I was in, and that I still had shampoo in my hair. But there was more. Being assaulted like that. Manhandled as if I was of no worth, and without my permission.

Five years earlier. Sshh, Witi. *You don't want anybody to find out what happened to you, do you?*

You are eleven. You are out shearing with Mum and Dad and your sisters. You are sleeping with your male cousins in one of the quarters. Halfway through the night you feel someone touching you and you wake with a start. Come with me.

One of the shearers stands there. His eyes are gleaming. He puts a finger to your lips.

You know this man. He smiles, hypnotic. You are trusting. You follow him out into the night, along the banks of the Waiapu River and into the woods. The moon makes beautiful patterns on the pathway, lighting a way to the hut through the dark.

He opens the door. Nobody will find us here. *Unbuttons his trousers.* Stroke me, Witi. *And, then, suddenly he hisses and it is as if something has leapt out at you, a ponaturi — an ancient webbed creature — from a nightmare sea. He strikes. Chops your windpipe. Pushes you face-down into the mattress. Rises above you. Pulls your pyjamas down.*

Panicking, you struggle. No.

Time to break your arse, cousin. He forces himself into you. The shock takes your breath away. And then all you can feel is his slamming into you.

You have never felt such pain.

I saw red. Somebody else in the shower stall.

My brain connected me to the time I had been anally raped. Ripped to pieces by the painful encounter I had ever since lived in fear that I had been scarred internally or externally. There had been so much blood. Dad had been there when Dr Bowker had wanted to make his medical examination. I had refused. No way would I reveal any scars to them both.

And now, somebody had *touched* me. Were boys laughing at me?

I recovered sufficiently to understand what had happened — the school jock and his mates in possession of the shower room — and my rage mounted. For apart from anything else I have told you, I have never tolerated bullies or bullying behaviour. I am like my mother, who one evening confronted a man who was giving his wife a hiding. Even today, whenever I read of another case of bullying in the newspaper or hear of a young person who has committed suicide because of cyber bullying, I can't stop the anger that brings me immediately to boiling point.

What I did was a provocation, I know, but in those days I acted spontaneously.

I didn't give a damn. Nor did I care that the school jock was twice my height and size. I went to the shower and turned the cold tap off. Whoever the bastard was who was in it, he yelped and came out fast. Stepping back in, I started to wash the shampoo out of my hair. I expected to be yanked out again, but not to be demobilised by a blow to the side of the head. What I planned was to make a good fight of it, but this was a king hit. I staggered to the side of the shower and tried to protect myself from the rain of blows and kicks to my head and stomach.

Uncle Jim saved me by arriving. He took in what had happened.

"You senior boys, hurry up, kai start soon."

He stayed with me while I recovered. I heard the jocks laughing and showering. The bell for dinner sounded, a shrill clanging invited the lords of the flies to dinner. They had all gone when Uncle Jim took me along the corridor to my room.

He patched me up and then, "Get dressed," he said. "You better have special meal with me and Sister Elkington. Boy know he deserve that beating. Better learn to get on. Take the chip off the shoulder."

"Which way is the dining room?" I asked.

I had enough sense not to accept a privileged kai and be marked out as somebody who was a pet.

The cafeteria was full with students. Young men and women, laughing and merry. I must have made quite an entrance. Not only was I the perennial new boy who didn't know anybody, but my eye was black and my lip was split.

I looked for an empty seat. Saw one. I was on my way to sit in it before I realised that on the opposite side was the boy who had brought me down in the shower room, with his mates. It would have looked too obvious if I changed direction.

"This seat's not taken, is it?" I asked. "Good," I continued before anybody could answer.

I sat down. I don't think the boy opposite believed that I would be so foolhardy; I didn't believe it either. But what was I to do? And if my appearance was putting him off his food, be my guest.

Staring around, I waited for my food to arrive. A plate with two sausages, a splotch of potatoes, carrots and peas, then another plate with raspberry jelly and ice cream, and a glass of orange cordial.

"You can have as much bread and butter as you want," the server whispered. "Though what you really need is a steak for that eye."

The matron, Sister Garlick, with her pet dog Suzy, could never understand why we always topped our meals with bread. "The menus have been scientifically evaluated by the best American dietitians as providing the exact amount of nutritious values and calories required for growing boys," she scolded us.

I could hardly chew. I looked at the bastard and thought, You were brave enough to yank me out of the shower with just your mates around. Try yanking me out of my seat with everyone looking on.

Auē, I was not to realise that our next encounter was just around the corner. After dinner there was mandatory study period. After that, evening prayers, where Uncle Jim introduced me to the other boys. Then time for bed.

Life suddenly got a whole lot worse when I saw among my three room-mates that my brutish assailant was one of them.

You'll understand why, therefore, I count my surviving as a male within a society of young boys the main triumph of my time at the Mormon College. Yes, I even survived the alpha male. How? He may have thought I was a smart-aleck third-former; after all, with my slight stature I looked like one. But I was saved from constant thrashings by the fact that I was a senior and that my qualifications from Te Karaka District High School vaulted me to twelfth grade, above him and his mates. Apart from which some of the boys at the college were cousins, some not so closely related but influential, like Wi Smith, who was the Student Court judge and Boysie Parata, who put the word out that I wasn't to be messed with.

Things got a lot more interesting when the bastard and I discovered we were distantly related. Whether he or I liked it or not, he stepped down and so did I. We learnt how to tolerate each other.

3.

Looking back, the thrashing I got from the bastard and his mates is a painful clarifying vantage point from which to look at my two years at the college.

Every such crossing of the paepae poto of life is fraught with challenges, and mine was probably more violent than most. I had to rise to the tests and survive, for there was no escaping the college's society. In my village of Waituhi I had taken iwi and whānau relationships for granted; so too, in Gisborne, my friendships at primary and intermediate.

In early adulthood, however, I learnt that I must seek it and, if I wanted to advance it, earn it. I found this difficult because as much as I wanted friends, farm life at Te Karaka had given me the habit of always relying on myself. The enforced separation from the family I loved, and the farm life I loved — not to mention Waituhi — created within me a huge sense of longing and loss that I had to live with. I was deeply in love with my family, my whānau, although that love was in recognition of all its flaws and ruthlessness.

I was, however, also on the cusp of manhood, those years of being sixteen and seventeen crucial to all of us. They were the years when we exited childhood, the time when all boys learnt not to cry. How we negotiated those years, and our success or otherwise in doing so, would set the pathway for the rest of our lives.

I had chosen to do so at Church College of New Zealand, although "chosen" wasn't quite the right word. More accurately, I had been placed within a co-educational context which put me in a community of young men and women with different and competing desires. How would I cope in my relationships? The proximity made me grow up, to test myself against others, to develop as an individual. Previously everything had to be on my terms — as old as I am now, it's upsetting that I still conduct my relationships this way. At the college I had to face the challenges that burst around me and negotiate them.

Not only that, but the context was a religious environment where our behaviour was prescribed. I could not have picked a better — or worse — location, if I tried, to orient myself towards manhood.

And there was the other matter. I was a boy trying to escape from the self that he was, who had decided to take on the Māori version of our surname — Smiler became Ihimaera, as if that alone would create another person.

First things first. Get rid of the attitude.

Next, develop the gift for friendship.

Chapter Seven

In the Land of the Latter-day Saints

1.

Picture this:

A bitter Waikato morning, and 5.30 morning prayers. The moon and sun conspired to be in the sky at the same time, conflicting discs, one fiery, one wan.

"Time for boys to go mahi do," said Uncle Jim after the karakia.

The college was a self-sustaining school producing its own fruit, vegetables, dairy products, poultry and meat. Uncle Jim was referring to the jobs all students did, mostly in the mornings from 6 to 7.30, in the cafeteria, office, or on the farm.

As a newcomer I was assigned to the *other* job with the ground crew. Some of the fields of peat swamp had to be "cleaned" of organic litter, so out we trooped, into a cold that made you feel so brittle you might snap in two. Low-lying fog covered the ground, unleashing pungent smells as if from an adolescent boy's dank and odiferous armpit.

And so we would begin, pulling out the sticks and branches which the peat, ever churning, delivered up from underfoot.

Yes, we also had to dodge eruptions of gases. You developed a second sense, heard a slight phut-*fart* and made like a GI in Vietnam who had tripped a mine. Otherwise one of those tongues of fire just might ignite and lick, as Americans would say, your *ass*.

Most mornings, in the early light, young visiting American elders played gridiron on the sports ground; Kiwi boys could never be persuaded away from their loyalty to rugby.

"Down. Set. Hut one. Hut two. Hut three."

The elders also had permission to play basketball in the gym until school began. While boisterous and sweaty in gridiron and basketball, they underwent a transformation when you saw them next. They proselytised in pairs, grave and intent young men always in sight of the other. Perfectly dressed in white shirt, tie and black suit, into Hamilton they would ride in bicycle convoys to go about God's business.

And then the college piano and organ teacher, Brother John Murphy, heard that there was a boy, just arrived at college, who was good at the piano. Before I knew it, I was taking music duties and lessons with him — and out went my job with the cleanup crew. While I missed the work, my first sight of Brother Murphy and Sister Boyack at Sunday church services playing "Come, Come Ye Saints" on the gigantic pipe organ made me salivate. Sister B pedalled like crazy, coaxing enormous grunts, groans and orgasmic squeals from the beast, barely keeping it on the road.

Did I want to drive that baby? Man oh man, did I what.

Indeed, most of my peers at college remember me as the school's star organist and pianist. They called me Liberace or, more dire, Fingers. Sometimes I was called in to give Brother Murphy or Sister Boyack a spell. But I blotted my copybook when, during one service, I impishly interpolated into "Come, Come Ye Saints" a less-than-heavenly song called "See You Later, Alligator". I thought I'd escaped notice but I hadn't and, although Brother Murphy would have forgiven me anything, Sister B was made of prim and more formidable stuff. She banned me from all further interference with the organ. Up to then I'd enjoyed blasting the congregation with the volume, making the floor quake (everybody hold your hats) and trying to bring the roof down.

I was forced to concentrate on the piano — Haydn, Beethoven and Mozart — where Brother Murphy became starry-eyed about my talent as a classical pianist. (I was very good at sleight of hand. One music examiner wrote of my performances, "The student uses the pedal in a most artistic way, letting it achieve tonally what his finger work should be doing.")

After one lesson, I stopped by the gymnasium. The American elders were at play and I realised that they were not much older than I was, maybe by two or three years. I felt a shiver of apprehension that I only had that much time before — if all went to my grandad Pera's plan — I would go on a mission.

One of the boys cajoled an opposing elder to take the ball off him.

Come on pal, make my day, you are my *bitch.*

He stretched, sighted and took the shot. In that moment of the ball's release, he became a vision of American wholesomeness — and the inspiration for Glen Harper in my novel, *The Uncle's Story* (2000).

2.

I know now, though I didn't know it then, that I did most of my growing into manhood at college — and this forced me into confrontation with the church's fundamentalist beliefs: the sanctity of the body; the relationship between man and woman; and one's relationship with God through the church. Why would I have expected otherwise? After all, I was at that powerful age when I was on the cusp of physical and emotional maturity — and I hope that I have conveyed the moodiness of the young man I was becoming.

This is why, in this memoir, I will be tracking my development not only as a Māori and a writer, but also as a man — and the decisions I ultimately made about manhood, and Measuring Up To Manhood. After all my sexuality was as much part of the helices of the spiral as everything else.

I will therefore, on your behalf and mine, make no apology for being a normal testosterone-filled young boy. For some strange reason, the seniors of my generation — not just Mormon, but also Māori and Pākehā — seemed to think that the natural urgings and voluminous secretions of teenage boys and our bodies were unhealthy. Therefore there were a set of prohibitions about what we could do and what we could not do, and what could be seen and what could not be seen. What was chaste and pure, and what was unchaste and impure.

Our physical responses were spontaneous, we could do nothing about it. "Blue balls" was the term that described the state of being in such constant sexual excitement that your testicles hurt, they were fit to bust. We had our own coded behaviour, flashing a secret smile, *It's okay,* to the boy who had a helpless boner sticking out of his pyjamas at morning prayers.

No use trying to hide being, well, normal.

One boy could never do that. I'll call him Peka, but I nicknamed him

King Dong. He was the boy who cured me of having any penis envy. Somewhere, someone would always have something bigger, so why worry about it?

Nights were filled with erotic dreams that sometimes were relieved unconsciously by what were called nocturnal emissions, or manually, which was shameful. I guess that's why, one night in the first semester, all the boys were herded into the David O McKay auditorium. None of us knew the reason. I was around the middle of the audience, and when our principal, Californian educator Dr Clifton D Boyack, husband of Sister B, ascended the stage we all stood. He wore a grim expression.

"College, sit," Principal Boyack called. "And keep your arms folded, so that they can be seen at all times."

Folded? Oh-kay.

Principal Boyack introduced a guest speaker. I can't remember what his name was, so let's call him Dr Darol K Johansen, I think he was a scientist in juvenile antisocial behaviour. Once introduced, Dr Johansen began a fire and brimstone lecture, to wit, "Cleanliness is next to godliness, boys, and God can see into the heart of every unclean youth. He can see *all* delinquents, everything that you do. Don't think that He can't. You must *save* yourselves."

Dr Johansen pounded the lectern, and we quailed.

"For the sake of your future wives, boys, do not deplete yourselves by *self-abuse*."

Imagine an assembly of over three hundred, patrolled by teachers and stunned to silence by the lecture. Meanwhile the male faculty nodded at his every point, looking us in the eyes and daring us to disagree.

"Every time you give in to your lust, your body needs two pints of blood to replace it. If you feel Satan urging you, think of God. If that doesn't work, think of your dear mother or your sisters. And if that doesn't work, have a cold shower."

Dr Johansen scared the living daylights out of us. Wow, two pints each time you whacked off? That meant six pints if you were relieving yourself three times a day . . .

And then Principal Boyack made the fatal mistake of asking, "Are there any questions, boys?"

I foolishly suggested one. I was the new boy, I was a senior and I was trying to be helpful. The habit of provocation had always been my downfall. Standing, I said, "Perhaps, Sir, Dr Johansen could explain what self-abuse is."

The school sighed audibly, hanging on the lecturer's answer.

"Why," Dr Johansen answered, growing scarlet, "it's . . . masturbation."

Few of the boys would have known what *that* was either. So, later, Elder Steve Hemi was despatched to the dorm to explain.

More was to come. The Powers That Be must have decided to reboot — and a second assembly was called. The auditorium lights were full blazing. Teachers patrolled the aisles. A film flickered on the screen full of bees buzzing around stamens and pistils, diving into the flowers and pollinating them. There were also shots of frogs croaking and hopping around and making a jelly substance from which, in fast motion, tadpoles spilled out. Ten minutes later, and the film was over.

Principal Boyack heaved a sigh, and nodded that the assembly could be dismissed.

"So?" I was sitting next to Sid Haig from Tokomaru Bay.

It was his droll delivery and crossed eyes that undid me. "Sex instruction," he said.

I couldn't help it. I was a farmboy after all. Nothing could stop me from laughing and, later, ending up with Sid in detention.

For a boy growing into his sexuality, you'd assume that a church school would be the most repressive environment to live in. The fact was that our entire society was repressive and, well, at the Mormon College, at least they *tried*. The truth is, we all had to muddle our way through to who we are today. Some of us managed. Others didn't. And of course, sorry Mum and Dad, some of us had long left virginity behind.

In that first term one or more of the boys caused an epidemic of what was known as crabs. The tiny parasitic bloodsucking wingless little beauties (*Pthirus pubis*) hopped and skipped a trail through the dorm. They required us to line up to be inspected by Brother Elkington.

"Okay, Brother Smiler," Uncle Jim said when it was my turn. There he was, sitting on a chair at groin level waiting with a magnifying glass. "Down your trou, turn around, bend over and give me your best smile."

3.

On my first holiday back at Te Karaka after first term, I got off the NZR bus in the township to find Dad, my sisters Kara, Tāwhi and Viki, and little Derek there to welcome me home. Kara was the first to tell me the news that our mother was pregnant, which, for a teenage boy of sixteen or a girl of fifteen, as Kara was, was most disconcerting — and Derek was eight years old now.

"How could they?" Kara wailed. "What will the kids at school say?"

Dad tried to derail my own view by asking, "Where's the boy we sent away?" I was a changeling child, and growing fast.

"You should get the snip, Dad," I growled at him, but I wasn't irritated for too long because, although I sometimes wanted to cut the umbilical to him, he could never take the hint. For instance, within two weeks of my starting at college he had turned up on his way to a Māori golf tournament. I saw him standing outside my class looking in, holding his familiar fedora in his hands. I said to the teacher, "Can I be excused a moment?" I went out and asked, "What are you doing here!" I was worried that something had happened on the farm.

"I never realised," he said, "until you left, how much I would miss you."

"Did you get our letters?" my sister Tāwhi asked. My sisters and I were like puppies sniffing each other, and they were jumping up for me to pat.

My attention was still on Dad. Whenever he had the mind to do it, he would say to Mum, "I'm going to see my son," and he would turn up unannounced, wherever I was. It was my sister Kararaina who organised an early warning telephone call, "Get rid of all evidence of illegal activity," she would say, "your father is due to arrive on your doorstep at any minute."

And then I turned to my sisters. "Yes," I answered Tāwhi. I think I had told her at some point, perhaps in a telephone call home, that mail call had been pretty lonely when everybody else's name was called out but not yours. After that, every two weeks, without fail, the letters had begun to arrive; carefully written by Tāwhi, and she must have dragooned Kara and Viki to write too. The ones from Viki were very sweet.

"Dear bruther, How ar you? We ar well. The cat had kittns in the siting room. Mum was cross. The Roos chased me, I wish Dad would put it in the pot. Love Viki."

I was puzzled that the one person I most wanted to see wasn't there. "Didn't Mum come with you?"

"You know what she's like," Dad said. "She told me to tell you she'll see you back at the farm."

My mother was Dad's helper but sometimes, when the male triumvirate of Te Haa, my Uncle Puku and Bulla got too much for her, she would go off on her horse and cut scrub so as to keep the gorse from claiming more of our grass. Once she started she never liked to put down her axe until the job was done.

The male trio would finish work at 5pm, but not Mum. "Your mother's still out there," Dad would say to my sisters and me when we arrived back on the school bus. "She's left the usual instructions to you to start making dinner."

My father always said that Mum chopped scrub like a man. He sometimes left the axe unsharpened to see if that would slow her down. They had a game going with that blunt blade. Sometimes she would chop a certain patch of gorse and then give the hatchet to him and say, "Now you cut out the same amount of scrub in the same time, with the same axe."

As soon as I was home at Maera Station, I immediately changed out of my good clothes, saddled my horse Stupid, took my own hatchet and some bread and water, and rode across the river to join Mum.

Don't get me wrong, I had just discovered on arrival that she had done something which put me into a psychic spin. She had painted my room completely with fucking yellow paint, proving that she could be as wilful and self-destructive as I was. All the stories that I had written on the walls, the great skein of words, had been obliterated. There was no trace of any of the kupu or sentences beneath.

"Bring your mother back," Dad said. "She shouldn't be doing hard work in her condition, and it's getting dark."

I heard the chopping sounds even before I saw her. There she was, halfway up a slope, going hell for leather, scything the earth, chopping the sky. My turning up didn't stop her rhythm. I stood level to her, raised my axe, and soon I was felling the scrub in unison. Even though she was carrying Gay Kathryn, my sister to come, her swelling belly did not stop the swing of the axe and, well, I guess that Gay just had to go with the flow. Indeed, Mum was typical of Māori expectant mothers. They kept working, no such thing as being "in confinement".

Chop, pull the gorse away, chop. Swing, baby, roll.

I didn't stop until Mum did. "So," she said finally, wiping the sweat away, "you're home then."

"Yes," I answered. I handed her the bottle of water I had brought with me.

She drank some, "Ah, water, wai ora, the gift of life." Grinning, she flicked some at me and, in a glance took me in. What she saw caused her face to become shadowed, withdrawn. She looked closer.

Sometimes my mother saw things in me that I never knew were there. And there were other times when I would hide myself from her searching gaze — the way that she could, like a dream swimmer, come upon my hidden fears — before she flushed me out. She knew that as much as I had been reluctant to leave the farm, part of me had decided that going to the college was a good way of escaping her, and of escaping myself too.

"Don't look at me like that," I said to Mum. "And couldn't you and Dad find something else to do at nights?"

"You've been in a fight, haven't you?" she asked.

"Yes," I answered.

"You better get your father to give you some boxing lessons." We started cutting scrub again. Then her voice curled around my heart and squeezed it. "We should never have let you go," she said.

Manhood came at a sacrifice not just for me but for everyone else in my life. And when my mother said "We" she really meant herself. Pregnancy may have made her reflect that day on me, her first-born.

Later, as we were burning the gorse I looked at her and saw her wiping the sweat and tears caused by the smoke billowing across us both. She would, eventually, have to let me go.

No, that's not quite true. Both of us would have to let the other go.

"Why did you do it, Mum?" I asked her.

"Do what?"

"Paint my room."

"It's not your room, son. It's Tāwhi's now. All those spiders. And all *that* world. Don't you like the colour?"

I couldn't blame my mother for being pragmatic. How was she to know that those spiders' webs, as she called them, were an expression of a creative unconscious reaching forward into the future?

When we were back at the farm, I left the dinner table early, lit a lamp and stood at the doorway of the room, trying to map my memory back over the walls. It worked for a while, the universe of words reappearing. They swirled out of Te Pō, sparkling cosmic clouds, merging into one another, the scripts trying to find coherence, phrasing, sentencing . . .

Failing that, the stars started to burn, galaxies flaming.

And the kupu began to wink out.

4.

A few days later, after a long afternoon of branding cattle, your father teaches you how to box. Or, rather, both he and Uncle Puku decide to give lessons to all the boys — you and your cousins Ivan, Miini and Banana. The first you know about it is when they announce that there will be another family sports day.

All your uncles had been sportsmen as young men, and Dad, Winiata, Puku and Michael had won trophies in rugby, hockey, wrestling, track and field . . . and boxing. From somewhere Dad finds two sets of ancient boxing gloves, so decrepit that when he shakes them moths fly out. He, Uncle Puku and Bulla construct a boxing ring on a dusty piece of ground.

"This is only an excuse," you say to Mum, "for Uncle and Dad to boast about their prowess as boys. Why does this have to be so public?"

You are hot and sweaty from holding down calves as your father applied the Maera Station brand. The smell of the seared skin is acrid in your nostrils. The bawling of the calves echoes in your ears. Your cousins and you, in turns, face off against one another. Ivan and Miini are heavier and more muscular than you are. The three men are having the time of their lives giving advice.

"These young fellas," Uncle Puku says to your father, "they have nothing on us, eh."

And Dad says to you, when you hit the dirt yet again, "Looks like you're going to have to lead with your head, not your hands — so you better start thinking up tricks to give you the advantage."

His suggestions on the day are to throw dust into your cousins' eyes, or talk to them so rapidly that they can't concentrate.

"You could always put them off by doing a fart," Bulla adds.

Over the years the tricks have become more sophisticated.

Your father's voice is the one that wings to you through the years from that makeshift boxing ring.

"Get up on the balls of your feet. Look your opponent in the eyes, they will show you what his action will be. Keep moving, weave; if you stand still you're easier to hit. Don't let your guard down, arms up, up, higher, higher. Wait your opportunity. Now lead with your right! I said right, Witi! Oh, I forgot, you're cack-handed, eh, then with your left! One two three jabs then let him have it with your right! Go, you little beggar, go!"

You would have done anything for your father. He scored you with his brand, seared you with his love.

And after the boxing lesson you decide to dig up the small trunk you had buried before you left for the Mormon College. You knew that you had dug a hole for the chest next to the lemon tree outside your bedroom window, but you can't find it. Maybe one of your cousins had seen you burying it and dug it up.

You thought that some of the texts you had written on the wall might be in the trunk. The box has moved, just as you have moved. You think that, had you been able to find the chest and open the lid, inside would be . . . a lost paradise perhaps. But you will never know. Later, you discover that earth moves and you now like to prefer to think that the box is somewhere near the small stream in the front of the house.

However, the stories . . . ah, the tales and narratives that might have been part of that paradise, have moved into your memory.

That's where they will be regained.

And in many ways, you have come to look upon the boxing lesson itself as being like the making of your career as a writer. Up on the balls of your feet, constantly on the move, waiting your opportunity.

Doing it all, like Māui, with a bias to the left.

Chapter Eight

Left-hand Drive and a Collision with Grandad

1.

By the end of 1961 I was on a high. As referred to earlier, John Kennedy had been elected President of the United States and the whole world *lifted*.

The years of Camelot began.

At the college I had learnt the gift of friendship. I have to admit, however, that I masqueraded a bit by pretending I was a sheep when I was really a wolf in fleecy clothing. Although baptised a Mormon and brought up in the church, I had my reservations. Those reservations still exist, but I am still a Mormon, go figure that one out.

I knew enough of two books of the faith — the Holy Bible and the Book of Mormon — to be able to pass. I already abided by the Word of Wisdom, sort of, and it was only when I was confronted with the intertextual Pearl of Great Price that my faith was truly tested; I'll come to that later. I traded on the college's goodwill and was let into the paddock to frolic and play with the flock.

But I resisted as much as I could, the touchy-feely stuff, the buddy-buddy putting of arms over your shoulders and the squeeze-squeeze handshake that promised friendship forever. You either beat 'em or joined 'em.

In my case I chose resistance. While most of my friends at school soon succumbed to the seductive Americana, I became impossibly clipped in my diction and kept as much distance as possible. How was I to know that only doubled the palsy-walsy attempts from all those baby blue eyes yearning for my attention?

The college, too, masqueraded a bit when it underwent New Zealand government inspection and became fully registered as a *New Zealand* educational institution. But did the college change its American teaching practices? Dr Boyack, the college's first principal, simply batted his own baby blues at New Zealand authorities, but kept on doing it Uncle Sam's way. On a preliminary visit to New Zealand he had observed several local high schools and was shocked by what he considered to be outmoded educational methods. And his successor, Dr Wendell H Wiser, blissfully maintained the clear American bias. For instance we attended semesters not terms. And an elected student-body government replaced the traditional prefect system.

Over the years I have come to realise that CCNZ's educational — or, rather, alternative — approach acted to my benefit. In particular, I was able to get out of the trap of the New Zealand provincial system. As those Muscovy ducks realised when they finally reached the dam on the farm and couldn't believe their luck, neither could I.

Indeed, I can still remember the shock of my first English literature class when, instead of being taught Mansfield, Sargeson or Curnow, I was introduced to Henry David Thoreau, Ralph Waldo Emerson, Walt Whitman and Emily Dickinson. Who were they?

American semantics was also in, so out went the *Oxford English Dictionary* and, heresy of heresies, in came *Webster's*.

Our literature teacher was Sister Elsie Wortley. She was a handsome woman, big-boned, who wore rimless glasses, and her hair, braided, was curled on top of her skull. All of the senior teachers were American and had been brought in by way of a very clever manoeuvre.

A skilled strategist, Dr Boyack had noticed the nationwide shortage of secondary teachers in the country and used this to his advantage. Loath to take New Zealand teachers from New Zealand schools he made a gesture that appeared (to our unsuspecting bureaucrats) to be magnanimous. He employed a core staff of eighteen Americans who arrived with their families on the SS *Mariposa* in January 1958 — and Sister (and Brother) Wortley were among them.

Sometimes Sister Wortley was so beatific you had no problem visualising her as one of those intrepid Mormons who trekked with handcarts all the way from Carthage, Illinois, to Salt Lake City, Utah. What was a small sea voyage but an extension of that epic pilgrimage?

She once began a class with, "Thoreau said simplify, simplify,

simplify, and every sentence that he himself wrote was the perfect example of his perfect art."

I sat goggle-eyed listening to her with Ray Solomon, Mere Kururangi, Lamia Hooper, Rewiti Brown and Edina Coulston.

Her voice often caught with unconscious drama as she quoted from poetry and story. She communicated absolute heartbreak or transcendent hope, lifting you up and gently setting you down.

Something of a shock was to be taught within a lecture-theatre format, with Brother William C Carr roaming around the raked auditorium and giving his lesson extempore. He taught us history and, forgetting that he was in New Zealand, began with Abraham Lincoln and the Declaration of Independence.

His lingo took a bit of getting used to. When he spoke of a period he really meant a full stop, and so on. And when he asked his usual question, Barry Smale, Iris Whaanga or Lloyd Te Ngaio — well, all us Māori students — would duck for cover.

The question was: "You've all done your homework and read the chapter of our text assigned for today?" There was a *New Yorker* cartoon that expressed the futility of the question. It showed a doctor saying to a man without hair and seeking a cure for baldness, "You have only one hope and that's reincarnation."

Nevertheless, Brother Carr would carry on with determined optimism. "Great, then close your textbooks, put down your pens and let's discuss the Gettysburg Address and its impact on the democratic principles of government of the people, by the people, for the people."

Whaa-at? Nevertheless, Brother Carr would try to draw us all into the debate, gently quizzing us to argue the subject in an interactive way. Actually, he became somewhat worried that students weren't keeping up on our homework requirement — he never questioned our incapacity to rise to his level — so he taught us a neat little trick called speed-reading where you read down the middle of the page rather than from side to side.

I still speed-read; friends watching me today sometimes accuse me of "not taking it all in".

You should have seen the textbooks we studied from! Especially those for Brother Morris Athay's general science class. No wonder boys like Waka Haig or Albie Te Maari carried the books of their girlfriends

Marie Hapuku and Terry Osborne to class. The texts were big buggers, curriculum packages five hundred pages plus, bearing evidence of the money put into education by the US Federal Government and private organisations such as Carnegie, Ford and Rockefeller. This was education as a social enterprise, with publishers such as Ginn & Company, Addison-Wesley, and Holt, Rinehart & Winston driving it.

The books were like American cars: left-hand drive, Cadillac with fold-down roof, two-tone tyres, aerial and other fancy doodads — and not quite right for New Zealand roads. They were workbooks with copious illustrations, questions and end-of-chapter sections that encouraged you to mind-map out of the text.

Whatever the class, the emphasis was not only on what you were taught during classroom hours but what you learnt during study hours. The library, therefore, became the hub of the college. One of Sister Wortley's first lessons was an introduction to the Dewey decimal system. As librarians will know, the Dewey system was an American book-navigation network. Sure, the college's holdings contained the historical literary works of the British Isles such as Shakespeare, the Irish poets, Thomas Hardy and all, but it disdained contemporary twentieth-century English literature for American.

Being culturally biased, the Dewey system meant that poor old New Zealand literature was way down somewhere on the library's branching whakapapa.

Not that I minded; I was constantly looking up the works of Sister Wortley's favourite author, Willa Cather, such as *My Antonia*, *The Song of the Lark* and *Death Comes for the Archbishop*. When Sister Wortley saw that I loved literature she encouraged me to read F Scott Fitzgerald, John Steinbeck and William Faulkner.

JD Salinger's *Catcher in the Rye* didn't mean as much to me as it did to American students, but when Harper Lee's *To Kill a Mockingbird* was published in the 1960s I responded to Scout's dilemma and the hanging of an innocent Black man.

I may have been bedazzled by it all, but the downside of an American curriculum meant comparatively few students passed the New Zealand public examinations. As a consequence, the college was unfairly criticised for its low pass rates for University Entrance. We were, however, low socioeconomic Māori students to start with and we had to sit the examination, whereas other schools were privileged with accreditation.

2.

It must have been around this time, while on holiday again in Gisborne, that I bumped into playwright Bruce Mason in the Gisborne Public Library. Tall, rangy, head tilted upward, he was the first real writer I had ever seen and I couldn't stop myself. "You're Bruce Mason," I yelped, surprised that he would be there in our hick town.

At the time, while he was known for his play *End of the Golden Weather* (1959), his first breakout success had been with *The Pohutukawa Tree* (1957). He had also been brave enough to call out Shakespearean actor Sir Donald Wolfit on what he considered a less-than-stellar tour of New Zealand; Wolfit had even made it to Hamilton, declaiming his scenes from Shakespeare across the footlights. In the darkened theatre we were a rapt audience who didn't know any better.

What Bruce Mason made of the eager young pup who bailed him up in a corner and panted all over him in a one-way conversation about God-knows-what, I shudder to think.

My relationships expanded when I packed my hockey stick in my bag and returned to the college with it after the holidays. I realised that if you played basketball, baseball, rugby or swam you would be part of the élite. You also qualified if you were into boxing, wrestling, rowing, track and table tennis. Brother Merrill Boothe was the typical American phys-ed teacher and coach, so tall that he didn't have to jump to make hoop with the basketball.

As a student, you were in The Vikings, The Knites, The Sadsacks, The Kiwis — or you were on the out. You either made the team or else you were a spectator. Mine had never been a passive personality, and standing on the sideline or sitting in the bleachers was utter boredom. And while hockey was not even played at the college (though non-American sports like cricket and soccer made the cut) a boy's gotta start somewhere. I therefore found other friends who played hockey and were as irritated as I was at being sidelined from school sports glory.

"Let's start up a team," I said to my friend Michael Pratt and cousins Rangi Te Maari, Hori McKenzie, Graham Smith and Lucky Walker.

We began to meet after classes had ended, found a vacant space at the far end of the sports arena, and started to fool around with the ball.

Very soon I realised we had enough players, eleven, odds and sods of various experience ranging from excellent to hopeless, to make up an incompetent but valid boys' team.

At the beginning, the only competition to be had was with the girls' team, which sometimes came down to practice. Maria Haeata knew me from the Māori hockey tournaments, and she was aware that playing practice games against a boys' team improved their form. While some of the jocks laughed to see us playing against the girls, I didn't mind. Dad was always getting my boy cousins and me to play against the village women's teams to help their game, so what was the problem?

I thought Pera Punahāmoa might help us — after all, he was the coach of the girls' team. I'm not blaming him that he didn't; after all how could he help, and for what purpose? And I had never asked him for anything so there was no reason to start.

Even so, there was no doubt that we needed a champion, somebody at the college in a top position who could put our case to the senior sports administrators at the school. I found that person in a tall, gangly American teacher, Elder Glen A Horspool. He owed me, as I was the rehearsal pianist for his student musical, *Julie*, the finale of which had, from what I recall, a snake up a tree that menaced the titular heroine. She was saved from it in the nick of time by the hero — or some cockamamie climax like that.

I asked Elder Horspool straight out, "Sir, would you take us on? We want to play schoolboy hockey against other schools in Hamilton."

You won't find our team listed in the yearbook for 1961 (the first entry for it is 1962), but you will find intimations of my clear attempts to create a college boys' hockey team on page twenty-eight of *Te Rongopai*, the end-of-year yearbook:

> Our music maestro, Witi, has given all who listen to him play the
> piano and organ a greater appreciation for the classics through his
> interpretation and dexterity at the keyboard. His artistic nature extends
> past his hands — it reaches into his heart and into his head and emerges
> in the form of poetry and prose. Witi also won honours for the school
> through his outstanding ability on the hockey field.

You'll have to trust me, therefore, when I say that I became captain and Elder Horspool our first coach, and our school hockey team was born.

Well, it would be great to say that we were a blazing success which surprised everybody — but in that first season we started out losing and kept on losing. Elder Horspool didn't know anything about hockey and so he didn't know how to coach us either. After a few more losing games, though, he started to worry about our (or his, or the college's) reputation and came up with some surprising strategies.

"You know, Widdee," he drawled, "I see some similarities between hockey and American football. They both have eleven players and what you call the circle is what we would call the end zone. And when you score a goal, that's what we would call a touchdown."

I looked at him, puzzled. Who was this idiot?

Elder Horspool began to sketch on the ground the play for an American football team on the offensive. I remembered what Dad had always told me about the Maori Agricultural College, which in the 1930s had been an earlier Mormon school in New Zealand — and that their rugby team had benefited from having American coaches. Maybe I should stop rolling my eyes at what Elder Horspool was saying and hear him out.

"So, Widdee, you are the centre forward and you usually try to win the ball and take it forward. But I want to change your position to quarterback or, rather, centre half. And I want Lucky, here, to take your position. Now . . . Lucky . . . when you win the ball, I don't want you to take it forward. I want you to flick it back to Widdee. Once you've done that, I want you to run up the centre and wait. Now, Widdee, you are the brains and the intelligence, you direct the play. You also have quick release, you don't hog the ball to yourself so, depending on your decision, fire the ball out to the wide receiver, either the left flat Rangiora or the right flat Hori. It's up to those guys on the wing to take the ball up the field and draw your opponents to stop them. And then, when it's time, they should fire the ball back to any of the eligible receivers but, most of all, send it to Lucky, he's the best we've got. And you take the touchdown, Lucky, got that?"

Again it would be great to say that the turnaround in tactics improved our game, but if you looked at the scores you could see that we were still losing. However, that doesn't tell the entire story because . . . we were going down by fewer points! Say, from 21–3, to 18–6, and then to 12–8 and so on. And even though we didn't really understand Elder Horspool when he shouted sideline instructions, "Z out, flanker right!"

or "Quarterback option, go left side of defence!", somehow we got the idea.

The team definitely improved when Tommy Taurima became the coach and we started to attract strong players such as Arthur Selwyn and Lloyd Phillips. We began to win the occasional game. But I'll tell you what, being on the losing team was more fun than being on the winning team. I never felt dispirited; rather, there was a greater sense of achievement.

We started as the underdogs, we remained the underdogs, but I will remember forever walking off the hockey field on a cold Waikato morning feeling more alive and victorious than I ever did when we won.

But, you know what? . . . The lack of my grandfather Pera Punahāmoa's support for our team catches in my craw. I brood about it so much, I just can't get over myself. And when, at the next Māori hockey tournament in Waituhi, he doesn't select me for the Waituhi Men's team in the seven-a-side tournament, I have had enough.

I ask him if I can form my own team.

He says, "You can do what you like."

I see Nani Mini Tupara and ask her, "Will you support me if I register a team?"

Nani Mini isn't a Mormon, but that doesn't matter. "Rebelling again?" she laughs. "Sure I will. But if your team wins, I don't want the trophy in a Mormon house. It comes to my house. Deal?"

"Put it there, Nan."

Okay . . . so the next step is to find a team. I already have a mate with me from CCNZ staying over the holidays — it may have been Lucky Walker but I have a feeling it was Michael Pratt — let's make it Michael. That makes two players, five to go.

I wrote about our team in *Bulibasha, King of the Gypsies* (1994). Here's the fictional account of that hockey tournament, slightly reshaped and edited. Not the same hockey sequence that I included in *Māori Boy* but the other, more subversive one.

3.
from *Bulibasha, King of the Gypsies*

It is all very well for me and my friend from college, Michael, to decide to field a team. The problem is where will we find players at this late hour? Out of sympathy Dad and red-headed Ben Milner say they will join us, but every other male in the village who can stand up without a walking stick has already been taken by other teams needing spares. I am running out of time.

Then my cousin Chantelle, who used to be Charlie, comes up with two other cuzzies, Donna and Cindy. "Nani Mini says you're looking for players," she says. "The women don't want us in their teams, so she said for us to try yours."

"Well—" I hesitate, dumbfounded.

"Honey," Donna says kindly, "we may shave our legs but we're your last resort. Take us or leave us."

"We can run faster than the men around here, too," Cindy says. "All that practice getting away from the police, eh girls."

"And most of the time in high heels," Chantelle adds. "Well?"

I look at Dad who, actually, is killing himself with laughter. And Ben is not exactly happy.

Oh what the heck. "I'd love to have you," I say.

The Waituhi Rebels are born.

As expected the best seven-a-side teams start to come through the ranks, and by Saturday afternoon bystanders are barracking for their favourites. In the women's division it is clear from the beginning that the major battle will be between Waituhi and YMP. But in the men's division, Pera Punahāmoa's Waituhi Men's team isn't faring as well. The team gets through the first and second rounds but in one of the quarterfinals — a ding-dong battle between Waituhi and Te Aowera — Waituhi loses. The semifinalists are YMP Men's, Te Aowera, Uawa and—

Did I forget to tell you that the Waituhi Rebels surprise everybody? If only Elder Horspool could see us now.

There are two semifinals. One between Te Aowera and Uawa, and the other pitches YMP against us, the Waituhi Rebels. The winners from each semifinal will compete against each other for the top trophy.

That's when Grandad and I have a showdown. Five minutes before Waituhi Rebels are due for the first semifinal he starts to heavy Dad.

"I want you to change the name of your team to Waituhi Men's and sack some of your players. You haven't a hope of winning against YMP. Not with those three takatāpui among you."

Pera's voice is loud and carries to where Donna, Cindy and Chantelle are standing. Māori homophobia has always been the worst part of their lives. When they hear Grandfather's words they change and seem to diminish. "I want them replaced," he says. "No ifs, buts and maybes."

My father could have taken the decision away from me, but he doesn't. "I'm just a centre-half, Dad," he says, trying to lighten Grandad's mood. "My son's captain."

"Then you tell Witi."

"You ask him yourself." And then Dad stands there, looking at me, wondering which way I will jump. He knows I am growing independent and can look after myself now. But can I man up — even to Grandad?

A crowd has begun to collect around us and Grandfather, aware of the attention, wants to get the matter over quickly. "Witi, you've heard what I asked your father," he says. "Change the name of your team and get rid of those three." Pera never asks. He commands.

Chantelle trots over and whispers in my ear. "We don't mind, honey," she says.

The trouble is, *I* do. "No change," I tell Grandfather. My heart is thudding in my ears. My mouth is dry. And I wonder, looking at Dad's face, whether he expected me to stand up myself; he looks startled by my decision.

"What did you *say*?"

"There will be no change in either the name or the team."

"You will make a laughing stock of me," Pera says.

"Have you ever taken the time to watch our team, Grandad?" I ask. What I really mean is: Pera, have you ever watched *me*?

Just then Nani Mini, alerted to what is happening, comes running over. The light of battle is in her eyes and her temper is up. "Are you trying to muscle in on my team?" she asks Pera. "They're registered under me, not you." She is enjoying having her brother on. She loves to get her own back on him for splitting the valley with that Mormon angel of his.

And Grandfather looks at me. "You love your Nani Mini that much?" What he really means is: Witi, have you ever loved *me*? "One day you and I —"

He walks away.

Ask anybody who has played seven-a-side hockey and they will tell you that it is a difficult and punishing game. With only seven players each team has to be fast and fit to last the distance — fifteen minutes first half and fifteen minutes second half and not just one round, either. In a tournament you play six times or more a day. No good pulling all the stops out at the beginning and running out of steam as the tournament progresses. In the individual matches, the main secret to success is having and keeping possession of the ball. As long as you have possession you can control the speed and destiny of the game.

Over the preliminaries I have developed enormous respect for Donna, Cindy and Chantelle's abilities to keep possession. I have every reason to expect that Waituhi Rebels will give YMP a good run for their money. What I haven't anticipated is that my cuzzies will be so devastated by Grandfather's dismissal of them that they will give up. From the moment they walk on to the field they don't even try. They think everybody is laughing at them.

The YMP team, led by Alexander Poata, swiftly takes possession. Despite attempts by me, Dad, Ben and Michael to stop the fast YMP men, they score one runaway goal after another. By halftime YMP is ahead by 15 to nil — a goal a minute.

"Chantelle," I plead during the break. "We've got to turn this game around." By now people *are* laughing at her, Donna and Cindy. All along the sidelines, men begin to heckle us. Some are making effeminate gestures and mincing along. Pera, having washed his hands of us, is looking on in horror. And sympathy too? Maybe.

Nani Mini comes over. "What's wrong with your players?" She asks me. "They better pull their stockings up."

Then my cousin Mohi blows kisses at us and I see red. I walk up to him and sock him in the mouth. "Whū . . ." the crowd rumbles.

"Why don't we just throw in the towel?" Michael asks.

"No," I answer. "If we keep possession of the ball we can keep the score down. I'll take over Chantelle at centre forward; Dad, you play left inner; Michael, you play right inner; and Ben, you play centre half."

Michael jerks his head at Donna, Cindy and Chantelle. "What about—"

I shrug my shoulders.

"Play ball!" the ref cries.

Tears of rage and humiliation are stinging my eyes. I barge back and push Chantelle away from the centre forward position. "You bitches," I say to her, Donna and Cindy. "If you don't want to fight for yourselves, get off the field. Go crawl back into your holes and die."

I settle down to bully against Alexander Poata. All I can think of is winning the bully, shooting the ball out to Dad or Ben, streaking into YMP territory where I will wait for the ball to come to me and—

I feel a hand on my shoulder.

"You better step aside, honey." Chantelle's voice is kind, but there's steel in it. "You're standing in my position and *I don't like it.*"

I look at her, uncomprehending. "Off you go now, there's a good boy. Me and my girls are going to work."

I move back to centre. "Are we ready, girls?" Chantelle asks.

"Any time, any place, any *way* you want it," Donna and Cindy respond.

"So why are we waiting?" Chantelle says. "Let's kick *ass.*"

The game takes off. Chantelle bullies so fast that Alexander Poata is left literally standing in the middle of the field wondering what the fuck happened. He looks like one of those cartoon characters who lose their pants and cross their legs: Eek. Chantelle pushes the ball past another YMP player and yells to Cindy, "Go, girl!"

The ball cracks from Chantelle down the middle of the field. Cindy takes off after it, picks the ball up and swerves and dips past the remaining YMP players. Like an avenging angel she sprints down the field and *slam—*

YMP 15, Waituhi Rebels 1.

"One down," Chantelle yawns, tossing her hair, "fourteen to go. Well...fifteen if we want to win."

The onlookers are stunned into silence. They let out a surprised roar. Nani Mini is laughing so much she almost loses her false teeth. Hockey one, hockey two, hockey three. Again the ball cracks from Chantelle but this time to Donna who hits it into the far corner and speeds after it. None of those YMP players has a chance. Donna is there to pick up the ball and dribble it into the YMP goal.

"What took you guys so long?" Donna says as the panting YMP players catch up.

Alexander Poata is so pissed off about being beaten by a takatāpui that he takes a swing at Donna who ducks, knees him in the balls and asks the other men, "Next?"

It's the kind of strength or bravado that people on the sidelines understand. They cheer and stamp their approval.

"Never mind about that," Chantelle yells. "We've only got another twelve minutes." YMP 15, Waituhi Rebels 2. We will never make it.

The game gets harder, but the crowd is with us all the way. People like to see born losers fighting back. Against all odds we manage to draw 15–15, thirty seconds before the game finishes.

"Extra time!" the ref allows. Now the game must continue until the first goal is scored.

Nani Mini is beside herself. "Why didn't you fellas play like this in the first half?" she growls Chantelle.

Chantelle looks at me with tenderness. "We can fight our own battles, Auntie," she says. "But sometimes it takes somebody to remind us what they are."

The story of the hockey game is a narrative affirming the underdog. In the fiction, the Waituhi Rebels go on to win the tournament but real life wasn't like that and, in the final, Te Aowera was the winner. But fiction can make anything happen, and in *Bulibasha* I could win, my way, through words.

Although the seven-a-side hockey game is treated satirically, the subtext is serious. It lies not in the game, but in the relationship between myself and Pera. What's going on there?

I just didn't know what my grandfather wanted. Obedience? I found the male structures of domination oppressive and it didn't matter whether they were Mormon or Māori. Imposing any stricture on my conduct by way of some hierarchical assumption of superiority or by holy writ didn't cut it with me.

When Pera said "You can do what you like" — and I did what I liked — he didn't mean that at all. What he meant was that I could do what I liked as long as it was what *he* liked. But if I did that, I would have to conform to his assumptions and values. And, of course, shut out the possible, in all its variations.

If I really considered Pera's words, "You can do what you like", they sounded suspiciously like "I don't care what you do." And yet, had that been him cheering our team at the end?

You could excuse my behaviour by saying that I had simply butted my head against the older generation. But it was more than that. Other people — Chantelle, Cindy and Donna — had forced patriarchy into the sunlight where I could see it.

Where did *that* buck stop?

Here. Now. We have been esteemed enemies ever since.

And apart from anything else, I was defending my team. Without knowing it, I was also defending the *me* that I eventually became. The bloodied boy, shambling away from a shed wondering where to go down a pathway coiling into the night, is just the beginning of my story.

Your father is right, sometimes you think too much. After the tournament you have a go at him, annoyed that he has not had your back.

"Don't come to me thinking I should have supported you," he begins. "Maybe *I* should have made the decision when your grandfather asked me to."

You're stunned. "And what decision would you have made?"

"Probably to change the team," he admits. "I know our Waituhi players, you don't. I would have taken the burden of making the decision off you."

"Don't make it sound as if you would have done me a favour."

"Stop right there, son," Dad says. "I would have acted according to custom. As head of our whānau your grandfather comes first, then me and my generation, and then you. But I passed, didn't I? So your grandfather's not the only one you should be thinking about. It's me too, how much I gave up to you."

And then Dad gives you one of his lessons about life, something you've carried with you as you've negotiated your way as a writer through the Māori world.

"Look, what you did was your decision. You made it. Now you *own* it. And *you* take full responsibility for it — especially for what you have done to your grandfather, to his mana. He's the spiritual as well as the temporal leader of the family, there's that. And he's been a referee, administrator, delegate and manager in Māori hockey for donkey's years. Without him there would be no hockey tournament. And then some little shit like you comes along and says no to him. Have more respect."

"Have more respect" sounds suspiciously like "Apologise to your grandfather or, at least, try to find a way of burying the hatchet."

While you could "man up", you aren't yet enough of a man to do that.

Chapter Nine

Return to Temple View

1.

In early August 2016 I drove from Auckland to Hamilton to begin production on *Flowing Water*, an opera I was writing with composer Janet Jennings. The production was to be based on Potatau Te Wherowhero, the first of the Māori kings of the Waikato. As a youth he had been marked out for greatness when, armed only with a garden hoe, he faced down twelve warriors sent out one by one with taiaha and mere to defeat him.

Potatau was an elderly man when he agreed to be crowned king. By that time, Māori were facing invasion from British settlers, and most Pākehā histories of the period consider that the King Movement was merely a last-ditch copycat attempt by an unsophisticated people to reinforce their tino rangatiratanga. Far from it. Waikato was following up on a recommendation, made by a tribal delegation to Queen Victoria some years earlier, that a king be crowned so that Victoria might be able to speak equally with him.

While in Hamilton I decided to call in to the Church College for only the second time since I had graduated 55 years earlier, in 1961. For many years President David O McKay's love of Māori and Pacific Islanders buoyed the college along. However, in the 1980s New Zealand's education systems began to improve and catch up with Mormon expectations, especially with regard to Māori. Oh, there were many successful graduates, Māori and Pākehā, including the young woman Jacinda Ardern, who would go on to become New Zealand's prime minister.

On 29 June 2006, the church therefore gave three and a half years', notice that it would close. McKay's vanity project was over.

Apparently, an ending comes even to eternity.

2.

The city of Hamilton's urban sprawl now enclosed Tuhikaramea. I found some difficulty negotiating the suburban growth that surrounded Frankton Junction and the highway that once ran through smoking and empty fields of peat. I didn't expect to see the temple from afar — that astonishing floodlit sight was best witnessed against the evening sky. However, I knew that I should expect the boys dormitories on a rise, a natural sports stadium to their left and an administration building to their right.

Not any longer. Gone were the residences and, when I topped the rise, all I could see was a building site where most of the college complex had been demolished. The shell of the magnificent David O McKay auditorium still stood, but that was about it; though, at a distance, there was the temple still leaning against a cold slate winter sky. Even the wide boulevards and the white white Kolynos overbright aura I remembered, as if angels' wings fluttered overhead, were gone. All had been replaced by overriding brown earth like a wound in the side of Christ.

The only other remnants of the past were the houses which had functioned as a faculty compound. They comprised an oasis of ranch-type bungalows on bright green lawns that the graders appeared to have missed.

I navigated between excavators and other earth-moving equipment and, after some backtracking, finally happened across a man at a roundabout. He opened a "No Entry" sign and waved me through to the administration building — it now functioned as a building-site office and research centre.

"I've been watching out for you, Witi," the man grinned. "I saw you driving past and tried to catch your attention. Remember me?"

When I opened the door to get out I was assailed by the roar of graders, diggers, trucks and jackhammers. "Halverson?" I asked.

"Ken Williams," he said. "I was a third-former when you were in the sixth form." He hastened me into the building. "The old school doesn't look the same, does it?"

Ken had been deputy principal when the school closed down in 2009. Odd as this might sound, I found his familiarity disconcerting. I always considered it was my role to remember, and I was constantly startled when *I* was remembered, especially when it was for something I had set aside many years ago — like my reputation as a classical pianist.

Indeed, as we were walking the deserted halls, we came across the college's grand piano. By that time we had been joined by Val Jones, Hana Haeata and Gillian McLean, three of the researchers who worked under the guidance of Mormon historian Rangi Parker.

"Feel like playing us a tune, Witi?" Val smiled.

I caressed the keys. Piano and farmboy was such a strange juxtaposition, but somehow I had made it work; artistry with artisan. And despite my initial reticence (who would want to be known as "Fingers"?) I had become one of the school's music stars. At one concert I played the finale of Mendelssohn's Piano Concerto no. 2 in D minor, op. 40. Brother Murphy played all the orchestra parts on the organ, a demented Energizer Bunny pulling the stops out, feet pedalling like mad. We managed to get through the Presto scherzando climax without self-destructing.

On another occasion, I had a featured spot when the college went on a tour of the North Island with the rugby team and an accompanying kapa haka party. Although the college syllabus didn't include classes in Māori language and culture, the church had proclaimed a mission edict in 1957 that "Each [LDS] district should have a Maori Culture Group". In the concert, variety numbers came first, including a snappy a capella group led by Harry Rivers, nephew of jazz singer Mavis Rivers, and me playing everything from Richard Addinsell's pop classic The Warsaw Concerto (I was accustomed to killing it) to Beethoven's absolutely classic Sonata no. 23 in F minor, op. 57. In the second half, the CCNZ Māori concert party took to the stage, performing Tommy Taurima's stunning and sophisticated compositions.

Mark Metekingi and Tommy took kapa haka performance classes at the college and they, together with the charismatic Albert Whaanga, were principals supporting the Te Arohanui Maori Concert Party which appeared in Elvis Presley's film, *Blue Hawaii*, in 1961. At the time Albert was a leading light in Mormon and Māori circles and may already have been a bishop of the church. In 1963 he led the concert party at the opening of the church's Polynesian Cultural Centre in Hawai'i; the group carried on to the mainland where they appeared on *The Danny Kaye Show*. Watching them on YouTube can be a disorienting experience. Compared to modern-day razzmatazz they come out of a golden age of beauty, classicism and glamour.

Back to that college tour. At most venues, the pianos were oh-kay, but the one at Parihaka was something else. Given the historic nature of the marae as the centre of one of the greatest Māori protest movements known in New Zealand, I planned to unveil my newly learnt Chopin Polonaise in A-flat major, op. 53. Not only was the upright out of tune, but some of the keys weren't working, and, here I was, wishing to execute the work with absolute perfection. I gritted my teeth and remembered what Beethoven had reportedly said: "To play a wrong [in my case a missing] note is insignificant; to play without passion is inexcusable."

The tour was notable for another incident. At Napier, on the way home to Gisborne, I planned to see an (anonymous) doctor to have the kind of physical checkup I had denied Dr Bowker. Whether I was physically okay or not was still playing on my mind and I should have put my fears to rest long ago. I told Tommy Taurima I had permission from Mum and Dad to leave the bus and stay a few days with relatives who didn't exist. I then looked up the telephone book and phoned a doctor at random and called myself, I kid you not, Mr W Smith. When I arrived in school uniform, the receptionist said, "Oh yes, Mr . . . er . . . Smith, the doctor will be with you soon."

Then *she* came through the door.

Curses. I had been expecting a male doctor so that I could talk man to man. I clammed up and told the doctor that I had made a remarkable recovery. On my way out I used my pocket money to pay for the consultation and fled the clinic. Now broke, the beach provided the only option to sleep at.

Came the grey dawn you would have seen a moody, disgruntled, boy with tousled hair, slightly sandy, sticking out his thumb. A sheep truck stops, he clambers in. Very cross.

Baaaa, he bleats. Mission unaccomplished.

3.

I had come to the college to look at the yearbooks for 1960 and 1961. Ken, however, was eager to take me on a quick visit to that other artefact of my life, the grand organ in the David O McKay auditorium. The organ itself was gone, but the massive pipes were still there.

Completely gutted, the auditorium looked like the set of *Phantom of the Opera.* But in its heyday, pianist Julius Katchen had performed here, along with violinist Alfredo Campoli, the Harlem Globetrotters, pianist Winifred Atwell and unicyclist Jacques Cordon. And then there were the mammoth extravaganzas like the Boy Scout production *Leave It To the Boys* (I went schoolboy drag for that) and *Circus Time*, and the huge balls where the gorgeous among us were crowned King and Queen of the Prom.

Returning to the research centre, Ken leaves me in the good hands of the ladies.

"Is this what you were looking for?" Val Jones asks.

She opens the yearbooks, and there they are: the studs, the chicks, the Basketball Champ, the Girl Most Likely To Succeed. The beauties like Barbara Marsh, Rangi Northover, Rona Riki, Rosemary Kohu and Mirinoa Reti. The brains like David Beecher, Barney Wihongi, Brian Hunt (Brian became the church's golden boy for writing *Zion in New Zealand*), Wallace Chote, Roland Josephs, Farina McCarthy, Mary Eleanor Carr and Louise Drummond. The hunks like Grant Amaru, Simeon Cruse, Oscar Broerderlow and Prince Collier. The sports stars like Sid Going, Ken Going, Kay Mitchell and Valetta Nepia.

And there *I* am. "Well, look at you," I say to my younger self.

Despite my cutting myself out of my mother's photograph album, there were group photographs that I couldn't avoid, class photographs, graduation photograph — or somebody photographed me when I wasn't looking, playing the piano or organ or in other candid shots.

And there was Hiria.

In the years of my Mormon juvenescence, I fell in love. Of course I'd had girlfriends before, especially in my last year at Te Karaka District High School. Two I liked a lot were Vienna Robin and ash-blonde sylph Jennifer Nicol.

Around 2010 I met Jennifer with her daughter in Gladstone Road, Gisborne. "Remember me?" she asked.

Did I what! I'm fairly certain it was Jennifer — after all, how many ash-blonde girls did I know? — who rang me at the farm, just before I left for college, to ask if I would escort her to a ball in Gisborne. She even came to pick me up in her father's car. I remember she was wearing a long blue dress which she hitched up around her hips while she drove.

We were speeding from the farm on a moonlit night when, suddenly, she braked fast.

"Hang on a minute," she said.

She stepped out, went around to the boot and opened it. Inside was a rifle, which I loaded for her.

"Shine the torch over *there*," she instructed.

I directed the beam to a tall gnarled gum. Up went the rifle to her shoulder and she squeezed the trigger. Following the loud report, out of the tree fell a dead opossum.

"I'm making my own fur coat," Jennifer explained.

Those country gals, you gotta love 'em.

I guess it was inevitable at a co-ed school that love would be part of my experience.

And this was *first* love, the love you always remember. Unlike Te Karaka and Gisborne, where I could only continue a love relationship with a girl like Jennifer or Vienna after school, between bus timetables and after hockey matches, I was in proximity to Hiria and we could see each other *every day*. Sometimes you got lucky growing up.

There were a few girls I had crushes on, and some who had crushes on me. Most became longstanding friends like Iris Whaanga, but there were two whom I romanced. Maxine Ransfield I found totally irrepressible and we were so utterly unlike; but I really admired her spirit and the way her personality glanced off mine at crazy angles. I went to see her in Rotorua one weekend during the holidays and she took me to a dance that was a Māori version of *West Side Story*. We necked a bit and, because beaches were getting to be a habit, I slept on the pebbly shores of the lake.

The other girl was Hiria. I always preferred young women of independent spirit, and she was certainly that. Actually she was taller than I was, slim, ponytailed, with a tilt of chin that made her look stubborn; a little higher the incline and she was imperious. A Hastings girl, she hung out with friends like Jewell Forbes, Halomia Chase and Janet Harris. When I showed interest they gave me the message: go look elsewhere, buster, this space is reserved.

Who for? Probably one of the sports studs who had sent a message of his lovelorn infatuation through the network of college female go-betweens.

Hiria had a simple, unadorned beauty. I was aware of her before I actually met her. There was often somebody sitting at the back of the auditorium watching and listening as Brother Murphy took me for piano lessons. Whenever I looked up, though, she — or he — was gone.

One day I wandered into the library and took a seat, and Hiria happened to be sitting opposite. I liked the look of her and said, "Hi."

She said, "Hi," back. Adolescent conversation was as monosyllabic in those days as it is now.

Time to put the move on. I introduced myself.

"I know who you are," Hiria began. "We're in the same English class with Sister Wortley . . ."

Were we? Had I been blind?

She picked up her books in a huff. "And I follow after you when I have my piano lesson with Brother Murphy. I have to wait and watch and, if you think I like to be showed up by you, I don't."

With that, Hiria left. Not a great start, but I never liked to be rejected. The following Saturday I made my second move.

The college had a great social calendar, putting on film evenings, concerts and, sometimes, a New Zealand equivalent of that good old-fashioned piece of Americana — the barn dance. On the Saturday in question Elder Horspool was screening one of the old films he had ordered up for us to see from some ancient film distribution outlet. I remember black-and-white classics such as *Citizen Kane* and *The Te Kooti Trail* (both Rudall Hayward's silent and sound versions), but, hurrah, there were the occasional bleached colour movies like *The Four Feathers* and *Blue Lagoon* (with a nubile Jean Simmons flashing a glimpse of breast).

What usually happened was that we were all trooped into the auditorium from the dormitories, girls in the front and boys at the back. Once the lights went down there was a sudden flurry of movement as boys snuck down to take seats next to the girl they were, er, dating.

This was my chance. I slipped from my seat and, having sighted where Hiria was, made my way over to her. "Hi," I said. "Can we talk?" Would one of her friends budge for me?

Nope. I stood there like an idiot, waiting for something to happen.

I felt totally exposed. Some of the students started to titter and whisper "Shrink", which was the current lingo for having been caught in an embarrassing situation. Meanwhile, Halomia Chase and Jewell Forbes and every other female in the neighbourhood was in conference, Oh, let him *stand* there.

Come on ladies, cut me some slack, willya?

Finally, with a sigh, Hiria nodded to Janet Harris, and Janet moved to another seat.

"You've got a nerve," Hiria said. "Count yourself lucky I took pity on you and didn't tell you to take a hike. And do not try anything."

From that moment it was battle stations as I tried to take Hiria's hand and she pulled it away. Throughout the entire film we battled. I took her hand. She pushed it away. I took her hand again. She smacked mine, ouch. But my persistence paid off.

Following the film, hallelujah, we became a number.

I count myself really fortunate to have known Hiria. You have to learn how to love, and I think one's first love is the place where you do most of your schooling. Hiria, by reciprocating my interest, enabled me to explore that difficult and sometimes confusing territory that lies between teenage boys and teenage girls. Within that college setting, and given the American mores that went with it, there were "standards" of behaviour that a modern generation would probably laugh at. They have the pill now; we didn't. They go all the way and often on the first date; we didn't.

You'll forgive me, I'm trying to do this from the perspective of the seventeen-year-old boy that I was in 1961. I have to say that the recall's difficult and I am fully aware that my experiences of love might not have been those of others.

All I can say is, well, the innermost chambers of my heart unclenched.

Whenever I was near Hiria, it would beat in a different way, di *der*, di *der*, di *der*. And I surprised myself by discovering a romantic self.

There came a time when I wanted to spend every moment with her. I even tolerated sitting in the bleachers watching her play indoor basketball, after all, she was my girl. Being taller than most girls at the college, making one of the top teams was a natch. My heart burst with pride as, ponytail swinging, she would dribble the ball towards the goal, looking for a team member she could pass the ball to. Her movements had an unconscious sensuality. When an opposing guard tried to take the ball from her she would hold the guard away with an elbow and then execute a spin, that ponytail whirling. If her team members were still not placed to receive the ball, you could see the look of resignation, and hear her inward sigh, Oh well, me again. She would sight and pop a jump shot. I would watch the ball in flight and will it to go in or, if it looked like it was not, by force of concentration I would bend that damn hoop the ball's way — or try to. I will always remember the way she shot a grin in my direction when she made a three-pointer.

And the envy in some of the boys. I knew they wanted her as their girl.

I let down my guard to let love in. However, with love came physical desire *and* the Mormon expectation of chastity! And I was a Mormon boy who had promised to abide by the church's constraints. A *good* Mormon boy or girl remained a virgin — what was known as "carnal knowledge" was out of bounds until connubial sex had been sanctified by marriage, preferably in the temple. Thus the idea of recreational sex, that is, sex for fun, may have been on the agenda for the sexually eager among us, but overriding that was the admonition that sex was to be associated with procreation.

That didn't mean my body was ... obedient. My heart made my feelings right, but the way my body reacted made them wrong. With Hiria, love was all mixed up with my "shameful" sex drive. My carnality mounted to such force that I was made excited and breathless by the strength of it. By any sexual thought that came into my brain. And it didn't have to be about anybody in particular.

But unclench? No, my body would not *unclench* in the same way my heart did. Because of the Mormon stuff. Because of the societal prohibition against sex. And because anybody who has been raped, whether a woman or man, knows exactly why your body can't relax. If it does, the rape will roll out of your hand and others will see it.

How weak you were. How damaged you are. How shameful you are.

And if you are a boy who has been raped by a man, he's done to you what is normally done to a woman. So add that one to the list.

Manning up. Being enough of a man.

Being unmanned.

4.

I have spent more time on the college than I should have. I wanted to show you where my time at the college fits and why it's important.

Life is always about learning, growing and adjusting one's moral approach, testing one's assumptions against what you are learning and making decisions as to whether you accept them or not. At the college, at the end of 1961, I was approaching graduation. Although I hadn't achieved a New Zealand University Entrance qualification, I had fulfilled the requirements to go on to one of the church's American universities. Pera Punahāmoa therefore arranged for me to obtain a prior blessing from a visiting Melchizedek priest.

The crunch time had finally arrived. Studies at the Brigham Young University, Utah, followed by a two-year mission.

I joined the excited bunch of graduates, being measured up for tasselled caps and gowns. I will admit that I had become perfectly happy as a student as long as I went with the flow. Removed by accident and not by design from the stultifying, conformist and — worse — assimilationist tendencies of the typical New Zealand state school system, I simply blossomed as a creative spirit. The college nurtured my questing spirit and provided me with a huge and capacious resource for my creative inventory that I otherwise would never have obtained. I have already, for instance, referred to *The Uncle's Story*, possibly the most American of all my novels, but there are also resonances related to masculinity in *Nights in the Gardens of Spain*.

There's an additional inflection, and it is that I don't care about looking foolish or making odd juxtapositions in my work. Something about the lunacy of Elder Horspool's notion that hockey was like American football worked its way into my practice. I wasn't scared to bounce my work off walls.

While the church, with its inbuilt monastic life, would be great for somebody who didn't have a life, I realised that it was seriously looking like Mormonism just wasn't for me. Church practices and beliefs were absolutely crashing into and colliding with my cultural and sexual defaults.

Regarding the cultural, had not my grandmother Teria been of the Ringatū faith? And the tangihanga practices, let alone the haka, while tolerated by the church, made them queasy.

At least, as far as my sexuality was concerned, I had found a girl, Hiria, who thought I was worth being loved. And her interest in *me* helped me to start believing in myself again.

Nevertheless, standing in line for the processional I realised I couldn't go on much longer pretending I was a good Mormon boy. Or a good boy. Or good. Or boy.

At the graduation ceremony I sang along with great gusto about my dear alma mater, our dear CCNZ. I promised to be staunch and true all through the coming years of smiles and tears to goals that lay ahead. I said I would be true blue, always to CCNZ true. But I didn't mean it.

A proud Pera was in the audience. So were Auntie Mary and Uncle Hape Rauna. I could see the stars in my grandfather's eyes.

Time for the tika.

I contemplated them while in London en route to the Aegis Salisbury Festival, June 2016. The buses whizzed past, and most of them were advertising a musical called *The Book of Mormon*. I had travelled across the rainbow to discover that the world had wagged on and all those verities I took for granted were no longer the same.

At the college I found myself actively in pursuit of a harder truth, a sharper reasoning. Be careful, boy, you could cut your throat. A number of things troubled me, in the case of the Mormon faith, concerning their doctrinal approach.

Black people could not hold the priesthood.

Nor could women. Not only that, but Mormon women on the whole seemed too passive. They were Stepford wives who existed as handmaidens to their husbands, and mothers who clearly held a helpmate status in the home.

Then there was the problem, for me, involving the Pearl of Great Price. I could accept the Book of Mormon being found on golden plates on a hill in America. But the idea of the manuscript of the Pearl of Great Price turning up as wrappings from some mummy found in a warehouse was a bridge too far.

At one of our film evenings, there was a movie shown about a young, rather plain single girl who, from the look of her, would never attract a mate. All around me I could hear sobbing and, when I looked, some of my young (unattractive) female classmates were crying and hugging each other.

The ending took the cake. In it, the young girl dies. During the final sequence of the film she is seen ascending to heaven. A tabernacle choir is belting out a hymn for all it's worth. And waiting for the girl is a stunning-looking boy, who opens his arms to her.

After the film, in the lobby, I tried to get out of there fast. I was detained by one of my friends who I knew had feelings for me. She said to me, "I am so happy. If I can't have you on earth, I know that my husband will be waiting for me in heaven."

Finally, there was the church's attitude to gay men and women. Mormons were clearly heterosexual, not homosexual. Gay men could be excommunicated. While I deeply loved Hiria, who was I sexually?

One night I was studying in my room when a friend from another dorm came over to talk after his indoor basketball practice. Coach had him on a weight-lifting programme, and he appeared to have damaged his shoulder in the workout.

"Would you give me a massage?" he asked.

I thought nothing of it. He was sweaty, he took off his white T-shirt, and I wiped him down. We were talking, perhaps about an assignment from Brother Swenson's science class that he was having a problem with. I was placing oil on his back and rubbing it.

My friend had great musculature and I could feel the muscle groups rippling under his skin. I realised too late that the world around me was shifting a little, turning on a different axis. I became mesmerised, kneading my friend's shoulders, admiring the way his lower back tapered to slim hips, and his legs were covered in a fine fuzz.

My heartbeat, instead of going di *der* di *der* di *der* began to go *di* der *di* der *di* der.

The atmosphere became hushed, breathless, that perilous time when, if you didn't watch out, all control was lost and you were damned forever. I felt myself slowing down, touch taking on a different frightening meaning. And then . . .

I stopped, dismayed. I don't think my friend knew what I was feeling. He sat up, working his shoulder. "That's better," he said.

5.

Following graduation I realised I had to dash the family's Mormon dream for me. It was now or never. On the Road Service bus back to Gisborne, I faced the fact that for me there would be no resurrection theology. Time for me to destroy Pera Punahāmoa's endgame. I just wasn't worthy.

Down. Set. Hut one. Hut two. Hut three.

When I unpacked my bags at the farm, I told Mum and Dad, "I don't want to go to Brigham Young University or on a mission." I did not want to continue to hold to their dream. Had I known at the time that the college was alarmed at the lack of uptake from students who showed promising potential for American study or a mission, I would not have beat up on myself so much.

"I'd better let your grandfather know," Dad said.

I wondered, Why? This was my decision, not Pera's.

Grandfather had every right to be furious. He didn't speak to me at all when he came over to see Mum and Dad.

"I am a kin chief, I hold the Melchizedek priesthood," he began, "and your son rejects God, denies the family and embarrasses me before my peers." He hit the dining room table with tremendous force, I had never seen him so angry. "Hei aha! If he wishes to live a selfish life, let him get on with it."

I know that Pera and my parents made due compensation to the Lord. They had always paid tithe, one-tenth of their earnings, to the church. I discovered they added an extra portion to their tithe, a penance offering.

My sister Kararaina was also in Mum and Dad's sights. She was seventeen now with a glory box and a sewing machine to set herself up in marriage, but having no School Certificate to go with it, she wasn't allowed to leave school either.

But even Kara could not deflect attention from me.

"We'll try again, son," Mum said. "Next time, we'll get it right."

Cut to February 1962, when you are eighteen.

The future pivots as Mum and Dad drive you to Gisborne Boys' High School, where you are to enrol. If they had not persevered with you, your life might have been entirely different.

Other cars have gone through the entrance to the sunlit buildings beyond. Parked in the leafy shade you sit silently in the cab of the truck between Mum and Dad. That way they can make sure you won't do a runner.

"This is where we should have been two years ago," Mum says. "Never mind, you can catch up, son." She looks at her watch and then at your father. "Well, Tom, we can't sit around all day."

Dad gets out and you join him; Mum stays in the truck. You walk through the sunlight to the headmaster's office. There are a number of other parents waiting with their sons. Dad gives the secretary your school records from Church College. One by one, the other parents go in; most return with relieved smiles; Sonny Boy is in. Half an hour later, it's your turn.

The secretary takes in your documents. Five minutes later she looks at Dad, "Mr Gray will see you now, Mr Smiler."

Jigger Gray is an imposing man. He always wears his academic gown, surely a garment to intimidate the bravest heart, and he suffers no fools. Dad is wearing a snappy fedora which he takes off as you both enter. The headmaster gets straight to the point.

"I have read the reports from your son's previous school," he begins, "and he showed good grades there. However, given the school's American teaching methods I have to evaluate their reporting criteria as well as your son's reports. Although I note that he didn't get his University Entrance, and that the school nevertheless would have recommended him to an American university, I'm afraid I can't take a positive view."

He gets up to shake Dad's hand goodbye. This is the kiss-off.

Dad refuses to budge from his seat or rise to shake Mr Gray's hand. "A New Zealand education is the right of every child," Dad says. "Witi decided America was not for him. He needs his UE, a New Zealand qualification, to go to Victoria."

Victoria? Dad was jumping the gun.

Mr Gray is taken aback. Did he think this ejection of a parent was going to be easy? "Your son is not a child," Jigger Gray reminds Dad. "He is eighteen and, if I admit him to the lower sixth he will be joining pupils who are mostly sixteen."

"Show me," Dad says, "in the education regulations where an age limit is set for pupils entering sixth form." He is bluffing.

Mr Gray's eyebrows arch, and he must admire Dad's attempt to finesse him. But he's firm, he's not a man whose decisions are questioned, and he goes to the door and tells the secretary to send the next parent and son in. As you and Dad pass him by, he says, "I suggest, Mr Smiler, that you take your boy home to the farm and put an axe in his hands. He's had his chance."

You walk back to the truck. Dad reports to Mum, "Well, dear, the headmaster won't admit Witi."

Your mother is made of sterner stuff. "You go right back in there, Tom. We are not leaving until our son is enrolled."

You return to Jigger Gray's office. "Tell Mr Gray that I am back," Dad advises the secretary. Inspired by Mum's obstinance Dad is fired up. You think you know why: as a boy he had been denied an education, even if, like you, it was partly his own fault. He wasn't about to let history repeat itself. The morning turns into a long procession of parents and pupils coming to see the headmaster. Dad overhears the secretary whispering to one of them, "We have a very stubborn parent here and he will not take no for answer."

At midday, three hours since you got here, Mr Gray appears at the door and is going to lunch — and he is clearly furious with you and Dad. He marches past and disappears.

"Maybe we could go and get some lunch too?" you ask your father.

"Better not," Dad answers. "Your mother would not be happy if we left our post. And I'd rather face the headmaster than her."

Lunch over, Jigger Gray returns. He goes into his room and slams the door behind him. And then, just as quickly he returns. He lifts his hands in capitulation, "All right, Mr Smiler, I will allow your son to enrol." And he looks you straight in the eye. "I'll be keeping my eye on you, young Smiler, and after the first term will ask your teachers to give me a progress report. If you are not doing well or are slacking and give me good reason to reverse my decision — and I hope you do — your feet won't hit the ground until you are on the street."

He turns to Dad. "Do we understand each other, Mr Smiler?"

Dad shakes on the deal.

"Then good day to you," Mr Gray says.

With that, you and your father join Mum.

"Don't let the headmaster prove me wrong," Mum says.

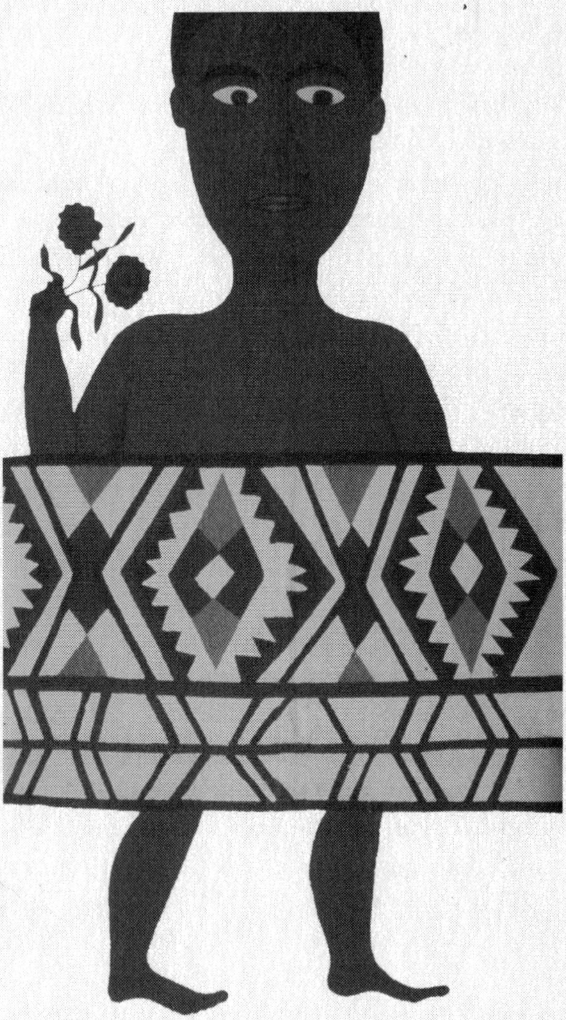

PART TWO

TŌRINO SPIRAL

Chapter Ten

Māui and Mahuika

1.

The demigod Māui has always been my mythic exemplar.

It was he who made my journey "Māui-esque". He kept challenging the way of things, taming the sun or fishing Te Ika-a-Māui up from the sea. However, there are two other stories told of Māui which show a streak of wilfulness, exemplifying the same qualities in myself when I became a writer. They have to do with the formidable guardians Mahuika, the fire goddess, and Hinenuitepō, the goddess of death.

In the Māui–Mahuika confrontation, Māui literally played with fire. For the story's sake, Mahuika has been elevated to the aforementioned "goddess" status, presumably so that Māui can be accorded a worthy competitor and thereby a greater victory. So we could say that in this story Māui began to challenge the power of the very gods themselves — but, really, Mahuika was an auntie. She has also been given the appearance of an old hag, made all the more frightening because flames glow at her fingertips and toes; they limn her extraordinary silhouette against the night sky. By such imagery sympathy for the hero, Māui, is increased. He is young, she is old; she is a goddess, he is only a demigod; and she has a frightening appearance whereas, presumably, he is handsome.

Well, I have never liked such patriarchal rubbish, especially since when Māui first meets the fire goddess, where she is dancing and scattering fire, she treats him with kindness. Therefore let me make her beautiful and desirable instead, like the Indian goddess Kali.

Māui is covetous of Mahuika's powers and says to all, "I will steal her magic fires."

He does not heed the reprimand of his mother, Taranga, who reminds him that Mahuika is his respected kuia. Oblivious to the heat and coals raining fireballs around him, he gives sly obeisance and makes his request.

"E kui, will you give me of your magic fire?"

The beautiful Mahuika willingly gives her mokopuna the end of one of her big toes.

Now, this might appear to be a rather mundane gift but, in fact, Mahuika is bequeathing to Māui an object of extraordinary power. In Māori culture, it's the big toe that the acolyte bites when the priest demands his obedience and subservience.

What does Māui do with this gift? He throws it into a nearby stream where, on contact with water, there erupts a huge gush of steam. Why does he do this? So that he can go back to the dancing goddess and report, "I lost your toe."

The myth tells us that again and again the greedy and arrogant Māui asks for more fire. He is testing his auntie to see how far her tolerance will go. At every request the goddess obliges, her dance a blinding kinetic whirl of embers scattering across the evening sky.

"Just one more toe, e kui, one more."

He is monstrous is our Māui! After Mahuika has given him all her toes, he starts to ask for her fingers. Not until Mahuika has only one finger left does she realise her love for this mokopuna has blinded her to his avaricious nature. She begins to truly rage at Māui's tinihanga, his deceit. Plucking the remaining finger she throws it, in a combustible fury, at her mokopuna.

Now the fire is on the other foot. The finger creates a huge forest conflagration and, as she dances, Mahuika fans the flames higher with her hands. At every step of her intricate haka, she opens the earth so that lava flows out. She shrieks her song, the oxygen setting alight the words.

Even the air sparks, scintillates and combusts.

In deadly peril, Māui must run from Mahuika, but she continues to whirl and send her fiery aura to chase him. Only when the mokopuna calls upon the (male) gods of storm and rain does he manage to escape immolation. Torrents of water put out the flames unleashed by Mahuika's pyromania. The phenomenon is called The Great Rain, The Long Rain, and it lasts for aeons. But when the fire is finally extinguished some glowing embers remain in certain rākau such as the kaikōmako.

It is this wood, the last gift of Mahuika, that the old-time Māori used when kindling fire from the embers within.

2.

When I am acting needlessly or selfishly, I think of Mahuika.

I don't believe she minds any of her mokopuna asking for her powers, as long as we do something with them.

There are lines, however, that should not be crossed.

For instance, in 1998, photographer Sally Tagg asked me if I would be interested in writing the text for her photographic book *On Top Down Under*. The book featured photographs of famous New Zealanders acting out their fantasies or appearing in fantastic layouts.

"You have to be photographed too," the actor Temuera Morrison said. "You can't opt out just because you're the writer."

I therefore found myself gloomily contemplating the inevitable — and decided that my photo shoot should feature myself as Māui. Naked. A thigh strategically lifted. A string of something around one arm. And a pāua shell taped over one eye.

The session was excruciating. You try to keep a pāua in place while looking as if you don't care you are in the nuddy. What Sally didn't tell me, and what I discovered when I was driving in Newmarket, was that she planned to exhibit the photograph, in an ornate gilt frame, in the front window of a local gallery.

Mahuika may have been sending me a message about consequences and to mind my impudence. I consider her to be the goddess of multiple chances in my life. She dances still, the fires arcing in circles around me as she dips and sways.

She has been forgiving of all the toes and fingers I have asked of her.

Chapter Eleven

Mā wai rā, e taurima
Te marae i waho nei?

1.

For Māori artists Mahuika is one of our important muses — the goddess figures in our pantheon that we can acknowledge as the source of our inspiration; Greek mythology has nine, inspiring European artists since antiquity.

I had great need of Mahuika when I began to think my way into the writer's life, in particular, as a novelist. This is the hinengaro I have already spoken of. It is the thought, the awareness, that all must have before they embark on anything, whether it is a career or some life-changing event. Māori say that one of the reasons why humans are like the gods is because we have hinengaro, an intellect, a consciousness.

It is not, however, the *why*, the reason that motivates.

Māori people call the reason te take.

In my case the take was a very simple one. Perhaps I can illustrate it by referring you to the harakeke, the small plantation of flax bushes that Pera and my grandmother Teria grew on the shady side of their house in Waituhi. Whenever the families went to visit — for Sunday dinners or Christmas or birthdays — one of my favourite games was to play Cowboys and Indians in the plantation with my cousins.

Oh, my achy breaky heart remembers it all. Playing Ngā Kaupoi and Ngā Iniana, me the cowboy hero Kit Carson or Hopalong Cassidy and my cousins as villainous Cochise or maiden Pocahontas. Puku full from lunch, we chased each other with stems broken from the flax as spears.

The flax bushes also attracted the korimako, bellbirds. They liked to sup at the throats of the harakeke for the sweet nectar within.

One day, Teria came out of the homestead and growled us. "Hika mā!" she reprimanded. "Stop playing in the flax bushes, you are trampling their roots! And stop breaking the stems! And how can all the korimako drink when you're making this racket and scaring them away? Hūtia te rito o te harakeke, kei hea te kōmako e kō?"

Now, some people might think I am a vatic writer; that is, one who can claim or hint at the possession of some secret or visionary knowledge. But I am not that, nor was my grandmother. However, Teria was a kuia who was deeply and spiritually embedded in her world. And she took advantage of the fact that her grandchildren were all there within the vicinity of the harakeke and the bellbirds to remind us of a larger truth.

"The flax bush must be treated with respect," she said. "If you damage it, where will the bellbird sup, where will it drink?" She made us hush and bend our heads to the flax. "Listen," she said. "The flax is asking us, what is the greatest thing in the world?"

There was sunlight all around and, in the breeze, the tall fluted blades were clicking together, *the greatest thing, the greatest*...

And Teria parted the interior of the flax. "Look."

Inside were slender leaves protecting the delicate growing shoot within.

"There resides the answer," she continued. "He tangata, he tangata, ā, he tangata. It is man, it is woman, it is children." She gave me a sharp look. "Therefore, e Wit*sh*, serve humankind."

And then she called a mihi to the birds, asking them to forgive children at play and to return.

2.

To make the above easier for those from elsewhere, let me give you a European way of looking at this.

"Je pense donc je suis," the French philosopher Descartes said, or "cogito, ergo sum," — "I think, therefore I am."

I've taken Descartes' approach throughout my life, personally and professionally. *I thought, therefore I became.* Keeping my eye on the prize, I visualised myself as a writer and then went on to te take, the reason. Indeed, when I look back on my life and career I often suspect that rather than conforming to the dictates of fiction by accident, it is doing so because that is the way I am writing it.

Thus, to paraphrase Descartes, "J'écris donc je suis," I *write* therefore I am: scribo, ergo sum.

Let me invoke the power of the spiral again. The gyre begins to spin, the helices whirling faster and faster. And I am propelled from the time I started high school at Gisborne Boys' to the years when I moved from writing short stories to writing the novel.

The helices thus take me forward again to 1968 when, after reading Bill Pearson's essay, "The Maori and Literature 1938–1965", I decided to become a writer. My brain was whirling so fast it's no wonder that in a nanosecond I was already at the threshold of writing a novel — no, a *Māori* novel — whoa, what was that! And to qualify, how different would it have to be to the master narrative — White literature — already written for the world?

From the very beginning I always thought of the master narrative — if you like, the master's narrative — as the product of "the European imperium". It was supported by industries, academies and cultural, political and commercial entities all designed to ensure the imperium's superiority. At international conferences on writers and writing I sometimes described it as an alien construct.

People at those conferences took my observation the wrong way. But Māori literature must have been as alien to them, surely! Different narrative structure, literary conventions and symbolism, underpinned by a different mythology. Comprising Māori thought and Māori vision, only accessible if you — at the time — were Māori.

What I was also trying to convey was that the imperium held the power. Despite whatever sympathy the masters might have to those within their empire, they would always privilege their own writers and not mine. It was the way of the world.

I turned to Mahuika for support, knowing it was a big ask. I pleaded for the flame from the treasured big toe on her left foot.

With her gift in hand I touched the flame to the European dominion. But, of course, it was not as easy as that. In New Zealand, I had arrived at a time of European omnipotence. It was so dominant that Māori in the European arts such as music, film or theatre were virtually nonexistent. Opera singer Inia Te Wiata, film actress Ramai Hayward and a smattering of actors, and that was pretty much it. We were doing better in the fine arts. There were no Māori painters working within the European landscape tradition — Māori were already part of the landscape so we didn't need to place ourselves in it — but Ralph Hotere was claiming his space as one of New Zealand's premier artists and sculptors.

The situation in literature was similar. The body of imaginative work in English in 1968 written by Māori was small. As Bill Pearson averred, "Hone Tuwhare's volume of verse and a handful of poems by others; and no more than one book and fifty short prose pieces, all of them, except for some by Rowley Habib, published in *Te Ao Hou* since 1955."

The volume of Hone's referred to was *No Ordinary Sun* (1964) and the book was Reweti Kohere's *The Autobiography of a Maori* (1951). The writers included superb Māori linguists such as Pei Te Hurinui Jones, who translated into te reo Māori both Shakespeare's *The Merchant of Venice* and Edward FitzGerald's English version of *The Rubaiyat of Omar Khayyam*, and who also wrote *Mahinarangi*. And there was journalist and cartoonist Harry Dansey, who later wrote a play, *Te Raukura* (1971), and whose work awaits championing.

Earlier Māori writers had taken to the English-language tradition, but they were more concerned with communicating anthropological and historical information to the reader — where Māori were being referred to in the past tense. I'm citing Te Rangi Hīroa (Sir Peter Buck) and his seminal works *The Coming of the Maori* and *Vikings of the Sunrise*, and Sir Apirana Ngata's *Ngā Mōteatea* collections of waiata. Locally, my granduncles Rongowhakaata Halbert and Hetekia Te Kani Te Ua had been involved in writing the stories of the Gisborne tribes to which I belonged. They spoke to the anthropological imperative, but I wanted to speak to modern Māori and create a new way of seeing.

I wanted to write survival.

And I felt I had a set of capabilities (yes, they were European, affirming infiltration as a methodology) that would allow the writing of something distinctive.

My first thought — the hinengaro — was to write something set in urban society *now*, you know, the "boy traversing the dominant society, preferably, coming to the city and confronting racism". My life would have been much easier if I had offered up that kind of text, but Europeans had already written — and were writing — that novel. I wouldn't flatter them by writing it myself because if I did, wasn't I condoning their work? And, frankly, I hadn't had the kind of experience to authenticate the urban Māori story. That would have to await the arrival of Alan Duff.

No, I was firm with myself. And I felt the responsibility of "the first Māori novel" very keenly. In previous indigenous fiction (and film) worldwide, the device of the outsider going into an indigenous community allowed the writer or filmmaker the opportunity to explain and see that "exotic" society — or, vice versa, to observe the indigenous character as the "other" in his own.

I wasn't going to replicate either of those outsider narratives. Mine must be a Māori story with a Māori character in the middle of it — an authentic, non-exotic Māori setting. Nothing less would qualify.

You can see, can't you, that I was advancing, in my thinking about my first novel, from the hinengaro to the formulation of a kaupapa, or more particularly, kaupapa Māori?

For Māori, everything has to have a kaupapa or purpose. It's the set of values, principles and plans by which you can justify, if you like, your actions. It can be a Big Question, such as, What is the purpose of your life and the work that you do? And the question might not be asked of you particularly, but of the community you belong to.

What is Witi's purpose?

I can tell you, having the whānau make your decisions about who you should be can be quite a daunting experience — and they don't take "No" for an answer.

Or the question might be small, such as, Why do you want to call me Miro and not Mini?

If it's your Nani who's the questioner, you better have a good reason, boy.

Whatever the case, kaupapa Māori involves, mostly, a question. And I have been to many meetings involving Māori and Pākehā where, after the Pākehā has brought out his nice spreadsheets and showed his visuals and computerised simulations on whatever the project is, Uncle Joe or Auntie Essie will put up their hand and ask, "What's the kaupapa?"

Bang. Right between the eyes. Down comes the (Pākehā) elephant in the room.

As for me, well, I've got those ancestors poking away at me in my own room behind my eyes. They are the tūpuna comprising my Māori cosmos, my map of the universe. We sometimes say of our ancestors, "Kua whetūrangitia rātou — they are the myriad of stars", and at a tangi someone who has recently died is often farewelled with the words "Haere ki Paerau — go to the threshold of the heavens."

Perhaps instead of ancestors, the room is a beautiful dark sky filled with sparkling, singing — or rather, bickering — stars.

And in my searching and threshing around for the kaupapa of my opening gambit as a novelist, I found myself thinking not only to a place but also to a time. Why was I surprised? My sense of excitement mounted as I was taken not to elsewhere but else*there*.

To the time in Māori history, the 1960s, before the great urban migration. And the hinengaro (thought) and the kaupapa (purpose) acted as a lightning rod to a question: Who would look after the marae after we had — so the experts were predicting — *all* left for the cities?

The image of my father, Te Haa o Rūhia, came into my mind.

3.

Born in 1915, my father was named after The Czar of All the Russias.

People also called him Te Haa, The Breath.

I could think of no better exemplar of a rural Māori leader than Dad. He was stocky, sturdy of body and mind, and his craggy face matched the mountains he was born in. Known popularly as Tom, he personified the concept of tangata whenua, a man of the land, representing Waituhi on the Wī Pere Trust and still *padrone* of the Smiler shearing gang. He was not afraid of confronting people — Māori or Pākehā, parliamentarian or public servant. And he thought nothing of walking into the Gisborne City Council — here comes Tommy — to harangue them about developments affecting Waituhi. Physically, Dad was still strong enough to keep the structures of life in their right places — a suitable metaphor. He was a patron for the Poverty Bay Hockey Association and, as coach and administrator of the Waituhi hockey team and a teenage indoor basketball team, a younger generation looked up to him.

And my heart began to overflow.

I decided the novel would be about Dad because he was the personification of all that was good and true about being Māori. And he was practical too: the kind of person who on the *Titanic* wouldn't tell you everything was going to be okay but would know the way to the lifeboats — and be able to lower them.

Yes, Dad would be representative of the life before, the time *in anticipation* of Te Ao Tūroa. He would be the symbol of rural Māoridom. And to put across how I felt at the "death" of rural Māoridom, the book would reflect that by being about the death of a father. That's how my mind, for better or worse, works. The electrical charges ricochet through the synapses until, bingo.

I decided, for instance, to ensure the novel would have a pito. Ever since, every one of my books has had a birthcord. The practice follows Māori custom. Traditionally the entire placenta, whenua, and the pito were normally buried at the ancestral marae of the parent; because the word for earth is also whenua, you will get the idea — whenua to whenua. However, whenua burial was not condoned at the time I was writing the first book — that had to wait for a revival in the 1980s — so my thinking applied specifically to the pito.

As an example from my life, when my first daughter, Jessica, was born in the 1970s, I asked the hospital in Dunedin to keep the pito so that I could take it home to Waituhi. I flew to Gisborne where Dad was waiting — and he officiated at the ritual at Rongopai. When Olivia was born two years later, I again asked the hospital, this time in Wellington, to keep the pito and I again took a flight north to conclude the ceremony; this time, I was assisted by my sister.

When our three grandchildren were born, times had changed and I didn't have to ask for the placenta and the birthcord. I understand that increasingly Pākehā as well as Māori parents have adopted the practice with newborn children. How good is that, Aotearoa?

And within the narrative framework of waiata I began by deploying the three unities of time, place and action. The story would occur over three days and nights, with a coda; the place would be centrally Waituhi. The action would be mainly confined to the tangihanga, with that event providing the atmosphere and symbolism.

I would sup from the throat of the harakeke flower and find my sustenance there, as the bellbird did.

And the novel would be called *Tangi*.

Chapter Twelve

A Son's Homage to his Father

1.

My father Te Haa o Rūhia is named Rongo Mahana in *Tangi*. In Māori mythology Rongo is the god of cultivated foods, especially the prized kūmara. Rongo's other names are Rongomātāne and Rongomaraeroa; "mahana" is the Māori word for warmth. Already I was establishing a pantheon for my work and my father as the Māori equivalent of Noah, the original man of the soil, husbandman and farmer.

He was also a shepherd in every sense.

One lambing season, we rode the paddocks on our horses to check the ewes and to intervene quickly if any were having birthing problems. Dad sometimes acted as midwife; he had an uncanny inkling when a mother was due to give birth, and when that involved twins or triplets he tried to be on call. One bright morning, however, we were too late. The ewe had given birth to a healthy lamb but a second one had died in her womb, and she with it.

All that morning, Dad and I carried the live lamb in a sling. I thought we would take it home where my sisters would feed it milk from a bottle. But Dad had other ideas. Just before midday, as we were cresting a hill, he grunted: a ewe, bleating over her dead child.

I had never before seen Dad do what I am about to describe for you.

With the mother ewe looking on, and me holding the orphan, he took the butcher's knife from his belt and began to skin the dead lamb. He slit the pelt at the neck, sliced the skin around all four legs and peeled the coat off in one piece.

"What are you doing, Dad!" The small, skinless body gleamed with extraordinary, moist, whiteness.

My objection faded as Dad draped the woollen coat over the orphan lamb, pushing its legs through the small holes in the pelt to secure a good fit. Nor was he going to take any nonsense from the grieving mother.

"Here you go, Mum." He pushed the bogus child towards her. She took a couple of sniffs — well this lamb kinda sorta smells like mine — and the lamb itself was hungry and wasn't waiting around for her to make up its mind. In it went for the milk, butting its head against her teats to drink.

My father was sentimental about some things, but about other things he wasn't. Every loss of a ewe or lamb meant our flock numbers would be down but the circumstances couldn't be helped. Meantime, he had an orphan lamb to care for and a grieving ewe, heavy with milk. And, as Dad grinned at me, a lesson was passed on about the role we sometimes have to take upon ourselves to make sure that while death is absolutely terrible to behold, life is relentless, pushing us through grieving — it must and has to carry on.

This is the subtext of *Tangi*. It's narrated by Rongo Mahana's son, Tama, "tama" meaning son. He has a government job in Wellington and receives a telephone call from one of his sisters that his father has died. Father and son are the same ages as Dad and I were in 1968, fifty-three and twenty-four.

Tama sets off at once by plane for his home in Gisborne, Poverty Bay. He travels from a "Pākehā" world in one of those border crossings, which prefigures a journey will be taken to the Māori world and back. In the journey — in all the journeys in my work — the dynamic of the koru, the spiral, takes over.

Ever since, most of my work has been structured on what I call te wā tōrino principles, narratives characterised by spirals of time. I felt that this would help me to escape the linear compulsion of the dominant literature and introduce circularity as the indigenous alternative.

As far as *Tangi* is concerned, this "spiralling time" operates as follows. In the first of the intertwining narratives, outward incidents on the flight home awaken Tama's memories of his childhood and, more particularly, of his father. The spiral is three-dimensional and its axis is the account of Rongo's three-day funeral, the intensely emotional tangi itself. The second interwinding — or contrawinding — narrative follows Tama as he returns by train after the funeral to Wellington, ostensibly to settle his affairs prior to taking on his responsibilities to the family and the whānau land. His father's death has left Tama a changed man and, as the eldest son, he is now the head of the family.

However, the reader never knows if Tama does return or doesn't, just as we who lived in the cities didn't know, just as *I* didn't. Indeed, I have always preferred "open" rather than "closed" endings to convey that while, for narrative purposes, a novel must come to an end, the spiral does not.

The tangi itself takes place in the village of Waituhi, Dad's wider whānau and the home of our family kin — the Smilers and the Peres and, well, everybody really. Even though Dad, Mum and my sisters and brothers lived on the farm, hardly a week went by that we didn't go out to Waituhi.

2.

Okay, so in this account of cultural formations apposite to writing and narrative practice, I had negotiated the questions of *why* and *what*.

I now needed to answer to the *how*.

How could I write a Māori novel in the English language? Could I achieve such a thing? Surely there would have to be some linkage to the reo, the Māori language?

I found the linkage in the basic component of all literature: the word or, in Māori, kupu. The Pākehā might say, "In the beginning was the Word, and the Word was God", but in Māoridom, we said, "In the beginning was the Word and the Word was Kupu." By that we meant that the reo was sacred. My view was that English had long lost its sacred qualities and had become profane, common. The challenge therefore was this: How could I join a sacred word to a profane practice?

And yet, once, English had had kupu! The closest European analogue to Māori literature was the narrative poem, and the most comparable English form to the art of Māori storytelling was the Icelandic or Anglo-Saxon saga. I found kupu's equivalent there, in the rune, which was talismanic. Sometimes the runes scattered over fire could, like bones, crack open and unlock all their hidden meanings, secrets and mysteries. I was sad that the figurative elements in English had become so hackneyed they'd lost their layered meanings, especially their sacred resonances. Instead they'd become plain porridge or — to illustrate with a cliché — as plain as a pikestaff, which was originally "plain as a packstaff", but few people today would know what either pikestaff or packstaff referred to.

By contrast, I was fortunate that Māori still practised the original language. Its meanings had not become diminished, demeaned or distorted. Nor had it lost its rhythmic intensity, propulsive force, poetry, richness, colour and, yes, sanctity. I knew that if I could do it, splice kupu into the English narrative, kupu would help me open up Māori history, a Māori world view, a Māori story within the English literary tradition.

But how? What personal imagery might I deploy to authenticate this process?

My friend and colleague John Huria offered a way of visualising this from a Māori — not European — point of view. "Remember when Mahuika was chasing Māui and setting the world on fire?" he asked. "Some of the coals lodged in the kaikōmako."

And gratefully I began to consider Mahuika's last gift as the implant I needed. I would insert kaikōmako into my English narrative wherever I could, in the same way as my ancestors did when kindling fire.

That would set the flame going, eh? But I still needed to keep it alight — to motivate the kupu to link one with the other. Not in any random sequence, but in a pattern which would precisely express, beneath the English appearance of the words, their Māori subconsciousness.

I therefore looked to the Māori oral literary tradition — te reo — for the textual and subtextual wording, the root system that would feed the fire. Rich and huge, the inventory mainly evidenced itself in waiata, haka and kōrero; if you like, through sung poetry, chanted dance and declamatory speechmaking. I absorbed the work of the great contemporary waiata composers Bill Kerekere, Tuini Ngāwai, Bub and Nen Wehi, and Tommy Taurima. Kapa haka and waiata and whaikōrero and pakiwaitara are the modern equivalents of kupu, and have become today the largest repositories. You can see them at their full glory at Te Matatini competitions every year.

In particular, I absorbed that particular class of traditional song called waiata tangi. Thus, in *Tangi*, the tangihanga ceremonials are re-created through the language, rhythms and symbolism that you find in Māori funeral waiata. I used Te Rarawa Kerehoma's beautiful Māori lament to provide the mnemonic to attach the kupu to.

I tried to create a poetic drama in prose, and *Tangi* became, literally, the novel that cries.

3.

In all the time I was writing the novel I didn't tell Dad about it. I didn't know how to.

I did, however, telephone Mum and I said to her, "I've started my first novel, Mum, and it's about Dad. But it's not really Dad because the man I am writing about is dead."

There was silence at the other end of the phone as my mother tried to process what I was telling her. And like my Nani Mini she was not averse to giving me a short, succinct and terse reply.

First of all, "I don't like this new career of yours, son," she said. The reason? Well, the writing she upheld was truthful, like the whakapapa on the hallway walls of 11 Haig Street. The genealogy was tika, factual, while in my writing I was looking at people in my life as characters inhabiting a fictional whakapapa.

Second, Mum acknowledged that no matter what her opinion, "You've always done what you want to do and I suppose nothing will stop you." In other words, when the world gave birth to a writer, and if he or she wished such a career, family must step out of the way.

And third, she laid down the parameters of tikanga. "All right," she said, "but you will have to finish and publish your novel before your father dies so that people at home can see that it's one of your usual make-believe stories, even though it is set in Waituhi. If Dad dies before the book is published, you are to pull the novel from publication."

I said "Yes," to Mum's third proviso.

Tangi was published in hardback in 1973. A brief introduction was recommended by either Dr Joan Metge or Professor Bruce Biggs, but I felt it was important for me to stand on my own two feet.

It could be said that I tried with the novel to give another *aperçu* into the hearts of those who shared a common location, and I think *Tangi* was good to go to from *Pounamu, Pounamu*. Greater glamour attaches to the novel than to a short-story collection and so the book garnered more attention. While the emotional amplitude of the book discomfited some stony Anglo-Saxon hearts, it was a *succès d'estime*.

When considering the cover image, there had been a stunning colour photograph taken at the funeral of King Korokī in May 1966, seven years earlier. Casket bearers were straining to take the Māori monarch to the resting place of the Waikato royalty on Taupiri Mountain. I had reservations about using the portrait: even though our family had whakapapa connections with the kāhui ariki, the funeral was Waikato-specific and the novel was set in the lands of Te Whānau-a-Kai. In the end I was swayed, rightly or wrongly, by the symbolism. My publisher wrote to the new monarch, Te Atairangikaahu, for permission. She agreed, and that began a lifelong affection between us for the forty years that she reigned.

My author photo on the back flap had a stronger whakapapa connection. I wanted to acknowledge that my inspiration came from my ancestors. One of them was Raharuhi Rukupō, the head carver of the beautiful meeting house Te Hau Ki Tūranga, the oldest wharenui in New Zealand. Although no photograph of Rukupō existed, his likeness was represented by the pou in the house which, at the time, resided in the then Dominion Museum, Wellington. In 1995, Dad was one of the kaumātua who escorted the meeting house to Te Papa Tongarewa on the waterfront.

One matter: if you have a train journey in your work, it pays to consult a rail enthusiast. A month before *Tangi* was due to go to Hong Kong for printing someone, it must have been my publisher, David Heap, suggested that we had better check the details of the train trip. Horror of horrors, I had written that the train left Gisborne railway station at 8.00 am; well, not on that day it didn't. I also had the times the train arrived at the various stations incorrect and, worse, I had plotted its course on a railway line from Palmerston North to Wellington via Upper Hutt that didn't exist.

The lesson is that there are trainspotters everywhere, and they know stuff.

In case you're wondering, Dad was not dead when the book hit the shops. Did I breathe a sigh of relief? Did I what. Had he died, I would have had to pay David Heap for scrapping the book or, at least, to personally purchase every copy in the shops.

When the book won the Wattie Book of the Year Award in 1974, I asked Dad to come to the award ceremony. I loved introducing him to people, some of whom gasped with disbelief. They had assumed that the novel was autobiographical, which it was and wasn't.

From that moment, Dad and I made a great literary team. I loved having him with me at some book function or another. It got to the point where people would say to me, "If you can't make it, do send your father," or even more blatantly, "Can Tom come and speak for you?" He attended the premiere of *Waituhi: The Life of the Village* (1984), and when I left after opening night, stayed on to offer the customary protocols and hospitalities of Te Whānau-a-Kai. One of the many occasions when he made the newspapers and I didn't was when he went to collect the Wattie Book of the Year Award for *The Matriarch* (1986). By that point he was literally asking me not to go; he would do it. He launched *The Whale Rider* (1987) and *Bulibasha, King of the Gypsies* (1994); Mum joined me at the *Bulibasha* launch. We stood aside while Dad took over with a pōwhiri.

"Five minutes, Dad," I warned him. "Just five minutes! And don't tell them about the time you left me to be looked after by those Pākehā ladies at the golf club when I shat my nappies."

Did he listen? Nope.

I said to Mum, "Just listen to Dad! You'd think he wrote the book himself."

"Let him enjoy the glory," she said. "He deserves it."

The Czar of All the Russias lived a long and full life, longer than the usual three score years and ten. Because of this, rather than give you an extract from *Tangi* which killed Dad off prematurely, I have decided instead to give you a glimpse of him in his later years.

Here's how I wrote about my father in my short story "Going to the Heights of Abraham", published in 2002. He was still, as ever, the husbandman, the shepherd, not worrying about himself but the whānau, the whenua, the iwi.

4.
Going to the Heights of Abraham

My father's voice whispers out of the stomach of the night, "Are you there, son? Are you there?"

Although spiders have spun me tightly into my dreams I tear the webs apart to reach for him.

"Did I wake you, son?"

It's three o'clock in the morning and, yes, he has woken me up but I lie, "No, you didn't wake me, Dad."

The telephone calls have been coming for over four years now. Dad rings from Maera Station, the family farm just outside Gisborne, far from where I live in Auckland. When he calls I look out the window at the moon and I realise that this same moon is also sliding low across our mountain, Maungahaumia, skipping the light like glowing stones into Mum and Dad's bedroom. Mum is asleep but Dad has crept from her side. He has been awake for hours and has gone into another room to telephone me. "I wouldn't have rung you, son, but I'm so afraid. Can you help me?"

My father is eighty-seven. How could he have become so old? None of us, my sisters, brothers and I, even noticed when it happened. One minute we were teenagers going to Te Karaka District High School and our father had dug a sandpit so we could practise the long jump for our school sports day. On that same day he taught us to run in hobnail boots because, according to him, when we took the boots off our feet, we would feel so light that we'd run on the wings of eagles. Somehow or other, between the time he called a practice run, "Ready, Steady, Go," and the time we ran back to him, laughing and arguing about who had come first, something happened to our god of a father, our laughing, muscled, carelessly handsome Daddy. Somebody took him away and put this other, older person in his place.

Who did this to him? Who turned his hair white, who trapped him in a different body with its musk smells, failing eyes, dry rasping breath and replacement hip? Who gave him all his fearful words, his querulous and anxious imaginings?

"I don't want to bother your mother about any of this, son. She's got enough on her own plate as it is."

I grasp for words with which to reply. "What is it, Dad? Why are you so afraid?"

"I don't want to close my eyes, son. If I close my eyes and go to sleep I mightn't wake up. I've got to stay awake. Will you help me? Will you?"

This is why he rings me, this father whom I love. He doesn't want to close his eyes because if he does Death's dark angel might sneak up on him and grab him unawares. He doesn't want to go, not because he fears dying; no, he's worried about how Mum would cope, the family, the farm, the whānau land at Waituhi, us, everybody. So he rings me up and we talk until dawn. He doesn't mind going to sleep in the day because he thinks that Death usually comes at night. He sometimes has strange ways of thinking and, I may as well say it, he has old-fashioned attitudes too, my dad. For instance, my sisters and I were often puzzled when we began to have boyfriends and girlfriends that Dad would always insist we were home before midnight. It was my sister Kararaina who guessed the secret. "Dad thinks that you don't do it, you know, *it*, before midnight."

When I had Dad up about it and suggested to him that you did, or could if you wanted to, at any time, he was absolutely disgusted.

My first inkling of Dad's anxieties came about seven years ago, just before he turned eighty. That's when he began to call. In those early days I simply humoured him, telling him he was stupid to have such thoughts, to go back to bed and go to sleep. Then one early morning, Dad said something that slammed me in the heart.

"Did I ever tell you, son, that I've always wanted to see the Heights of Abraham?"

His words really broke through my defences and, shivering, I said to my friend Murray, "I think this is really serious. I think my father's giving up. He wants to die."

Murray calmed me down. "You've got it all wrong," he said. "Your father wants to go to Canada. He wants to go to Québec."

I was puzzled and asked, "Why Québec?"

Murray answered, "That's where Britain's Major-General Wolfe fought the French during Canada's Anglo–French wars. The battle took place on the Heights of Abraham."

In a subsequent telephone conversation with Dad I asked him, "Why didn't you tell me you wanted to go to Canada!"

He answered, "I thought you knew. I've always wanted to go, ever since I learnt about the battle at school when I was a boy." However, his own words triggered his fears and worries again, reminding him of how far ago his school days had been. Where did this capacity to frighten himself come from? He never used to be like this. What first reminded him that the moon was lowering onto the horizon, the tide was turning and ebbing out? Was it my Auntie Joey's funeral? Or three years ago when he buried Hani, another younger brother? At every death in the family it has always been Dad who has said, "Oh well," loaded up the truck with his shovels and gone up to the family graveyard to dig another hole. "Better me to bury my brothers and sisters and cousins, uncles and aunties, than some stranger."

My dad has always been the one who digs the graves. What happens when the digger dies? The thought is inconceivable.

So what do you say to a father who is so old and frightened? Four years ago, I had tried laughing it off. Then three years ago I thought being angry with him might do the trick. "Dad," I would say, "I'm tired, I have to go to work tomorrow and I won't talk about this. Of course you're not going to die." I tried diversionary tactics like, "Why don't you wake Mum up and bother her instead of ringing me up and being such a nuisance?" Or I would say, "Go and have a glass of water and watch television," or "And stop worrying about us, we'll be okay."

But there were times when he began to chip away at my resistance and make me afraid and, forgive me, but I let the telephone ring and ring and ring. Then I would get angry with myself for not answering the only telephone in the world that was ringing and I would take the handset off the cradle and say, "Yes, Dad, I'm here."

The trouble is I have always thought my dad was indestructible. This was the father who, no matter his ageing body, I regarded as invincible. Even at fifty he had still been playing rugby. For God's sake, he was still shearing at sixty. I had always been good at playing the game of Let's Pretend as far as my father was concerned.

"Look," Kararaina scolded me, "this is your wake-up call. Is anybody home? Your father's been growing old for years now. The trouble is that you've been stuck up there in Auckland and never been around to notice it." True, when you're living somewhere else you think that time only ticks by where you are and not everywhere else.

To complicate matters, Mum rang. "I think your father is seeing another woman," she said. "He gets out of bed in the middle of the night and he goes to telephone her. He thinks I don't know what he's up to. I wonder who she is, pae kare, when I find out I'll . . ."

I reassured Mum. "It's me that Dad's been ringing."

My mother paused and then her voice came down the line, "Are you two jacking up some story behind my back?"

I answered, "No, Mum, it's true. Dad rings me up."

Mum was still suspicious. "What about?"

I answered, somewhat ridiculously, because Dad was the one who should be telling Mum what it was all about, not me, "It's . . . it's . . . a male bonding thing."

There was another long silence, then, "I'll never understand about you and your father," Mum said.

"Son, I'm so frightened, so worried." It is so difficult to listen to a father calling across the night and to listen to the panic in his voice. "What will happen to your mother when I go? Who will look after the farm?"

With surprise I have realised that once upon a time I was the one who used to run to Dad but now he's the one — and he's running to me. I the son have become the father. He the father has become the son. Surely this is not the way it's supposed to be! The father who was always there for me is now the child wanting me to hold him in my arms. The man who hugged me when I ran my races is now the boy who needs to be embraced.

"See? Wasn't I right about the hobnail boots? You had the wings of eagles, son, the wings of eagles."

Two years ago, I tried another tactic. I told him, "Dad, we all die sometime," and then, to get his mind off death, I began to tell him how much he is loved in his life, because isn't that what people really want to know when they are fearful? I told him he was the greatest father that anybody could possibly have and that he was my best friend. I reminded Dad that his own father, Pera Punahāmoa, had a long life and the likelihood was that he would have the same. And that he shouldn't worry because he had brought his children up well and we all knew what to do with Mum, the farm, the land at Waituhi, everything, don't worry.

Despite our reassurances, Dad was still concerned. The trouble was that he had been head of the family for so long. And he was the longest-living member of our tribe, Te Whānau-a-Kai. And so every small thing, any newspaper report, any incidental occurrence had surrounded him with darkness and taken him away again into the dread stomach of the night.

For instance, the frogs stopped croaking in the dam on the farm. He hadn't heard a weka calling for many nights. Worst was when he read a report that the Department of Conservation had closed Ninety Mile Beach and now you had to have a permit to transit the beach.

"How am I going to get to Te Reinga, son? Will I need a permit so that my soul can fly across Ninety Mile Beach?" He began to rail against DOC and the Māori people of the Far North. "Don't those people up there know they're the kaitiaki, the guardians, and that they're supposed to keep the airways clear for us? You better get me a permit just in case I need it."

The telephone rings. The sticky threads of the webs are not sufficient to restrain me in sleep, not strong enough to keep me from answering, "Yes, Dad, I'm here, I'm here."

He begins to talk and I can hear his heart beating in his voice and his lungs breathing air through his words. "So afraid, son, so worried."

With a great sense of awe I have to come to realise that loving my father in his autumn years has become my greatest gift to him as a son. I never thought it would be like this and that I would have the privilege of being so strong for him. A year ago, listening to my father spinning his fears across the night, I realised with shock, "I think Dad wants me to save him somehow. But how can I do this? Can anybody combat Death himself?"

But I have figured out a way of at least stalling those dark angel wings.

"You won't die, anyway, Dad, because we have to go to see the Heights of Abraham."

And so the questions my father asks have changed. "When are we going, son? When are we going?" I have begun to answer, "Next year, Dad, next year."

At first I made this promise for him. Now I realise, however, that whenever the telephone rings and I hear his voice once again, "Are you there, son? Are you there?" I am also making the promise for me as much as for him. And why?

Oh beat the drum slowly and play the fife lowly. This man, my father, is the Lord of my life. He represents all the people I come from, my life's kings and queens, princes and princesses. They tamed the sun, pulled islands from the sea and separated the earth from the sky so that I might stand upright on the bright strand between and claim my world's inheritance. This man, my father, my Lord, made me from strong loins so that I would continue to carry the great stories of a people who were Vikings of the sunrise. These, my people, came to our savage islands far to the south to the valley where my father lives. They fought and died for the valley, spilt their blood to the last man, woman and child standing — against guns, ghosts and strangers who already had taken everything but wanted ... *everything*. No matter who I become or where I go in the world, I will become a prince only because I am of such royal stock and have a valley in my life, a sacred mountain at one end, a fortress at the other, and a river running through it — and a father keeping up the sky.

I need my dad to keep holding on to his last breath. As old as I am now, I cannot bear the thought of running back to him on my wings of eagles and not finding him waiting with all his masculine pride and fatherly admiration. God-like, I have found a way of keeping my father alive.

"When are we going, son? When are you going to take me to see the Heights of Abraham?"

My father's voice reaches through the spiders' webs of my dreams. The filaments shiver and are suddenly drenched with dew.

"Soon, Dad. Next year. Yes, let's make it next year."

5.

I never did take Dad to see the Heights of Abraham. I guess I was too afraid to, scared that no sooner had I taken him there, he would die.

The Czar of All the Russias was ninety-five when he left us on 6 September 2010. He was a wonderful father and truly a man among men.

My cousin Haare Williams told me a lovely story about the pīngao (*Desmoschoenus spiralis*), the golden sand sedge which can be found at the tops of dunes on Ninety Mile Beach all the way to Te Reinga. The sedge has a tangled, clumped appearance because as the spirits journey to Te Reinga, the ones in the morning twist the pīngao together so that the others who come later can follow the path.

As the sun begins to set, the pīngao makes a noise as latecomers rush through the twisted signposts before the coming of the dark.

I like to imagine my father carefully knotting one leaf after another for me, *Don't be afraid son, come this way, this way.* After all, he who shepherded me all my life would surely not want to lay derelict his duty by not guiding me in death.

One thing more. My sisters and I liked to say of our parents that although we owed our lives, career and ambition to our mother, Julia, the one we really loved was our father. I think this was because our mother was often very dogmatic whereas Dad was malleable. For Mum, life was black and white, no shades of grey, it was either Yes or No, you did it or you didn't do it, and she disliked people who rationalised with all their "Yes, but" or "No, however" or "Maybes".

What's ironic was that I had told Mum that the novel was about Dad. Even so, the revealing aspect of *Tangi* is that although it is about a boy thinking of the death of his father, the last chapter is, in fact, about his mother.

Chapter Thirteen

O, Clouds Unfold!

1.

Let's spiral back to my return to Gisborne from CCNZ in 1962.

And first of all, allow me to bring you up to date with my three sisters.

We were, of course, overjoyed to be back in each other's company. During the time I had been at CCNZ they had become spirited and independent young women; in these qualities they have all these years remained unaltered. They had been nurtured well by our mother, Julia, who did not allow gender to delimit anyone's mana.

Kararaina was seventeen, slim, a stunner, and her sisters looked up to her as the eldest girl. Tāwhi was fifteen, bright-eyed and held to her views — in this she was more like our mother and, as such, could sway decisions. As for Viki, although she was only fourteen, her opinions could not be discounted simply because she was — at the time — the youngest.

My sisters were a tight trio who loved each other's company and defended one another.

And while the fact that I was the oldest sibling was something they respected, that did not stop them from demanding they should be treated equally. In this they were supported by our mother. Indeed we all remember a particular negotiation — we laugh about it all the time — that has become our origin story.

It was the first time equality was demanded — and given. And it set the course and terms of our sibling relationship for the rest of our years.

The family is in Gisborne from the farm for the weekend, and I plan a date with my friend from CCNZ, Iris Whaanga. My sisters ask Dad if they can go out too and he says no.

However, Mum countermands him. "If Witi is able to go out," she says, "the girls should be allowed as well."

Now, I love my sisters more than they know, but taking them out with me is a totally different story. However, Kararaina is wanting to see her boyfriend from Te Karaka, one of the Robin boys. And Tāwhi always thinks she is my equal anyway, and she has caught the eye of Billy Tahata, a garage mechanic. Viki, at fourteen, is much too young to be out on her own but, "You can take her to the pictures with you and Iris," Mum says.

Despite my protests, I find myself driving the car to Iris's place and when she sees my three sisters with me, she giggles, "I should be surprised . . . but I'm not," whatever that means.

Meantime I have already decided on a movement order. That night Iris and I *are* going to a movie, so I park the car outside the King's Theatre and I glare at the three darlings.

"Right," I say to them, "Viki, you are the youngest, so you're coming with me."

But Viki has other ideas. "I've got my own plans"

What can I do? "Okay, but I want you to be here at the theatre when we come out at 10.30." I turn to the other two. "Tāwhi, you are next eldest, so I will pick you up at the clocktower at eleven. Kararaina, what are you up to tonight?"

A brother should never ask, and she doesn't reply.

"Oh, all right," I say. "I'll pick you up at 11.30 at Roebuck Road. That way, we can all be back at Haig Street before midnight."

"Before Dad thinks we can have sex with our boyfriends, eh?" Tāwhi giggles to her sisters.

Of course, when the movie is over Iris and I discover Viki isn't waiting at 10.30. Nor is Tāwhi at the clock tower at eleven. They are both at a dance at the War Memorial Hall. By the time I am able to drag them away from their mates — cousins and hockey players all — it is already 11.30 and Kararaina is nowhere near Roebuck Road.

"She must be up Kaitī Hill," my dear younger sisters say, referring to the local lovers' lane.

A loving brother's word of honour disallows me from telling you where I eventually find her or the car of the boy with her, but Iris and I drive like heck to get back to Haig Street before midnight. Dad is waiting for us, tapping his foot and looking at his watch.

"You're late," he says.

"Still up?" my sisters answer, kissing him on the cheek and running into the house. And then they turn to me. "Goodnight, brother."

Sometimes that's all it takes. Two words: Goodnight, brother.

Fortunately for me, Dad's watch is running fast and I am saved by the chimes from the clocktower announcing from far away the witching hour.

And it is Iris, after you take her home, who confers the title on you and your sisters.

She calls you all, "Witi and his sisters."

When your youngest sister, Gay, becomes the fourth girl, she reverses the label by saying, "His sisters *and* Witi."

It's been like that ever since, and just as your sisters have been, and are, in your life, they are *everywhere* in your fiction.

2.

I began a year in the lower sixth at Gisborne Boys' High School in Stanley Street. My childhood friends, such as Maarten van Dijk, had already achieved scholarships and gone on to university. I knew some of my classmates — Peter King, Victor Mackey, Haupai Henare and his brother George — but most I didn't. So what was new about that? Gisborne Boys' was my third high school in three years and, what with umpteen primary schools earlier, I was accustomed to starting again.

But I never made the connection between my parents' insistence on education for their children, and schooling itself, until I went to New Delhi, India, in August 2016. Actually, Mum and Dad supported education for as many young Māori children as they could fit into the house in Haig Street, in those years before we moved to the farm.

After all, Haig Street was large enough. And it kept on getting bigger because Dad, as padrone of the family shearing gang, centred his business there. "The House That Tom Built" eventually became three main bedrooms as well as extra rooms that could provide sleeping places for shearers who wintered over with us. There was also a huge garage, an outside hut for any visiting Mormon elders, kennels for dogs — and a paddock for livestock, as the property became a place for animal overnighters too.

An extra couple of school students? No sweat. My cousins Ivan and Tom were boarders for a time, and people still come up to me to tell me that they stayed over because their parents lived too far away from the city. The boarders came in handy going after the sheep and cattle that sometimes leapt over the fence.

Dad's attitude was that any career that advanced us in the Pākehā world was better than his as a farmer and a shearer. When I sometimes complained about how hard it was to be a writer he was very pragmatic about it.

"Beats digging in fenceposts," he said.

In 2016 I met journalist Debarshi Dasgupta and my old colleague Sudeep Sen. Both had been recipients of the largesse of parents who insisted on education. Debarshi told me, "You can be the poorest peasant in Bengali, yet you will ensure an education for your children. It will give them the opportunity to make their way in the world." Debarshi was called by Mahesh, his driver, "Sweet Boss", and indeed he was.

Mahesh, who was a Tamil from southern India, had his own views on the subject. "The parents and the teachers, they are the most important people in the bringing up of the child. And with schooling, the child is able to make money, buy gold and jewels, so that everybody can see. Yes, of course the child can become wise too, but wisdom you can't see!" And then he added, "The parents never know. And because they don't know, they must continue to hope."

My visit to New Delhi was moving and spiritual. Sweet Boss and Mahesh drove me through hair-raising traffic to sites of Mughal architecture. The mausoleum of the Taj Mahal, Agra, was the most recognised, but New Delhi had many other notable examples. The Moti Gate of Sher Shah Suri, Bahlul Lodi's tomb and Humayun's tomb were all examples of Indo-Islamic architecture.

I spent a day at Humayun's Tomb, the Indian subcontinent's first garden vault, going on to inspire such places as the Taj Mahal. Built in 1565–66 by his grieving widow, Haji Begum, it typified Persian design, with its octagonal shape, and it was notable for its double dome. I walked through a grove of orange trees and saw people sheltering under neem trees (*Azadirachta indica*), grateful for shade in the beautiful paradise garden.

Equally affecting was a visit to the Agrasen ki Baoli. An ancient step well where people used to draw water on a daily basis, it was accessed by 103 stairs. I know, I counted them and, eager to help, so did Debarshi. At the bottom was the well; above, was a roosting place for hundreds of bats.

Baoli were built to cope with seasonal fluctuations in water availability. I love anything to do with water, and the whole idea that millions of people over the centuries, mainly women, had descended daily to draw water from the storage and irrigation tank — and offered gifts to the goddess of the well for her blessings — filled me with humility. In some related wells, known as johara, ramps were built to allow villagers to take their cattle down to drink the water.

"That sounds like what Mum and Dad were doing with me," I said to Debarshi as we rested during our ascent from the well, back into the full light of day. "Prodding an unruly calf into education who, at the ripe old age of eighteen, continued his schooling at Gisborne Boys' High."

No wonder then, as I was resting, that I saw a woman coming out of the sun and down the steps. I shaded my eyes and, in that moment, I sensed my mother approaching.

I was not surprised. After all, my mother, Julia — whose Māori name was Turiteretimana — was a dream swimmer.

I can only presume that the conversations I had had during the day with Sweet Boss, Sudeep and Mahesh had vibrated the air sufficiently for it to open and for my mother to step through. Not just from one culture into another but also — because Turiteretimana had died in 2008 — from one time to the next. She was dressed in a sari, she was one woman, but she was all women who had come to draw water.

I left Delhi on the birthday of Lord Krishna with a great sense of gratitude for my parents.

"You never know," my mother had smiled, and I had felt the touch of her lips on my brow.

At the top of the well, Debarshi and I joined other tourists and, together, we sought relief from the daytime heat.

3.

My parents were unfair to foist me onto Gisborne Boys' High School, but they, the school and I survived. The school heeded its own motto: *virtus repulsae nescia,* courage knows no defeat. I was moody and morose, yes, an unruly calf. Returning to black shorts, grey shirt, pull-up socks and school cap was a bit of a shock, and when I went with Mum to get the new uniform from McGruer's I baulked. After the American glam of the Mormon College duds, I felt that removing my butt from long trousers and putting it into a bumbag was a retrograde step. The axe in my hands recommended by Headmaster Gray was the more attractive bet.

Mum and Dad were adamant. "Get used to cold knees," Dad said.

"You've only brought this on yourself," Mum added, whatever that meant.

A closer look at the architecture of the school — stately, ivy-covered, Edwardian with a capital E, and were those oak trees fronting the main building? — confirmed I had also travelled back in time on Chitty Chitty Bang Bang to an educational practice reeking of Crown and Empire. Centuries of history joined Gisborne Boys' with the quadrangles of Albion.

The civic-minded descendants of those venerable ancestors of "Home" must have watched, alarmed, the approach of the darksome barbarians at the gate. Unlike us, they saw the school in a different light as one of the city's crown jewels, Great Britain's last stand in the far-flung colony. This glittering status was shared with the clocktower, Masonic Hotel and Barker's Castle, orienting Gisborne to time according to Greenwich, affirming freemasonry as the arbiter of civic morality — and, well, every English city must have a castle.

And then there were the three bridges built by Frederick Goodman — Peel Street, Kaiti and the Railway Bridge — that kids still jump from. The three rivers triangulated a very English-looking market town.

Let's add Poho-o-Rāwiri meeting house, though, to give the town a Māori look.

The school was into its seventh year as a boys-only institution, the girls having been separated out to attend Gisborne Girls' High across Gladstone Road. Mum and Dad contemplated settling me at the school's rectory, as the farm was too far away for me to make the trip to Gisborne and back every day, but, fortunately for me, the residence was fully booked. I had not relished being the hori in the woodpile. Alternative boarding arrangements were therefore made with one of Dad's brothers, Uncle Hani, and his wife, Auntie Lena, in their new house in Valley Road. My younger cousin Tiopira was also boarding with them.

Uncle Hani was Hephaestus, god of fire, in the family pantheon. He had just returned from a stint in Hawai'i at the Hawai'ian Cultural Centre. Auntie Lena's claim to fame was that she had appeared in the movie mentioned earlier, *Blue Hawaii*, with Elvis Presley. There she was, swinging her long poi and singing her heart out, as Elvis and Joan Blackman kissed in the final reel. Auntie was from a high-flying Māori family, and one of her sisters, Queenie, became an accomplished composer and stalwart of the kōhanga reo movement. I had the pleasure of teaching Queenie's daughter, Linda, at Manukau.

As for Tiopira, he was as hyperactive and manic then as he was as an adult. He had a brain that must have looked like an electric storm discharging bolts of lightning over the Tallahassee River. If you ever connected with it, watch out, you would crash and burn but . . . a cuz was a cuz.

Uncle Hani was what Māori would have called poto, very short. He was certainly south of five feet tall, and that made him immovable in hockey games. In the goal he was like a tree stump, planting himself in the ground and nothing could get past him. Like Uncle Win, Uncle Hani had a BA and I knew that Dad had him on my case: make sure Witi steps up. I baulked at boarding with him and Auntie Lena as there was a perfectly good house that I could stay at — our family house in Haig Street, lying vacant; my sisters and I liked to call it our "town house" as opposed to the farm. I had an ulterior motive when I argued my case to relocate. A certain amount of welcome freedom was waiting at Haig Street, as Mum and Dad and the family came into Gizzy only during the weekends to play sport. But the school authorities nixed that proposal. They preferred me to sneak out Uncle's window rather than walk freely out the door at Haig Street.

That didn't stop me from plotting.

On my first day at Gisborne Boys' I joined my classmates at school assembly. Over eight hundred students watched as the staff trooped onto the stage and waited for the main attraction: Batman, also known as Headmaster, in his flowing cape. Mr Gray took one look at us and shuddered.

Bring me my Bow of burning gold:
Bring me my arrows of desire:
Bring me my Spear: O, clouds unfold!
Bring me my Chariot of fire!

I had definitely returned across the paepae poto back into New Zealand provincial society.

From a Māori perspective, it was a society that was being driven by Pākehā. They were in control, and their aspirations for Māori could all be seen in the Hunn Report I have earlier referred to. Among those aspirations, education was regarded as one of the main ways for the model to work. Therefore picture me, sitting in class feeling rather like the pushmi-pullyu in Hugh Lofting's *The Story of Doctor Dolittle* (1920). The gazelle–unicorn cross had two heads and two sets of legs and it could go either one way or another and, most often, confused, just stood there and didn't go anywhere.

If I advanced in Pākehā education, what would happen to me as a Māori?

I would have to chance it. Those two heads have been constantly braying at, snarling at and spitting at each other ever since. And the gazelle–unicorn cross has been spraying shit all over the place (where was the orifice, I wonder?) Balancing the concerns of both heads would become a lifetime pursuit.

Pity about the excreta.

I was, therefore, suspicious of Gisborne Boys' High from the start. There was no doubt in my impetuous brain that the education mindset was assimilationist. Yes, it was benevolent, but even so there were low(er) expectations for Māori students — that hadn't changed — and they were reflected in the division of the lower sixth into two classes. Those who were likely to have University Entrance accredited (they wouldn't have to sit the end-of-year exam) were in one class, 6B1 natch. Those who wouldn't be accredited (and would therefore have to sit and maybe they would pass but most likely they wouldn't) were in the other, 6B2.

You don't have to guess which class I was in, and to reinforce the obvious our form teacher was Māori, George Marsden; he also happened to be the history teacher. The first thing he said in our introductory class was: "They don't expect you boys to pass but, pae kare, you're going up and over the top and through No Man's Land even if I have to pull you over myself."

He had all the credentials. In World War II he was Captain George Marsden, A Company, Maori Battalion, and later he married Pare Saxby of Women's Services. The received wisdom was that the male leadership among Māori suffered by the grievous loss of men in World War II. While that might be true, there was also a vanguard of Māori who, on their return from battle, obtained career jobs in education, the church, Māori affairs, social and community welfare, the armed services and even diplomacy. Among them were Canon Wi Huata, chaplain, Harry Dansey, specialist, Charles Bennett who became New Zealand Ambassador to Malaya, Sonny Waru, Kahi Harawira, Ngātai Wanoa, Manu Bennett who became Bishop of Aotearoa, Norman Perry, Monty Wikiriwhi intelligence and later senior welfare officer with the Department of Maori and Island Affairs, Roy Te Punga, Charlie Shelford who became a Māori warden, John Rangihau who spent some time in the New Zealand Air Force before transferring to the Maori Battalion — and of course Pita Kaua who married my beautiful Aunt Mattie, my mother's sister.

I settled down to my school work. Gone was the joy of studying and enjoying contemporary American writers in the English class. In came the absolute boredom of Shakespeare's *Hamlet* (or *Omelette* as I called it, with its eggy existentialism); the study of an English novel (I can't remember what it was, but something non-arousing for schoolboys by a male writer who probably never had an orgasm in his life); and lyric poets, again male only, such as Keats, Wordsworth and Yeats, as the received opinion was that women never wrote good poetry or, for that matter, good anything. Instead of discussing history, we watched as Mr Marsden wrote some facts on the board about English history during the Reign of the Tudors — women existed only to get their heads chopped off — and asked us to underline passages in our set text.

We were advised to learn these passages by heart so as to regurgitate them in the end-of-year University Entrance examination, should we have to sit it.

At least science under a harassed Mr Jowett provided the possibility of an explosion which would enliven my life. There was also Derek Bird's drama class. He was tall, thin and could have stood in for actor Christopher Lee. He had one of the most beautiful voices I had ever heard, as well as the knack of being completely surprising.

I also had hockey to fall back on, as I was picked for the first eleven. I worked out my frustration by whacking the ball at some opponent's head.

4.

To be frank, all I have ever been is an uninteresting boy and, later, man, but life and the people in it are what have made me interesting. In this retro frame of mind, let me therefore introduce my English teacher Mr RN Grono, my "Mr Chips".

Readers of old and dusty novels picked up in secondhand book stores will recognise the reference to Mr Chipping, the schoolteacher in James Hilton's novella *Goodbye, Mr Chips* (1934). Mr Chips guided generations of schoolboys at the fictitious Brookfield School, modelled on Hilton's own master of classics and education at a private élitist school in Cambridge. The playwright Terence Rattigan later created a different and altogether more anguished kind of master, Crocker-Harris, in his acidic play, *The Browning Version* (1948).

Mr Grono had known me from Te Karaka District High School as well as Gisborne Intermediate, where he had been headmaster; who was following whom, I don't know. He was a small, round man with thin lips, squinty eyes, and he was always a natty dresser. When I turned up in his English class at Gisborne Boys' High, one eyebrow raised, his eyes blinked once (and Mr Grono *never* blinked) and, for the rest of the year, he never asked me for my scholastic backstory or paid me any special attention.

Great. Leave me alone. Let's get on with it.

In temperament, Mr Grono was a cross of both Mr Chipping and Crocker-Harris, and although he was forced to teach the curriculum he took us, willing or not, beyond it. He found a ready disciple in me as well as others, such as a former schoolmate, Norman Maclean, who has characterised Mr Grono as a pedagogue, a strict and pedantic one.

Norman published an essay on our old master in the *Dominion Post*, 5 January 2010, which he has given permission to be reproduced here. It captures both the sentimentality of the students' affection for him and the astonishing nature of his teaching.

> Because I was something of an apple polisher, I would sit at the front in fifth form English. My desk abutted Mr Robert Grono. Bob, we called him — behind his back, naturally. From where I sat, I could look up to him, as it were.
>
> He had a way of standing his right hand on the desk top: five plump and bandy ballet dancers' legs that sprang in the air to emphasise a particular point. Throughout each lesson, this troupe pranced and lightly thudded, inches from my nose.
>
> There were many favourite prejudices aired and a wealth of esoteric knowledge offered, despite their irrelevance to the November burden of School Certificate. But how he endeared himself to me, the first time he said, 'Now boys, you cannot hope to pass the examinations without a thorough knowledge of the Greek myths and legends.'
>
> I knew this was a lie, an absurdity — a preposterous endorsement of what he held dearest to his considerable heart. It was repeated several times throughout that year with a certainty that brooked not the smallest doubt and presumably made the dullest shudder at the prospect of assured failure. I adored him for it. With glittering eye and right hand rising, falling, rising again, he insisted that there was no educated man who did not understand the symbolism behind the rape of Persephone, the flaying of Marsyas, the allegorical significance to be mined from the slopes of Mount Olympus.
>
> Bob's rages were notorious. Crimson visaged and spraying the first two rows with furious flecks of spittle, he would roar condemnation of those who interrupted him when he spoke or dared to question how the amorous exploits of Zeus could possibly bring a higher percentage on the results slip.
>
> I found enough voice to tentatively request book titles. He approved of the fact that I was a reader and wrote enthusiastic essays on every topic he set.

Bob lent me *The Ingoldsby Legends* which he deemed to be a student's finest introduction to classical mythology. He endorsed the Bible, too, and Shakespeare — naturally — and practically everything venerated in the canon of western civilisation's literary achievements.

Bob boomed approval of my English results the following February when I joyfully went up into his sixth form class. Of course there hadn't been as much as a glimpse of the Greeks in that three hour mish-mash that had seen us so recently ploughing through dense thickets of comprehension and exposition of rather dull short stories studied. I didn't care. I was immersed in a realm peopled by deities and heroes; extraordinary realms where anything was possible and everything — everything that I read, somehow connected with the world I was coming to know in my stumbling teen years.

Unlike Norman and my other classmates, I could never call Mr Grono either Robert or the more familiar Bob. But he joins the whakapapa of teachers to whom I owe gratitude. In Norman Maclean's case, he returned to Gisborne Boys' High to teach classical studies. When Mr Grono died, Norman gave a eulogy for him to the massed ranks of students, none of whom had ever heard of him.

The strong vein of Greek classical mythology that flows through my work, especially in *The Matriarch* (1986) and *The Dream Swimmer* (1997), definitely comes from those long and stirring diatribal asides that emanated from Mr Grono's English classes. From there it was only a short hop, step and jump from the gods of Olympus to the mountains of Māoridom. I therefore join Norman in thanking him.

Frater ave, atque vale.

5.

I can't remember how I did it but I managed to persuade Mum and Dad that it would be better for all concerned if I stayed at Haig Street. I always had the habit of provocation so I probably bullied Dad into it.

More to the point, I had returned to Mrs Cole, my piano teacher, to continue my brilliant career as a pianist — and Uncle Hani and Auntie Lena didn't have a piano in their house. Mrs Cole was overjoyed to see me, and I her, although she didn't approve of some of Brother Murphy's innovations to my technique.

"Your hands are too low and in the *American* position," she said. "They need to be higher," she continued, which I took to mean the superior, English position.

I clearly needed remedial work. "Why don't you bring the piano down from the farm and put it in Haig Street?" I said to Dad.

Once the piano was moved in, so did I.

I was sequestered in Haig Street by Easter. One of my disappointments in leaving Uncle Hani's place, however, was that I hadn't known he was researching to write a book on our ancestor, the parliamentarian Wī Pere Halbert. I sometimes wonder about the interesting conversations Uncle Hani and I could have had over his manuscript which, I understand, is still under a bed in Haig Street.

Easter came, and the annual Māori hockey tournaments were held. In that year, the Hana Konewa cup and other shields and trophies were to be fought for up the Coast. You think that the Māori part of my life was put on hold while I was at Gisborne Boys' High? Nope. It was exhausting being a Māori and, when I look back, I am amazed at its continuing fullness. There were so many hui that my family went to. Sports tournaments, birthdays, weddings and funerals saw the family zipping and zapping across the country, and me with them.

However, that particular Easter I had my own plans and I pleaded, "Do you mind if I don't come to the tournament this year?"

I used homework as an excuse and expected the usual reply, "You can do your homework afterwards". *Afterwards* was a concept unique to Māori, referring to some nonexistent time you had to do the thing you should have done except that reciprocal commitments meant that you didn't.

Instead, Mum and Dad said to me, "Okay." They really wanted me to finish high school.

At the time Dad had both a Holden and a farm truck and, with a cheery wave, the folks left in the car to play hockey, heading northeast. As soon as they were out the gate I jumped into the truck and zoomed south to see my girl Hiria in Hastings.

It was Dad's own fault. What had he been *thinking*?

I stayed in Hastings with Hiria and her family for three days, relishing the chance to get to know her parents, brothers and sisters.

I liked her Dad, Te Waru, a lot, he had been a boxer in his early days. And Hiria's elder sister, Naumai, was on my side in enabling Hiria and me to spend as much time together as possible. But Hiria's mother was distrustful of me for good reason — loving Hiria had turned in my case to lust. There was only one thing I wanted during that visit and her mother made sure I did not get it. Frustrated, I kept delaying my return, and Hiria in the end virtually pushed me out of her mother's house.

On the way back to Gisborne, I was travelling so fast over the Whareratas that I couldn't take a corner and ended with the truck down a bank. Luckily for me some Māori forest workers saw my plight and towed me back onto the road. I arrived back into Gisborne an hour before the family was due to return home for the weekend, washed the pickup, good as new.

"We lost," Dad said, referring to the hockey tournament and blaming me.

Then he looked at the truck, saw some chips and dents in the paintwork and suspected something. Next thing I knew he had put a minder on me. Charlie Mohi, 28 Maori Battalion, Bren Carrier Platoon, was one of Dad's mates at church.

Under the guise of being my Mormon home teacher, Charlie knocked on the door, dapper with his pencil moustache.

"Thanks, Brother Mohi," I said, "but I don't need looking after." I already had Mummy and Daddy Waugh next door checking me in and out.

The next week, hullo, his son Lester turned up. "Gidday, Witi, feel like a movie?"

From that moment on Lester and I became good mates, along with Turei Whaanga from college and Maude Ngaira.

But Charlie had his uses. He became the adult to whom I turned for intellectual stimulation. For instance we had a conversation on whether the universe was deterministic or not, and he used mātauranga Māori — the knowledge and understanding of everything in the universe — to take the worrying affirmative. I, however, never liked the idea that you could not affect your fate.

More specifically, Charlie became the farmhand Bulla's replacement in my quest for information on the meaning of life, on love and sex — and, in particular, being male, on male performance and all those issues around what is known today as sexual health. I think I must have been a challenge to Charlie because my questions were often, er, clinical. Frankly, I've never liked learning "on the job" in any endeavour, and he was the only male nearby who could respond precisely to direct questioning. Poor unsuspecting Charlie turned out to be better with information than I had been expecting; I think he had to do some crash-course research and cross his fingers that he could stay in front of my persistent probing.

Mind you, my focus was not as narrow as the above might imply. Sex, birth, life and death were inextricably linked with wider issues. For instance, one night Charlie and his wife, Blossom, kindly invited me to their house along with other members of the local congregation to meet new Mormon elders; actually, Blossom had an inkling about my unorthodox inquisitiveness and kept trying to pull me into (Mormon) line. I created a ruckus when I asked a simple question: "When does life begin?"

At the time the Mormon and Māori opinion was the same. "When the first breath is taken," the newly-minted American boys said.

Smart-arsed me looked at them and the star-struck gathering, chomped on my leg of lamb, and let the elders have it between the eyes. "Oh, so abortion is all right then."

I said goodbye to my hosts and tried to get away fast. But Blossom Mohi came out shaking her fist.

"You come right back here, Witi. Don't think you can drop your stinkbomb and get away with it."

By then I was down the street and away, leaving the elders to justify their position.

Later, when a complaint was made to the bishop — Albert Whaanga had continued his brilliant rise in the church — Charlie took my side. He was the closest I had to a mentor in the Mormon community.

6.

I had to knuckle under that peculiar practice of New Zealand schools called cadet training. This hangover from English regimental schools enabled senior students to brush up on their command skills, should they decide on a military career. Every Thursday they had us "square bashing" as we called it, reinforcing to all that if we followed the rules we were in for a pleasant education experience; if we didn't, life would be *un*pleasant. One of my colleagues, Ivan Carswell, went into the army as a commissioned officer from 1967 to 1989 and subsequently taught educational psychology at Victoria University of Wellington and Massey University. And, of course, many of the Māori at Gisborne Boys' High joined up after they left school.

I don't want to come down hard on Gisborne Boys' High. After all, the school library is now named after me. I made good friends regardless, and some of them I still see around, like Basil Sharp, Chair in Energy Economics at the University of Auckland. I've already mentioned my cousin George Henare, one of New Zealand's greatest actors, and others included pianist David James who, the year before I arrived, won the Junior Prize for Piano Concerto with his playing of the Mozart Concerto in B-flat minor. But it is Norman Maclean who seems to me to be the best example of the Gisborne Boys' High Everyman, and I have fond memories of others such as Michael McIvor, Richard Ivess and Vern Owen.

I have to admit, however, that I never went out of my way to cultivate their friendship.

Nor did I know it then, but I do know it now, that being at Gisborne Boys' High was a retrograde step for my imagination. I must have parked it somewhere as it was not being nurtured. On the other hand, perhaps frustration and boredom are just as important in the stimulation of a life of the mind? Whatever, I know that I was driven by despair to, finally, join the public library rather than visit it from time to infrequent time.

I felt like a Māori Oliver Twist asking for a plate of gruel. But a writer's education must include a place where you can go for reference as well as for pleasure. Today, while libraries often close or merge, there are still institutions which honour knowledge; but in the 1960s in Gizzy, the public library was *it*. I had been intuitively feeling my way through my reading towards this understanding, and I guess I had reached the point where I had to strike out beyond school resources.

I can still remember those mixed feelings of shame, anger and excitement when I made that decision to go through the glass doors and approach through the silence the Head Librarian, bespectacled, her hair in a bun, waiting at her desk.

"I would like to join up," I said.

The library became the place where I was able to expand my world. I discovered, for instance, a nascent interest in the arms race, fuelled by my movie-going — such films as *On The Beach* (1959), *The Day the Earth Caught Fire* (1961) and *Panic in Year Zero* (1962). And *Dr Strangelove* (1964), *Fail Safe* (1964), *The War Game* (1965) and *Planet of the Apes* (1968) were just around the corner.

And I discovered that someone in Gisborne belonged to the infant New Zealand Campaign for Nuclear Disarmament and dropped pamphlets off while the librarian wasn't looking.

It was impossible to grow up in New Zealand at that time without having concern for the future of a world which looked to all intents and purposes as if it was heading for a nuclear war between major powers. Such a war might be fought in the northern hemisphere, but it could impact on us down at the bottom of the world. *On The Beach* was about civilisation's last gasp in Australia, and on the night of 9 July 1962, East Coast skies were lit up by the American high-altitude tests at Christmas Island, just north of the equator. They revived memories of the twenty-kiloton fission bomb detonated at a height above Hiroshima, a city about the size of Christchurch, seventeen years earlier. That act might have ended World War II, but did a hundred thousand civilians have to be killed for it? And what about those who were injured or suffered radiation-induced illnesses?

People sometimes forget that New Zealand received more fallout from bomb testing than the equatorial regions.

I was in China in March 2017 and I heard Rod Oram, at the Shanghai Literary Festival, describe the 1960s from a geological perspective as the beginning of the Anthropocene epoch. In that decade humans became the defining agent in changing the ecology of the environment. The clear signal was the creation of a blanket of definable man-made radioisotopes around the earth.

Have we learnt anything? Back in New Zealand in July 2017, I turned on the news to hear that Pyongyang had tested its first intercontinental ballistic missile (ICBM), affirming that North Korea had become a country with intercontinental missile capability. For some months tensions escalated among its neighbours — South Korea, China and Japan among them — and some clown in the White House threatened to rain "fire and fury" on little rocket-man. Fortunately calmer counsel prevailed, and by the end of April 2018 the world breathed a sigh of relief at seeing North and South Korean leaders pledging peace between their two countries.

The point is that humankind are truly masters of the earth and its future wellbeing. Of the land, seventy-four per cent, excluding perpetual snow and ice, is managed by humans, and we've long passed the point where nature has much of a chance to restore herself.

In this scenario, however, we are still being held ransom by grandstanding men in positions of great power. In 2019 we can only hope that they turn their attention away from their toys and focus on saving the planet.

Chapter Fourteen

The Art Gallery of the Mind

1.

From the beginning, my purpose was to write Māori into existence. The eminent French writer André Malraux, who became Minister of Culture under De Gaulle, wrote on the subject in his book *Le Musée Imaginaire* (1947). His theory was that everyone had the freedom to create their own museum of the mind and that there was no need to be intimidated by the scholarly displays of the real museum.

Over seventy years have passed since Malraux's view. Today I would want to update it and write that Māori writers have not been intimidated. However, rather than offering their own work for display in a museum, they exhibit their work in the art galleries of the mind. There on show are not only artworks which show hinengaro, kaupapa and kupu but also aroha, meaning love, sympathy or affection.

In most cases, aroha is something that is offered to another person. But when it comes to the writer, Kāterina Te Heikōkō Mataira, in *The Maori People in the Nineteen-Sixties*, refers to aroha as a gift, not just from person to another but also — as in the phrase, "aroha ki te iwi" — as a koha to all peoples of the world.

Kāterina also points out something that should have been blindingly obvious:

> He (the Maori artist) does not need to create or seek situations from which to draw inspiration, for he already has a wealth of material to draw upon. The rich heritage of his forebears, the constant struggle of his people to keep their identity and integrity, the stresses and strains evident in the problems of the day, the never-ending stimulus of nature and the elements, as well as man's own struggle to find

himself, his purpose, and his God. All of these and much else are at his fingertips, requiring only the sensitivity, the strength of feeling, the power of expression (which I believe is innate in the Maori) and the skill (which I believe he can acquire) to bring to fruition works which may be a constant inspiration to man.

2.

I now turn, very quickly, to my second novel and third book, *Whanau, The Life of the Village*. Published in 1974, the book literally fell out of the air in a surprising way while I was writing *Pounamu, Pounamu* and *Tangi*.

It had initially been a novella, "Village Sunday", and was planned for inclusion in *Pounamu, Pounamu*. However, my publisher David Heap at Heinemann Educational must have consulted Maurice Dowthwaite of Heinemann NZ Publishers on the length because, on 29 May 1973, Maurice wrote to me as follows.

> From a rough count it looks as though it will be about 50,000 words and this makes it a short novel. As you will appreciate, there are some problems in marketing a thin book no matter how good. I do wonder therefore if you would consider either extending this or putting something else with it. I would prefer the former if this is possible.

In later discussion with David, he thought that another 20,000 words would do the trick.

Now, I am only telling you all this to convey that becoming a writer isn't just all about the writing; there's a lot of backstage negotiation that takes place in the editing process.

Wine out of water, three books out of two, who would not be tempted?

Immediately, I saw the benefits of expanding "Village Sunday" as a narrative. I had in mind a particular kaupapa: that the book could go head-to-head with one of the main proposals of the Hunn Report (January 1961), authored by Jack Hunn, then Deputy Chairman, Public Service Commission and Acting Secretary for Maori Affairs.

You can blame those ancestors in the room behind my eyes. At one point in my life, I had been taken by a Māori proverb which went, "He pai te mahi, ahakoa hū, The work was done well, but noisily."

Those ancestors must have liked that whakataukī too. They were just about to start a ruckus.

The most popular image of the Hunn Report was that government wanted "to put a motor on the waka". Why? Well, the country was in the middle of that unprecedented rural to urban movement of Māori to the cities I referred to earlier. Since the previous stocktake of the relationship via the Maori Social and Economic Advancement Act of 1945, no matter how hard Māori were paddling, we hadn't kept up. We were considered ill equipped in terms of housing, social skills and education.

The report was therefore an attempt to look at government's — and our — assets to ascertain how they could be capitalised on to ensure our faster progress. For instance, Māori housing should be doubled, even trebled. Māori studying at university would be increased as numbers were only one-eighth of what they should be. The Māori crime rate was three and a half times the European rate and an effort could be made to reduce it. And Māori land development should be brought in at a rate of 50,000 acres of good farming stock annually rather than the present 10,000 acres.

Shoulda, woulda, coulda.

The report pointed out that intermarriage was integrating Māori and Pākehā, and it predicted that by the year 2000 the Māori population could reach 700,000 — a bit of an overshoot as the 2001 census figure was 526,000; and moreover, "Māori" were no longer identified by blood, but by their own preference, and all those Māori intermarrying complicated the question.

Extrapolating from the figures, the report proposed a model whereby Māori comprised one of three groups: 1) a completely detribalised minority (aka living in cities and Pākehā already); 2) the majority more or less at home in either society (aka living in the cities and on the way to Becoming Pākehā); and 3) the rest, "complacently living a backward life in primitive conditions" (aka Māori still down on the farm and exiting out the Back Door.) In the report was enshrined the notion of two peoples having two different pasts but one common future.

The devil was in that ideal of "one common future".

This was the future on Pākehā terms, but, as we know from history, Māori had other ideas. Part of the problem of the report was that it looked only at those "assets" it liked and ignored those it didn't — like the political sharing of power and returning land to Māori. And Jack Hunn and his report were demonised for notionally embracing the idea that the sooner Māori became Pākehā the better.

Two choices were offered up — integration or assimilation — with brown Pākehā as the endgame.

Where all this related to *Whanau* was that the Hunn Report had looked at multiple ownership of Māori land in a negative, Pākehā, way. What with booming population growth it was likely that whānau owners on any one patch of land would increase, leading to further title "fragmentation". Surely, the report asserted, this would create a "serious bar to the proper use of land in the interests of the Māori themselves — and in the national interest also"?

The report therefore decided that land-ownership reform must be implemented to bring about sole ownership.

Oh yeah? Dad and Nani Mini had a different view. The report had completely missed the point that Māori land was not just an economic resource, but also a cultural resource. In *Whanau* I therefore set out to create a human document, a Māori twin, to offset the official one.

More important, some Māori actually agreed with the proposed reform, so I also wanted to track the turmoil as a community responded to change within as well as without.

I set about adding those 20,000 words to the quotidian lives of Waituhi. I tried to show the social imperatives that inspired people to solidify those same structures and, if necessary, to die for them.

As it happened, the novella's structure allowed the insertion. Set over the course of one day, the "Sunday" of the title, the novella occurred in real time with members of a Māori family returning to Waituhi after a wedding. The 24-hour period was one of the Aristotelian unities in neo-classical drama — in *Tangi* I had expanded it to three days — and one of the best examples of a local book which conformed to the unities was Noel Hilliard's *A Night at Green River* (1969); the conflict between Pākehā Clyde Hastings, and his Māori neighbour, Tiwha Morris, takes place over one day and night.

Green River became the model for *Whanau*. I admired the way

Noel's book performed as parable, and I tried to port that sense of allegory over to my book. And right at the centre of the story was Rongopai, the meeting house — the axis — affirming the equipoise of the marae as spiritual and physical hub of the iwi.

Personally, I have always acknowledged Rongopai as playing an important function in making me the kind of person that I am. Its combination of traditional Māori motifs and contemporary scenes (contemporary with when they were created in 1888), its dual spirit of tradition and modernity, of seriousness and irreverent wit — all carried over into my writing. And, because the elders were horrified when they saw the pictographs the younger generation had painted, that too — the licence to comment and critique — I added to my armoury.

As a writer "in my own right" there's something else. I admired the work of Janet Frame and decided to use the "I" perspective and, as she did, to write from the then unusual present-tense position. At the time this mode of writing wasn't much used in the New Zealand novel, which tended to be predominantly written in third-person past. In my case — and this references both *Tangi* and *Whanau* — there were two crucial Māori reasons for writing this way: the modality would allow me to tell my story from inside a Māori consciousness, as an insider, not as an outsider; and I would be forced to be always "in the moment" of personal witness. In the case of *Tangi*, this caused a reduction in scale of the story to a more intimate, emotional staging, but perhaps that's a reason why it is still read today. And almost fifty years later, writing in first-person present is the mode of choice, especially by creative-writing class graduates who think it's new.

One more stylistic note — and it refers to my first four books. All of them use the quotation-dash instead of quotation marks. James Joyce and William Gaddis had used this form overseas, and Janet Frame may have introduced it in New Zealand. I wanted to signal that Māori could be as innovative as any other and that our writing needed to be liberated from expected practices.

3.

The publicity for *Whanau* invited the reader to "Follow them [the villagers] out by bus to their community. Haere mai, come and meet them. Come and walk down the road which runs through the village. You will meet: Rongo Mahana, alone in a landscape altered by Pākehā values; Miro Mananui, fighting to retain her land; Andrew Whatu, who must leave the village to follow his ambitions; Mattie Jones, who came back to the village defeated by the city; Nanny Paora, escaping the present by living in the past. These are some of the village people. There are more. Together they are *Whanau*, a vision of Māori rural life as it is now and its values now."

Whanau became the first tangible expression of my tribal self. From it I developed the idea of myself as writing for and on behalf of the collective whakapapa — Māori living and dead, present and past. I tried to amplify the social commentary and, in the process, *Whanau* became filmic, a kind of docudrama. In many ways it was a geographical survey, and Brian J Murton in 1979 wrote a very interesting article for the *New Zealand Geographer*, "Waituhi: A Place in Maori New Zealand", which mapped out Waituhi according to the novels and short stories I had published to that point.

The book begins with a description of Waituhi. In the early morning, the villagers are seen coming home from a local wedding. A series of short chapters follow, in each of which one or other of the various householders is briefly observed. Then as though from the bird's-eye view of a child's kite — I am referencing the manu tukutuku in Waituhi's own mythology, put up by Kahutapere to find the twins murdered by Tūpurupuru — I give an overall sight of the whole village. At close of day the kite darts and sways in the wind, pulling all the narrative strands of *Whanau* together — and then it swoops down on an old man and his grandson, Paora and Pene.

If ever the book is rewritten in a contemporary way I'll update the kite to a drone. I think Kahutapere would like that.

Throughout the novel Paora and Pene, representing the old and new generation, are walking through a reality composed of past and present into a future that is not terribly optimistic. It is Paora's disappearance that brings the entire village together in a common purpose to find him. His discovery provides the parable for the story.

When it was published, *Whanau* had its admirers.

Among them was filmmaker Aileen O'Sullivan who, accompanied by Māori director Larry Parr and actor–director Ian Mune, knocked on my door and asked if she could make a movie of the book; she had fallen in love with the old man and his grandson. Director Patrick Cox was also involved in writing a script.

Another admirer was composer Ross Harris who, with producer Adrian Kiernander, thought the novel would translate well into an opera. In 1984, *Waituhi: The Life of the Village* was premiered at the State Opera House, Wellington.

But was *Whanau* really a novel? Just because the book was novel-length didn't make it into one. Sure, *Whanau* was tidy and economical, vivid, lively and engaging. Being close-packed gave it clarity of form and lent an unimpeded propulsion to the narrative. The shape of the book, together with its compactness (the unity of time) contributed to its impact.

But one of the criticisms of *Whanau* was that I did not provide the signifying individual of Western literature to hang the story onto; my tribal response had led me in the other direction. There are no "characters" as such in *Whanau*; they are instead representatives of certain aspects of the whānau. They have no shading or moral ambiguity.

Really, the main character in the book is the village, Waituhi itself.

As well as that, *Whanau* presented challenges to readers accustomed to a Western linear, rather than spiralling, narrative. The book only works if you read it in one sitting because then the unity of time extends to include the reader. The use of the kite is what saves the structure, and at least it is a Māori device which I am deploying in the story. And while the writing is virile enough, it lacks suppleness.

The real problem is that, while *Whanau* has political resonance, I hadn't learnt yet how to go for the jugular. All around me the context was the small story well told, and the politics were mainly implicit. I was not equipped as yet to break out from that straitjacket. In the very best books the *thought,* in particular the political thought, should continue long after you've finished the book. Over the years I therefore came to realise that the attempt had not been good enough. Sometimes you can sense this, even though people try to convince you that you have done a good job.

But the universe tells you.

How did I know that? Aroha can be given to the iwi, and it can also be received. The reciprocal nature of the exchange only happens, however, if the subject of your attention wants to return it. You can try as hard as you like to fool yourself, but the universe just wasn't feeling it.

Try again.

Rex Turnbull provided the evocative painting for the cover, *Last Puha Before the Rain*. In the painting a Māori family is pictured in a village crop plantation; it's the symbolism of the approaching storm clouds which turns the painting from representational to predictive.

When the book appeared in bookshops, the title was a handicap. People asked, "Have you got the latest novel, I can't pronounce the name, by that Māori author whose name I also can't pronounce but it's something like Wacky Ickimakericky?"

Readers complained about the lack of a glossary.

Despite the criticisms, *Whanau* is the book where you can see my ancestors driving me more strongly from the room behind my eyes. In the end, they were the ones who told me that the novel was always "the novella you added 20,000 words to". This was why, thirty years later, I took the opportunity — when my publishers planned to reprint *Whanau* (1974) and needed a new typescript to do it — to rewrite the novel as *Whanau II* (2004). I playfully called the second iteration 'Revenge of Whanau'. The difference was not only marked in the expansion of pages, with the second version almost double the size. It was also marked by a stronger kaupapa.

In the first version, my ancestors had given me due warning that they would scrape my skull out if they had to. In the second version, they did that.

Chapter Fifteen

Things Fall Apart

1.

I haven't told you everything.

I know now, but I didn't know it then, that there was a reason for my questing nature.

Frank O'Connor speaking to the BBC in 1961 hinted at it.
"Towns and cities have a mental age of their own," he said.

> The mental age limit defines the period after which a young man or woman of talent ought to pack his bags and get out. I don't know exactly how you judge the mental age of a town, but one way is by its bookshops and libraries, art galleries and theatres and concerts.
> I had a feeling that, at one time, Cork, for a short time at least, during the reign of Cormac McCarthy, was a real European capital. It has ceased to be that and the problem now is how it's going to recreate a life for itself, a life in which a man can live completely from the cradle to the grave; that I think is a problem not only for Cork, but for the whole of Western European civilisation. Life has to start flowing back into the smaller places. Metropolis ended with Hiroshima. People have got to start living a much less specialised form of life, a much more community form of life and my feeling about this city is . . . either people make a success of it or Western Europe is finished.

I had reached the mental age of Gisborne without knowing it. The city was at least five years behind the rest of New Zealand, and that's being charitable; the enclosing mountain ranges and sea were to blame. Mind you, there was always some comfort in living in a place that didn't appear to alter too much or, at least, changed more slowly than anywhere else. Gisborne was the place where *Biggles* comics, Baby Austins and planes with propellers came to die.

On the other hand, Gisborne's time delay was also a provincial trap, and I suppose my visits to the library and to the movies were attempts to escape it. I needed a greater life than Gisborne could provide. During the week I oscillated between school, hockey practice and the Mormon community. The school wasn't giving me much joy, and while I had great friends from the chapel like Iris Whaanga, Charlie Mohi and Lester, there wasn't much to give my life frisson there either.

But there was a greater fear — yes, I'll call it that — driving me to clutch . . . at straws, really.

I think I was trying to find in everything — my world, my society and particularly in my *self* — affirmation that everything was all right and that I was okay.

The truth was that I just felt so unworthy. Of Mum and Dad. Of having a family. Of having a girlfriend. And, no matter the soporifics with which I sedated myself, of not keeping faith with the masculinity of my whakapapa.

It was at this particular moment that I met a boy I shall call Jackson. Hitting my head against the ceiling at Gisborne Boys' High, I found my primary friendship not from my classmates or the Mormon community, but in him.

I had decided to go to Waikanae Beach for a swim. Jackson was there, sitting on the sand. He was slightly older than I was, having left high school behind, a stripling with rich black hair. When he saw me taking off my clothes, he said, "You're not going in, are ya?"

The waves were high and a rip was running along the shore, but I nodded my head.

I was down to my swimming trunks when, merry, he said, "I better come too."

He shucked off all his clothes. He didn't have togs and just stood there, buck naked. Cars going past. People walking along.

And he posed, gave them the finger and said, "Who gives a shit."

Jackson caused a tonal shift in my life. Tall, impudent and cheeky, he was fun — and I was desperate for a friend who could match my own adolescent insanity. Because sometimes keeping myself all straitjacketed made me want to be reckless, yes, *who gives a shit.* That's the only way I can explain myself — and him.

He worked for the Railways and, when he was off-duty, I would meet up with him after school to play pool, smoke and hang out at the Lyric Café or have coffee in the local coffee bar.

Yes, Gizzy had all the mod cons.

Jackson wasn't gay. He wasn't straight either. I don't know what he was. His view was if it moved, fuck it. I should have known that he had no boundaries. Then one night, after drinking, my gender binary was smashed into little pieces. To put it bluntly, Jackson was a taker and ... he took. We were sitting in the front of his car, laughing about something or other, and suddenly he leaned over from the driver's seat. Before I could say no, he unbuttoned my trousers. My adolescent sexuality was always spontaneous — just the thought of sex was sufficient to trigger a response — and before Jackson could go any further, I climaxed.

Startled, he asked me, "How long have you been waiting for *that*!"

I was gasping for breath — what had just happened? And then I began to get angry.

"We'll wait a few minutes," he said, as he began to pull his own pants down, his penis pulsing out. "Meantime..."

"Meantime *what*?" I said. "Is this a game to you? I don't like to be touched without permission. Next time, ask."

Something pent up and now released, made me double over with grief.

"Hey," Jackson said, "I'm sorry. Hey ..." But the thing about Jackson was that he never, really, had a conscience. Very soon, as cool as, "You wanna smoke?" he asked.

On later outings he often asked. "Always willing to help out a mate," he would say, which he knew always made me mad. Clearly I must have been affected by Jackson in some way to let *go*. But because he was amazingly open about sex and it meant nothing to him, it meant nothing to me.

By this I mean that love did not attach itself. "Good Mormon boy, you," he mocked once. "Keeping yourself for the wifey, eh."

2.

Jackson was the Dionysus figure in my life. As the Greek divinity could bring joy and ecstasy into relationships, so did Jackson. He was such a dedicated follower of fashion, too. His clothes were loud but never square, and he definitely bought the best. For a brief time, in my search for my own personal style, I even purchased with my own pocket money a half-red, half-green shirt under Jackson's influence — I looked like a traffic light having an identity crisis — and some wicked grey winkle-pickers. By the time of the young man on the cover, however, the florid style had long gone. Instead, I went colonial-Mod, showing that anything they could wear I could wear better.

Jackson and I had great fun and I found joy in our relationship. But with such joy there came, on reflection, great self-loathing.

He asked me to go to a party and may have been grooming me, for all I know. The weekend of the bash, he was the ticket collector for the service from Gisborne to Napier. When the railcar arrived at Napier he got off and operated the northbound service back to Gisborne. Jackson met people on the railcar, travelling salesmen or women, or tourists looking for a friend to show them the sights in an overnight Gisborne pit stop.

By the time Jackson got back to Gisborne he had the guests for the party. They were likely girls — and lads — looking for action. In me, Jackson had already found a congenial companion. First stop was the nearest chemist shop to buy condoms. Jackson was never put off by the glare of the blue-rinsed lady counter clerk or the bald-headed coot in the dispensary. "Ones that don't break," Jackson said, saucy as, "and I don't want lamb skins."

The next stop was a local hotel to buy some booze for the party. Jackson saw a bottle of wine on the top shelf, but the proprietor looked at him and said, "Oh, you boys won't be able to afford that," and he turned his back on us.

Jackson didn't blink an eye. He simply got the hotelier to take the bottle down and, slowly as, peeled out the notes. "Is that enough?" he asked, staring the proprietor down. "Now open it."

You had to be careful about Jackson. Sometimes his bravado could turn nasty. But the hotelier popped the cork and Jackson took a couple of gulps and put the bottle down.

The wine was spilling from his lips. "You expect me and my mate to drink this shit?" he asked.

Outside, with the proprietor looking on, he poured the rest of the wine in the gutter.

I could hardly stop laughing. "You're as mad as a meataxe," I said.

"And bugger me," he answered, "now we've got no money for the booze."

You might have expected that Jackson could exorcise me of my demons. But when we got to the party and, two hours in, everyone was pairing up — and Jackson and I were about to join a threesome, two boys and a girl — I froze. I would have nothing to do with the other boys, although they clearly wanted to have everything to do with me — forget about the girl.

Jackson smoothed things over, signed to me, Okay.

"I don't know, mate," he said afterward. "You have to let go of whatever it is that's fucking you up."

3.

This telling is getting tricky because I am trying to convey how much my life was yawing between school, family, church, friends and Jackson. Spinning off its axis, it plunged into the perilous.

It's also too easy to say that my stress levels started going up and into the red. But I do know that there came that moment in my life when, fuelled by the self-loathing I earlier spoke of, I had to find a way to obtain release.

Thank God drugs were hard to get in Gisborne. Instead, Jackson showed me how to use a razor — but I'm not blaming him. Small, silver-edged, sharp, a razor was such a beautiful thing. It sliced. Opened. Just a little pain but, ah, it gave the sense of punishment I so desired.

I hadn't even heard of self-harm. Did it exist in those days? All I know is that, really, Jackson and I started to do it for laughs. Giggling, he demonstrated by, first of all, passing the blade over the flame from his cigarette lighter; I don't know why he did that, perhaps it was part of the ritual. Then he cut himself on his left forearm.

"Nothing to it," he said as the blood welled out.

I watched him, the orgasmic joy on his face; I wasn't the only one with demons, because he had sticking plasters over previous cuts. Why hadn't I noticed them when I had met him for the first time down at the beach?

And then I tried it myself . . . heated the blade and found, after the sting of the cut, that it was comforting. It felt good to hurt myself, and I knew I deserved it.

"Better start wearing long sleeves," he said.

You'll forgive the lack of detail as I have spent many years trying to forget this part of my life.

But whenever I succumbed to slicing my skin there was first of all the pain and then a huge rush of elation. Chasing quickly after it, however, was depression and the need to cut again.

I would think, I can't escape, maybe the universe was determinate after all.

The razor's cut was also an act of blood-letting. Panicking, I went through a period where I thought my rapist's spermatozoa, viral, were moving around inside me. Eating up my universe. Extinguishing the nebulae. Soon I was slicing my chest, my thighs, my arms to rid myself of them.

Too late. Stars began falling from the sky. There came an evening when the spores reached my dreams and *struck*.

And a dawn blossomed around me and I heard chanting in the dark. I found myself in a lambic zone of myth and surreality, the world of moemoeā. The dream was interlaced with the symbols and signs of the Māori darker myths; a maelstrom of activity burst around me, terrorising and alarming, and I was at the centre of it.

I knew this dream. I had been to this place once before. Aharon Appelfeld wrote of himself, "My nights are a nightmare, quite often, but the nightmares are rich. I nourish myself on those nights."

My dreams often became nightmares and, sometimes, they came from the Māori world of moemoeā.

The sky was blood red, and I was standing at the edge of a tall cliff. The wall was sheer black, and a thousand miles below, the sea of dreams was swirling, opalescent and luminous. An errant draught caught me and I began tumbling over and over. Disoriented I saw the surface of the sea rushing up at me. And then, above and around, I saw birds coming out of a blood-red sun, thousands of birds. When they flew closer I saw that they were half-men, half-avian, winged ponaturi with clawed hands and wings jagged as a bat's.

Quickly, I sliced my chest again. See? That didn't hurt at all, did it?

The slice of blade. The astonishment at the relief the sharp pain brought. The beauty of blood, the blood-letting, the liquid redness and glow before the blood dried, rusted over, lost glamour.

The desire to cut once more. Ah, so good.

And people were tumbling in the infinite air. We were a tangled mass of falling men and women, soundlessly screaming. I watched afraid as a flock of ponaturi caught my companions by their ankles and soared with them to some eyrie to feed their young. Three of them peeled back and, wings folded, pursued me. With mounting terror I felt their ravenous beaks flailing at my feet. One of them nipped my left ankles and I screamed, fearful that it would carry me away with it and with one strike kill me, no no no.

I forced myself awake. Whimpering, cut myself again. Come out, come *out*. In a dazed moment, disoriented, I saw something perched on my bed looking at me — and I cried out in fear.

Hello pet, the ponaturi said.

Chapter Sixteen

Blood-red Sky

1.

I was doing well at Gisborne Boys' High and Mr Marsden's reports to Headmaster Gray must have been positive because, when I saw him in the corridor, he nodded as we passed each other.

During the August holidays I tried to persuade Mum and Dad to leave me at Haig Street to "study" again, but Dad needed me up at Maera Station; Uncle Puku had taken his family to Wellington for a break — I don't know where Bulla was.

There was a day when Dad and I were taking fenceposts across the gully. The palings were roped to two packhorses. I was on my horse leading another, and Dad was on the mare doing the same.

Normally, we would have taken the packhorses across the swing-bridge, but rain was falling and wind was gusting down the valley. Suspended in space, the cables pitched and yawed in the wind currents. Whenever the strain threatened to snap them, sharp reports like rifle shots would ricochet, crack, crack, *crack*. Some of the boards that strung the bridge looked slippery.

The rain, dripping from the wire frame, transformed the bridge into a shivering, jewelled cobweb spun in the air. It made the arching span of it look so deceptively beautiful that I didn't realise how dangerous it was. I wondered why Dad was hesitating; I was cold and wet and I thought he was waiting for me to go across first.

He stopped me. "I think we better cross over the river today," he said.

"It will be faster if we use the bridge," I answered. But Stupid, my horse, kept on rearing, whinnying and backing away. I was feeling reckless and past caring.

"Yes," Dad said, "but you're with me."

Before I could protest he kicked his horse and we continued further down the track to the river. Even so, after we had forded the torrent, I took it up with him.

"The overpass would have been quicker," I said.

"When you're a man," he answered, "and have the capability of getting yourself out of trouble, then you can cross whatever bridge you want to. You'll be old enough to make your own decisions, stupid or not, and if you do get into trouble you won't be able to blame anybody else except yourself. But you're still a boy and I am your father and this is my watch. Apart from which, kill yourself if you want, but not your horse."

This was Dad's shift, I know, but I wouldn't have been bothered if the span had collapsed beneath my weight. Death by drowning seemed good to me and, being accidental, would be acceptable to any coroner.

2.

At the end of the year, Mr Grono must have realised I was tearing my hair out with frustration. He is responsible for my second short story and the first ever published, "The Prodigal Daughter". He told me that the end-of-year school magazine hadn't received any entries for the fiction prize and encouraged me to submit something. Not only that, but he suggested that three of his better students — Norman Maclean may have been among them — come to him for writing classes after school.

Even though I went, I was reluctant to be singled out. But to compensate I deliberately stayed away from Gisborne Boys' on the day that the class photographs were being taken. I bought one nonetheless — I wanted to remember who my schoolmates were; I couldn't have cared less if I wasn't remembered.

Wonder of wonders, I was accredited University Entrance. I can remember the look of relief on George Marsden's face; he never lost faith in me. Mr Gray had the grace to congratulate Dad. Later in life I made a close friend of Mr Gray's son, Murray. In my literature I might not have treated his father kindly, but I did respect him and honour him.

Not only that, but I won the prize for "The Prodigal Daughter".

To celebrate, Mr Grono invited me to afternoon tea with Mrs Grono.

They lived off Chalmers Road near the Elgin Street shops. I didn't want to go, my world was swinging off its axis. I kept having headaches that I couldn't shake off.

But I kept the appointment, and Mrs Grono — I couldn't bring myself to call her by her first name, Gwen — had made delicious little jam and cream-topped pikelets to have with our tea. I was pissed off with myself for buckling under. Even though I was grateful to Mr Grono, I thought of the visit as a chore. If he picked up how uncomfortable I felt, he did not comment on it.

The lounge had a beautiful Persian carpet and a glass cabinet in which were displayed the curios collected during their world travels. And there were books everywhere. I hadn't realised that Mr Grono was such a lover of poetry and, indeed, literature in all its forms — and that he liked writing poetry himself. At the end of the afternoon he asked me what I planned to do with my life. I said I wasn't sure, but what I really meant was that I didn't want to tell him. He must have been irritated at my answer because, at the door when I was leaving, he looked at me straight.

"What happened to you, Witi?" he asked.

Shocked, I didn't know what to say. Then I realised that Mr Grono, having taught at three of my recent schools at the same time I was there, was probably the best witness of the years when I was growing up.

Had he been spying on me all along? Fuck off, Mr Grono.

"I don't know what you mean," I answered.

But he wasn't about to let me go so easily. "No, son," he said. "What *happened*?"

A boy wearing shirts with long sleeves in summer, even if unbuttoned at the cuffs . . .

Before I could stop him, he pushed up my sleeves. Saw the sticking plasters.

And something gave up inside me.

So that's it then.

3.

I returned to Haig Street after the afternoon tea with Mr and Mrs Grono. I was calm, anyone looking at me would have thought I was okay.

For the rest of the afternoon I kept thinking to myself: if Mr Grono could see who I was — and now knew I was harming myself — then everybody could.

You don't think I enjoy this level of disclosure, do you? I have no option. When I wrote the first volume I found myself forced to go deep, make incisions into my memory and not sew up the stuff, throw away the needle and forget about it. My mother and Nani Mini weren't the only ones who didn't like my chosen profession; sometimes *I* didn't either.

You think this is easy? Fuck *you*.

I was teaching a creative writing class once. Alice Te Punga Somerville was in the group; she is now one of Māoridom's leading academics. One of her fellow students put in a story about a young boy who commits suicide by slitting his wrists. I pointed out that this was a method that girls usually do, not boys.

"Boys," I said, "either shoot themselves in the head or get in a car and drive it into a tree."

I felt no triumph when the student walked out of the room; Alice went out to support her. The student's brother had shot himself and, rather than revisit the pain of that event, she had chosen to distance herself from it in her fiction.

How did I know? This is how.

I gave up fighting.

I tried to kill myself. Why do you think I wanted to stay by myself at Haig Street?

So that if I wanted to, I could do it. As they say, off myself.

A car was my weapon, but I didn't drive it into a tree. Dad had conveniently installed a new roller door on the carport. I can remember the whirring noise as it went down and the clunk as it hit the concrete floor. I felt I had come to the end and that if I continued living I would give in to . . . what? I might have saved myself if I had somebody to talk to, but I didn't. I couldn't speak to Dr Bowker because then he would know. I couldn't talk to Dad because then he would know. I was glad that Teria was dead because now she would never know. The only person, ironically, that I could have spoken to was the rapist because, ha ha, at least he knew my shame already.

My thoughts filled with my father, Te Haa. The weekend before I had watched him coaching my sisters Kararaina, Tāwhi and Viki how to shoot the ball for a goal in indoor basketball. I marvelled at his instructions to shoot high, not flat, so that the ball would fall into the hoop.

I could never aspire to his masculine strength and surety.

4.

All right, then. Best for you to end it.

You get a garden hose and put one end in the exhaust pipe of the Holden. You close all the windows of the car except the driver's side window — that one you leave till last, once you have put the other end of the hose inside the Holden. Then you start the engine and sit there with the motor running. Very soon, the interior begins to fill with petrol fumes. It doesn't take long.

Hurry up, you think, as the smoke billows. Let's get this over with.

You're an utter failure. Your parents wanted you to go on a mission, you refused. They then said that you could go to Brigham Young University, and the local chapel had already begun to raise money for you. Your grandfather wants to arrange a marriage for you to a nice girl from Tūhoe. Your teacher has high hopes for you.

You keep on letting people down, over and over again.

Could you be gay? No, not that. Never.

Don't let anybody tell you that suicide by asphyxiation is a good way to die. Your body goes into paroxysms. Your mouth fills with bile, you are retching.

Just before losing consciousness, you think of your mother.

The sky is blood red and ponaturi are wheeling. Below, an opalescent sea. As you plunge through the surface you see yourself as a young child going into Mum and Dad's bedroom. You watch as your younger self opens Mum's sewing kit. He takes out her scissors. He finds every photograph of yourself and cuts you up, the scissors slicing through your head, decapitating you, dismembering you, disembowelling you.

Smoke builds, the vapour fills the car.

But while your younger self is cutting the photographs Mum returns earlier than you expect her.

"What are you doing, *son?" she asks us.*

"Oh Mum," you murmur to her as the smoke billows. "Surely you who uphold whakapapa don't need to be told? I'm doing you all a favour. Cutting myself out of our family tree, can't you can see that?"

And then you knife into an ocean that stretches to the edge of forever. Fuck off, Mum. *All around you are other swimmers, holding their breath, because if they resurface the ponaturi will grab them. But there is no escape because the ponaturi plunge into the sea too. They fold their wings, their hair catches flame from the last of the sun and through their bodies you can see their veins pulsing.*

The ponaturi are everywhere, grabbing victims by ankle, wrist or throat. Some, already ravenous, are feeding. They begin to drag their prey not up to the broiling surface but down to a different destination — an undersea kāinga, lit by subterranean fires.

And the sea is a liquid sky and you are plummeting through it. Out of the light and into the dark. Swarms of ponaturi are pulling you down and churning a bloodied wake. And the ocean is filled with a haze of blood.

You try to hold your breath. Your heart is beating fast. In. Out. In. Out. The pressure is building, threatening to split your skull apart.

The undersea kāinga draws nearer. Protecting it is a grim palisade. Right at the centre of the kāinga is a huge meeting house. It is constructed of black timbers and appears to be sleeping. But as you approach, suddenly, the pāua eyes studded in its timbers open wide. And then the water is filled with ponaturi in a frenzy of feeding.

Some other fate awaits you. You're dragged out of the house and hauled to the gable. Nailed to it so that all can see. This is the boy, the one who sins.

The blood spurts as the nails go through your flesh.

All around, the vapour hangs heavy in the air, filling the carport.

But sitting there watching are ponaturi, silent, curious. Chittering and chattering, they fold and unfold their gleaming wings.

"Won't be long now," you tell them.

You lose consciousness. You don't know how long it is before, without knowing it, you call for your mother. A hundred years? A thousand? And then you see a figure swimming through a luminous sea, shafted with sunlight stretching to the end of forever. She is Turiteretimana, and she is wearing a white gown; her hair, unpinned, flows around her. Her qualities are sacerdotal; she is anointed by the dawn. Her courage is fashioned from the ancestral women figures of Māori myth. In her hand is a butcher's knife, a symbolic weapon.

She is not alone. Another woman, or rather, a taniwha companion, the merwoman named Hine Te Ariki, is with her to carry her from one side of the world to the other if ever such a journey is required. In this case the journey has been from the real world into the world of moemoeā. Hine Te Ariki is twenty feet tall, with eyes that flash like pāua. Her giant flukes churn the water.

Surrounded by the sound of swelling, triumphal karakia and tumultuous sea, you hear the dream swimmer say to you, When you were born, you were the first thing I had ever truly owned.

A shaft of light. As soon as you see it, you know that your father — not Mum — is there. He is pulling away the wooden slabs of the meeting house so that the sun can stream in. Its rays crown the roof and *flame* upon the wharenui. They lace through the walls, ever descending upon the sleeping ponaturi. And then the sun completely irradiates the interior. The ponaturi begin to scream and writhe, burning in the light.

Your father is a man of immense innocence. You often puzzle him because of your behaviour and anger. One day he says to you, "You know what the trouble is with you?" He puts a finger to your temple and taps it, "You think too much."

You reach up to your father and, weakly, put your arms around him.

5.

It wasn't Dad.

It was poor unsuspecting Charlie Mohi.

He must have sensed some disruption somewhere, and ended up at Haig Street. Or maybe he had finished night shift at his job and was walking by. Occam's razor, the simplest answer, was always the best.

"Witi," he asked, terrorised, as he pulled me out of the vehicle. "What are you doing, boy?"

My eyes were flooding with tears. I was vomiting my guts out. Even after the first paroxysms were over and my body had poured its fluids out — sweat, urine, shit — flush after flush, it still tried to cleanse itself.

The poison kept me heaving, every dry retch bringing up the fumes.

I don't know if Charlie told his wife, Blossom.

He took me to counselling. Mum and Dad didn't know about it. Later, in Auckland where I was going to university, I did some counselling myself to young teenagers at Middlemore Hospital.

You mustn't feel sorry for me; I wasn't. Save your sympathy for those boys who try to commit suicide and succeed. Those beautiful young men, all lost to families and friends. And how many of them were gay? Oh, all those gorgeous boys.

New Zealand has repeatedly ranked among the worst countries in the world in rates of teen suicide. A 2016 OECD report revealed that our levels were the highest in the developed world. Twice as many young men kill themselves in New Zealand than in Australia. And as far as Māori boys are concerned, John Snowden, using Ministry of Health and Australian Bureau of Statistics data, compared rates between Māori and Aboriginals, and noted that the suicide rates were, dangerously, equal.

But here's the irony. It's life, not death, that hurts.

Die young, stay pretty? How appalling and indecent that idea is. After you've been revived, and when your body is forcing you to breathe in, every rasping gulp tears you apart.

Chapter Seventeen

The Great Mother of Te Pō

1.

It is death it is death
It is life it is life . . .

I referred earlier to the confrontation that Māui had with Mahuika.

He escaped with his life, but, in a second confrontation this time with Hinenuitepō, he was not so fortunate.

The "goddess" of death has already appeared in *Maori Boy*, my memoir of childhood, where I gave her whakapapa. Some texts refer to Mahuika as being the younger sister of Hinenuitepō. And therefore Hinenuitepō is another of the muses Maori artists and writers can look to for guidance and inspiration. She is the senior among them.

Her father was the god Tāne, and her mother was the woman he fashioned out of earth, Hineahuone, whom I have called "the stone woman" to convey her ancient origins.

A daughter was born, Hinetītama, known as the dawn maiden. Her name, like her mother's, was resonant of the time when the world was just beginning. Tāne mated with her and from that union sprang children. The children in turn mated with one another and thus were on their way to becoming a different kind of being — the less-than-godly humankind. Therefore I like to think of Hinetītama as being the mother of humankind or, more correctly, the Māori subspecies.

In other cultures such as the Greek, Jewish, Indian and Chinese, their own gods were at play in the fields of the celestial lords.

I have to add here, however, that there is another Māori story that posits Tāne as also creating a first man, named Tiki. We will come to him later.

By the time Māui appears in the history of the world, half-god half-man, a throwback to his godly origins, humankind has proliferated and spread on the face of our earth. And Hinetītama has undertaken a huge transformation. Discovering that Tāne the father is also Tāne the husband, and that her children are the consequence of incest, she has fled from him. She runs from Te Ao, the world above and beseeches Te Kūwatawata, the gatekeeper, to let her enter Te Pō, the world below.

"Haere atu, Tāne," Hinetītama farewells Tāne. "Hāpai a tātou tamariki i te ao. Goodbye, Tāne. Raise our children in the light. I will take them to me when they die."

In so doing Hinetītama also acknowledges the terrible inheritance that has come from the female side, following that first mating of god with stone woman. All the children have inherited a fatal genetic flaw: unlike the gods who live forever, they will die.

So far so good.

Hinetītama establishes her domain at Rarohenga in Te Pō. There she takes on her new name, Hinenuitepō, but, auē, because the narrative is written by men, she undergoes a sinister change. They crown her the chthonic queen of Hades, goddess of death, and give her all the imagery of malevolence. Teeth like a barracuda, the eyes of a Medusa and hair of writhing snakes. Vaginal dentata, a sexual cleft filled with rows of sharp, obsidian, gnashing teeth. Like Mahuika, she becomes a suitable goddess for Māui to conquer. After all, death is to be feared, isn't it?

As for Māui, he is given a noble purpose. He braves Te Kūwatawata at the gate and enters the realm of the Below World. He comes across Hinenuitepō, sleeping. For the sake of reversing the genetic flaw, he embarks on a quest to seek her manawa, heart, and manawa-ora, life-breath, and thereby reacquire what has been lost — eternal life for humankind.

To accomplish the task requires Māui to do nothing less than invert the process of childbirth. In an episode that has all the elements of comedy, he must enter Hinenuitepō's toothed vagina, make his way up her body, and snatch her heart and life-breath as he passes.

Although I have sometimes seen people guffaw at the physical notion involved, what's powerful about the narrative is that there's a kind of logic to it, albeit tinged with a sense of the absurd.

Māui takes as companions a number of birds, including the pīwakawaka, fantail, warning them not to laugh as they might awaken Hinenuitepō who is sleeping. However, the pīwakawaka can't help himself and starts to sing with hilarity. And Māui is only halfway through Hinenuitepō's puapua.

Aroused, the "queen of Hades" closes the doors of her labia and Māui is impaled, crushed and killed. Some people see a sexual subtext in the story, the triumph of the vagina over the penis.

In a trice, comedy turns to horror and the life of the great Māui ends in tragedy.

2.

And now the *tika*.

Nowhere in the usual telling — at least, the version that has come down from Victorian times — is there any sign of remorse concerning a sleeping woman and the attempt to violate her. After all, she is the goddess of death.

Nor is there any reference to the woman as she really is, the female parent who, with great love, takes her children to her when they come to her bosom, to be cradled by her forever. The narrative obscures the understanding of Hinenuitepō not as queen of Hades but as the great mother. In this dazzling role as matua she is also muse, presiding over her court at Rarohenga and granting us access to the inspiration from Te Pō.

Does she ask her children's forgiveness for having passed on to them the mortality gene, do you think?

Be that as it may, there's something comforting about the possibility that Hinenuitepō waits in the world after this, not as death goddess but rather mother, to embrace us when we leave the world of light for the darkness.

As I will do, when I eventually go to her.

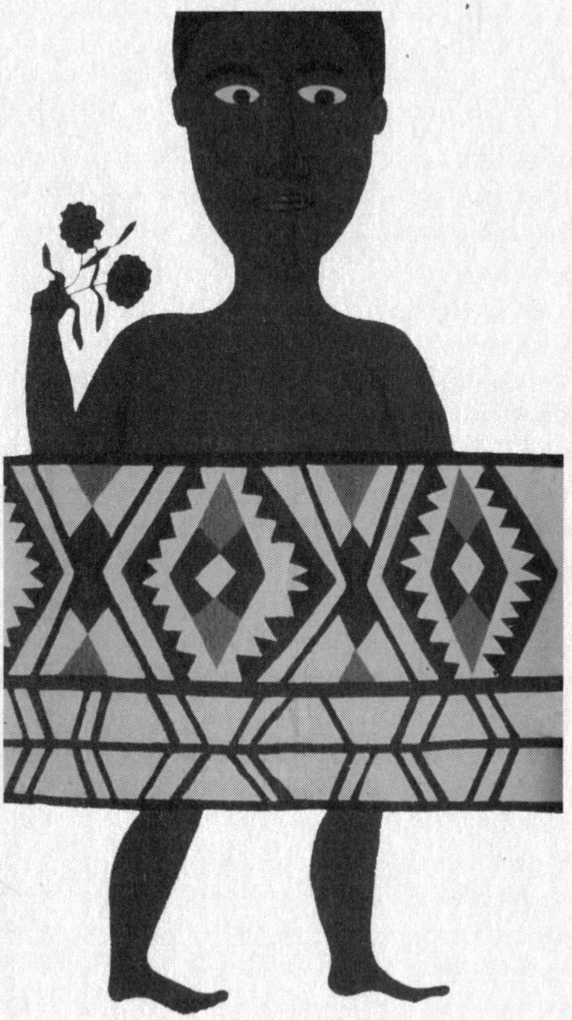

PART THREE

TE AO TŪROA
THE WORLD

Chapter Eighteen

Whaitiri and Her Grandson, Tāwhaki

1.

The ancient texts don't tell us, but it is clear that when news reached the myriad men and women about the death of Māui, all the tribes of the world went into deep mourning.

After all, Māui had been the hero of heroes, the champion of champions. He had tamed the sun, fished up islands from the sea and confronted the very gods themselves. All this he had done to ensure a better world for humankind, a world of greater expanse and longer days, limitless and endless.

Finally, he had attempted to gain sovereignty over death so that ngā tangata could live forever. Can you imagine what it must have been like for them to realise that, instead of obtaining immortality, Māui had bequeathed to them the death gene?

"The great Māui has failed? And in the attempt he has lost his own life? Auē, taukiri ē!"

It was a double tragedy because nobody else but Māui, then or later, could ever have established for us a world without limitations. There had been just the one shot, the one opportunity.

Humankind was now condemned to live within a limited space–time continuum. Infinity would never be ours, nor a world without end. And there would come a time when we *would* die.

For a generation after the death of Māui, the Māori world tried to come to terms with its own mortality.

What they really required was a saviour.

2.

We come to the remarkable story of the grandmother, Whaitiri.

Yes, another grandmother figure — Māori mythology is full of them!

But Whaitiri was someone very special. She was regarded as being the most potent figure of Polynesia and was known as Hina-hana-ia-ka-malama in Hawai'i and Ina-ma-ngurunguru in Rarotonga. Her celestial powers were formidable. Some said that without her to perform the appropriate karakia, the great god Tāne would not have been able to separate his male parent Ranginui from Papatūānuku, the Earth Mother. Thunder always attended Whaitiri and, where thunder was, lightning strikes were not too far away.

What's fascinating was that the story of Whaitiri was somewhat similar to that of another world mythology: the narrative of the Christian God who sent his beloved son down into the world to bring salvation to humankind.

Why did Whaitiri intervene in this way?

Throughout the world, all had lost the will to live. "Why live at all, when we are born to die?" the people asked each other.

So it was that Whaitiri came down from the heavens and set up the circumstances by which humankind was able to accept the inevitability of death and, nevertheless, go *on*. Her arrival can be dated two generations after the death of Māui and her task was to provide the saviour.

This was how Whaitiri went about it.

In the second generation after the death of Māui she married into the human race, a warrior known as Kaitangata, which some translated as Maneater. By this union they produced, in the third generation after Māui's death, two sons. One of them was Hema, known by this name in Hawai'i, Tahiti and the Tuamotu Archipelago. He is 'Ema in the Cook Islands.

Good, a child had been born possessing both godly and dynamic human elements.

But Hema was not actually the one to save the world. Who can tell why not?

For her own reasons Whaitiri guided him to a woman of the highest status in Te Ao Tūroa. Her name was Urutonga and two sons were born to them — Tāwhaki and Karihi. Through Urutonga was added further mana and, in particular, love for parents — for Hema and

Urutonga are at the heart of one of the most thrilling rescue stories in Māori mythology.

Again, so far so good. And I hope you are following carefully, because whakapapa demands intelligence and close attention.

Of the two boys it is Tāwhaki, Whaitiri's grandson in the fourth generation since Māui's death, who becomes her agent.

He is the awaited saviour who is required to lift the great pōuri — the great darkness or sadness — that has fallen upon the world. Now here's something interesting. Some people such as Mohi Ruatapu thought that Te Kore, usually the very first incarnation of the creation myth — from Te Kore to Te Pō to Te Ao Mārama, and so on — came *after* Te Ao Mārama. Could the great pōuri be Te Kore?

But back to Tāwhaki, and let's leave my question to scholars.

Whaitiri makes certain that he will become a great leader, an ariki having strategic decision-making skills. She instigates a cycle of challenges and tests whereby he becomes famed as the fearless Kaha'i in Hawai'i, Tafa'i in Tahiti, Tāwhaki in the Tuamotu Archipelago and Taha'i in Rarotonga.

Tāwhaki's thrilling achievements establish him as the brave aristocratic figure of our early literature and one of the icons of our history. And his arrival marks the high point of a cycle of myths, already three generations in the making, tracing the fortunes of the same family.

Meanwhile, Whaitiri waits from afar.

Chapter Nineteen

The Fishing Lines Go Forward to Te Ao Mārama

1.

Hinengaro, kaupapa, kupu, aroha.

Te wehi (dread), te ihi (energy), and te mana (strength) were also among the qualities that I had to bring to my task as a Māori writer.

With these qualities added to my skill set, let me tell you about the writing of my fourth book, *The New Net Goes Fishing* (1977).

The book was my second short-story collection. It was published three years after the pastoral trilogy of *Pounamu, Pounamu*, *Tangi* and *Whanau*. I went from stories of rural Waituhi to stories of urban Wellington — my songs of experience — and the first-edition hardcover artwork by a mate, Ray Labone, tells it all. Ray sketched a silhouette of Evans Bay–Mount Victoria, the monastery prominent, and, above, an arching rainbow.

The crescent did double duty as both a Māori and a literary symbol. It represented the god Kahukura accompanying the waka *Takitimu* during its long ocean voyage from Hawaiki to Aotearoa. I appropriated the rainbow for the book, because I considered that its main theme — the rural to urban migration — was as profound as the mythic waka odyssey of the first Māori voyagers to New Zealand.

To mitigate the punitive nature of that marae-to-city demographic event, I also used the rainbow in the Ringatū manner (and the biblical one), as the sign of deliverance.

And Kahukura had further, European, literary meaning. In *Pounamu, Pounamu*, I had included a story called "In Search of the Emerald City". The reference was to L Frank Baum's *Wizard of Oz*. In my story, a boy named Matiu wants to take his favourite — Baum's — book with him. Ergo, the Emerald City became Wellington.

In *The New Net Goes Fishing* I kept the Baum references going with the stories "Yellow Brick Road" and "Return From Oz". Over the years the *Oz* symbolism continued to haunt me as a trope, and I wrote a further story, "Kansas", about descendants of the original family leaving Wellington and going back to Waituhi; that one's in *Kingfisher Come Home* (1995).

Recently, in 2017, when asked by the Auckland Writers Festival to provide a story for their anthology for school students, I updated the story again as "Seven Waka". This time, seven canoes — or, rather, a fleet of space ships carrying migrants to New Earth — are about to leave Old Earth and Māori families are among the settlers. They include, yes, a young boy who wants to take his favourite book. No prize for guessing the book's title.

There were eighteen stories in *New Net,* which took its themes from the proverb, "Ka pū te ruha, ka hao te rangatahi, the old net is cast aside, the new net goes fishing." The reference was not just to the questing nature of Māori as they turned from the greenstone landscapes of rural Māoridom to finding new lives in Pākehā society — to their rejection or acceptance by it. The net also referenced my own attempt to create a different literary approach to the craft, indeed, a new set of trailing hooks.

The pastoral trilogy had been set in the early 1950s; *New Net* was set in the late 1960s. The trilogy had been such an outpouring of easy lyricism, but now I had to bring a different consciousness to the writing — get street-smart. After all, the kind of young man I was in Wellington in my mid-twenties was not the same young boy who had lived in Waituhi a decade earlier, singing his full-throated, passionate songs of innocence. I needed a new voice to render the political didactic. While *Whanau* had the glimmerings of social commentary, *New Net* was an attempt to craft the work as social documentary. In the collection I therefore set out to fashion a new way of writing, one that would cope with reflecting what was happening to Māori now: urbanisation, loss of land and the status of Māori as statistic.

Here's how the reflection showed itself in one of the stories, "Big Brother, Little Sister". As background, I was inspired to write the story when photographer Warwick Teague gave me a large, stark, black-and-white photograph of two Māori children, hand-in-hand, at Wellington Railway Station.

The setting was no longer rural. Māori could no longer rely on whānau.

And where was "Home" in the story?

That was the question.

2.
Big Brother, Little Sister

He burst out of the house and was halfway down the street when he heard Janey yelling after him. He turned and saw her on the opposite pavement, appearing out of the night. As she passed under a streetlight her shadow reached out like a bird's wing to ripple along the fence palings towards him.

"Go back, Janey."

She cried out his name again, and pursued her shadow across the street. A car shrieked at her heels and slashed her with light as she fluttered into her brother's arms. "I'm coming with you." She wore a jersey and jeans over her pyjamas. In her hands she was carrying her sandals. She bent down and began strapping them on.

"You'll be a nuisance," Hema said. "Go home." He pushed her hand away.

"No." She wrapped her arms and legs round him.

He wrestled her, "Get off of me," and she fell on the pavement. He began running again, down the long dark street of shadowed houses towards Newtown.

"Don't leave me, Hema."

He turned. His face was desperate. "You're too small to come with me," he yelled. In desperation he picked up a stone and pretended to throw it at her. She kept on running. He picked up another stone. "Go back, you'll hold me up."

"No." She gritted her teeth, closed her eyes with determination and launched herself at him. Hema felt her trembling in his arms. She shook his rage apart.

"You'll just be a nuisance," he said.

Hema had been asleep when Janey began to peck at his dreams. He had turned on his side away from her. She began to shake him. "Hema."

The two kids slept in the same bed in one of two bedrooms in the flat. There was the sound of a crash. Hema sat up. He saw a crack of light under the closed door. Mum and Dad were back from the party. They were quarrelling again.

"Don't be scared," Hema said to Janey.

He went to the door and pushed it open. How long Mum and Dad had been fighting he didn't know. He'd never heard them as violent as this and he had to close his mind against the pain. He went back to the bed and sat on it. Janey crawled into his arms. They watched the light stabbing past the edge of the door and, alarmed, listened as their parents fought.

"Don't you talk to me like that," Dad said.

"I'll talk to you any way I like, you rotten bastard."

"And stop answering me back, Wiki, I'm warning you."

"You don't own me," Mum yelled. "You and your white bitch were made for each other. And keep your hands off me. Get away. Get out."

Hema could hear his mother panting and struggling in the bedroom. There was a ripping sound. A helpless woman-cry. The sudden crack of an open hand. Mum had spat into Dad's face. He slapped her again and threw her against the wall.

"Damn bitch," Dad said.

Janey gripped Hema in fright. Hema saw Dad's shadow cut through the lighted crack of the door. He heard his father walk down the passage to the front door. And his mother's voice changed as she began to plead. "No, John, don't leave me."

Dad laughed at her. Stung by his scorn their mother cried out, ran to the bedroom and began to pull open drawers and throw clothes at Dad.

"Here then. And here. And here. See if I care."

Dad turned the handle to leave. Their mother looked up at him and her body became limp. And then, "You bastard," she said, "well two can play your game."

She picked up the telephone in the hallway. "Taxis?"

"Can't wait to get rid of me, eh," Dad laughed.

Then Mum dialled another number. "Pita?" Dad's laughter stopped. There was a sound of scuffling in the passsage and shapes flicked across the crack in the doorway. "You been playing around, eh Wiki? You and Pita? Eh?"

Hema ran to the door and opened it. Dad had forced Mum against the wall and his hands were squeezing her throat. "Dad, Mum, don't."

"Go back to bed, you damn kid." The door cracked shut against the faces of his father and mother — her face wide with anger and blood streaming from her mouth. "Leave them alone, you arsehole."

Then Hema heard Mum fall heavily to the floor. He pushed the door open again. Dad was standing there, his fists clenched, kicking the shit out of her. Hema tried to shield his mother and lay over her. But Dad kept kicking until, exhausted, he backed away.

Mum beckoned to Hema. She opened her arms to Janey. She looked up at Dad. "Don't think we'll miss you, John. Now get out."

He lurched out of the flat.

Uncle Pita came to stay.

Janey tugged at Hema's hand. He looked down at her. She was squirming and fidgeting and holding her other hand across the front of her jeans.

"I knew you'd be a nuisance," he said.

They were just passing Wellington Hospital. A taxi swerved into the kerb in front of them. Hema could see a man inside with a smashed face. As the taxi driver took him to the main entrance he began to scream through a red hole where his mouth used to be. "There was a lav a few streets back," Hema said to Janey. "Why didn't you go to the ladies there?"

"Because you were in a hurry," Janey answered. "And I didn't want to have a mimi until *now*."

Newtown was busy. Cars had double-parked all along the main shopping strip, impeding the stream of traffic. A trolley bus had snapped its poles, and the showering blue sparks made it appear like a giant red beetle writhing in pain. Shopkeepers spoke in strange languages. Crates of fruit, bolts of cloth, boxes of secondhand clothes spilled onto the street. Two small children sold evening newspapers. A Salvation Army band exhorted passers-by to come to God. In a fish shop, the fishmonger swung a cleaver and cut the head off a flapping, gasping cod.

"Hema," Janey wailed.

"Hold on a bit longer," he said. He pulled her through the littered pavement towards the lights at the corner of John Street. He glanced back at the hospital clock. It was still early. Not half past seven yet. Mum and her new man would be in the pub till ten and afterwards they would go to a party. There was still plenty of time to get away, even if Janey might slow him up. Not that Mum would miss them. She'd probably be glad they were gone.

The traffic punched to a stop as the lights turned red. "Come on," Hema said to Janey. Car motors revved and roared at them and unblinking headlights watched them cross. Then the lights turned green and the traffic leapt through the intersection.

For a moment, Hema stood undecided on the opposite pavement, wondering whether to stay on Adelaide Road or get off it. Better get off it. Adelaide Road would take them past the Tramways Hotel, and Mum might be drinking up large there. Be safer to go up John Street. He pulled Janey after him — and saw some trees. "You can have your mimi over there."

Janey rushed into the shadows. Hema kept a lookout. Across the street faded billboards announced an industrial fair. Garish fairylights were strung across the dead facade of the Winter Show Building. Then Janey came back, hitching up her pants. Hema tucked her clothes in. There were mimi stains on her jeans. "Well, you told me to hurry," Janey said.

They hastened on. All along Wallace Street the lights from the houses shone down. "Where are we going?" Janey asked.

"You'll see," Hema said. His mind was working fast. He'd previously planned to make for the railway station and get a ticket for Gisborne. That was where his Nani George lived, Mum's father. But now that Janey was with him, his money wouldn't stretch to two tickets. Perhaps he could put her on the train by herself and follow later.

When he told Janey that the railway station was their destination, her eyes widened. "Are we going to walk all the way?"

"You said you wouldn't get tired."

Her face set with determination. They walked on, past the lighted windows, the rows of singing windows, towards the city.

When Uncle Pita had come to stay Mum started pushing Hema and Janey away from her. It happened slowly at first and with only small things. "Hema, dress Janey for me, eh?" Or, "Can you take Janey to school today . . . and bring her home afterward?" Or, "Me and Pita are going out tonight, can you get your own tea for you and your sister? Go away now. Go."

Hema didn't mind but Janey was confused. She asked, "When is Daddy coming home?" Or, "Is Uncle Pita staying with us forever?" And then she stopped asking Mum anything. Daddy was never coming back And Mummy had Uncle Pita now.

Actually, Uncle Pita was quite nice at first. He seemed to like the kids or be amused by them anyway, as if they were a novelty in his life. But he wasn't interested in them really, only in Mum. Sometimes, when he was fondling her, he would dart them a look of irritation and whisper in Mum's ear.

"Go away, kids," Mum would say. "Uncle Pita and I want to be alone now."

Her anxieties about pleasing Uncle Pita began to affect Hema and Janey. They became careful when he was around, treating him with as much caution as their mother did. Trying to please him. Trying to please Mum because she was happy with this man and wanted him to stay with her.

But Uncle Pita was much younger than Mum. His lips were moist for pleasure and his eyes reckless for fun. One day, Hema felt, Uncle Pita would leave Mum too. And he knew, watching Mum and the little nervous things she did, that even she knew he wouldn't stay. Uncle Pita, knowing her fears, would play on them and twist their mother round his finger whenever he wanted to. Tight like a rope. Tighter.

He frowned one night when Janey clambered into Mum's lap. "Do these kids always have to eat with us?" he asked at tea.

After that, the kids began having dinner before he came home. And watching television in the sitting room. When Uncle Pita came in with Mum, Hema would take Janey by the hand. "Come on, I better get you ready for bed."

One evening, Mum managed to sneak into the bedroom to say goodnight. When she stroked Hema's hair, he turned away from her. "I'm sorry, son," she said. "I was always lousy at picking my men."

After she left, Hema crept to the windowsill and looked out. Across the road he saw people sitting behind lighted windows.

And then he glanced at Janey where she fluttered in her dreams.

The night cracked open. Through the gap the bikies rode, helmeted on high silver-chromed wings. Their bodies were carapaced with leather and studded with silver, and they rumbled through the dark trailing black scarves from their necks like clotted blood.

"My foot is sore, Hema," Janey said. They had come down Taranaki Street and were at Pigeon Park.

"We'll go and sit over there," Hema answered. He pulled Janey after him across the busy street, where Janey sat on a bench and began unstrapping her sandals. "Let me look," Hema said. He found a small sharp stone in one of the sandals. "Why didn't you tell me before?" he asked as he rubbed her foot.

"I've already been a nuisance."

They rested, watching laughing people walk past and the traffic glittering in the streets. "I like your maxi coat," a girl giggled at Hema through her thin painted lips.

Hema flushed, but he didn't really care. The park seemed littered with people like him and Janey, and he had a strange sense of being part of them. Then he saw a policeman coming, jabbing at others, hustling them on. "We'll go now," he said to Janey.

Janey pointed to a bus standing at the corner of Cuba Street. On the front flashed the destination: Railway Station. "We haven't got enough money," Hema said.

"I've brought some," Janey answered. She reached into the pocket of her jeans and brought out some coins.

Hema smiled, there wasn't enough for two fares. "Better keep your money for later," he said to her. "We might need it for something else. Okay?"

She grinned proudly and put the coins back in her pocket. At the corner, while waiting for the lights to change so that they could cross, Hema saw a man thumbing through green notes and stuffing them carelessly into his wallet. Maybe he would drop some.

"Now hold on tight," Hema said to Janey. "I don't want you to get lost. If you let go my hand you stop right where you are and don't move. I'll find you."

Ahead, the pavement was crowded with people. Thrusting through them was like struggling through a land of giants, of people who did not look and see the boy and his sister. "Are you holding on tight?" Hema asked.

His sister nodded back, scared. Her fingernails dug into his arm. Heavy bodies slammed into Janey and loud voices boomed around her.

Along Manners Street the children went, and into Willis Street. From a movie billboard a grim-faced man pointed a gun at them. On a television screen in an electronics shop a woman was being stabbed to death.

They came to an intersection. The lights changed and the crowd was moving. From the four corners of the crossing they came to merge in the middle, jostling, shoving and pushing their way across the road. And Hema felt Janey's hand wrenched out of his.

"Hema," she yelled. He looked back and glimpsed her fluttering in the crowd. He tried to get back to her but the rush of people pushed him onto the opposite pavement. The lights were changing. The cars began to move. Janey was still standing there, turning round and round looking for him. Round and round. A bird in a cage. Looking.

"Janey." He rushed out from the pavement and put his arms around her. Drivers were shouting and horns were booming, but he didn't care. Then a car braked in front of them. The traffic came to a stop.

"Get your sister off the road, boy," a voice called.

He picked Janey up in his arms and carried her to the pavement. He heard a bystander mutter something about mothers who let their children roam the streets at night.

"You told me to stay right where I was if I lost your hand," Janey said, "so I did."

"You did good," Hema said. "Come on, not far to go now."

They hurried down Lambton Quay.

It happened slowly at first, their mother pushing them away.

But it increased as Mum's life twisted more and more around Uncle Pita. Her kids were her own — she owned them — but she did not own her man. Her need for security made her attempt to possess him and she pushed her children further into the background. They became as unsure of her as they were of Uncle Pita. They tried to read the signs that flickered over her face. Once they thought they'd known everything they needed to know about Mum. The signs became strange, clouded. It wasn't that she didn't love them anymore; it was just she had to make sure to always please Pita. Her moods became inconsistent. Sometimes she laughed and played with the kids; other times she growled and lashed out at them. There came a time when they could never tell what she might do.

One day Hema returned home late from school. "Where's Janey?" he asked Mum.

"How should I fucken know," Mum said. "I gave her a slap and she ran off."

Hema knew instantly where Janey was. He went into the bedroom and looked under the bed. "Come out, Janey," he said. "No use crying."

"Mum hit me. And don't tell me she didn't mean it. She did."

Hema crawled under the bed and put his arms around her. Although he consoled her, he felt Janey comforting him too. He thought of Mum and realised he and Janey were secure only in each other. And, as if to confirm, from that moment on Mum was always telling him to look after his sister.

"We're having a party tonight, Hema. *Look after your sister.* Pita and I want to watch television. *Look after your sister.* My darling wants me to himself tonight. *Look after your sister.*"

Mum had always been careless about keeping the flat clean. After Uncle Pita came she was more careless. Hema began making breakfast for himself and Janey, washing their clothes, doing the dishes and sweeping the floor. Sometimes his mother noticed, sometimes she didn't. Not that it mattered. It had to be done. Mum was busy enjoying herself. As long as she was happy, Hema was happy.

Yet he couldn't help wondering whether or not Mum was *really* happy. He wondered constantly what his mother really meant to Uncle Pita. Whenever parties were held at the flat Uncle Pita often flirted with other women — kissing and fondling them — and they would treat Mum with amusement. *Why not sneak out on your old bitch and have a good time with your young bitch, eh?*

Mum began to drink more. She sat on other men's laps. Hema watched her sometimes through the crack in the bedroom door. She was very pretty and gay. Yet when she danced by herself while everyone clapped and told her to dance faster, *faster you desperate cunt,* her hair swinging free, sweat dripping down the neck of her dress, thighs grinding, *Look at me Pita honey,* Hema wanted to go in and say, "Stop. Mum. Stop."

After one such party, the children cleared up the flat. Took the flagons downstairs. Opened the windows to get rid of the smell of cigarette smoke and beer. Mopped the floor. Uncle Pita had made it to the bed. But Mum was sitting on the lav, still drunk as, her pants down around her ankles. "Come to bed, Mum," Hema said.

She looked at him. Saw where she was. Told him to turn around. Kissed him on the back of the neck as she flushed the toilet. "You and your sister are too good for a rotten bitch like me," she said.

But she wasn't rotten. She was Mum.

Fists thudded in a sudden fight outside the main entrance of the railway station. Two men argued over ownership of a taxi at the rank. Within the pillared shadows thin faces gleamed.

"Yay," Janey said. "We made it."

The station was crowded. It was half past eight. Late-night commuters rushed to catch their units to the Hutt or Porirua. Above the clamour, the loudspeaker announced departure times, platform numbers, welcomes and farewells to passengers. Everyone seemed to have a place to go, a destination.

"You wait here," Hema told Janey. He sat her next to a middle-aged Māori woman. The woman looked at them with eyes shattered by tiredness. "Can you keep an eye on my sister?" Hema asked.

She shrugged her shoulders. Free country, anybody can sit anywhere they like.

Hema walked to to the ticket office and joined one of the queues. Every now and then he looked back at Janey. Would she be all right travelling by herself? What happened if . . .

"Next customer," the man on the other side of the glass said.

"Can I have a ticket to Gisborne please?"

"What day do you wish to travel?" the man asked. "No Gisborne service tonight. Next train's tomorrow morning."

I should have looked up the railway timetable, Hema thought. He stepped away. Went back to Janey. What would they do? They couldn't go back to the flat. Not after last night.

Last night. Hema, Janey and Mum sat in the kitchen having tea. Mum's face was tight and her hands kept smoothing down her dress. She was moving her thighs together, brushing the room with tension. "Mum—" Hema began.

"Just eat your kai," she answered.

Last weekend, Mum's new darling had moved in. Uncle Pita had pissed off a fortnight ago. The new man's name was Rapper and he had been to some of the parties Mum used to go to. Just waiting for Pita to move on so he could move in. He belonged to a gang. Didn't work. Mum was his pay cheque. He cashed her in every day and night. Sweet as.

They were waiting for Rapper to come home. Hema was feeling sick at his mother's weakness for this new man.

The door opened downstairs. Mum gave a cry and ran down the steps to Rapper. He came up and saw Hema and Janey sitting in the kitchen. "What the fuck are youse two doing here?"

"Go to bed now, Hema," Mum said. "Look after your sister." Her voice was deep-throated, purring with happiness. She wanted to be in this new man's skin, lick it all around her and nestle in it.

But Hema had had enough. "Why don't you leave my mother alone?" he yelled. "You're just a loser." Mum looked at him, shocked. "We don't want you here," Hema said to Rapper. "And I don't take orders from you."

He was looking to Mum to support him. But she had not understood. She had not seen Hema or Janey at all. Her eyes were filled only with the new man standing next to her. But she knew what the new man meant to do when he took off his belt.

"No, the kid doesn't mean it," she said to Rapper.

"He needs a lesson. He needs to know who's the boss around here. I *am* the boss, aren't I, darling?" And Rapper threw Hema into the bedroom and kicked shut the door.

"Mum . . ."

The *pain* of the belt. It slashed, struck, slashed again. The buckle scored the skin, opened it. Hema realised that Mum didn't need them anymore. And if she ever had, she couldn't look after him and Janey any longer.

They sat in the concourse, watching train after train pull out of the station. Carriage after carriage of lighted windows flowing past like dream after dream. The old Māori lady had gone to sleep beside them. The police had come by now and then but thought that Hema and Janey were with her — and left them alone.

The station became a derelict place strewn with cigarette butts, spilled food, used condoms. Someone had used a corner as a toilet.

Then the shops in the concourse closed down. Only a few people remained. The old Māori lady woke up with a start, shivered and, without a look at the two children, wandered off into the night.

"Do you think Mum will be home yet?" Janey asked.

"Too early." *Mum had just stood there. Let Rapper give him a belting. She had let him.*

"We can't stay here." Janey was rubbing her legs. They were cold.

But when Mum gets home and sees we aren't there, she'll cry out our names and run from room to room looking for us, and then she'll go into the street. Where are you Hema? Janeeee.

No, they couldn't stay at the station much longer. "We'll have to go back," he said. A patrol car screamed along the street. The lights of the city tightened around them.

"Home?" Janey asked.

And Hema gave a deep sigh. *Our mother's a weak woman, Janey. She needs men, and after Rapper there might be others who will come and go. One day when the men have all left her, Mum might need us again. But there's always you and me, eh?*

"Yes, home," Hema said.

3.

The world was changing. *New Net* records the difference and was successful enough to go into three reprints. The third 1993 edition sported a new cover: a still photograph from the Roger Donaldson–Ian Mune Aardvark Films adaptation of the story "Big Brother, Little Sister" for the television series *Winners and Losers*. Indeed, following the screening, I always planned to rewrite and expand the story, as I finally have done here, for *Native Son*.

"Big Brother, Little Sister" had enough of my personal stamp to become, like "A Game of Cards", one of my calling cards as a writer. Future Māori novelist Paula Morris watched the television adaptation as a West Auckland schoolgirl in the late 1970s and wrote, "I'd never seen anything like it — an urban setting I could recognise, kids I understood, a story about here and now, startling in its familiarity, in its lyricism and its ugliness."

I wish the reviewers, both Māori and Pākehā, had seen the adaptation in the same way. They were damning of the representation of Māori as abusive hard drinkers, and of the story as revealing a violent misogyny towards women. But in 2018 *Big Brother, Little Sister* has been rereleased in remastered high definition, so it will be interesting to await critiques today. Perhaps we've grown up sufficiently to accept the hard truth about the consequences of the urban drift happening way back then.

In reality, Hema and Janey would never have made it home. Like as not they would have been picked up by the cops, removed by the courts from their mother and placed by the state into separate foster homes. There, they would have become lost to the system and suffered further repetitive domestic violence and sexual abuse. Hema would have ended up in prison and on release found, in one of the gangs that had begun to proliferate in Aotearoa, the only home that would take him in.

Apart from "Big Brother, Little Sister", two other short stories were also adapted for television. "The Truth of the Matter" was adapted as *Against the Lights* (1978) by director Sam Pillsbury, and *The Makutu on Mrs Jones* (1983) directed by Larry Parr. I wish I could see *Against the Lights* again, but it seems to have disappeared. Its base story, "The Truth of the Matter", was inspired by the work of the Japanese writer Ryūnosuke Akutagawa, whose two stories "Rashomon" and "In a Grove" were made into the film *Rashomon* by the famed Japanese director Akira Kurosawa. Whenever I feel the need to think high quality, in terms of writing, I always turn to Akutagawa's stories for guidance. And the use by me of the word "truth" in the title of my story is prescient. All my work since has, in one way or another, placed that concept under scrutiny.

In 1990, Alan Duff wrote *Once Were Warriors* and the lid was really blown off the domestic abuse and gang violence happening to and among urban Māori. And when the film version was released four years later, New Zealand — and the world — really sat up and paid attention. I am hoping that there will be a film version of the latest novel to authenticate this urban experience: Apirana Taylor's *Five Strings* (2017), which was longlisted for the New Zealand Ockham Fiction Awards.

What's interesting was that kupu changed. You only have to listen to the cadences before, and after, 1970 to know I am right. As young Māori borrowed from Black music, reggae and other international influences the rhythms and vocal emphases strengthened kupu, gave it a stronger shell, and took its whakapapa somewhere else. At the time I wasn't sure whether kupu would survive. Ways had to be found to allow it to do so.

The "new net" I went fishing with in 1976 became the prototype for the kind of Māori literature and other work that I would continue to write from that point onward.

All my subsequent works have had a political streak built in to their infrastructure. The personal equation I developed to ensure tikanga and kaupapa was the following:

Aesthetics + the Politics of Difference = Māori Literature.

I felt that aesthetics alone could not guarantee the moko.

And what's interesting is that at that time I felt I had a choice as to what direction I could write to. As I have earlier noted, I could have favoured the right, te taha matau — after all, I was already moving that way — and developed a contemporary urban Māori world in my fiction. Indeed, my archive at Victoria University of Wellington has in it verification that I planned a novel, *Wilson Street*, set in the Wellington suburb, Newtown. I proposed to use the same format as *Whanau*, depicting the lives of young urban Māori as they revolved around an infamous party house during a volatile weekend.

Instead, auē, cack-handed, I veered to the left and *Wilson Street* became The Novel That Got Away — although scraps of it exist in stories like "Four on a Bus" and "Dustbins".

You can see the swerve in "Big Brother, Little Sister", which is the kind of narrative known as "The Hero's Journey".

The mythologist Joseph Campbell, in his book *The Hero with a Thousand Faces* (1949), is the pre-eminent expert in tracing the development of this archetype. In it, a hero is called to action and goes on a quest. There are a number of crises that he has to endure, but through his successes or failures he is changed, learns some important lessons and returns home transformed.

In Hema's case, the boy is called to escape from a violent situation. He has somebody to save — Janey — not just himself. His journey involves a number of perilous situations that must be negotiated, both in the past as well as in the present. On arrival at the railway station he has faced the challenges and been transformed by them. He is able to return home with Janey to his mother to eventually, if he can, rescue her from the cycle of circumstances which keep her trapped.

But the hero's journey is more mythic, more metatextual than that. It wasn't until I had put myself through a lot more life and learning (my next book did not appear until eleven years later) that I finally introduced the mainframe of all my later work.

Rather than go forward from *Tangi* into an urban present I began to walk backwards into the future.

I started to look at the novel in a tribal way.

After a lot of thinking, I realised that the best way to encompass all I wanted to say about being Māori was by writing the contemporary but multigenerational Māori family saga that traversed our mythologies and histories.

That iwi novel was *The Matriarch* (1986) and, with it, I felt I was onto something reflecting my engagement with whakapapa within the context of literary modernism and internationalism.

Nevertheless, I date the time I wrote *New Net* as the moment when I stilled the waka and let down the net into the sea.

Today the grappling hooks still trawl the ever-changing currents of time and race politics.

Chapter Twenty

Sacrifice to the Volcano God

1.

In early 1963 I needed to make some money fast.

A failed suicide doesn't want to stick around, he or she has too much shame to do that. Therefore I decided the best thing to do was to take myself out of Gisborne.

Something else motivated me. One weekend I saw someone familiar. *Hello, Witi, enjoying your life?* I was at the hockey grounds in Stanley Street, Gisborne. I had just finished a game and I saw the relative who had raped me walking on the other side of the field. *Even if you think I can't see you, I can smell you, sweet boy.*

He was always there. Somewhere. Everywhere. On the marae at Waituhi, whenever I saw him I turned my back and retreated. At weddings, birthdays and funerals, there was always the possibility of moving out of range. How long could I keep it up?

This time, however, I couldn't walk away. He had a young boy with him, as youthful as I had been when he had taken me into the hut at night. Was this taitamariki to face, as I had done, an assault on his mana?

The sweat popped onto my brow. Although seven years had passed, I honestly don't know how I got the strength. I walked swiftly over to him, tapped him on the shoulder and, when he turned, let him have it with my hockey stick.

"What the hell—"

Surprised, he put up an arm to fend off my second strike. And then he saw me, laughed — he *laughed* — braced, and struck. I staggered back and when I wiped my face I saw that he had drawn blood.

I went at him again, up on the balls of my feet, trying to get through his defences. Kept moving, wove, my guard high, and waited my opportunity. Jabbed and then hit him in the stomach. I was just about to follow through when I felt myself pulled back by onlookers.

I turned to the boy with him. "Has he touched you?" I yelled.

The taitamariki looked confused. "Uncle," he said to my relative, "are you all right?"

His parents, hearing my yell, arrived, alarmed.

"Has he molested your boy?" I asked them.

They didn't know what I was talking about. And by now I was losing whatever adrenaline I had mustered to follow through.

"Don't listen to his bullshit," my relative said.

"Make sure he doesn't," I warned the parents. Kneeling to the boy, I forced him to look into my eyes. "You know who I am. Contact me if ever you have to."

I had just enough strength to walk to the changing rooms. When I got there, I went into one of the stalls and sat there, shivering, trying not to moan. I still wasn't free. Still hadn't confronted him.

Later, I took the keys of the truck without Mum and Dad knowing, and drove out to Sponge Bay. The stingrays were threshing in the moonlit water.

Yes, time to get away. I sat there, looking out to the horizon, and wondered — hoped — that something might be waiting for me beyond the towering cloud worlds, something that was *good*. But was I only prolonging the inevitable? Another suicide attempt?

I would have to negotiate my way through those lashing barbed tails, and maybe I would survive or maybe I wouldn't.

2.

If you have been raped, you know what it means to always be in the physical presence of the person who destroyed you.

You can therefore imagine how surprised Mum and Dad were when, after the euphoria of knowing I had got my UE, they asked me, hesitantly, "What do you want to do now, son?"

"I'm going to uni," I answered.

When Pera Punahāmoa was told he grunted, "You had the chance to fulfil my ambitions for you and go to an American university a year ago. Are you mocking me, Witi?"

Mr Grono, whom I met on Gladstone Road, was delighted. He kept pumping my hand, glad that no matter his glimpse of what was troubling me, I was not letting it hold me back.

To be frank, my decision to take on university training had also been arrived at by a humiliating process of elimination. I had earlier gone to Army Headquarters across the Peel Street bridge to sign up and was surprised when they turned me down. Teacher's training college was also an option, but Ardmore declined me too. I turned to the possibility of an AFS scholarship, and even went for a job with Volunteer Service Abroad serving in the Solomon Islands — still no takers.

The first question was: which university?

"I'll ring brother Win," Dad said. "If you go to Victoria University of Wellington I'm sure he and Margaret would love to have you at their place, and Win can help you with your assignments."

Since leaving Murupara, where I had last seen him, Uncle Win had become a welfare officer for the Maori Affairs Department in the Levin District and a teacher at the Wellington Correspondence School; later, he taught at Naenae College. He was the Vice-President of the Ngati Poneke Young Maori Club and treasurer of the Ngati Poneke Maori Association, and also chairman of the Taurarua Maori Tribal Association. You only had to hear him talking to know he was well educated. His utterances were eloquent, his vocal delivery resonant, something like actor James Mason's, and he couldn't have put a badly constructed sentence together if he tried.

I had the feeling, however, that Uncle Win would prove a hard taskmaster. Given his volcanic temper and that he was an inspector of education, I thought he would not be forgiving of any intellectual lapse on my part. As well, I was seeking a greater anonymity than Wellington could provide. There was also the embarrassment of turning up at Victoria Uni where most of my Gisborne friends, such as Maarten van Dijk, were completing their undergraduate training. I was already three years behind them and they were ready to graduate when I was only starting.

I told Dad, "I'll go to Auckland."

There were fewer family members up there to spy on me — or so I thought. That was the main factor in my decision.

The next question was: how would I support myself? The shearing income and small amounts from Māori land trusts such as the Wī Pere Trust, Mangatu, Waerenga-a-Hika and Tahora covered my fees and books. But I was still too proud to take money from the family, and so my living expenses would have to depend on the Maori Education Foundation.

Set up in 1961, the foundation was a government education initiative, following the Hunn Report, to provide scholarships so that more Māori would get into tertiary study. Financed from public and private donations, it was launched in a heady, exciting atmosphere and, in Gisborne, Keith Bracey on the local radio station 2XG presided over a radio fundraiser. The bicultural buoyancy of Gisborne was such that both Pākehā and Māori rang in to pledge donations; I promised £5 sterling.

Two years later I hoped to take advantage of my investment.

You could say that by deciding to go to university I ran away from Gisborne, hoping to escape from myself and find that self elsewhere where nobody was looking; I'm not ashamed to admit it.

I said goodbye to Jackson, and he said, "Hey, maybe I'll come up and join ya."

When I told him "No" he shrugged his shoulders.

And then he grinned. "Whenever you come home, I'm always here to help a mate."

"Bloody idiot," I smiled.

I suspect Jackson contributed more to my life and career than I have realised — I'm still trying to work that one out. I suspect I will have to thank him, and I'll do that if ever I see him again.

I spent the rest of my time beforehand apologising to Nani Mini, her husband George Tupara and everyone at Waituhi that I was going. It was cousin Sammy who rolled his eyes and answered, "What are ya, cuz? You're nothing like us, you can do better."

And Nani Mini said, "You can tell all those girls up there that you got a girlfriend."

She wasn't exactly what I had in mind.

I told Dad, "I'll catch the Road Service bus to Auckland."

He answered, "Well, as it happens your grandad Pera is travelling to Hamilton and could take you part of the way —"

Thank God he was kidding. "I'm taking you," he said.

On the day I left, my sisters and I hugged each other tight. "You're always leaving us," they said. My farewells from my mother were the hardest. We just looked at each other without saying anything. If she had said, "Stay," I would have stayed. If she had cried, I would have said, "I'm not going."

Anything, Mum, anything. Just one small teardrop. But my mother never cried and I never asked.

Finally, "Time for Witi to go," Dad said to her.

He loaded my two suitcases onto the back of the truck, we said a prayer, Mum flicked water over me and Dad trucked me personally to Auckland.

3.

We arrived in the Queen's City around midnight. Dad drove the truck off State Highway 1 and found a dell shadowed by pine trees where it was so quiet we should have been suspicious. He parked under the trees. "This will do us," he said, and we bedded down.

As it turned out, the place we slept was the Symonds Street cemetery at the corner of Karangahape Road.

The next morning, disconcerted, Dad quickly took us off to find his cousin, Uncle Jim Pere. He and Auntie Elsie had a boarding house in Gibraltar Crescent, Parnell, a big rambling villa overlooking the railway tracks below and the Domain. Despite my telling Dad that I could find my own digs, I had to stay somewhere meantime and, as it happened, I boarded with them for the first year. Uncle Jim told me I could work at the boarding house if the scholarship didn't come through.

The following day, Dad said, "Well, we better get enrolled."

Not *you*. We.

This was my first time in the Queen's City, though our family had driven through it at night in convoy with other Gisborne tribes journeying to the annual celebrations at Waitangi. In those quieter pre-protest days, iwi liked to travel as ope to meet — together with curious tourists — and affirm Ngāpuhi's position as the kaitiaki of the Treaty. Māori were the main attendees, and only later were there significant sightings of our Pākehā treaty partner.

Auckland was just a place to pass through.

Dad was like a shepherd pushing a rebellious young ram from one department to another, waiting in the queues for my enrolment and allocation to tutorials. Auckland definitely made me feel frisky. I didn't think anything of his being with me, though, until we went to enrol in geography.

A beautiful young woman stopped me and asked, "Your dad's with you? Cute."

She was Tanya Cumberland, daughter of one of the professors, Kenneth Cumberland.

Meanwhile, Dad was bedazzled by it all and I couldn't help thinking that he was the better candidate than I was for higher learning.

The most important interview was with the Music Department, where I was hoping to enrol in an Executant Diploma in Music. I was a late entry, as the entrance examination had already been held in September, but, after playing two compositions for Professor Charles Nalden and doing a bit of sight reading, he didn't rule me out. He asked Dad a pertinent question: "What does he want to take the diploma for?"

Not me. Dad. You would have thought I was arrogant enough to say, "I want to become a classical pianist," but the cat got my tongue.

Dad and Professor Nalden were getting on like a house on fire and Dad told him about learning the violin. Very soon the kōrero turned to alternative careers open to a successful student — none of which I had thought about — including work in an orchestra or in radio; it was either classical pianist or nothing. However, somehow or other, I had ceased to exist.

"I suggest you take a BA conjoint with the Executant Diploma," Professor Nalden said to Dad. "You're good at English, you say? There you are then! If the diploma doesn't work out, you can switch to a BA, majoring in that subject. Why, you could be an English teacher."

Professor Nalden assigned his wife, Felicity, as my tutor. Dad shook hands with him and we left the office. "I liked that Professor Nalden," Dad said.

And then Dad started to ask questions designed to find out what I knew about you-know-what, as if I might still need the father-to-son lesson before he abandoned me to the wiles of the wicked city. I took the same approach as my friend Gavin Strahan's daughter. When Gavin found her reading a book about the Marquis de Sade, he asked if he could read it after her. She said no. Gavin thought it was because she was embarrassed for him. The truth was that if he did, he would know what she now knew after having read it.

Dad stayed on in Auckland, delaying his departure. Sometimes he could be as bad as Pera, taking me here, there and everywhere, visiting relatives who had migrated to Auckland years ago — even those who had been living away from Waituhi for generations.

He had promised the parents of two boys who had got into trouble with the police that he would visit their sons in Mount Eden prison. I will never forget that visit when, hat in hand, Dad signed us through security and we waited for them to appear. I couldn't help noticing how most of the visitors and inmates — even guards — were Māori. At the time there were more of *us* in the prison system than Pākehā. There still are; that hasn't changed.

The boys had been in Dad's shearing gang and, when they saw him, they began to weep.

"Thank you for coming, Tom," they said. And then they began to ask about their families. Afterward he left some cash for them. After all, he had been their padrone. And then he left *me* money, saying, "You come back here and visit the boys, give them this money, do it for the family."

Finally, "I have to go back to your mother," Dad said one morning.

He was looking somewhat embarrassed and with good reason. Mum was pregnant . . . again.

"Oh no," I said. My sister Kararaina and I had barely forgiven him and Mum for having Gay the year before; with Dad in his late forties and Mum in her late thirties they were, after all, middle-aged. Having Gay was just oh-kay but another child was definitely carelessness. What was worse was the clear evidence that Mum and Dad hadn't learnt from their mistake and were still doing *it*.

"Well," Dad tried to justify, "Gay needs a mate to grow up with."

The mate turned out to be my youngest sibling Neil Lamarr Gillen Ihimaera Smiler. When he was born he was twenty years younger than me, and I've always thought of him as a son rather than a brother. Now we were eight: me, Kararaina, our brother Thomas who died when he was a baby, Tāwhi, Viki, Derek, Gay and Neil. At least this was evidence that life was renewing itself, if not in my life, in my parents'.

Another brother might even help to replace the useless, defunct eldest one.

The day after Dad left I had my appointment for the Maori Education Foundation grant. The interview was conducted in a large sunlit room in a small house off Wellesley Street. I walked across the wooden floor, the boards tolling loudly at every footstep, to a table at which were seated four people. I wished Dad had come with me, he always talked to people whether they wanted to have a kōrero or not, and they found themselves signing papers without realising it.

The selection team looked bored, and asked for evidence that I had enrolled and that I needed their financial support. Sometimes I am not quite *on,* and my oblique responses to their rote questions — "What would a grant mean to you?", "How will you serve the Māori people once you complete your degree?" — must have made their day. They got up my goat.

"Look," I answered, "I'm Māori, there are not many of us here, I'm perfectly happy to go out and work, I'm all you've got, take it or leave it."

I didn't like having to bow and scrape for the money, I just wouldn't do it. I cut the interview short by walking out.

But the committee must have forgiven the crass action of a moody boy, because a letter came in the post a couple of weeks later to say that my application had been successful. To be frank, I had been waiting on tenterhooks for it.

Cheque in hand I walked to the bank and deposited it. Then back to Uncle Jim and Auntie Elsie's boarding house. I had dinner with the other boarders and went to my room. It must have been around eight, the summer days still long. As I went up the stairs, one of the boys yelled out to me, "Feel like doing the town?"

"How about tomorrow night?" I yelled back.

"You could be dead by then!"

I shut the door, locked it, and opened the window to the Domain opposite. It looked so beautiful out there with the sun slanting golden through the trees.

And then I heard the boy in the park opposite before I saw him.

Can you hear him now? The running boy?

He is still far away but if you put your ear to the ground you can hear the faint thump of his feet. Listen to the pattern. It is erratic, it is fast, as if he doesn't know where he is going. All he knows is that he must get away. Must escape from the hut where something monstrous has happened to him.

And now can you hear his breath on the wind? It is hoarse, it is rasping, he is breathing deep and dragging the air in, keeping it there, and then expelling it out. Hsss. Hsss. HSSS. HSSS.

The boy comes running along the coiling path. Can you see him now? The boy, running so speedily that he is just a blur in the moonlight? He is even faster when darkness shrouds the path. He fears the shadows and seeks the light.

He bursts out from the forest. He is on the riverbank of the Waiapu River. He runs along it, stumbling, falling, rising. Not far away is the wide moonlit space where the river meets the sea. He runs through the sand, running, running.

Splash, splash, splash. He runs right into the water, it cascades around him. And when he can't run any more, he wades out, the sea waist deep.

He can't see it, but you can, the tendrils of blood that swirl around his thighs. From the attack. From the mounting. From the tearing. From the breaking.

Whimpering he washes himself, but the wound still hurts. And the salt from the sea stings.

And then he gets out. He finds some sedge and uses it as a poultice. Sits in the dark, the sea soughing, hush, hush.

What should he do now? At least the night is warm. He can't go back to the shearing gang yet. He should wait here. Go back when the sun rises.

"Yes," I murmured. "Wait for the dawn."

I closed the window and pulled the curtains against the sunlight. Stood there a moment before turning to the wardrobe. Still hadn't unpacked everything from my suitcase.

"Go back to the shearing gang in the morning. Don't tell anybody. They don't have to know."

And then I gave a deep moan . . . and, fainting, fell to the floor. You'll know why.

I had been keeping myself together by sheer willpower.

Chapter Twenty-One

Tāwhaki and the Hero's Journey

1.

When I had been leaving Waituhi to come to Auckland, my mother, Julia, stroked my cheek and said, "Ah, you are following in the footsteps of Tāwhaki."

And then she said, "After all, you had Teria for your grandmother."

No matter that Teria had died when I was eleven, she had already prepared my pathway through life; her influence has continued to inform my decisions over all my years.

Throughout Polynesia there is no greater example of the multi-generational monomyth — the hero's journey — than the story of Tāwhaki, set into operation by Whaitiri two generations before. The cycle is the Polynesian equivalent of *The Epic of Gilgamesh*. Originating from ancient Mesopotamia, *Gilgamesh* dates from 2100 BC, and is written on twelve tablets. This epic story of the king of Uruk and his marvellous adventures is universally accepted to be the earliest surviving work of great literature. It is the Father of All Epics that others have borrowed from (think *Lord of the Rings*) and has such shapeshifting characters and ambivalent heroics — not to mention variant sexuality and gender — that you/he/she/they will find that you were authenticated, like, way back.

During my early manhood, Tāwhaki became my exemplar. For all of us who left our kāinga in Aotearoa or motu throughout Polynesia for the metropolitan centres in France, the United States, Australia or New Zealand, he was the hero whose journey we were encouraged to emulate — "Whaia te ara ō tō tātou tupuna a Tāwhaki" — particularly if we were embarking on university careers.

We were never told, "Follow in the footsteps of Māui".

Ours was to be a more difficult *human* journey.

2.

Like all heroes, Tāwhaki's story is preceded by predictions of greatness. It was said that no infant had such gleaming skin as his. The sheen of it was taken to indicate that he was set apart to accomplish great tasks. As he grew to boyhood most people were not aware of anything abnormal about him until he threw aside his garments and "clothed himself with lightning".

His nobility and generosity also set him apart, arousing jealousy. Like most boys he had small wooden waka which he would race in competitions against the canoes of other boys. He kept on winning. So much so that his cousins gave him a hiding, beating him until they thought they had killed him. The forbearing Tāwhaki got up and followed them home.

I like what he did next. Instead of telling on them, he turned them into pāpahu, porpoises.

In New Zealand we tell an adult version of this story. In it Tāwhaki is not a child but a man married to Hinepiripiri. While fishing, he falls out with his brothers-in-law who fight him and leave him for dead. But Hinepiripiri discovers him still alive and they escape together, retreating with their followers to a fortified kāinga on the top of a very high mountain.

By the time Tāwhaki was a young man, his beauty and aristocratic bearing as an ariki had already made him the cynosure of all eyes — the gaze of all Pacific peoples was on him. The people of the Tuamotu Archipelago — almost eighty islands and atolls — claimed that the very sight of Tāwhaki made women "distraught" with love. That's an interesting description — in the reo, the sense is conveyed by the phrase *e pōuri*.

Interest elevated when lightning was seen flashing from his armpits!

Tāwhaki's unearthly radiance seems to have created much envy. In Mangareva, the largest of the Gambier Islands in French Polynesia, rival warriors turned themselves into fish and, during a diving competition, waited underwater to tear his shining skin off; I love the logic of water cooling the "lightning". But Whaitiri, his grandmother, guessed the warriors' plan, and she too hid underwater where she gathered the bits into her basket. She is reputed to have stuck them all back on her grandson again, but couldn't find enough to cover the soles of his feet. Humans weren't the only ones to covet Tāwhaki's skin — the whē, the stick insects, had managed to steal those bits for themselves.

And, of course, Tāwhaki attracted not only human but divine interest. A celestial woman, Hāpai, was attracted to Tāwhaki and floated down from the heavens to be with him. She became Tāwhaki's second wife and they had a daughter.

3.

So far so good, but every hero requires a great "search and rescue" mission to elevate his narrative from the ordinary to the extraordinary.

Tāwhaki had three such missions that stand out. The first was to do with seeking and finding imprisoned parents, leading to the classic parental reunion. The second involved searching and locating Hāpai and his daughter, leading again to a classic reunion — this time of husband with wife and child. And the third required him to climb into the heavens and bring back fabled baskets of knowledge, leading to his promotion by humankind as their saviour.

To accomplish all three missions Tāwhaki risks his life and places himself in immense danger.

Let's look at how his saga plays out in the first mission.

Some years earlier Tāwhaki's parents, Hema and Urutonga, had gone missing without a trace. All that was known was that they had set out to seek a birth gift for their son. This suggests that their disappearance occurred when Tāwhaki and his brother Karihi were children. The two boys become the classic orphan siblings of myth.

We don't know when Tāwhaki decided to search for his parents. But he — and Karihi — must have been only adolescents when they were told the rumours that Hema and Urutonga had trespassed on the territory of the fierce ponaturi. These were the savage and pellucid gillmen and -women who served Tangaroa and lived in the sea. Some were also winged like bats, able to fly as well as swim.

I knew them well. They watched me from the shadows as I slept, waiting for me to fall from my cliff of dreams into the sea of nightmares.

"The ponaturi seized your father," Tāwhaki was told. "They gouged out his eyes to light their sleeping house, and then they killed him."

"What of my mother?" Tāwhaki asked.

"She is probably dead also."

Now, for ancient Māori it was imperative to recover the bones of relatives and bring them back to their own ūkaipō, homeland. Only then could the appropriate ceremonials be performed to enable them to cross over into the world beyond this one. Meantime, as spirits, they were condemned to a living death.

"Will you come with me?" Tāwhaki asked his brother.

"Yes," Karihi said. He became the sidekick, the clumsy one, whose brashness and incompetence highlight the hero's dignity and skill.

Tāwhaki answered the call to danger: variations include the summons to adventure or the requirement to fulfil a prophecy. Thus the two boys leave their kāinga to find the bones of their dead parents. In so doing, they cross the paepae, the threshold of their homeland, and venture into the unknown. They already have Whaitiri as a spirit guide but they must rely on their own resources of intelligence to survive in the lands of the ponaturi.

Now, there were as many tribes of ponaturi in the ocean as there were human iwi living on land. Eventually, Tāwhaki and Karihi were guided to a meeting house called Manawa-Tāne, which was the last place their parents were known to have been before they disappeared. The wharenui was actually on dry land rather than under the ocean. All the gillmen and -women were swimming in the depths of the sea. Together they chased shoals of fish, surrounded and fed upon them. They only returned to the meeting house to sleep when it was dark.

The one person at Manawa-Tāne was an old woman, sitting at the door. She saw the two boys coming towards her and began to weep.

"Are these my sons coming at last?"

The woman was Urutonga. While the ponaturi had killed Hema they had kept her captive. They could not afford to oversleep and be caught by the sun — direct exposure to sunlight will kill them — and Urutonga was their watchwoman. She warned the ponaturi when dawn was coming so that they could descend further into the dark, subterranean grottoes of the sea.

"They call me Tatau," Urutonga told her sons bitterly. "They keep yelling to me during the night, 'Hey, Door, is it dawn yet?'"

A door is a portal from an outer world to an inner world. Tatau is the guardian of the door and, when the two brothers enter, they will forever be transformed. In symbolic terms, it is the innermost cave, the central ordeal. They will leave boyhood behind and, as they confront the terrible reality of what has happened to Hema, their father, enter adulthood.

After being captured, Hema's eyes had been torn out. Then he was killed, his body eviscerated and thrown into a cesspit. When the flesh had wasted away, his bones were suspended from the ceiling of the ponaturi's whare. But his spirit still inhabited the bones.

Imagine Urutonga's grief at hearing, through all the years of her captivity, her husband's soul calling out, *Find me release, wife.*

And Tāwhaki and Karihi went through the doorway. To their horror they saw hundreds of skeletons intertwined one with another, interlacing the rafters. Hema had not been the only one to be captured and killed in the lands of the ponaturi. Which bones were their father's?

Tāwhaki chanted an incantation, *Where are you, e Pā?*

From within the dense skeletal mass of skulls and bones he heard a rattling reply, *Here I am.*

Tenderly, the two brothers extricated Hema's remains from the skeletal cemetery. They cried over the bones and washed them.

The next challenge was to find their father's eyes. But there were so many glowing eyes through the interior! However, only one pair was crying — Hema's.

The boys trussed their father's remains together and made ready to take him back to their homeland. But darkness was quickly falling.

"Oh, sons," Urutonga cried. "The ponaturi will be returning soon. We must get away *now*."

The ocean's surface was blood red with sunset. The ponaturi rose in their many thousands, yes, mano maha ngā ponaturi. The surface seethed and broke apart as they rushed through the surf or flew up through the waves.

But Tāwhaki paused. He looked at his mother and brother.

"No, we will not go yet. I must avenge my father."

4.

Tāwhaki's decision is a revelation.

It brings him to the edge of an abyss. How can three human beings defeat the monstrous thousands?

"We must hide," he says to Karihi. "Climb into the ceiling."

"The ponaturi will smell you," Urutonga interrupts. "They will soon know where you are."

"My brother and I have a spell that will make us invisible to them."

"But then what?" Karihi asks. "How do you plan to kill them?"

The ponaturi are swarming onto the beach. They are chittering and chattering towards Manawa-Tāne.

Tāwhaki turns to his mother. "You say that sunlight kills them? All right, when the ponaturi are all inside and the door is closed we will put a plan in action. While they are sleeping, Karihi and I will come from our hiding place and stop up every chink we can find. Meanwhile you, mother, will keep on telling them that it is still dark — even after dawn has risen. Once the sun is high, open the door."

Tāwhaki and Karihi have just enough time to hide themselves in the thatchwork of the interior. They are almost detected by the vanguard of returning ponaturi — but the rush of the remaining ocean monsters obscures the human scent altogether.

At length, after feasting and drinking, the ponaturi fall asleep. And, as always, throughout the long night some call out, "Hey, Door, is the sun rising?"

"No," Urutonga answers. "Moe mai, masters."

Meantime, invisible, Tāwhaki and Karihi creep stealthily around the meeting house, closing any gap they find.

The ponaturi sleep on. Outside, the sun rises hourly towards noon. And when it has reached its zenith Tāwhaki gives the command.

"Mother, whakatuwhera te tatau, open the door."

With a cry Urutonga does as her son has bidden her. She has great bloodlust in her heart against the ponaturi for murdering Hema and badly mistreating her.

The sun pours in like lava, blazing upon the thousands. In a trice they are burning, every gill and wing aflame. There is no darkness anywhere, no place for the horde to hide, for Tāwhaki and Karihi are moving like whirlwinds to open every chink to the sunlight. The sleeping house is interlaced as if with glowing lasers, striking the ponaturi down and incinerating them.

Afterwards, exhausted, Tāwhaki tells Karihi, "Let us take our father home now."

Imagine them, two brothers and their mother, carrying the bones of Hema back to the ūkaipō. On their arrival they are able to release Hema's spirit to the afterlife. *Thank you, son.*

Tāwhaki's courage in destroying the ponaturi enables him to reach apotheosis as an ultimate hero in the Polynesian world.

When Whaitiri receives the news she has, alas, become blinded by small birds which, every evening, scratch her eyes as they fly through her whare. She feels great elation at her grandson's triumph. Very soon he will be ready to embark on his ultimate mission.

How does Whaitiri know this? Tāwhaki's decision to fight the many thousand ponaturi has revealed to her that he is prepared to go against impossible odds and confront death.

Not only that, but he has been willing to sacrifice his mother, his brother and his father's disconsolate spirit, to do it.

Chapter Twenty-Two

In the Abode of the Ponaturi

1.

The Tāwhaki story became the mythic context for my aspirations as a university student.

Not that I appeared to be in any hurry because I promptly spent the Maori Education Foundation money flying back to Gisborne every weekend, £5 7s return airfare.

I was homesick, and I missed Maera Station and my sisters.

Dad dutifully came to Gisborne Airport to pick me up, he never complained. After about a month and a half, however, around Easter, when we were de-horning calves, he took me aside. "This has to stop, son," he said. "How will you get through your studies if you keep coming home?" He was waving the hot cauterising iron around dangerously, and I thought if I didn't heed his admonition I would be next.

Mum was more to the point. "You can't keep doing this, Witi. It hurts both of us."

Thus, from Easter onward, in Auckland whenever I felt homesick I would say to myself, "Witi, you heard Mum. Stay."

The only way I got through my loneliness was to look for Mount Hikurangi. My first memory had been of the dawn, my mother's profile limned with the blood of a rising sun — and the maunga. Chanting was coming from the marae on the other side of the river.

"Don't be afraid, son," Mum had said, "it's only the old people and they are at their prayers."

By the end of the first term, I was finally able to swap Hikurangi — temporarily — for the forty-eight volcanoes that lay within a twenty-kilometre radius of downtown. By degrees, Tāmakimakaurau and I came to suit each other.

I like to think we sensed the turbulence in both of us.

2.

In those early Auckland days I climbed Maungawhau (Mount Eden), Maungakiekie (One Tree Hill), Takarunga (Mount Victoria), Maungauika (North Head), Pukekawa (Auckland Domain) and Māngere. They truly demonstrated New Zealand's vulcan potency on the "Ring of Fire" comprising the Pacific Rim.

More to the point, if I was to spend my foreseeable future in Auckland, I wanted to take my bearings. Of all the cones Maungakiekie was easiest to access, and a Monterey pine stood in the place of the original tree, Te Tōtaraiahua — at least until Mike Smith took a chainsaw to it in 1994. However, Rangitoto was difficult to get to, floating out there in the gulf, and sightseers were banned anyway. Not even Māori were allowed there.

Climbing Maungakiekie would have to do, so one morning I walked to the top and watched the sun come up from the east. There I made obeisance to Rūaumoko, the volcano god, a propitiation that must have worked. No matter that I have lived in many other cities around the world, and although I still call Gisborne "home", Rūaumoko has been kind and I continue to live under his volcanoes.

What did I see from the top of Maungakiekie?

A city which Māori called Tāmakimakaurau, the Place of a Hundred Lovers. From the very beginning Māori had coveted Tāmaki Admired by Many. Straddling two harbours, the Manukau and Waitematā, the region's strategic position made it attractive; whoever held Tāmaki controlled movement north or south. Not only that but Tāmaki's fame as a grower of kūmara and other agricultural products meant that it was one of the most populous places in the Māori world.

Babylon may have had its hanging gardens; Tāmaki boasted cliff-face vines of the fabled sweet potato.

Then migrants mainly from Great Britain took possession. They established the port and township of Auckland with British troops to secure it. Over time, their safety was assured when further real estate was confiscated from the tangata whenua. Suburbs such as Herne Bay, Ponsonby, Parnell, Remuera, Ellerslie and Mission Bay established the pioneers as the new owners.

In the process, Auckland's Māori history was obliterated. Nor were the local Ngāti Whātua people acknowledged as tangata whenua.

Indeed, before Dad had left Auckland we had driven to Ōkāhu Bay to pay our respects to the elders. "I have to leave you in their care," Dad said. But when we arrived at Bastion Point he was disconcerted that the generational and historical trauma of colonisation had led to this: a shockingly small landholding of less than one hectare and the needle approaching zero. A people bleeding and impoverished — and no chance to put on a sticking plaster because new migrants kept streaming in to find work.

The writing was already on the wall. A second-class Māori population destined for dependency. Institutional gatekeepers and insidious practices that would keep them that way. There, down in the ghetto — so the song that Elvis Presley was to sing in 1969 had it — unemployment would rise and so, too, crime, domestic and sexual violence, and drug and alcohol abuse. Oh, a lost generation would rise of urban Māori who had once been healthy and now crowded the hospitals. Oh, a gang culture would arise and boys would go from patch to prison. Oh, another lost generation would arise, this time of children taken into state care. And another generation after that, the destitute mokopuna, unless, *unless.*

Dad sometimes had a beautiful way of saying things. "The embers of Rangitoto still smoulder under the ash," he said as he kissed me goodbye.

Those cinders burst into fire when police tried to move Māori off what was known as the Ōrākei Block in 1977. Ngāti Whātua had had enough and they hunkered down for 506 days. My friend Merata Mita directed a powerful documentary that showed the people in full protest.

But how difficult it was to turn around history!

And it's still difficult. The needle of the Sky Tower dominates the downtown skyline and the city has all the requisite trimmings: art gallery, museum, city centre, universities, theatres and a café culture. A calendar of arts and literary festivals, celebrating the new fusion population of young entrepreneurs from around the Pacific Rim, goes with that; super yachts and sailing hotels ply the glittering sea. However, although the city fathers of Auckland — all of them in their separate council jurisdictions — assume they have found protocols and ways of involving Māori, Māori have not achieved equity in Auckland.

It is still White Man's Isthmus or, rather, *rich* White Man's Isthmus.

Meanwhile, on nearby Waiheke, real estate has gone through the roof and boutique vineyards abound. White Man's Island — a name, I hasten to add, not given by a Māori but a Pākehā risibly affirming ownership — is an appropriate pendant to the city.

As for me, not many Māori own homes in the exclusive millionaire enclaves of Remuera and Herne Bay. In the latter suburb I have a whale windvane on the roof. Some fancy of mine inclines me to believe I am the only Māori who possesses his own house here, and the weathervane is my sovereignty flag.

In the abode of the ponaturi I have claimed a sovereign Māori space. And Māori identity still flares, magma ceaseless and shifting.

3.

The gift of friendship that I had learnt at the Mormon College stood me in good stead as I began to negotiate my new life in Auckland.

Three boys my age at Uncle Jim's boarding house decided to take me under their wing. They knew I was supposed to be going to university, but were dedicated to ensure I did anything but. Ron was a Pākehā boy whose main objective in life was to "pull birds", and so he and I plus our two mates would go downtown. I adopted an alter ego whom I called Bill and, even today, there are people who still stop me in the street to ask, "Is that you, Bill?"

Whenever I did manage to get to university, I met up with Gisborne mates. Some, like my Gisborne Boys' High friend Wyn, were at Ardmore Teachers' Training College, but came weekly into the university campus to take a unit or two for their teaching qualifications. Wyn was as broke as I was (though not for the same reason) and suggested we hitchhike back to Gisborne at the end of the first term; those were safer days when hitchhikers weren't molested or murdered.

Alec Luen was a Chinese boy taking economics, and I could never quite figure out what we had in common — perhaps Chinese were as thin on the ground at university as Māori. I owe Alec for getting us tickets to the Beatles concert at the Auckland Town Hall the following year; he had the same mop-top style hair, and whenever I see a manga comic I think of him. We sat downstairs, second row front, in the middle of screaming young girls and, well, I think we screamed a bit ourselves.

More compatible friends were to be found at Māori Club, where

Māori weren't anthropological case studies. The atmosphere was raucous, the guitar was strumming and students sang a love song, "Ten Guitars". They crooned it Māori-style, the muscle-bound brown jocks encouraging the few trophy Pākehā girls hanging off their muscles to come hula and haka with them — which was a not-so-subtle invitation to fuck.

With all due respect to my fellow Māori students, you could meet people, sing a few songs and then go to a flat and "make out", as my generation quaintly called it — if you weren't too impatient and found a bush before you got there. The Māori Club was not alone in this pursuit of sex. If you really wanted to get lucky without trying too hard, word was that the Tramping Club afforded better prospects for a hump in the hills.

Most male students never used condoms. Unless you were Mormon, gay or sterile, mine was the generation that got married because you had to. And what better choice was there than a nice girl of intelligence, blue eyes optional, with a university CV that Auntie Puti would approve of?

I first saw Bill Pearson at the club. The author of *Coal Flat* and English lecturer was totally drunk — but, after all, everyone was drunk after six, and he had probably come from the local hotel favoured by older literati and students. Bill liked to hang out with the Māori crowd, especially young Māori boys he admired such as Pita Sharples. Even in those days Pita, who later had an illustrious political career, possessed the kind of charisma and glamour that you knew was going to take him into politics. Bill always considered Pita, and author Albert Wendt, as the closest he ever had to sons. I came a doubtful third.

The closest female friends I had were Maree Papesch, Lauren Hunia and Georgina Kingi. Like me they were taking English, and we had a study group going for a while. Georgina went on to become headmistress of St Joseph's Māori Girls' College, and in 2017 was made Dame Companion of the New Zealand Order of Merit for services to Māori and education.

4.

My first real university friend, however, was Kit Withers, who was grey-eyed, curly blond and not, well, colour-coded. I had glimpsed Kit on occasion on my way to swim at Mission Bay. The climate was good for my breathing problems — only when the days were very sultry did I start to feel my lungs battling for air — and I have always loved the sea. From Uncle Jim's I often walked up Parnell Road to St Mary's Church (Kit lived close by), turned left into Stephens Avenue, past Queen Victoria Maori Girls' School and down the hill skirting the Parnell Baths to Tamaki Drive. An easy hitchhike took me to Mission Bay, where I would shuck off my clothes and dive into the water.

I finally said "Kia ora" to Kit at a Māori Club hui. He was a little like my friend Jackson, not in being dangerous but in the sense that I have always craved friends who can make me breathe life in a deeper way. In Kit, I discovered someone who was immensely empathetic of all world cultures. The university was like a mini United Nations, with many students from the Colombo Plan. Like as not, there was Kit in the middle of Black, Indonesian, Thai or Singaporean men and women, birds of paradise fluttering through the dour grey halls. Kit was intellectually brilliant, with an inquisitive nature that was more exhausting than mine! When he discovered I was going regularly to swim at Mission Bay, he came along — and other friends of his, such as Iaveta Short, would occasionally come with us.

Kit's academic interest was in mathematical sciences. I remember once at the beach he started scrawling numerical figures all over the sand, muttering, "No, that's not it" — and I left him to it. If I had a bedroom scrawled with stories, Kit's room would have been one constructed of mathematical theorems.

After the swim and sunbathe I sometimes trekked back to Kit's house, where his mother would scold him for some offence or another. Mrs Withers found her son to be utterly captivating and always wanted him to be more attentive. I wondered whether she liked the fact that he was making friends with unsuitable brown company.

Kit later went to Stanford University where, throughout the sixties and early seventies, we kept up a correspondence on thin blue aerogrammes. He wrote that he had found a stunning girl, Guyanan Mona Williams. When they married, he sent me a photograph of them both, resplendent in their ceremonial dress, on a white horse. Mona became a fabulous storyteller with many books to her credit, including her autobiography, *Bishops: My Turbulent Colonial Youth* (1995). She's the kind of person you want to come across on a cold winter day.

They had two daughters before they divorced. I thought Mona would return Stateside, but she taught me a quick lesson in the facts of life for a Black woman. "It's better for me to bring up my daughters here in New Zealand," she said, "where they won't be sexually molested the first time they step out onto the street."

In Rarotonga in the early 2000s I met up with Iaveta Short again, my erstwhile swimming friend. Iaveta had had a fantastic career as a distinguished lawyer, diplomat and cabinet minister in the Cook Islands. After dinner with his wife and family, he asked me, "What would you like to do?"

Remembering those days at Mission Bay I answered, "Let's go for a swim."

5.

How was I getting on with my studies? Pretty well actually — as far as the BA was concerned. In those days, as long as you did the required essays, students were left alone. Coursework that you were marked on during the year and that was credited towards your final mark was still in the future. In my first year I took English, geography and biology. I guess, given my resultant career as a writer, that it was no surprise that I took to English like a frog to water; it was, however, a surprise to *me*.

But, after all, look at the faculty. Professor Sydney Musgrove was head of department. Poet, public orator and classical scholar, he had been at the university since 1947, a venerable scholar for a venerable institution. The affable John Cowie Reid was a student favourite, breezing into lectures with a pipe in his mouth and an imperturbable smile on his face. Teaching staff included Allen Curnow, Bill Pearson and Karl Stead, lecturers who were not only teaching literature but creating it.

More important, Curnow had turned himself into the oracle of what was and what wasn't New Zealand poetry by editing *The Penguin Book of New Zealand Verse* (1960) with its contentious essay. And Karl Stead had edited Oxford's second series of *New Zealand Short Stories* (1964).

You'll recall that I had read the Oxford first series (1954) during Miss Bradley's library period at Te Karaka District High School. At the time, Pākehā were writing Māori stories, and one called "The Whare" by Douglas Stewart made me angry; it constructed Māori as living in flea-infested conditions and having sinister motives. As my Māori schoolmates ducked for cover I was incensed enough to ask Miss Bradley, "Why have you made us read this story?" — and then I threw the book out the window.

To be fair, Karl Stead offered me another point of view on the story and the incident. In early 2019 he read an interview in which I mentioned "The Whare" yet again, and he wrote in an email:

> Your interesting piece in the *Canvas* sent me in search of that Douglas Stewart story, which I probably hadn't read before. It's interesting — much less sensitive to Maori feelings than any writer now would be, but possibly more honest, do you think? The Maori community he was writing about must have been almost half a century before any you would have experienced, and at a time when Maori were at a low ebb. It feels as if he's reporting it just as he experienced it, and is puzzling out why the old couple appear to want him to stay. The old woman in the story keeps promising to do something about the fleas but doesn't get around to it. When the narrator leaves he writes them a very nice apologetic note; and the tone overall is not disrespectful. More than anything puzzled — which might be an accurate reflection of the (intelligent) Pakeha view of Maori at that time.

Given that Stewart's story is so foundational in my career, I appreciated being prompted by Karl into viewing "The Whare" through a more reasonable lens.

Karl goes on to observe:

> Of course none of us learned much of NZ history and nothing of NZ lit — so we were all colonised; but you were doubly colonised. And I can see how a Maori boy would have been offended by the story — or perhaps embarrassed by it — embarrassment seems more likely. But I found the bit about throwing the book out the window and being caned for it and resolving to write a book about Maori people that "would be placed in front of every school child in NZ" all rather improbable — a case of gilding the lily. Of course you *have* done that, and fully deserve every accolade it has brought you — but the idea that you foresaw your own success is positively Shadboltian. Am I wrong to be such a skeptic?

Curnow and Stead (especially Stead) were just the right teachers for a young man out to discover where Māori literature was within the literary canon: no great surprise, it wasn't (although Karl's editorship of Oxford's second series did feature Māori writer JC, or Jacquie, Sturm). As Karl has noted above, *New Zealand* literature itself was not central to the canon either.

And should Karl — or you — be sceptical of my story? Or any other written in this memoir? I'll leave that up to you. While I am writing my life as I saw and felt it, I'm not averse to being considered an unreliable narrator.

Putting that aside for now, there's no doubt that the training I received in the wider semiotics of English was hugely advantageous. Not until much later did I realise the benefits of obtaining the kind of "back to basics" instruction that very few writers obtain today — they just start writing.

For instance, JC Reid's lectures took me *inside* the language to discover the science of literary discourse. How meaning was created. The ways by which the meaning was communicated physically via sentence, paragraph, clause and so on. And then imaginatively by way of simile, metaphor and allegory. I was an embryonic apprentice being handed the screwdrivers, saws, spanners, spirit levels, plumb lines and glue guns that I would use, later, in the construction of my work.

The lectures tied the semiotics to a quick history of the language as it had been practised in *Martin Chuzzlewit*, *Wuthering Heights*, *Return of the Native*, *Portrait of the Artist as a Young Man*, *The Common Reader*, and Browning, Eliot and O'Casey.

More revelatory were Dr Elizabeth Annie Sheppard's preliminary introductions to Anglo-Saxon and Middle English. Dr Sheppard was a small, birdlike woman, her bones wired together with fierce intelligence. As soon as the lecture theatre opened, we rushed to take the front seats because her chirpy voice was so thin and tiny you had difficulty hearing her from the third row back. When she appeared, silver-haired and glaring, we all fell silent.

I often wondered how Dr Sheppard ever managed to pull herself together every morning. Where most of us were assisted by nature, I felt sure that the only way she could ever rise from her bed was by some rage against the world that could only be appeased by revenging herself on those sent to torment her — her students. In later years, retired, she still could not disentangle herself from the university. At nights she walked wraithlike through the dark halls of the English Department.

I credit her with a singular epiphany. In taking me back to the origins of English literature — to *The Dream of the Rood* and *The Wanderer* — I discovered that many Pākehā had completely forgotten that at the beginning of *their* tradition was an oral literature similar to the Māori spoken inventory.

While I did expect to learn where English literature came from, I did not expect to find, at the source, poetry that was akin to waiata.

After the Anglo-Saxon lectures my head was in the clouds. I would spend time studying at the Auckland Public Library, where the Auckland City Art Gallery is now situated. There, a small coterie of us, including brilliant student Michael Gifkins, international theatre producer and actor Arne Nannestad, and future advocate for neglected and abused children and dame Lesley Max would meet. Much to my surprise, Michael later turned up in my life as an editor at Heinemann's, editing *Whanau*, and he then became the author of a number of short-story collections. I was actually on the periphery of the trio which revolved around the kinetic Arne. I didn't do much talking, how could I? My head was still whirling with Grendel and Beowulf and other Anglo-Saxon sagas.

Ever since, I have been a ravenous devourer of Anglo-Saxon literature. In an early unpublished story called "The Tree" I wrote a sequel to *The Dream of the Rood.* The tree upon which Christ had been nailed is filled with remorse and has fled Jerusalem. It is now located in a New Zealand forest. I thought I was being clever.

In some of my subsequent work I replicate the device deployed in *Rood*, which is to give voice to an inanimate object. In one of my latest narratives, "Whakapapa of a Wallpaper" (2017), a piece of wallpaper chronicles the history of Pacific colonisation. Thus two of the hallmarks of my writing come from those university years: the habit of resiting stories in Māori settings, and allowing the environment to speak.

And regarding my other studies, geography's Kenneth Cumberland was a magisterial teacher you dared not argue with. There was, however, a Mr Fraser who took us on a bus trip to South Auckland to analyse the socioeconomic impact on the urban landscape, street by street, house by house, of Māori urban settlement. Listening to him as he pointed out the second-rate dilapidated housing and ghettoisation was humiliating. Literally one new house per day was being completed for parents plus up to six children — sowing the seeds of trouble for the future. He was objective but, at the time, I wanted to punch him in the mouth.

6.

My world was in a state of constant expansion. I watched a young David Lange holding forth in the Student Union quadrangle on New Zealand's nuclear policy. I did so without realising I was witnessing a history which would end with Lange as prime minister and New Zealand as a country with a stronger anti-nuclear position.

I wasn't just absorbing the local. I was also taken up in the international. It didn't matter that I lived and was going to university in New Zealand, the way I was thinking about life was also being determined overseas. And it should not come as a surprise that, in my case, things American kept on determining a particular world view.

For instance, on 10 June President Kennedy, speaking at Washington University about the arms escalation, said:

> Total war makes no sense ... in an age when a single nuclear weapon contains almost 10 times the explosive force delivered by all the Allied air forces in the Second World War. It makes no sense in an age when the deadly poisons produced by a nuclear exchange would be carried by wind and water and soil and seed to the far corners of the globe and to generations unborn. I speak of peace, therefore, as the necessary rational end of rational men. I realise that the pursuit of peace is not as dramatic as the pursuit of war ... But we have no more urgent task.

Kennedy was speaking not only to American students, he was also speaking to *us*. And, as far as a starry-eyed Māori student was concerned, when Martin Luther King gave his "I have a dream" speech at the Lincoln Memorial, Washington DC, his televised image and sonorous voice spoke not just to Black experience of race inequity, but also to *us*.

Never forget that Black personalities like King and Malcolm X were heroes as much for Māori as they were for Black Americans. And because I love the singing voice, add the inspirational activist Paul Robeson and Marian Anderson to that list.

More important, for me, was the influence of Black writers such as Richard Wright, Ralph Ellison and James Baldwin. Today, any writer can plug their iPhone into world literature for exemplars, and they would think nothing of it. But in my day Black writing — any alternative discourse — wasn't that easy to find, even in libraries. Wright's *Native Son* (1940), Ellison's *Invisible Man* (1952) and the work of James Baldwin, especially *Notes of a Native Son* (1955), were seminal American texts, and the title of this memoir is a homage both to Wright and to Baldwin. Wright, for instance, showed me the possibilities of telling my story through Māori eyes as he did through the Black American eyes of twenty-year-old Bigger Thomas. And Baldwin, in his essays, showed that "I am not your Negro". He inspired me to always be firm about my position that I would not be your, or anybody's, Māori.

As a footnote, I wish I had known the work of Wright's gutsy contemporary, Zora Neale Hurston. We have Alice Walker to thank for reviving interest in this remarkable novelist, folklorist and anthropologist who battled her way through a writing career — and suffered for it — including from Wright. He wrote a damaging criticism of her novel, *Their Eyes Were Watching God* (1937), in which he said that "her novel is not addressed to the Negro but to a white audience whose chauvinistic tastes she knows how to satisfy", and "She exploits that phase of Negro life which is 'quaint'."

Both sound suspiciously like comments raised by some Māori about my early work.

Yes, I also tried marijuana. I didn't think it did anything for me, until Kit asked, "You don't remember what you did?" The second time I *did* remember and gave it up completely. I was so self-constructed that I couldn't allow myself to be seen by anybody, including Kit.

Then two events happened, not necessarily related — or perhaps they were.

The first occurred when Dad telephoned to tell me that Uncle Win had died at age 46. Poseidon, gone? A life cut short, a proud family's dream for a favourite son over? I took the train to Wellington and on the way thought about my fabulous uncle who, since gaining his BA in social science, had carried all the hopes and dreams of the Smiler family.

"You can carry on in brother Win's footsteps," Dad said.

Uncle Win left Auntie Margaret a widow and their seven kids fatherless. He and Auntie Margaret had lost a young child and, rather than go back to Waituhi to be buried, Uncle had wished to be buried next to the dead baby.

Urban migration was not only affecting the living. The dead were also being buried away from the wā kāinga.

The second event was the assassination of President Kennedy on 22 November. My sister Kararaina and I were walking down Queen Street when a young man came running towards us, his arms windmilling, his mouth agape. He was like a horse bolting, yelling, "Kennedy's dead, Kennedy's dead!"

"Tell me it isn't true," I asked my sister as we stood holding each other on the sidewalk. Kennedy had stood for so much that was hopeful in international politics.

The times were a-changin' . . . Lyndon B Johnson succeeded Mr Kennedy — and paradigm shifts kept pushing me relentlessly into a world facing huge transformation.

7.

English, tick.

Geography, tick.

General science, tick.

The Executant Diploma, however, was a mess. I was required to have weekly individual lessons for thirty-six weeks of the year. Felicity Nalden was a wonderful tutor, but I didn't have a piano. I was so accustomed to practising at night, and the opening hours of studio rooms were impossible for me.

I was also supposed to take weekly two-hour ensemble classes with other music students and get further experience through the university Music Society and other orchestral and choral groups. How could I do that, not having a piano to practise on? And while I loved the lectures on aural training and harmony, again, lacking a piano meant I had to do a Benjamin Britten and complete my compositional exercises by carrying a "ghost" piano around in my head.

Very quickly, I fell behind. I panicked and became so whakamā, so ashamed, that I stopped going to classes. I realised I had to give music up and so withdrew from the diploma. I didn't know how to tell Mum and Dad, so I didn't.

On my next visit to Mission Bay, I was so shattered by the decision that I swam almost to the middle of Auckland Harbour. Kit came to warn me, "You're out too far."

What I said to him was, "My grandmother bought me my piano, Kit."

He mistook the sea drops on my face for tears.

I am not the first young man, nor will I be the last, for whom things don't work out. Aren't these the years when early aspirations and ambitions crash and burn?

When I went home for Christmas, Mum and Dad asked me to play the piano for them. I began a few bars of Beethoven's Piano Sonata no. 23 in F minor, op. 57, also known as the "Appassionata". I managed the first two pages of the score and then my errors compounded. I started crashing out the music, smashing the keys, everything descending into discordance.

I slammed down the piano lid. I should have kept my fingers there and broken them.

"Well, that's the end of that," I said to them. And then I told them the bad news.

From that moment I rarely touched the keys.

Chapter Twenty-Three

Stairway to the Stars

1.

As well as following in the footsteps of Tāwhaki, my generation — especially those few who went to university — were told to climb the poutama, the stairway, to academic success.

I am reflecting on the second exhortation from the vantage point of 2019 because, in my house in Herne Bay, a large woven panel has pride of place on the first landing of the stairwell. The tukutuku is made of reeds and was woven by my beloved aunt Te Ao Muhurangi Te Maaka Jones née Delamere, and framed by her husband, Pax.

Maaka, as she was known, was a Ringatū priestess. She was another surrogate for my grandmother Teria. Her father was Paora Delamere, then reigning as pou tikanga of the Ringatū church. He passed on his knowledge to his daughter; in 1968, together, they produced the first published text of the faith, *The Book of the Eight Covenants of God*. The publication also printed all the prayers of the church.

My friends Judith Binney and Gillian Chaplin included Maaka as one of the eight Ringatū women they interviewed for their book, *Ngā Mōrehu: The Survivors* (1986). In many respects their book is a companion piece to my novel, *The Matriarch*, published the same year. It's the real version of the fictional one, uncanny timing that.

I had got to know Maaka about ten years earlier, although she told me, "I've known you all your life, Witi." Her husband Pax was a Jones from Waituhi. At one time Maaka taught with (and loved) my sister Kararaina, but sometimes I was careless and didn't see everyone even when they were standing right up close. Well, when I finally focused on Maaka, her penetrating green eyes looked straight through me and I realised, *Damn, I can't hide from this person.*

Maybe that was why I had been avoiding her.

I don't want you to get the wrong idea, but Maaka was one of those people whose spirit self you saw first. That is, at our first meeting I could see Maaka, but I could also *see* her. I'm not saying she had a visible aura — she may have — but I am saying that whenever I was with her I always felt in the presence of a person who was like . . . splitting atoms is the only way I can describe the sensation. They were colliding all around her. Not scary, but you had to duck.

Conversely, Maaka was very earthy, and once I had adjusted to being in her presence, we soon were laughing and joking together. I couldn't help feeling, what took us so long?

Oh, she was such a majestic lady with a great sense of style! And she had an extended family who served her and who were, most of the time, obedient. They were always chanting karakia and were observant to her every instruction. I was awed that such a family, practising in such Old Testament ways, could still exist in the twentieth century.

In the 1990s, Maaka asked me to go down to Christchurch for a hui and that was where she gave me the woven panel. That night, I was privileged to join the family at karakia and then we went to bed. Maaka on one side, Pax on the other, and me, a grown man of almost fifty, squeezed in the middle.

Pax was snoring and Maaka was doing her nuclear fission thing, whispering karakia and going back to sleep again. In the morning, they took me to the airport and, on the way, I saw that a thread was sticking out of the back of the tukutuku.

Sometimes I can be awfully obtuse. I said, "There's a piece you haven't finished."

Maaka stiffened, looked through me with those green eyes of hers and said, "That's because *you* have to do it."

She didn't add the word *dummy*, but I felt the reprimand.

Those atoms are swirling again, as I look at the panel. Okay, Maaka, settle down.

The panel has wooden slats and the pattern is known as the poutama. The profile is of a staircase — or rather multiple staircases — and Māori say that the pattern symbolises Tāwhaki's climb into the heavens to obtain the baskets of knowledge.

I still have to tell you the story, so be patient. The vertical stakes that form the scaffolding for the poutama are slender culms of kākaho, the stem of the toetoe plant; the dark half-rounds that make the horizontal surface are kaho. The kākaho represents the knowledge the student brings to the task and the kaho symbolises the superior contribution of the mentor. There's a group of stitches at each step, called tuhi, which represent the training that must go on between a mentor and student before the student can carry on and climb the riser to the next step. In between one set of staircases and the next, Maaka and Pax have woven stars.

The multiple staircases honour the many genealogies of humankind which have contributed to the sum of our achievement as we know it.

As for the poutama, it symbolises that every generation must continue the search for knowledge or must strive for excellence. The pattern has both spiritual and educational connotations, because perfection cannot be attained the one without the other.

In a wider sense, the stairway to heaven is a metaphor for the growth of humankind and that we must always strive upwards. If we do so, generation by generation, we will access and add — pass on — the wisdom, the sum of all human knowledge, and increase the ways in which we can better serve the iwi.

The way I interpret the loose thread is that I have to keep weaving all the knowledge I accrue between my generation and the next. And then leave a loose thread so that they can continue to weave the sum achievement of humankind into the future.

Maaka, this dummy finally got it.

2.

Let's go back to 1964 now.

I returned for my second year at Auckland University with other Gisborne and East Coast Māori students by NZR bus.

How far I had travelled from Mount Hikurangi! It seemed only yesterday that I had left my Nani Teria standing by the road waving goodbye to me on the first day of school. Sitting in the back of the bus watching rural New Zealand go by, I had already transited childhood and arrived in Te Ao Tūroa.

Sitting in the back with me and other Māori students was a girl with blonde hair, sparking blue eyes, stunning skin and, shame, she was the only one with a guitar. Her name was Anne Thorpe, her mother Joyce was a fabulous lady and her dad owned Columbine Hosiery, which employed some of our aunties. Anne and I have subsequently had tandem careers. But there was a time when I would pick her up in Dad's truck and take her out — before she became Dame Anne Salmond.

No question, she climbed the poutama faster than I did.

While I was away, Uncle Jim and Auntie Elsie had sold the Parnell boarding house and bought a small dairy near the top of Symonds Street. For a while I stayed with them, helping to open the shop at 6 am, bringing in the milk and papers and serving the early customers. Around 9 am, I'd hop off to classes and to study. I loved the walk past the Symonds Street shops and down the hill to the university.

However, the flat at the back of the store was small and, after a while, we were getting on one another's nerves. Time to get out.

I was fortunate to find board a third of the way through the year with Mr and Mrs John Potter, 33 Komaru Street, Remuera. They had three children, Toby, Binns (Belinda) and Jiggy (Giles) Potts, and they were the Darling family from *Peter Pan* sprung to life. The Potters took in two boarders and I was one of them, sharing a room first with a Canadian and second with a Welsh boy. I outlasted both of them.

What surprises me about staying with the Potters was that, while I was with them, they never noticed I was Māori. We might have all been too busy debating "the meaning of life"; our conversations at the dinner table probably got too rowdy — one of us storming off in a temper — that there probably wasn't time for them to take a good look.

I think being a Māori was okay but, when I confessed to writerly ambitions, Mrs Potter went, "Oh no." There was a literary connection through her sister, Felicity, who was going through a messy separation from the writer James McNeish. Whenever Felicity came to visit, it was always the opportunity for the sisters to get into a huddle about James, and for Mrs Potter to go into a blue funk about writers, artists and other odd sods.

With music left behind, literature became my major. But of course music was not really "left behind". Like everything else in my life, it simply found expression in the musicality of my fiction. In this respect, I have found an exemplar in the Spanish poet Federico García Lorca; he was a pianist as well as a poet (and revolutionary) and he worked with the composer Manuel de Falla. On one project he memorably wrote:

> The melody begins, an undulant endless melody. [It] loses itself horizontally, escapes from our hands as we see it withdraw from us towards a point of common longing and perfect passion.

I guess that's what I have been trying to accomplish myself, using every influence of my life, in my own way: to follow the beat of my heart.

I enrolled in English II, Geography II, History I and a non-degree subject called Preliminary Maori. In English I did Early English and Chaucer, the *Anglo-Saxon Primer* by Sweet, Shakespeare's tragedies *Hamlet*, *Antony and Cleopatra*, *King Lear*; also Pope, Byron and Johnson. MK Joseph was back from leave, Elizabeth Sheppard was on leave, and Mac Jackson joined the staff.

History was my new subject. Keith Sinclair was a top New Zealand historian and so was MPK Sorrensen. In Stage I, I studied modern European history, where Judith Petrie lectured on Russian history since the Revolution. She was also my tutor, and I simply became obsessed with the study of Russia's economic transformation after World War I. I fell in love a little with Judith, who was bright, curly-haired, a clone of my primary schoolteacher Miss Hossack. However, she was stepping out with rising star Michael Bassett.

Preliminary Maori was primarily for Pākehā students without a good working knowledge of the reo. When I turned up, I met Patu Hohepa, who looked at me and said, "You're Smiler? Oh, I didn't know you were Māori."

He asked what I was doing in the class and I told him that my reo was basic. I took only one day to convince him.

It was an exciting period to be a student in New Zealand. The zeitgeist of the times was, as ever, balancing between the kind of creativity . . . and chaos . . . that attended a world undergoing massive change. I guess for every university student life is like that. In my particular reality I experienced my first sit-in in the University of Auckland quad — not about any New Zealand event but about the American escalation in the Vietnamese War; President Johnson had increased troop numbers, and air strikes in Southeast Asia were massively reinforced.

And although New Zealand was not yet militarily supporting the United States, Keith Holyoake was certainly starting to think us into the conflict.

Here's the thing. The international surges of anti-war, indigenous rights, Black consciousness and women's rights movements impacted on Māori thinking. No Māori student going through university during the 1960s could help but see themselves within a world setting and our absolutely terrifying minority status.

Already rising from within, there's no doubt that Māori sovereignty was also inspired from without.

And then came the day that illuminated, for me, my position in this incredible collision of worlds.

I was running to class and Pat Heremaia tackled me as if we were in a rugby game and said, "They need some Māori students for a photo."

The photographer was from *Te Ao Hou* and he was taking the snap for a story on Māori students; the magazine was published quarterly which explains why the photograph didn't appear until the September edition, no. 48. Hone Tuwhare was on the cover and there I was, inside, ready to follow him into literature. The flash of the camera caught me startled and unprepared — or maybe that's to do with lack of sleep from having come back late from a club.

In the photo I was in shirt, tie and a nice olive-green jacket with a rollover collar. The caption went as follows:

> The group of people in the photograph on the opposite page are students this year at the University of Auckland; six of them are of Maori ancestry and one is Rarotongan. They are among the 65 enrolled, 39 of them full-time students, 21 part-time and five of them graduates studying for higher qualifications. In addition, there are 75 Maoris at the three Teachers' Colleges in the Auckland area. Because three of four of the student teachers are also on the roll of the university, the total number of Maoris at institutions of higher learning at Auckland is about 134.
>
> This total, though certainly not as high as racial population proportions would indicate as a figure comparable with other students, is nonetheless most encouraging after hearing that Victoria University of Wellington this year had only seven first-year Maori students and that Wellington Teachers' College had no Maori students.

In the photograph were Maree Papesch, Te Awamutu; Mary Perenara, Whakatāne; Sherill Beattie, Dargaville; Rangi Moekaa, Rarotonga; Kingi Houkamau, Hicks Bay; Patrick Heremaia, Pātea. That year other Māori students were Roimata Sinclair, Rau Kirikiri, Robert Mahuta, and possibly broadcaster Derek Fox may have begun his studies. There's another photo, same page, of Polly Hopa, commonly known as Pare, who had just gained a diploma in anthropology at Oxford University and, at the time, was believed to be the first Māori woman to graduate there.

I am the boy captioned as "Wite Smiler" from Te Karaka.

In the same month that the photograph was published, news came that Nani Graeme, my mother's father, had died. I took the daylong bus trip back to Gisborne. Mum and my sisters were already at Uawa, and Dad met me at the bus station.

"Your mother is grief-stricken," he said.

Nani Graeme was seventy-two. The tangihanga was held at Puketāwai marae and it rained heavily. Every now and then I would watch my mother and her brothers and sisters. They had retreated into a circle of siblings, grieving over their dad. Sometimes, when they were with their mother, Hoana, the daughters would huddle like young girls in her protecting arms.

"There, there, children."

For some reason, I felt it was better to leave them alone, and not to interfere. I think most men feel this way, respecting women their right to weep and in so doing shed tears for us. But I remember my mother's face peering through the rain, as if she had pushed it aside with her hands. Her face has always haunted me: the habit she had of lifting her cheekbones to the light so that her eyes were illumined and within them someone else staring out from within. Mum was looking for something.

Maybe she was looking for Hikurangi. I caught her glance, pointed, and she covered her eyes to look to her mountain. The rain fell through her fingers. She blinked. Saw.

Recovered. Ah, terā te maunga.

3.

Now let's return to that photograph taken for *Te Ao Hou*. As students, although we were a small cohort, we were among the brightest hopes of Māoridom.

The photograph is tangible proof that I was at the University of Auckland.

And this is what I looked like at the time. Not handsome, but good-looking enough. A big skull atop a small body. Hair, black, lying this way and that across my scalp of a morning, requiring combing before looking like anyone else's. Eyes burning bright, like a tiger in the night; "You can see them across a room," someone said.

Oh yeah? Better watch out before I pounce.

The face not quite balanced. High forehead, low chin, big lips, wide cheekbones, but in certain lights I could force that visage into equilibrium or, at least, a pleasing symmetry.

A fine chest and slim stomach; in those days young men never went for ribs and definition. Good shoulders to drape skin on. Could I flash any lightning from those armpits? Nah.

Arms tapering to hands with beautiful fingers. Crook them for ugliness, stretch them for beauty. Not much use to me now.

Small waist, strong buttocks, head of the hammer. One leg still shorter than the other, easily disguised by a careful way of walking. Nine stone maybe? Fleet of foot, hard to catch hold of.

This is what the photograph reveals. But what it does not tell anybody is that two nights earlier you finally get enough courage to look up Middlemore Hospital in the telephone directory. You are in luck, there is a men's clinic this evening.

Why not during the day? They only come out at night, eh?

Here comes the bus. You know, you could have saved all this trouble going to Student Health at Uni. But you don't want them to know.

At the hospital, you go round and round trying to find the clinic. Ah, there is the waiting room. Quick, go in. You register with the male nurse. *First time here?* he asks. *What are your symptoms?* He is a bit bemused that you have come simply for a check on anatomical and sexual function, but they see all kinds here. *We'll take a urine sample just in case, eh?* That requires a visit to the men's toilet along the corridor.

When you return you give the sample to him. You sit and continue to wait. The first time, when Dr Bowker wanted to examine you for Church College, you refused. The second time, when you were in Napier, the doctor was a woman. Third time lucky.

You wait and wait. Other men go in to see the doctor and come out. You start to sweat. What if there really is something wrong? And then the male nurse signs to you. *Second door on the left.*

The consulting physician turns out to be an ex-Navy officer. He looks at you quizzically. *So I understand that you are here for nothing in particular. No symptoms?* Clearly you are wasting his time. You should apologise and leave. But, like the male nurse, he is kind. He makes a general inspection, looks into your eyes, inspects your tongue and all that. Then, *All right*, he says, *undress behind the curtains, everything off.*

You slip off your underwear. Strong thighs that surprise for such a thin boy. Must be all that farmwork. You return to the doctor. The walls of the room are puce yellow. When you get back he is sitting on a chair. You try not to laugh and remember Brother Elkington at the Church College asking you to give him your best smile.

No, you don't have to lie down. On the walls are charts and medical illustrations. *Now let me take a closer look.* You close your eyes. You feel his hands pressing your stomach, your groin area, your thighs and inside your thighs. *Turn around please.* You feel his hands again, examining your buttocks. *Now turn to face me again.* He gently slides his fingers over your balls and then holds them. *Look to the side and cough.*

You do as ordered. *You can get dressed now.* After putting your clothes back on he tells you, *Well, young chap, everything appears to be in order.* But he asks some more questions about erectile problems, none, problems with ejaculation, none, blood in your faeces, none. *Then you're all set to go out there and enjoy yourself.*

You thank him and return to the waiting room. *If we find anything in your urine sample*, the male nurse says, *we'll let you know.*

You leave the consulting room. Catch the bus back into the city.

You are all right then. So why, in the photograph, aren't you smiling?

The photographer hasn't been quick enough to catch your Anatolian smile, eh, because you are really, really happy. You've been cleared now.

There is no impediment to joining them. Becoming one of them.

That's all you've ever wanted.

Chapter Twenty-Four

Tāwhaki, the Sky Walker

1.

The Tāwhaki Cycle could very well lay claim to being the Father of All *Our* (Polynesian) Epics. Tāwhaki was no less a king than Gilgamesh, so it comes as a surprise that very little scholarly attention has been paid to him. When such investigation begins, I think people will be astounded by the richness of the saga as well as its pan-Pacific reach because every island had its own stories of Tāwhaki. They carried to all quarters of Polynesia and even reached Melanesia. Often, the stories of Tāwhaki were not the same motu to motu. Even when they were, there were variant tellings or details within tellings: different names, different places, different reasons, different outcomes.

Oh, there are so many stories about Tāwhaki! The consequence of all this amazing variation, one story engendering another, is that Tāwhaki has become a complex and ambiguous figure. This makes him all the more compelling as a character.

For instance, did you know that following the murder attempt by his brothers-in-law, he had his revenge in a somewhat pitiless way? As a child he might have turned his playmates into porpoises but, as an adult, he was more unforgiving. He called upon his ancestors — the climate gods — to let loose upon the earth all the waters of the heavens. The event, known as te hurihanga i a Mataaho, the overwhelming of Mataaho, led to the drowning of all the iwi of his would-be murderers.

The narrative concerning Hāpai, Tāwhaki's second wife, also has special complexity; in some versions of the story she is known as Tangotango or Maikukumakaka. She was a woman descended of a heavenly race, and she had come down from the skies to marry him.

On her return to her people with their child, Tāwhaki was filled with longing for them both. His amazing odyssey among the iwi o ngā rangi, the tribes of heaven, to find them, is truly Ulyssean.

2.

Then there's the story of how Tāwhaki obtained the baskets of knowledge. It's a narrative pertinent to this memoir and, in the metaphor of climbing, it installs the poutama as the most striking symbol in my life and work.

In those first days of the world, the oral traditions tell us that both Tāwhaki and his brother Karihi committed to the climb. They travelled to a dark, forbidding primeval forest. In the hero's journey, the forest equated with the soul's adventure, going down into our unconscious depths where there was no way or path. The hero must blaze his own trail.

However, in a small clearing the brothers find a helper, a wayfinder. She is an old blind woman, a seer, and she is counting out twelve kūmara, a crop favoured among Polynesians.

Tāwhaki gains her attention by upsetting her tally; he takes away a kūmara, and then another kūmara, and she has to count again. It is an affectionate piece of byplay between kuia and mokopuna of the kind I experienced with Nani Teria.

At the end of it, "E kī!" the old lady says. "So the ariki child wishes for the royal kai, nē? All right, you shall have it, for it is the only food to sustain you as you climb the poutama."

Her words identify her to Tāwhaki as his grandmother.

No doubt about it, Whaitiri is a third muse whom we can look to for inspiration and guidance. And I like the way she applies tests and challenges so that we can find our own way to advance in our aspirations, don't you?

Tāwhaki rubs kūmara sweetened by his own saliva on Whaitiri's eyes and, lo, her sight is restored. And among that forest of trees and vines she shows him the aka matua, the parent vine.

The vine has another name, the toi huarewa, meaning "the suspended way". It will test Tāwhaki's resolve and take him and Karihi into the realm of the perilous.

"But wait till morning," Whaitiri tells Tāwhaki. "And be sure to climb only by way of the aka matua and no other, for it is the true pathway." She gives him and his brother karakia with which to accomplish the task. But not only that: as the brothers begin to climb, Whaitiri utters powerful prayers to assist the hero.

> Piki ake Tāwhaki
> ki te rangi tuatahi
> ki te rangi tuarua!
> Ascend on high, Tāwhaki,
> to the first heaven,
> to the second heaven.

Whaitiri keeps up her incantation throughout the climb, but notice one point. Its function is to "secure the way, spiritually" and to invoke a meditative focus for the task. And Tāwhaki's brother, Karihi, is not mentioned in the karakia. Why this omission?

Once the brothers are out of hearing, Whaitiri stops. She hears with relief that Tāwhaki has taken up the chant.

> Piki ake ahau
> ki te rangi tuatahi
> ki te rangi tuarua.
> I climb on high,
> to the first heaven,
> to the second heaven.

Good, the mokopuna is measuring the way himself.

Swiftly she levitates and flies ahead of the two brothers to the uppermost sky to await, hopefully, the successful completion of the climb. And from there she continues the karakia.

> Keep climbing grandson,
> through the first heaven,
> now the second.

3.

The description is thrilling, isn't it! It attests to the old-time Māori as being fabulous conceptual thinkers. They considered Tāwhaki's climb not as a physical journey but a metaphysical one. And the true magnificence of Tāwhaki's accomplishment is this: where Māui tested the parameters of life and death, Tāwhaki and his brother retested the parameters of creation.

What were the possibilities for humankind and where were the boundaries set?

   Where did space end?
      Where did time begin?
         What lay beyond Te Pō, the great darkness?
            What lay ahead in Te Ao Mārama, the world of light?
               Was there such a thing as an uppermost heaven?
                  What gifts resided in all the unknown dimensions?

What's interesting is that with all these challenges women — Tāwhaki's grandmother, mother, wives and other female relatives — played an important function in the outcome.

Therefore let it not be said that Tāwhaki's success was attributable to him solely or — because the story relates to the hero rather than the heroine — to men collectively.

Chapter Twenty-Five

Grandfather and a Third Brother

1.

I need to bring my grandfather Pera Punahāmoa back into this narrative.

He returned to Gisborne soon after I had left for Auckland. His church labour mission in Hamilton was over, and he stayed in town with his daughter, my Auntie Alice. His Mormon activities developed an international dimension — he was truly affirming his Melchizedek priesthood as a "light bearer" — when he started to travel to the Polynesian Cultural Centre at Laie, Hawai'i. He became the kaumātua of the 136-strong Te Arohanui Maori Company concert party, led by Māori culture expert, Albert Whaanga.

Perhaps that's why he came through Auckland. All I know is that Dad telephoned from Gisborne to say, "Your grandfather will be in Auckland with your Auntie Mary. He wants to spend time with you."

With me? Dad had to be kidding.

"Well . . ." Dad conceded, "there's something's important he wants to discuss with you, he won't tell me what it is." Then Dad coughed. "And there's also something he needs help with . . . men's business."

My eyebrows lifted. Men's business? At least I knew the way to the clinic, ha ha.

Dad told me that Grandad, Auntie Mary and other faithful were sleeping over at the church's Auckland headquarters. When I turned up, Pera was waiting at the gateway, surrounded by an adoring throng. I waited until he noticed me and he smiled and introduced me to the others.

"This is my grandson," he said.

I was surprised at his warmth so I kept my guard up. Grandad had a habit of shifting the goalposts — as well I knew from our long-ago trip together when I was expected for enrolment at the Church College of New Zealand.

"Don't keep Tolo out for too long," Auntie Mary said. "Kai is at six."

Oh no, she was expecting me to keep Pera with me all day.

As it happened, the "men's business" turned out to be simpler than I had expected. Ever since he was a young man, Grandad had bought his pink flannel longjohns from a shop in Gisborne — but it had closed down a year earlier. Although he still kept wearing his old ones, the situation was getting, er, desperate. But I could see that this wouldn't necessitate our spending, well, hours on; what a relief, I could get him back early to Auntie.

Was I ever wrong. "Okay, Grandad," I said to him. "I know just the shop."

We took a taxi into Queen Street to Smith & Caughey's and, I have to say, Pera attracted everyone's attention. He had a dramatic style with his colourful bandana, tweed jacket and walking stick. For comparison, think Tūhoe nationalist Tame Iti, in his dandyish Victorian Māori gear. One of the most recognisable faces (full facial tā moko) in New Zealand, Tame was arrested twelve years ago, accused of running terrorist training camps; the criminal charges were later dropped. Grandad had the same stature and appearance as Tame — if they had ever met, each would have recognised the mana in the other.

In those days Smith & Caughey's had a major-domo and, when the taxi stopped at the front door, he helped Grandad out as if he were an important foreign potentate and took him through the revolving doors. When I enquired where the men's department was, he escorted Pera to the lift where an elevator attendant sped us to the required floor. And when Pera arrived at the appropriate counter he sent the female staff a-fluttering.

"We know exactly what your grandfather is looking for," they said to me. And they proceeded to show us every kind of longjohn that they stocked. Except that none of the styles were flannel or pink.

I became the go-between. "Tell them," Pera said to me, "I just want the pink kind."

"Oh, they went out of production years ago," I was told. "These modern ones are lighter, softer on the skin and more attractive to the eye."

I gave Grandad the news. "I don't want anything that's attractive to the eye," he grumbled. "Nobody else will see them except me."

We made our way from Smith & Caughey's and walked into every men's shop on Queen Street. They all stocked longjohns for the discerning elder gentleman, but none that were Grandad's style.

"I think we'll have to try the secondhand shops up on K Road," I said. "Some of them may have the discontinued stock that you want."

But as soon as Pera saw some interesting-looking ladies standing on the corners he told the driver not to stop.

The entire shopping expedition was a failure. However, by the time we gave up, I was laughing so much, and I thought Pera found it funny too. In hindsight, maybe I was wrong — he could have thought I was laughing at him.

When I took him back to the Mormon headquarters in a taxi he sat in the back seat for a long time. He seemed to want to say something to me — didn't Dad say there was something important he wanted to talk to me about?

Then, "You doing good at university?" he asked. *One potato.*

"Yes," I answered.

Two potato. "Do you need money?" he asked.

I don't want you to think that our relationship was without affection or caring. "No, Grandad," I answered. "I don't need anything from you."

Nothing from him? *The mokopuna does not wish the sacred kūmara.* He closed his eyes and nodded.

And then Pera took me completely off guard.

"One more thing then," he began. "Through the priesthood I hold I am able to offer you the keys that pertain to the kingdom of God on earth."

I shook my head, not so much stunned as saddened. "Where's this going, Grandad?"

Surely he knew how ashamed I was at not being able to fulfil his wishes, as far as his Mormon aspirations were concerned. Did he have to rub my nose in it?

He was silent for a while, his lips were trembling. "You know that there were two congregations in Gisborne, Te Hapara and Mangapapa, that pledged to support you to Brigham Young University, don't you? And for you to go on a mission later?"

No, I had not known. I thought I had made it clear to Grandad, to everyone, that that Mormon dream was their reality, not mine.

I began to get angry. "I won't be held responsible for their expectations," I said.

"Okay," he answered. "But you turned your face from them when you chose to come to Auckland. And you also turned from me."

He opened the door of the taxi and got out.

"Goodbye, Witi," he said.

I resumed my studies, sat the examinations and passed English II and History I. I must have had a sympathetic history tutor in Judith Petrie because I answered only two questions out of four in the exam, and both were on Russian political and economic history following World War I.

I asked Judith about it once and she replied graciously, "Two perfect answers are worth more than four mediocre ones."

There's a DNS for Did Not Sit for Geography II, which, at least, is not an F for Fail. That's because a mate, Billy Tahata, arrived from Gisborne on his motorbike on the day of the examination and said, "Fuck your exam." And we took a run up to Russell.

It's the first inkling of alarm. In my case, the poutama had started to malfunction.

Something else was also disturbing my universe.

The dream swimmer came to warn me that it was lurching near.

2.

I realise that my narrative is swaying in the wind quite a bit, like the vine that Tāwhaki climbed, but hold on tight. Take shelter on the side where the wind is not blowing. All safe now?

There has always been the presence of the mystical in my work and I will not apologise for it. After all, it was there in my life. No more so was this evident than when my dreams began to be haunted by a figure who I would see as through a luminous sea, shafted with sunlight, stretching to the end of forever.

I knew something was happening when I saw one evening my mother, who was also the dream swimmer, ascending slowly towards me from the depths.

She rose to the foot of my bed. She was wearing a white dressing gown, her hair was unpinned and flowing around her. Her eyes were wide open and her feet were paddling.

"Yes, Mum?" I asked.

Now, it is of no concern to me whether you believe me or not. You may live in your world constructed by its own mathematics and metaphysics, I will live in mine. But I'm glad that I am not the only writer to admit to the mystical. Sherman Alexie, the Native American author, was on an author tour in early 2017 promoting his new memoir, *You Don't Have to Say You Love Me*, when visions of his dead mother Lillian appeared in one of his dreams, "holding a sign that [said] STOP". Maybe only indigenous writers are able to confess the unconfessable. He had been trying to medicate his sadness, his complicated grief over his relationship with her.

But in my case, I wasn't seeing a "ghost". I was seeing my mother, a living substantial being, in her dream-swimming persona. Māori always say that people are able to travel in their dreams. They do so, most often, to visit loved ones, especially those on the point of death, or to say goodbye before they die, or to warn. I started to panic.

"What is it, Mum? What *is* it?"

I didn't know it then, but I do know it now, that my mother visited me because she felt I was at the greatest risk I had ever been. Oh, it might not seem such a big risk to you, when I tell it, for it was not physical but, rather, one to do with whakapapa.

Knowing my mother's great respect for genealogy, I can imagine Mum lying in bed with Dad, her feet beginning to paddle, swimming through the latticework of the names on the wall of the corridor. And then away from 11 Haig Street to come across the midnight sky, the womb of all dreams, to me in Auckland and then, Waiouru — I'll explain that destination soon.

Her warning was about the third brother in the story of three brothers. As written about in *Māori Boy*, my father had acknowledged one brother, Puke, born before he met Mum and whom my mother, sisters and brothers accepted and loved. I was the second brother, the one born legally to Dad.

However, there was a third, but my siblings and I knew nothing of him until my sister Viki met him. Of course in time my parents were to have two more boys of their own — Derek and Neil — but this was another born out of wedlock. He was my coeval, as I was told that we were born within three hours of each other but, in fact, he was eighteen months older.

Whatever the story, he had suddenly gained the support of my grandfather. And, because of this, in my novels *The Matriarch* (1986) and *The Dream Swimmer* (1997) I called him Toroa, to acknowledge his and Tolo's fond relationship.

3.

At the time, New Year, 1965, I was oblivious of the manoeuvring Pera was making, having joined other university students on compulsory military training for the summer, with one difference: I had volunteered instead of waiting for the ballot. You can blame my penchant for self-destructive behaviour. At least cadet training at Gisborne High School would come in handy.

I had also wanted to test my masculinity with other boys. I joined an unruly bunch who made our commanders' lives a misery by questioning every shibboleth they held dear about defending New Zealand just in case the war in Vietnam ever managed to get as far south as New Zealand; among them were Russell Fairbrother, Matt Campbell and Mandy Manderson.

I wasn't exactly on the same wavelength as my parents. My twenty-first birthday was coming up and, at Waiouru Military Camp, I kept on getting messages and telephone calls from Mum and Dad asking me if I wanted to have the celebration at Poho-o-Rāwiri marae. Sometimes the messages were delivered to me by relatives in the army stationed at Waiouru.

"You better telephone home, boy," they threatened.

I knew if I didn't I might be made to do a forced march carrying four backpacks.

The iwi planned to make a fuss over me. In Māoridom such birthdays were huge events, the whole tribe turning up. But I just didn't want it.

"Won't you come home, son?" Mum asked. "Your father and I want to give you the key to adulthood."

I realised my capacity to be cruel. "I can't, Mum, I'm busy."

Dad got on the telephone. "What's wrong with you, Witi? Can't you do this for your mother? Is there something we've done?"

Mum did call me on my birthday. "Happy birthday, son."

How could I tell her that, full of self-hatred, I couldn't celebrate myself?

I now know that the underlying reason why Mum wanted me home was to establish my physical presence among the iwi. A birthday party would have proclaimed my status as Tom's son, the one who mattered. Why didn't she or Dad tell me about Toroa?

Instead I had to find out in an indirect way. This is how it happened.

My sister Viki was in the family shearing gang working in the South Island, doing contract work around Mataura. She was fourteen at the time and, unlike me, was a favourite of Pera Punahāmoa.

"Nani Tolo had taken to picking me up every year," Viki told me, "and I would join Uncle Danny, Auntie Mary and Uncle Hape as well as my cousins Josephine, Arihia and Tiopira. I enjoyed going south and making some money for myself and I had bought myself some white flared trousers for a dance to go with my white Aran jersey. Anyway, one night after shearing, Nani Tolo was talking to a young man, maybe he was your age, who I had not seen around. Nani called me over and he said to me, 'This is your brother.'"

The boy was powerfully built, striking, adept in the reo. "When Nani told me," Viki continued, "I thought, 'This is fun.' But at the dance I kept thinking, 'How can Toroa be my brother?' and I started to feel sorry for Mum. The next day, upset, I rang Dad to tell him what had happened. I said to Dad, 'Please don't tell Mum.' Of course she already knew, she had known for years. Dad said to me, 'That's not your brother.' From that year onward, Mum and Dad began to come shearing too, and I was always with them, not Nani."

I didn't know anything of this until I was back from military training at university in Auckland. It was Kararaina, not Viki, who phoned to tell me. She was always the one who communicated family business to me. "There's something you should know."

I realised then why my mother was disturbing my dreams, and the first thing I did was to ring her.

"I've been waiting for your father to tell you," she confessed. "Had I known about his other sons, I would never have married him. If your father won't stand up to this, you must. It is your birthright that is being threatened."

I told Mum to put Dad on the phone. "Tell me straight, Te Haa, is this true? Why do I have to hear it first from my sisters and mother?"

And Dad said, "I was going with a woman who was Toroa's mother before I met your mother. So Toroa would be about your age, if he was my son — but he isn't. So it's wrong of Pera to be bringing this up, especially now. I'll talk with him."

Not good enough. I rang Grandad myself. Having had such a good day together in Auckland, I was puzzled and disappointed at his actions. "How long have you been planning this?"

"I don't know what you are talking about."

"You introduce my sister Viki to another son of Dad's when he isn't. Why didn't you tell me the last time we were together?"

"I don't have to answer to you, Witi. Your father should have told you and your sisters long ago that you have another brother."

"He denies it."

"You know nothing."

Something clicked into place. My memory went back some ten years to a day in the early 1950s when I was on a visit to Waituhi.

I realised my grandmother had tried to warn me then about Grandad.

The rain was falling lightly across the village, like a benediction. My grandmother and I were sitting together in the front of Dad's truck. We were parked at the gateway at the back of the Blue House where Dad was talking to Pera, probably about the stock that he was grazing in the foothills. From out of nowhere, Teria said, "Never trust your grandfather."

When I mentioned it one day to my Uncle Sid, he said, "Mum would never have said that." And Pera, in his own hand, writes in his whakapapa book: "In my married life we were happy. We tried our best to educate our children one of them got the degree of b.a. And m.a. And the other one is (a) teacher." I am quoting this because others have better memories of Grandad and I am prepared to accept that there are other bases from which to consider him.

I would, however, rather give my grandmother the richness of saying something inconsistent because people are not always consistent. The point is that she did say it and she said it to me, and I have wrestled with that phrase all my life. She didn't say, "Don't trust your grandfather"; she said "Never". But maybe she was really talking about a matter of distrust between them, that had nothing to do with me.

My cousins may forgive me this memory if I say to them that I think it had to do with Teria having given me her blessing and Grandad favouring another. That other was Toroa. Ever since he had been born, Pera had known about him.

Known about his family. Known his mother.

The matter of the third "son" made our family story messier. As time went on, I began to realise that the entire village of Waituhi had known all along with Grandfather.

Even Nani Mini.

When I talked to her about it she said, "I'm on your side, mokopuna," but she knew I was hurt that she hadn't told me long before. The more I thought about it, the more sick to my stomach I felt. Childhood was the time when children are either protected from, or not told, the truth.

But when adulthood arrives, and power plays are made, somebody makes a move . . .

And there it is, whatever it is, out in the open.

Oh, I could have pretended it hadn't happened, but dissembling had never sat well with me. Actually, I wouldn't have minded if this had stayed between Pera and Dad; let them sort it out. But the more I thought about it, I realised I couldn't stay behind my father.

People had already taken sides. They were complicit, even by being silent and assenting to Pera's declaration. Among them all, who was *for* me, and who was against me?

The matter of Toroa soon began a strand of conflict in the extended Smiler history that would impact on all our lives.

And I would be brought to face down my grandfather.

Chapter Twenty-Six

The Hope of Humankind

1.

Back to Tāwhaki's (and Karihi's) climb. And yes, the parenthesis is intentional for Karihi's status in the story of the hero's journey is already subordinate to that of his brother, the ariki. He is the sacrifice, the price to be paid.

Now, most people say that there were ten heavens to climb; some say twelve, others say twenty. In Sāmoa, they say there were nine. Collectively they were referred to as ngā rangi tūhāhā, "the bespaced heavens". They were of three kinds: the lower heavens, the inaccessible heavens and the distant heavens. I often amuse myself by thinking, wouldn't it be funny if, when astronauts make it to the end of the universe, they find that it has been a Māori construct all along.

Twelve, of course, equates to the twelve stages of the hero's journey, so let's go with that total. And don't forget that Whaitiri was counting out twelve potatoes when she played her little game with Tāwhaki. Tekau mā rua also happens to be the number given by the Takitimu people leading to Io, considered by them to be the god above all gods.

Each of the twelve heavens had its own series of celestial bodies, or luminaries, its own sun, moon and stars, clouds and flowing waters.

And of all the heavens the lowest, twelfth, was the one familiar to our old-time tūpuna. Known as Ranginui-a-tamaki, this was the Sky Father's domain, having our moon, sun and planets. In fact Māori studied the stars and had names for over a thousand of them.

Now, some versions tell of a jealous rival named Whiro who felt he was the one who should be climbing the aka matua. He sent plagues of insects, reptiles and carrion birds to attack Tāwhaki, but the winds enabled our hero to escape the attacks.

We can picture easily enough the climb of the two brothers through our solar system, because it involved a known heaven. Indeed, the ascent is described in the oriori *Pinepine Te Kura*, a chant for young children, usually of ariki status. While Tāwhaki obeyed his grandmother and went by way of the main vine, his brother Karihi made the mistake of climbing up the aka tāepa (hanging vine). This took him into the western part of the sky known as Ururangi where the celestial winds were very fierce. The winds swooped upon him and blew him down once, twice, thrice and, on the fourth occasion, he lost his grip, fell, and was killed.

Tāwhaki had already reached the eleventh heaven, Ranginui tamaku (remember, I am counting from the lowest heaven as the twelfth) and thought Karihi had been following. He let down a rope but, when his brother did not grasp it, he knew he had fallen. What should he do? He decided to face his fears and carry on.

So it was for Māori students climbing the ivory towers of academia.

From this point Tāwhaki's ascent took him from the known world into the unknown world. When he reached the tenth heaven, Rangiparauri, he was already moving from the ordinary into the extraordinary.

They were not empty regions but, rather, peopled with many celestial beings. In the ninth, eighth and seventh heavens — Rangimairekura, Rangimatawai and Rangitāururangi — there were as many tribes living in each stratum of eyries and cloud kingdoms as there were iwi of mankind. Whaitiri herself had come down from one of them and so, also, had Tāwhaki's second wife, Hāpai. They were kingdoms of art, science, language, mathematics and spiritual learning. And as Tāwhaki went higher, passing through the sixth heaven, Rangimataura, so the tapu (sacredness) increased. Consequently, at each crossing from one heaven upward to the next, he was set challenges to ensure he would survive. He travelled on through the fifth heaven, Ranginuikatika, to the fourth heaven, Rangitewawana.

Wasn't he fortunate that he had extra protection from Whaitiri by being descended from her?

2.

We don't know how long Tāwhaki took to pass through the third heaven, Rangi naonao ariki, to get to the second heaven, Tiritiri o matangi, but we do know that, by this time, Tāwhaki's advancement had culminated in a number of personal transformations.

> From corporeal to spiritual.
>> From unschooled to literate.
>>> From human to superhuman.

Nor do we know how long the hero's journey had taken as he had sojourned along the way among the various whare wānanga located in each heaven. What we do understand, though, was that the objective of his learning was to ensure that he could abide and survive in the uppermost heaven — Te Toi o ngārangi — the most sacred of them all.

His sacredness had to be equal to that realm, and his mortality had to match its intense purity.

Tāwhaki literally had to become a being of light within that place of incandescent brilliance, where all there was, was luminosity.

Why? Because in this empyrean resided the Supreme Being of All. And with him were two companies of supernatural attendants, known as whatukura and mareikura. They acted as messengers to the lower heavens, and to all other realms, and they were not averse to zapping any puny human being if he was unequal in any way.

Only an equal person could ask for the baskets of knowledge because, by reaching God, he had shown that the possibility existed for others to follow.

Let's imagine Tāwhaki kneeling in Matangireia, the temple that was situated in the sun's pathway, to make his request.

"E Io," he asks, head bowed. "Your servants petition you, we seek enlightenment."

His grandmother Whaitiri watches on. All around creatures of light are dancing in a dazzle of illumination.

The heavens begin to sing.

Let the baskets of knowledge be theirs.

This is the reward stage of the hero's journey.

Within the three (some say four) baskets were the gifts of wisdom that would help humanity to save *itself*. In the first basket, Te Kete Aronui, was the knowledge to help all humankind — not just Māori — in the peaceful pursuits, including community building, and practising arts and agriculture.

Te Kete Tuauri, the second basket, contained the ancient rites and ceremonies to ensure the tapu reinforcement of the knowledge of Te Kete Aronui — again not just for Māori.

The third basket, Te Kete Tuatea, had further knowledge of incantations, war, magic, and the lessons learnt throughout history — again, for all races to learn from.

The baskets together provided the syllabuses for improving whēkite (observation), whekaro (learning), te werohia (analysis and investigation) and te whakairihia (application of new knowledge). Although divisible, their ultimate power multiplied exponentially when they were operated together for the benefit of all.

As well as the baskets, Tāwhaki brought back two sacred mauri kōhatu. These physical objects, in the form of powerful talismanic stones, held powers to protect and preserve the health and wellbeing of humankind. They symbolised the partnership between the animate world and the inanimate world.

3.

On his return Tāwhaki — as the Hope of Humankind — was fêted throughout the Pacific for having brought back the knowledge that would allow us transcendence.

Universities and other schools of learning were instituted so that the syllabuses could be associated with sound training of the highest order.

The knowledge from the baskets was divided into two categories: kauae runga (upper jaw), which dealt with sacred knowledge; and kauae raro (lower jaw), which encompassed human traditions. Kauae runga matters were most tapu and needed to be handled by tohunga; specialists in such knowledge who were therefore closely associated with the gods. This detailed knowledge was learnt and passed on by tohunga in the whare wānanga, schools of learning.

Wharekura, Tangitewiwini and Whararaurangi are numbered

among the universities established in Raʻiātea (French Polynesia). Takapaurangi, Te Mahurangi, Te Kauwhanganui and Te Hauhungaroa are among the schools of learning that were established in Tahiti and Hawaiʻi. In New Zealand, the most famous whare wānanga on the East Coast was Te Rawheoro at Uawa, whose tohunga included Mohi Ruatapu; it was he who set down the practices and histories of Ngāti Porou in the 1870s. Another was Tokitoki in Gisborne, which established the lore for Te Whānau-a-Kai and Rongowhakaata; my ancestor Wī Pere Halbert had attended Tokitoki as his Māori training, to set alongside his education in the Pākehā world.

Students were selected and put through courses to enable them to climb to the very heights, as Tāwhaki had done. To complete the process was to become Pou Mataaho (knowledgeable and appreciative of all perspectives.) To be an ambassador. To be a mentor. To bring holistic training. To bring balance and order.

To pass the knowledge on.

The old people say that these gifts of Tāwhaki re-energised the people by showing that although humanity could not defeat death, they could hope for transcendence in their mortal lives. They could strive through their whare wānanga for excellence, attain extraordinary heights and, the gifts of achievement in hand, pass them to the next generation. This cycle of gifting became the overarching aim of all humanity. In embracing it, death became redundant and was made meaningless.

Our own universities proliferated in Polynesia. They were the stairways destroyed with the coming of the Pākehā.

Chapter Twenty-Seven

Decline and Fall

1.

At Auckland University for the third year, my downhill slide continued. That didn't change. Indeed, my view is that my experience reflects an alternative history of Māori at universities in New Zealand that has still to be written. When it is, my bet is that the history will reveal a different pattern to that of Pākehā attending higher study. It will not show the traditional success story but, rather, that for every successful Māori student exiting proudly through the front door would be fifty or more being shown the back way out.

Consider the optics. Academic, political and institutional power transferred to New Zealand via Commonwealth structures meant that Western modernity was imposed on all students, so it wasn't just a racial thing. Goodness knows, it also had to do with class and gender. University education was a matter of privilege and it was normally the province of males from the upper classes. Like Māori, women and the lower classes had also battled getting through the hallowed gates.

But Western higher education was also a Darwinian theatre. The University of Auckland, established as part of the University of New Zealand in 1883, taught a syllabus already prescribed, authorised and dominated by the "fittest", where they triumphed and the losers were subordinated or destroyed. Yet, when Māori had signed the Treaty of Waitangi in 1840, they had every expectation of an equal transfer of the Māori intellectual inventory into the cultural partnership. Indeed, Māori land went by way of reserved endowments into establishing the University of Auckland: 10,000 acres in Taupiri, Waikato, 10,000 acres in Karamū, Pirongia, and 10,000 acres in Waimana, Whakatāne, along with 354 acres in Ararimu, up at Kaipara. The 1885 Auckland University

College Reserves Act vested these lands in the college council, then headed by Auckland politician Maurice O'Rorke, with the promise that the reserves were not to be alienated in any way, by gift, by sale or by reserve for any purpose other than education. Until required for their original, specific purposes, these Auckland reserves, plus an additional 20,000 acres at Tauranga and 10,000 acres at Whenuakurī, Taranaki, were to be administered by the government and the revenues derived from them were to be applied "for the purposes of higher education".

The supreme irony was that the assigned acreages had been confiscated land acquired following the New Zealand Wars. The Māori "contribution" went into building an academe for their conquerors. You can still see physical remnants of the military past within the university's precinct, in particular, the Albert Barracks bluestone basalt wall circa 1846–1851 (Heritage New Zealand Category 1) that once was part of the quarters for the British Army Royal Engineers during the time they were in defence of Auckland town.

White curricula sustaining White culture, it was as simple as that. The "Other", including Māori, just did not figure in the demographics of success and achievement unless on Western terms. I came across a mention of one such Māori who attempted in 1931 to scale the academic heights — which, in those days, was success at obtaining one of two Rhodes scholarships to Oxford. James McNeish mentions the attempt in his book *Dance of the Peacocks* (2003, p. 35). Six candidates presented themselves: two each from Wellington, Canterbury and Otago — and "a Maori graduate from Te Aute College," James writes, "a leader of his tribe".

James does not give a name and, given that the Rhodes scholarship was a White boys club at the time and that success required patronage, one can understand that the anonymous leader of his tribe was unsuccessful. Not only that but the "Other", in the Rhodes' view of the world, was not the one who would solve the problems of Empire. He was, rather, part of the problem and supposed to be the recipient of White largesse.

Not until after 1948 was Māori introduced at the University of Auckland — as a subject within anthropology. The first lecturer to teach Māori language was Bruce Biggs in 1951. In 1983 a tent marae was erected in front of the Registry Building to protest the lack of a marae on campus; Waipapa was duly opened in 1988. Finally, in 1991, a Maori

Studies department was established as a standalone entity but, as they say, I had long left the building.

Whatever gains have been made at Auckland, they have been hard won. Most have been achieved by protest, such as the confrontation by Māori students in 1978 over the incredibly offensive engineering student tradition of lampooning the haka. Despite the fact that the Pākehā students had perpetrated the offence, the Māori students were the ones who were charged with a number of illegalities including rioting. Any successes have therefore had to be accomplished by persistent race politics or by stealth — infiltration, moving into the machinery of governance while the Pākehā wasn't looking and throwing the occasional spanner into the works.

Most of all, strong radical leadership made the breakthrough by way of the development of Ngā Tamatoa — the Young Warriors — on campus, and through the activist teaching methods of Hirini Moko Mead, Hugh Kawharu, Merimeri Penfold, Pat Hohepa and Ranginui Walker.

The first Professor of Maori Studies finally appeared in 1977, but not at the University of Auckland. He was Professor Hirini Moko Mead at Victoria University of Wellington. And it was through his vigorous work that the first Department of Maori Studies was established — again, at Victoria University — in 1981. Never doubt that Māori education was lifted up on the shoulders of giants.

And over time, it was all in the numbers.

2.

Ride the elevator of my life down with me. We'll be missing some of the contextual stuff that was happening, but that's the way it goes as we plummet down the shaft.

I obtained my scholarship monies, great, that would keep me in cash. I then gave notice to the Potters. We had a very sad parting and the children couldn't understand why I was leaving them. From my perspective, they were getting to like me too much.

I moved out to South Auckland near Homai College to stay with my Uncle Arapata Te Maari and "Mum" Mereana Te Maari. Why? Other indigenous students of the time might recognise the syndrome. I wanted

"She called me e Wit*sh*."
Witi's paternal grandmother, Teria Pere, with her
husband, Pera Punahāmoa, at Waituhi, late 1940s.

From left to right: Mini Tupara; her husband, George; Witi's father Te Haa (Tom); and Tilly, Mini and George's daughter, late 1940s. Mini was Pera Punahāmoa's half-sister, but Tom always called her Sis.

Witi Teka, 1940s, Tom's best friend and Witi's namesake. Three Witis were named after him.

Tom and Julia Smiler, Gisborne, 1950s.

"The Queen of Hearts." Mini Tupara with her daughter, Tilly, on a Gisborne Street, 1940s. She was the inspiration for Miro in Witi's story "A Game of Cards".

George and Mini Tupara,
Gisborne, 1940s.

Mini Tupara and her son
Nick at bottom, Witi's
mother Julia Smiler and her
sister Polly Kaa at right,
probably Waituhi, 1950s.

Mini Tupara, who
took on the role of
Witi's kuia when his
beloved grandmother,
Teria, died in 1955.

Witi Ihimaera, as always, looking sideways
at the world. Aged 16, on the eve of going
to the Mormon College, Hamilton, 1960.

"What is that thing?" The Church College of New Zealand
(CCNZ)(college in foreground and temple behind it),
in the lush green landscape of Hamilton. The temple
glowed at night like a celestial wedding cake.

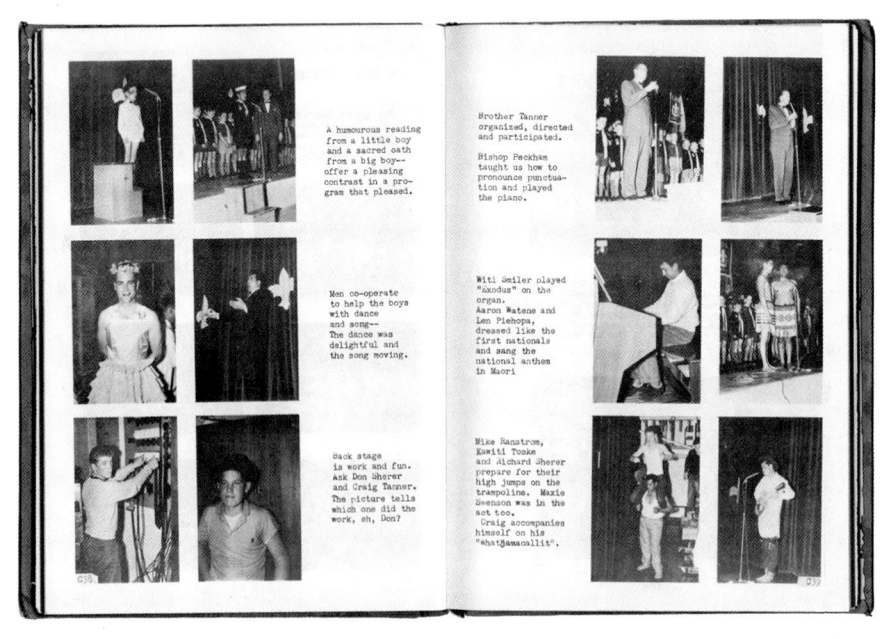

Two pages from "Beehive", CCNZ's yearbook, 1960.
That's Witi, playing the organ, page right.

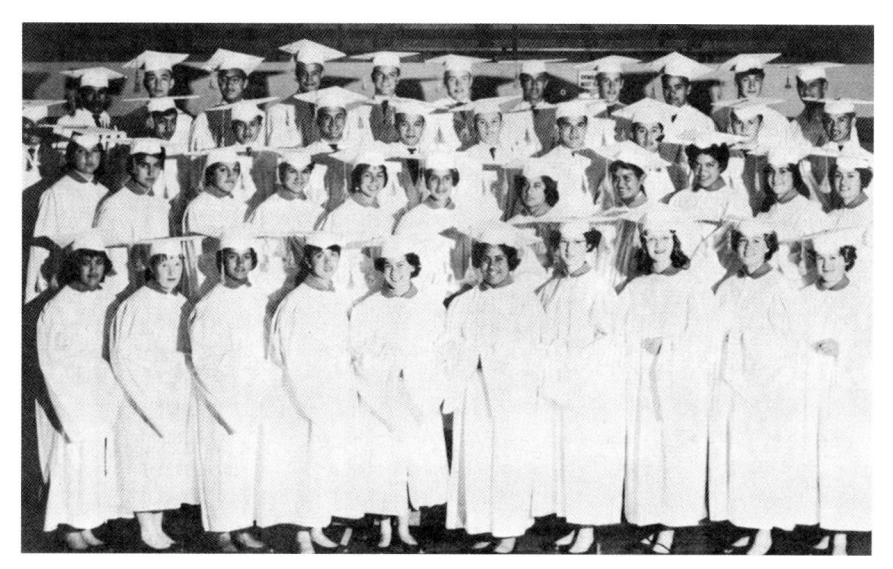

Graduation Ceremony, CCNZ, 1961.
Witi Ihimaera top second row, second from left.

WITI SMILER

Our music maestro, Witi, has given all who listen to him play the piano and organ a greater appreciation for the classics through his interpretation and dexterity at the keyboard. His artistic nature extends past his hands - it reaches into his heart and into his head and emerges in the form of poetry and prose. Witi also won honours for the school through his outstanding ability on the hockey field.

LAMIA HOOPER

Never afraid to express her own opinion, Lamia has played a prominent part in C.C.N.Z's history. If she wasn't driving the "Bomber" on some errand, then she was working on the annual as co-editor, or memorizing lines for her part as grandmother in "Julie". Lamia is extremely capable in the field of art as demonstrated by the mural on the music room wall and sketches throughout this book. Besides, she can "blow her own horn"!

BARRY SMALE

Barry surprised us all when he emerged from his shell and proved that mathematicians can be actors as well (Remember "Julie"?) He reads books in quantity and quality but don't let this rare habit fool you, 'cause "you can't tell a book by its cover."

BOYSIE PAERATA

One of New Zealand's future leaders, Boysie has shown much aptitude and ability in his studies. One of his avid side interests is collecting records. (He's noted for having the largest stock in the school.) Boysie has also cut a name for himself in the field of football as a member of the 1st XV.

Page from "Beehive", CCNZ's yearbook, 1961. Note the little graphic of Witi playing the piano! Instead, his career went sideways from music into writing.

"A descendant of Mormon followers who trekked to Salt Lake City." Sister Elsie Wortley, English teacher, CCNZ, with her husband, Lawrence Wortley.

"THE TWO WRITING MENTORS WHO TOOK OVER WHERE MISS HOSSACK, HIS PRIMARY SCHOOL TEACHER (SEE MĀORI BOY), HAD LEFT OFF."

"I always called him Mr." Mr Grono, second from left, Witi's English teacher, 6B2, Gisborne Boys' High School, 1962. At his encouragement Witi wrote his first short story, "The Prodigal Daughter", published in the 1962 GBHS annual magazine. That's his wife, Mrs (Gwen) Grono, next to him.

The Tom Smiler-Robbie Cooper shearing gang. That's Tom, bottom row, second from left; Julia, fourth from left; cousin Betty and her husband, sixth and seventh from left; sister Viki in the top row, fourth from left, and brother Derek just above Julia. Plus all the Pākehā and Māori boys, who totally adored Mr and Mrs Smiler.

"MEANWHILE, BACK ON THE FARM."

Tom Smiler, centre, Shearing School, 1968. Jim Leach on the left and Jim Tawhai on the right. When Witi was living in Wellington, Tom and Jim turned up one night and cooked tripe and pūhā. It's a wonder the city didn't die of asphyxiation.

"CLIMBING THE POUTAMA OF THE PĀKEHĀ."

Photo published in *Te Ao Hou*, No. 48, 1964. "The group of people in the photograph are students this year at the University of Auckland; six of them are of Maori ancestry and one is Rarotongan. They are among the 65 enrolled, 39 of them full-time students, 21 part-time and five of them are graduates studying for higher qualifications. In addition, there are 75 Maoris at the three Teachers' College in the Auckland area. Because three of the four student teachers are also on the roll of the university, the total number of Maoris at institutions of higher learning at Auckland is about 134."

Witi is middle back row, with, from left to right: Maree Papesch, Mary Perenara, Kingi Houkamau, Sherill Beattie, Rangi Moekaa and Patrick Heremaia. In the photo Witi was captioned as "Wite Smiler".

Te Ao Muhurangi Te Maaka Jones and Pax James with their son Nigel on his 21st birthday. A Ringatū tohunga, Maaka carried on the work of her father, Paora Delamere, the pou tikanga of the Haahi Ringatū. Her inspiration and karakia were crucial in ensuring the tikanga in all of Witi's work.

THREE MORE MENTORS.

Photo published in *Te Ao Hou*, No. 55, 1966. Joy Stevenson and Margaret Orbell, editors of *Te Ao Hou*, published by the Department of Māori Affairs. The publication featured many of Witi's fellow writers: Hone Tuwhare, Patricia Grace, Arapera Blank, Kāterina Te Heikōkō Mataira, Hirini Mead, Mason Durie and others. Joy Stevenson became a close friend, editing and correcting Witi's early work.

HAIL

THE NEW EDITOR of *Te Ao Hou* is Joy Stevenson, who comes from the teaching profession. For the last six years she has been teaching primer classes at the Department of Education's Correspondence School, where she assisted in the writing of a new two year primer course, wrote many radio scripts, and was for the last two years, co-editor of the school's magazine, *The Postman*.

Several times she acted as one of the school's visiting teachers, meeting many Maori and Pakeha pupils in their homes.

Miss Stevenson's main interests are in music and young people. She is keen to accept the suggestion made by many subscribers, and establish a section especially for *Te Ao Hou's* younger readers.

Joy Stevenson

and FAREWELL

Miss Margaret Orbell recently resigned from the position of editor of *Te Ao Hou*, which she had held for the past four years.

Miss Orbell's interest in traditional Maori literature has been reflected in the translations that have appeared in the magazine. She also continued *Te Ao Hou's* policy of encouraging the work of contemporary Maori short-story writers and poets. Her other special interest is in the field of Maori art, and many of the photographs of carvings and paintings which appeared in the magazine were her own work.

Margaret Orbell is now teaching Maori at the Correspondence School in Wellington.

He porporoaki poto noa tenei ki te Etita o *Te Ao Hou*.

Tena koe, e hine, i to kaha ki te kohikohi ki te whakatikatika i ta tatou pukapuka. Kei te mohio atu hoki, i whakapatua e koe to kaha kia tika ai a *Te Ao Hou*. Na reira, tena koe.

Margaret Orbell

"A Gathering of Maori Linguists." Witi's granduncle, Rongowhakaata Halbert, fourth from left, was the family's paramount iwi linguist. The photograph, published in the 1950s, depicts "... some outstanding speakers of the Maori language. In the back row, from left, are Kepa Ehau, Rongo Halbert, Bruce Biggs, Canon Dan Kaa and Pei Te Hurinui Jones. In the front row, from left, are Morris Jones, Rangi Royal, Michael Rotohiko Jones, Wiremu T. Ngata and Eru Pou." As well as Rongo Halbert, Bruce Biggs and Pei Te Hurinui Jones had important impacts on Witi's life.

Witi's uncles Winiata Smiler (left) and Hani Smiler (above left) with Tom and Julia. Both uncles were university-trained; Winiata was a linguist and Hani was a historian.

LEFT Hetekia Te Kani Te Ua.

BELOW Turuki Pere, one of Teria's (Witi's grandmother's) brothers.

Two iwi leaders — genealogists and orators — who, with Rongowhakaata Halbert, inspired Witi in his own writing. Te Kani's son, Henare, was a Māori broadcaster.

"IF YOU WANT TO KNOW WHAT MY HEART LOOKS LIKE, LOOK TO RONGOPAI."

Witi Ihimaera, within the interior of Rongopai meeting
house, Waituhi. He is looking at the representation of
his ancestor, the Māori parliamentarian, Wī Pere Halbert,
painted circa 1888 when the house was being constructed.
Wī Pere is shown with his mother, Riria Mauaranui,
on his shoulder, always whispering advice to him.

Photographer Warwick Teague gave this large photograph to Witi as a present, and Witi, in return, wrote "Big Brother, Little Sister" as a thank you to his friend.

That's Witi's auntie, Joey Te Omerengi Smiler (left of Paul McCartney), on the front cover of the *New Zealand Listener* during The Beatles' visit to New Zealand, 1964.

Second place-getter, Wyn Smiler, at the piano

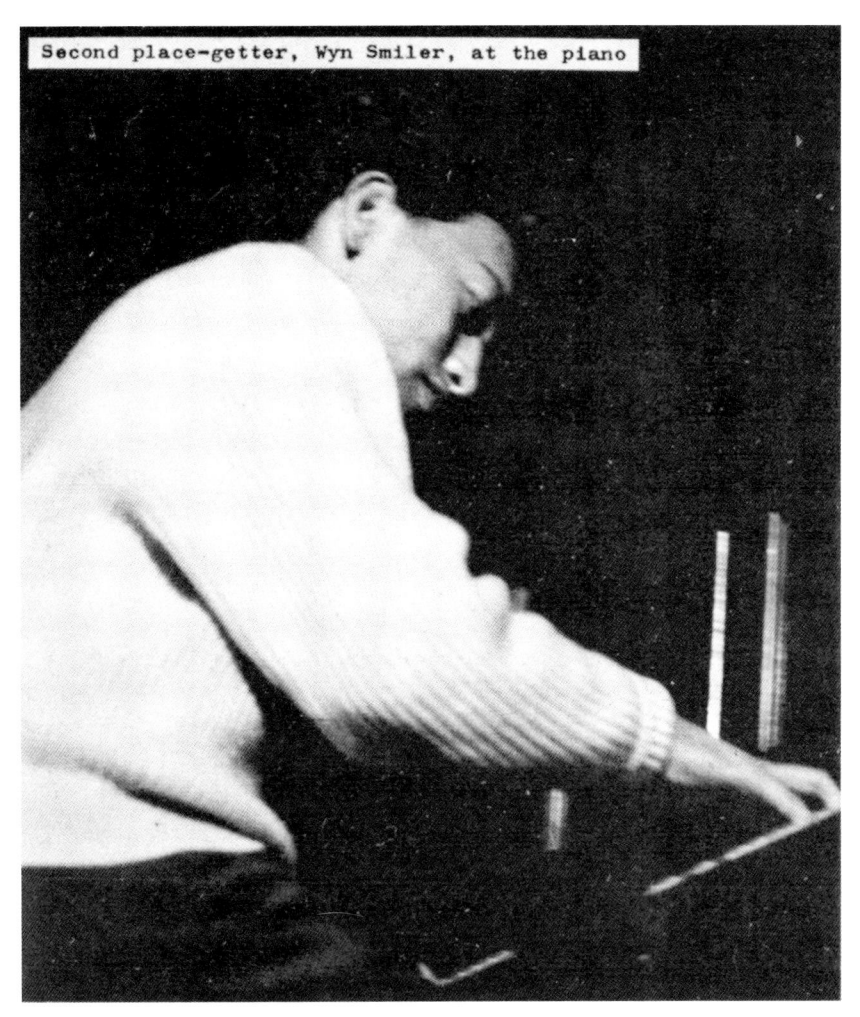

Variety shows were the rage throughout Māoridom during the 1960s. One that Witi entered was the Johnny Cooper £200 Talent Quest in 1962. He called himself Wyn Smiler and needed the money. Witi survived four months of weekly elimination rounds, and popular voting, to come second. The winners were an East Coast quintet called the LPs.

Wellington, 1968. Witi on the job as a journalist in Post Office Headquarters. ABOVE Covering for national news media; the construction of the Satellite Earth station, Warkworth, which eventually opened in 1971. BELOW Posing for a story written on safety in the workplace — in this case, occupational noise exposure — for the *Post Office News*, the monthly staff journal he edited.

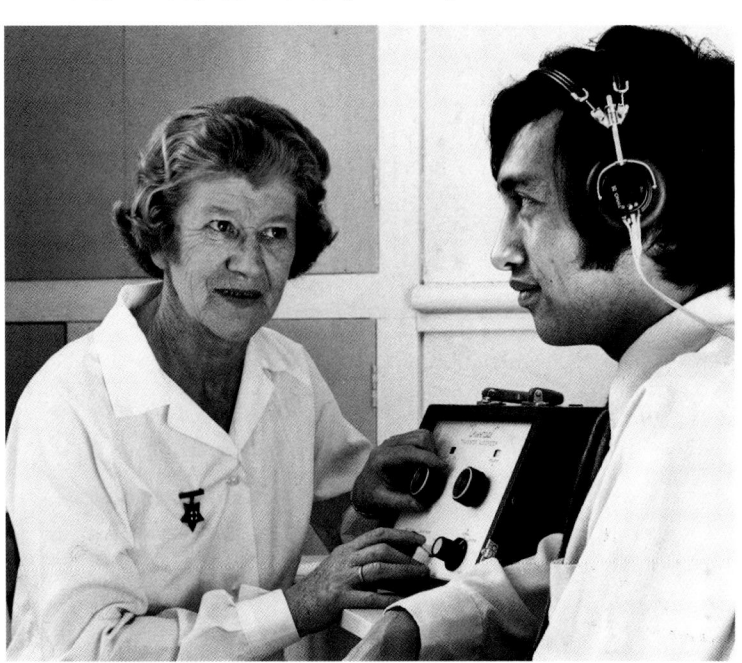

"She lived in a world of moral certainty."
Turiteretimana Tikitiki Keelan, Witi's mother, circa
1968, in her mid-forties. When Witi left Gisborne to go
to Wellington she said, "You're running away from me
. . . or something. What is it, son? What is it?"

Three glimpses of Jane Cleghorn with Witi, around Wellington. **ABOVE LEFT** With flatmate Dixi (Ian Dix), going to or leaving some pub where there was a rock'n'roll band. **ABOVE RIGHT** With photographer Ray Labone.

"Hello, dear," Nancy said to Jane. "And is this Witi?" Nancy and Tony Cleghorn, Jane's parents.

Witi's grandfather, Pera Punahāmoa Ihimaera Smiler, the patriarch of the Smiler family, as he was in old age. He wore a bandana and like all the men in Witi's life, when he was in public, he was always impeccably dressed.

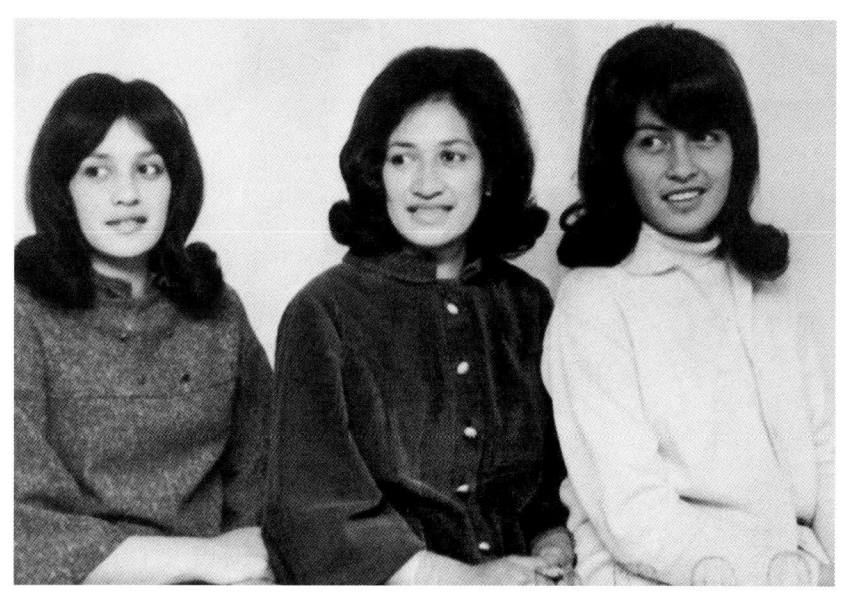

Witi's three sisters from left: Tāwhi (Polly), Kararaina (Caroline) and Viki, circa early 1970s. They were joined by Derek (ten years younger than Witi) and Gay and Neil (twenty years younger than Witi), pictured below with Julia and mokopuna Carol Crawford.

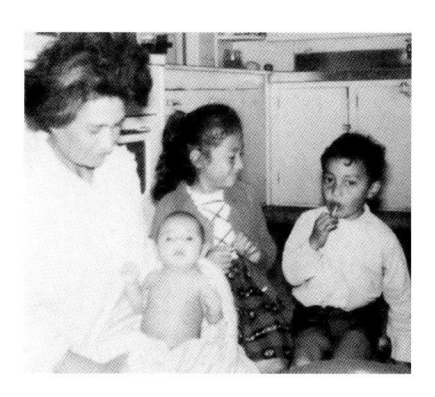

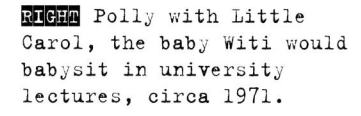

RIGHT Polly with Little Carol, the baby Witi would babysit in university lectures, circa 1971.

"Whenever I was with her I always felt in the presence of a person who was, like . . . splitting atoms . . . They were colliding all around her. Not scary, but you had to duck."

Te Ao Muhurangi Te Maaka Jones. Along with Teria Pere she was Witi's other inspiration for Riripeti in his novel, *The Matriarch*, 1986.

"THE JOINING OF TWO WHAKAPAPA."

The only photos of Witi and Jane's marriage, 9 May 1970, the same day as a letter arrived from the *New Zealand Listener* accepting his story "The Liar" for publication. Bottom row shows best man Francis Hemopo and Jane's maid of honour, "Tat", now Anthea Simcock.

Witi and Jane.

Tom Smiler on the right and David Heap, Witi's publisher, on the left, when Witi's first book, *Pounamu, Pounamu* (1972), was placed third at the Wattie Book of the Year celebrations in 1973. Witi had his foot on the first rung of the ladder.

Friend Lou Rivers sculpted Witi's head at the home in
Johnsonville, 1970. The head is in Witi's study, still young.

"Still hitched to the same star." Writer Dame Fiona Kidman,
at the time that she and Witi became friends forever.

"OH, GRANDAD, HASN'T YOUR WORK AND MINE ONLY EVER BEEN ABOUT THE MAKING OF A GENEALOGY?"

POLE PRESENTED

The magnificently carved Maori Pole was officially presented to the city at a brief ceremony outside the P.R.O. building, in Grey Street, where the pole has been ideally sited. The carvings trace the genealogy of Maori and Pakeha history, from the coming of Maui to the first landing on the moon. The pole is a commemoration of the Cook Bi-Centenary and a gift of the Maori people to Gisborne.

ABOVE—At the official ceremony were, from left, Public Relations Officer Allan O'Donnell, Mrs H. Waihi (convenor), Mr Bill Mou (carver), Mayor Harry Barker, Mr Ian Miller (president, Greater Gisborne), and Mr Tom Smiler (genealogy).

RIGHT, FROM TOP—Some of the carved sections on the pole. LEFT—The pole on its site. BELOW—The J. L. Primrose crane lifting the pole into place.

Witi's grandfather Pera Punahāmoa was the genealogist for a carved pou, presented to Gisborne City and tracing the history of Poverty Bay from the coming of Maui to man landing on the moon. He died shortly after the presentation and was mourned as having been the last, or one of the last, full-blooded Māori in the district.

Witi with Patricia Grace and Hone Tuwhare,
at Writers' Week, Dunedin, 1991.

With mentor, novelist and fellow Gisborne writer Noel Hilliard. Witi says, "Of all the photographs ever taken of me, this is the one which is the most truthful. I was always so relaxed in Noel's company that I forgot to be wary about life, about who I was and what I was trying to forget."

Dunedin 1998: The writer in mid career. The Robert Burns
Centennial celebrations photograph, with past fellowship holders.

Back row from left: Ian Cross, Philip Temple, Hone Tuwhare, Roger Hall. Second row from left: Witi Ihimaera, Keri Hulme, Bill Sewell, Christine Johnston, Owen Marshall, Ruth Dallas, Ian Wedde, John Dickson, Brian Turner, Peter Olds, Bernadette Hall. Third row from left: David Eggleton, Michael King, Elspeth Sandys, Paddy Richardson, Lynley Hood, Cilla McQueen. Front row from left: Michael Noonan, Janet Frame, O.E. Middleton, Maurice Gee, Graham Billing.

LEFT Witi Ihimaera.

BELOW The sisters and brothers, May 1993. Photograph taken on the occasion of Tom and Julia's 50th wedding anniversary. Back row: Witi, Derek and Neil. Front row: Carol, Viki, Julia, Tom, Gay and Polly.

to be at university but I also didn't want to be there, and so I removed myself physically as well as mentally from it. After all, in climbing the Pākehā poutama was I not implicitly endorsing it? Complying with its own objectives? I was the correct (male) gender, sure, but I didn't want to be a brown Briton. Or, to ascribe a more abusive term, an Uncle Tama.

I duly enrolled in English III, History II, Geography II and, now that I had Preliminary Maori under my belt, I felt competent to tackle Maori I. In English, my fascination with Old English and the late plays of Shakespeare — *Pericles, Cymbeline, The Winter's Tale* and *The Tempest* — kept me turning up on campus. *The Tempest* took me completely by surprise. I couldn't help but read the situation of Māori in Aotearoa into the play, and saw in Caliban the dilemma of the indigenous university student under the domination of Prospero, the white wizard. And although Caliban's mother, Sycorax, hardly appears in the play, I related her to Teria, my own sky goddess and witch grandparent.

Aphra Behn's novel *Oroonoko* also captured me with its indigenous text. But the real surprise was to discover that my own realisation of the similarities between English and Māori literature had been commented on many years beforehand by Governor George Grey. In an academic paper delivered to the Ethnological Society of London, January 1870, Governor Grey found homologies — similar structures — between Polynesian myths and the work of Edmund Spenser, whose *The Faerie Queene* had been published almost three centuries earlier. Grey makes the observation that "Spenser must have stolen his images and language from the New Zealand poets, or . . . they must have acted unfairly by the English bard." The governor was such a wily character; you can read that comment whatever way you wish.

In history, I had a tutor, I'm fairly sure it was Mr WT Roy, with a degree from Lucknow. The course was in the history of Medieval Europe and the Renaissance: the Feudal Kingdom of England and the History of the Church. It was all an auto-da-fé, and I found it monstrous.

Nothing was going my way and things got worse for me in Maori I. While Roger Oppenheim gave me a great mark for an essay I wrote to the question: 'Māori Leadership: Inherited or Earned?', I had a run-in with Professor Biggs. Just prior to the end-of-year exam he called me in.

"I see you haven't been to any tutorials this year," he said.

He was a severe-looking man and had had a difficult pathway himself as a Māori student, let alone endeavouring to establish a Department of Māori Language.

"I did them last year," I answered.

"You should have done them this year."

He wasn't about to let any Māori student go through without their navigating the required process, and why should he?

We went round and round in circles. Apparently Roger Oppenheim and Patu Hohepa had both spoken up for me, and I think Professor Biggs would probably have taken their views into account if I had gone up onto my two hind legs and begged a little. I didn't want to do that.

Finally, clearly exasperated, Professor Biggs asked, "What do you want me to do, Mr Ihimaera Smiler?"

I have often been my own worst enemy, unable to get over myself. It was entirely my own fault that Professor Biggs didn't approve my sitting the exam.

"Fail me then," I said.

While I passed English III, as I had requested, so was it done: I failed Maori I.

I was so disconcerted by my interview with Professor Biggs that I decided not to sit History II and Geography II, fuck it.

Three units in my first year, two in my second, one in my third.

3.

I know now, but I didn't know it then, that I was trying to find another way through the monolithic educational structures of Western learning. There *had* to be another way out — or through. Not finding it, in 1966, the brakes came off the elevator; watch the sparks fly as we descend.

I didn't want Mum and Dad to know what was happening to me, and why I was failing. I decided not to go home for Christmas. One look, and they would find me out. Sexually, too, I didn't want them to see the struggle I was having with my masculinity. They held assumptions about me. I was trying to conform to their high Māori, as well as Mormon standards. Better for me to sort out my shit alone.

And so I found it blissful to be back at Waiouru for the summer, still escaping from the folks and, well, everything and everyone. I proved to myself in every possible way that physically I was the equal of every sonofabitch who woke up at six, humped weapons across rugged terrain and rivers for a military day, and slept in a tent on the tundra that was swept by winds coming from the mountains.

But there were moments of sheer beauty in simple epiphanies. Bringing up the back of a platoon, I watched as they climbed a slope crushing white alpine flowers with their boots. I found the agony on the faces of boys trying to help exhausted colleagues to the finish line during a long route march profoundly moving. And there was poetry in the moment sleet hit a backpack and spread spray like a shroud.

I began university for a fourth year. I hadn't been home for six months.

An absent son is always terrifying for a parent.

"Where are you, son?" Mum asked on the telephone. "Can't you come home to see us? I'll send Dad up to Auckland to get you. Have you run out of money?"

Money? I was rolling in it, the scholarship funds ready to pay for the academic year. By now I had completely opted out of my studies. I also stopped going to Maori Club as I preferred not to go in to Auckland campus.

The Maori Education Foundation got on my case and tracked me down.

"Why aren't you attending your lectures?"

They put me on probation. I had to show up regularly at their campus office. However, once I checked in, I went back out to Manurewa. I was really happy in the rapidly growing Ōtara–Manurewa–Papakura Māori–Polynesian triangle. I met at the Te Maari house many important Māori such as Whina Cooper, Bill Herewini, Bill Nepia and others, including John Waititi who later had a marae named after him.

I was also closer to Ardmore Teachers' Training College, at nearby Papakura, where my sister Kararaina had fetched up, together with Hiria as a teacher-in-training. I had loved Hiria at the Mormon College and I still loved her, and we resumed as much of a relationship as could be allowed. At least Papakura was closer to me than Hastings had been when I was living in Gisborne.

Yay, 3, 2, 1, and now zero units natch.

Back for a third tour of compulsory military training, two boys were found fucking in a tent. We were told the offence was serious, they would face a military court and if found guilty — as they were sure to be — they would be discharged with dishonour.

Maybe the two boys did it so that they could get out of military service and, if so, they wouldn't have given a damn. But, "If you want to do that," our sergeant said, "don't get found out."

Yes, anything went as long as you weren't found out. While the world hadn't quite got into the swinging sixties, a new hedonism and permissiveness in New Zealand allowed freedoms, albeit mainly practised at the night-time strip clubs, bars and private establishments that flourished in "secret" Auckland. Doors were slowly opening in recognition that, sexually, New Zealand was freeing up. The Crimes Act 1961 determined the grounds for an abortion. The Dorian Society, established in 1962, was the first organisation for homosexual men. The Women's Liberation Movement was kicking into gear.

As for my own personal sexual history you can be sure that nobody — well, other than the other person involved — would find that out.

And I mean *nobody*.

4.

On return to university for my fifth year, the Maori Education Foundation told me they would give me one more chance.

Well, after all, it was their money.

I repeated history, geography and Māori; they were all that I needed to graduate with a Bachelor of Arts. But instead of going in from Manurewa on the train, I got a job as Bill Smiler working at a battery-packing factory. I lifted batteries off one conveyor line, put them into a slatted box on another moving belt and then hammered down two slats to make the top of the box. All day. Every day. I think it was self-inflicted punishment, but it made me feel good.

I wasn't getting along with Mum and Dad Te Maari by this stage, so I started flatting with my friend Turei Whaanga in a number of dodgy places in Grafton. I should have received an "A" for the efficient and capable way I was trying to destroy myself.

At least Grafton was closer to uni, but I had already tuned out. Ennui set in — I just hated being a passive recipient of knowledge. During the small amount of history study I did, however, I came across the story of the Children's Crusade. It captured my imagination — and made me think of doing something active. I decided to try a novel which I called *To Find Jerusalem*. I didn't get very far with either finding Jerusalem or writing the novel, and the existing pages are pretty dreadful.

I also wrote numerous unfinished short stories. At least I was trying.

But I wasn't studying what I was supposed to. I completely lost the plot. Perhaps my downward trajectory might have stopped if the university had creative writing courses (established in 2002) — but I make no excuses. My father remembers how I pleaded with him to understand how untenable I was finding university, and how I was facing a personal crisis.

I was becoming totally bankrupt as a person.

"I should have rescued you then," he said, blaming himself.

At the end of the year, zero passes again. I was excluded from the university and told not to return.

So it was finished with. Done. Kua mutu.

The whē, the stick insect that had taken skin off the soles of Tāwhaki's feet, had been waiting for me also. By degrees, they had managed to entirely denude me of my gilded skin and, because Turei was a barman, through him I started to live at night — all-night clubbing on K Road and partying wherever — and sleeping during the day.

The self-destructive, reckless behaviour I had got into with Jackson resurfaced. Drink dulled it, though, so that it didn't hurt as much — or at least I didn't develop a conscience about it. And I had learnt how to party and to love it.

But one thing I was not: vulnerable. I can be clinical about it. I disallowed myself from becoming vulnerable to anyone, anything, even to myself. And, fatally, I must have been spending at least fifty per cent of my life watching myself.

You can do this, but you can't do that. You can be this, but you can't be that.

Stop. Go. Yes. No. Someone help me. Please?

There's a line from Dante's *Inferno*, Canto 34:

> *Io non mori', e non rimasi vivo.*
> *I did not die, yet nothing of life remained.*

For some time that's how I felt about myself. Although I still lived the world was of no interest to me so I may as well have been dead. I was a pilgrim interposed between life and death, salvation and damnation, light and darkness, good and evil. And the guilt of the rape was still weighing me down.

I was at the extremities of exhaustion. When people are like this, they have to find a way of dealing with the trauma, somehow, to recover. They find a deep, dark hole in their psyche where they can bury it: stay.

In Māori mythology there was such a place. It was called Te Kore, The Void, the Nothingness. But how would I get there?

I resolved my dilemma in my dream world. One night, when I went to sleep, I summoned my ancestress Hine Te Ariki. The sea was the colour of greenstone, of pounamu. It stretched higher than the highest heaven and lower than Rūaumoko's domain.

Far away there was a silver flash. Hine Te Ariki rose through my subconscious. She was over six metres long. Her face had the form of a woman's but the features were inhuman, unearthly. Her skin was dark and mottled. She had rudimentary breasts and thick hair at the armpits and groin. Her lower limbs gleamed with scales. At the extremities the scales became splendid crystal flukes of immense power. They were out of proportion to the rest of her body, flicking back and forth in that shimmering sea.

"Take me to Te Pō," I commanded. "Beyond space and time, find Te Kore, the black hole where stars and moons are showering."

Of course she didn't know my intention. Riding her, I watched as we swam through the universe to our destination. If she had known what I was going to do she would have stopped me. I farewelled her in the hongi.

"E noho rā," I said.

And then I stepped off the rim of Te Kore, ah, the thrill of falling. I closed my eyes with the bliss of it.

Now rest, my soul, rest in the bosom of oblivion.

5.

The end came quickly and mercifully.

My money rapidly running out, Turei and I rented a room in a migrant hotel called The Rembrandt at the top of Queen Street. The other rooms were filled with newly arrived Fijians, Indians and Chinese, and this was their first rung of the ladder upward; for Turei and me, it was the last rung on the way to the bottom. Our room was small, dark, two beds, shared washroom down the hall, no cooking allowed. We ate canned food on our laps. Cockroaches were optional.

One night I returned to the hotel, stinking drunk, to find my father waiting for me. He was horrified at what I had come to. "Let's get you home, son," he said.

I was so angry I took a swing at him. "What took you so long, Dad?"

I know now, but I didn't know it then, that I had been waiting for him ever since the day he had brought me to Auckland.

Not until some years later, after I had read Frantz Fanon's *The Wretched of the Earth* (1961, translated into English 1963), did I figure out the malfunction. A lot of it was self-driven, I will accept some of the blame, but there was another reason.

Fanon was the leading anti-colonialist theorist of my time. His work eviscerates colonisation so that the whole stinking, appalling trauma of it is laid out for all of us to see, to recognise and to take action against. His propositions are truly surgical; he got under my skin with his theories, he will get under yours. It's a blood-letting, and I still shiver whenever I read his books and essays.

The introduction to the English edition, by Jean-Paul Sartre, contains a paragraph that was pertinent to my dilemma:

> The European elite undertook to manufacture a native elite. They picked out promising adolescents; they branded them, as with a red-hot iron, with the principles of Western culture; they stuffed their mouths full with high-sounding phrases, grand glutinous words that stuck to the teeth. After a short stay in the mother country they were sent home, whitewashed.

And so I look at that photograph again, at "Wite" Smiler, and now I find the intent of the snapshot slightly obscene. My student friends and I are framed within a context of success. The Western education system and the reigning European hegemony will not defeat us. There we are, happy and confident, appearing in a photograph to place in a Pākehā master's photograph album. Shaking the hands of the Māori students. Or with a part-Māori student who clearly obtained his brains from his Pākehā ancestry. Perhaps to accompany proud mention in the alumni magazine that said student was now the recipient of a scholarship to Yale or Oxford.

The real story for the Māori student would be like mine. Two years of gliding and then three in uncontrollable descent before being excluded, C for Coconut passes for those courses I successfully completed.

On the day that Dad collected me from The Rembrandt hotel I vowed I would never enter the gates of Auckland University again. Ever. While Māori students of my time aspired to be like the hero Tāwhaki, we were not climbing the Māori stairway to excellence, but the Western, Pākehā, one.

It was all a matter of destination.

We belonged to the generation climbing the wrong poutama.

Chapter Twenty-Eight

The Price to Pay

1.

Almost thirty years later, 1994, although our paths had crossed in between, Professor Biggs and I finally revisited those university years. I had become an academic as well as a writer, and we were serving on the same committee overseeing Waitangi Day celebrations. With a rather pained expression on his face he asked, "There was an Ihimaera Smiler who did Māori at Auckland University in the 1960s. That wasn't you, was it?"

"I was an arrogant arsehole," I answered. "Don't worry about it."

I didn't mention to him, though, that my not knowing the reo — and undoubtedly I would have gained proficiency — contributed to my self-loathing. Isn't it ironic that one of the skills I should have as a Māori writer — the reo — is something I still don't possess?

Am I therefore equipped for the role that I have taken upon myself? No.

And yet I still write, why? After all, I must have been the only Māori in the history of the University of Auckland to enrol in first-year Māori two years running and not pass the examination.

2.

At the University of Auckland I ended my calamitous career in the throes of great and intense emotions.

What was my way out or through?

I found it in the compulsion to *breathe.* An inner voice spoke to me: "You know how to breathe, don't you? You breathe in, let your blood begin to sing, and then breathe out the waiata."

While university had allowed the possibility of pursuing an academic career within the Western European model, and many Black and indigenous men and women would pursue careers within that context and grasp the Pākehā baskets of knowledge with brilliant success, that was not for me. The alternatives were to find success artistically in theatre, film, dance or literature, or in sporting achievement.

This is where I found my way forward. There, through *creative expression*, I was able to access the Māori baskets of knowledge. In my case, Māori imagination — the sovereign world of Māori thought and intellect — would provide the escape, the alternative pathway, I was looking for.

But to do it, this is what you have to do. The price you have to pay.

Now rest your soul, rest in the bosom of oblivion? No, it will not rest.

You've checked out physically at Middlemore Hospital, but mentally and emotionally you are still a helluva mess. Throwing your soul into Te Pō won't cut it. You have to find the solution nearer at hand. You must stop spiralling down to whatever death wish is in your psyche — call it the virus that has lodged there, always waiting. You cannot allow whatever malevolent urges you have felt in the past to take you to that same self-destructive destination. You have to lock the memory away. Your damaged younger self away.

And so you imagine a house far from anywhere, in a shining valley hidden from the world. There's a fortress at one end to protect him, a sacred mountain at the other to watch over him and a river running through the valley to sing to him. You conjure up your younger self to stand beside you at the gate to the house.

This is for you, *you tell him. He smiles and takes your hand. The sun sparkles all around.*

The house has three bedrooms. A back door and a front door. Windows.

You go through the front gate to the house. You take your younger self into one of the bedrooms. You have a special surprise for him. Remember the box of treasures we buried up at the farm? It's under the bed. *He opens the lid and uncovers all your boyhood delights and mysteries.* Look! *You both play with the contents together for a while. And you have a game with the sky-blue marbles. You let him win.*

Then you cradle him in your arms and tell him that you love him, not to be afraid. I will come back for you, you tell him.

When? *he asks. His eyes are trusting. He has always been this way.*

Soon. *You make him lie down on the bed, push your hands through his hair and tuck his head under your chin.*

When is soon? *you hear him say. You don't know yourself, how can you tell him?*

You realise you've forgotten to bless him. You dash into the bathroom and come back with a handful of water. It becomes a game, he runs away laughing but you catch him, and sprinkle him with the water.

Then, Soon is soon, *you tell him.* Now be a brave boy. Don't cry. You know we never cry.

You kiss him again. I have to go now. I can't take you with me, you understand?

He watches you as you leave the bedroom.

You close all the windows. Pull the curtains. Check that all the kitchen cupboards are full of his favourite food and drink. Then you lock the back door. Check it. Yes, locked.

Out the front door now. Lock it. Check it again. Yes, locked.

No, don't look back. Your younger self will be all right. You will leave the tohu, the sign of what happened to you here with him, and you will never from this moment admit it into your life.

But your younger self calls out your name. Witi! Witi! *He is watching from the front window. He waves. He will be all right. He will be the sleeping prince and walls of towering pōhutukawa, blossoming red, will spring up around him. Nothing and nobody will harm him any more. His dreams will be sweet and good.*

You call to him, Close the curtains. *You have the feeling that he is more concerned about you than he is for himself. He smiles such a hopeful smile.*

You call again. Go bye byes now.

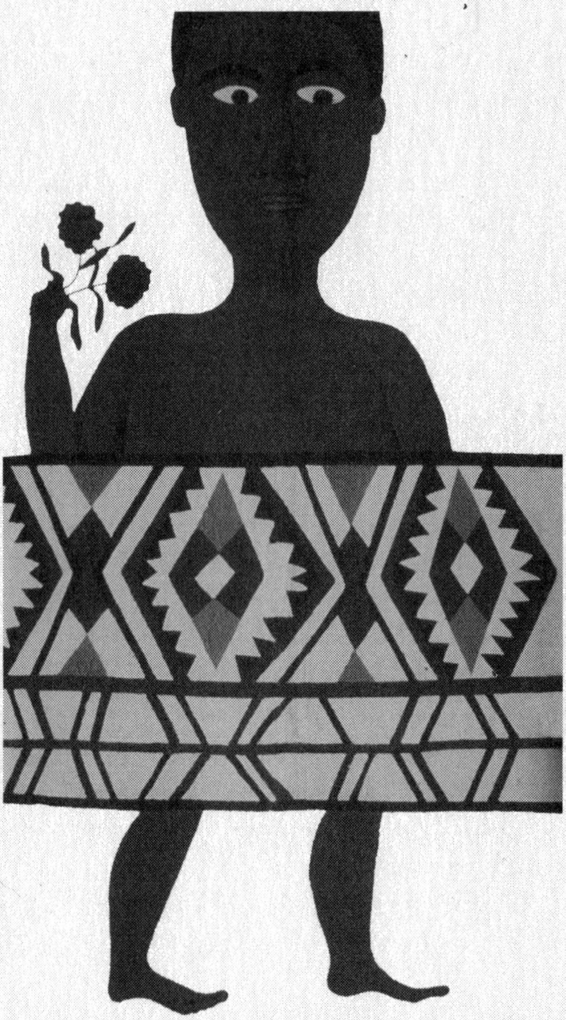

INTERLUDE

MANA INHERITANCE

Chapter Twenty-Nine

Tamatea, the Eidolon Ihimaera

1.

Let me now turn to *The Matriarch* (1986).

I had, in my previous work, tried to work out what the Māori Story was or, at least, what I thought it was. To do with *whakapapa*, genealogy. To do with *iwi*, tribe. To do with *tangata*, humankind.

I was really answering to the very first question a beginning writer asks of himself, which had to do with *what*. What was I going to write? And I had decided to write stories located in Turanganui-a-Kiwa (Gisborne and Poverty Bay) in general, and Waituhi in particular. The Smiler and Keelan families — whether they liked it or not — would be the fictional subject.

But *what* was not necessarily the most important question. There were also *why*, *how*, *where* and *when*.

In the early 1980s, the pātai that I constantly kept asking myself had to do with the *how*.

In terms of narrative, I have already mentioned (in writing about my novel *Tangi*) how I adopted te wā tōrino, spiralling time, as the structure for indigenous work.

This is how that operated in *The Matriarch*. The simplest way to pictorialise the process is to look at a spiral on the page. It first presented itself on the horizontal, where I was spiralling from the centre or axis of Waituhi outward and back and outward again. This was the prescription for *Tangi* and *Whanau* and the collections *Pounamu, Pounamu* and *The New Net Goes Fishing*.

However, rotate the spiral on the vertical. The possibilities present themselves differently in other ways, don't they! The corkscrew can widen both upward or downward like a cone, or an inverted cone, coiling upward or downward.

With *The Matriarch* I decided to construct the novel on this vertical. The very reconceptualising of Māori Story as being written this way, as well as in the horizontal, allowed me to enlarge the scope of spiralling time — bringing in past, present, and future — as into some spinning black hole in my creative universe. I was therefore able to explore kōrero as a multidimensional form.

Example: draw a square on the page, a circle and a triangle. Now draw the object three-dimensionally so that it becomes a box, a sphere or a pyramid.

Invest kupu, ihi, wehi, mana and aroha into the process and something interesting happens. The object becomes prismatic, able to disperse light and darkness. The energy frees it to move through time and space, and past, present and future. There, forwards can also be backwards. Up can be down. Along can be sideways. The dimensional permutations are endless.

The light allows all this to coalesce. It refracts, warps, bends and blends the perspectives. Locations collide. Present and future flow through one another. Change the ratios of ihi to aroha or wehi to mana and other permutations present themselves. Nothing is singular.

Indeed, I once talked with John Huria about this notion of spiralling time in Māori narratology, and he mentioned the Russian formalist view of a literary text comprising *fabula* and *syuzhet*.

"Perhaps," John began, "the Māori way of how we tell story — the syuzhet — is how we subvert the linear chronological sequence — the fabula. Aren't we fortunate to have spiralling time to allow us to dance on the thresholds of so many dimensions! And by way of its permutations, we have all these immense carved and complex doorways that allow us access into the Māori whare of the mind."

Yes. Well. John knows stuff. All we were doing was having a simple espresso in a Wellington café. And out of a beautiful summer day came the opportunity to thrill the intellect with theoretical kōrero on a meeting house of the mind, illuminated by multitextual experience, and set spinning by kaupapa and tikanga, toi, toi, toi.

Oh, I could go on with the metaphysics of Māori thinking but that will have to wait for a different opportunity. Here, in this moment, I simply want to show how one of these syntheses, metamorphoses, permutations — call it what you will — took me to te more (the taproot).

It was the taproot that took my work into pūrākau (mythology).

In the case of *The Matriarch,* the pūrākau anchoring the novel there was the multigenerational Tāwhaki monomyth. *The Dream Swimmer* (1997), being a sequel, also owed its mythic structure to Tāwhaki. *The Whale Rider* (1987) has, as its mythic text, the saga of the original whale rider, Paikea. And one further example, *Sky Dancer* (2003) has, to give its contemporary story resonance, the pūrākau of the division of territories between the manu moana (seabirds) and manu whenua (land birds).

The Uncle's Story (2000) is possibly the most loaded of my novels. The Tāwhaki cycle is its mythic basis, but Michael Mahana is a "Tāwhaki" who never existed — a gay Tāwhaki. The mythology surrounding Tūmatauenga, god of war, is contested by deploying my gay hero against the then prevailing image of the male as warrior.

In modern parlance, the mythic template is called the urtext (kōrero pūrākau). It's a word of German origin, circa 1932. One definition of urtext is "the earliest form of a text as established by linguistic scholars as a basis for variants in later texts still in existence". I apologise for having to use modern theoretical definitions to describe Māori processes but, until someone comes along to create a new theoretical discourse to quantify those processes, I'm probably as good as it will get.

Thus, just as was happening in my life, the Tāwhaki cycle became the kōrero pūrākau for *The Matriarch.* My hero Tamatea Mahana, like Tāwhaki, is set on a quest. The first instigator of the search is his grandmother Riripeti. In the prologue, Tamatea as a child remembers sitting with her, sometime in the 1950s, on Ramaroa Mountain, Waituhi, awaiting the dawn. Like Whaitiri, Riripeti is associated with the sky world and, metaphorically, invokes the sun to rise.

However, the real catalyst is Tamatea's Uncle Alexis. The location shifts to Wellington, 1974, and Tamatea is now a young man. It is Alexis who voices the kupu in the book, and he also establishes the kaupapa that precipitates Tamatea's journey.

Here is Act One, Scene One, of the book.

2.
from *The Matriarch*

It was Uncle Alexis who started it all — this imaginative reconstruction of the woman who wore pearls in her hair, Riripeti, the matriarch who ruled the Mahana family for three generations. Poor Uncle Alex. The Italians would have called him un superbo uomo, a superb man, and so he was. And it was he who without knowing it started this journey into the past and into the dynamics of an astonishing family.

Father Blain said that all families are somewhat like jungles. So it is with mine, but I have made it even more of a jungle by mingling fiction with fact, like saprophytic vines twining the trunks of already dead trees. I think the matriarch herself would have approved of this. After all, she was the one who turned my own life into fiction.

It was July 1974. Wellington. I had arrived late to see my Uncle Alexis who was going blind and after two hours I realised that I was committed to stay longer. It might have been better had I not gone to see him at all. But Regan, my wife, said I ought to go, and my father, Te Ariki, was expecting me to see his younger brother. Dad was cross that I hadn't made the effort before this. "You've been back from London for a year now," he had said the previous weekend when he'd telephoned from Gisborne. "Surely you can get in your car and drive down the hill to Oriental Bay. Take your daughters with you. Your uncle's expecting you. He's wondering why you haven't been to see him. I told him last week that you must be busy. Well, Tamatea, try to un-busy yourself for a couple of hours. Go and see your uncle. It's not easy for him, being blind." My father always called me Tamatea when he wanted to remind me of my family obligations.

It wasn't that Uncle Alex and I didn't get along together; just that the gap between the last time I had seen him and now was as wide as the ocean and as treacherous to navigate. Almost three years had gone by. How can you cross three years of sea in a few hours? On top of this we'd never really known each other very well and I was inclined to suspect that he didn't approve of my successes — the diplomatic career and public achievements had established a reputation which, for him, was all too good to be true. But I like to think that he admired me and, perhaps, was fond of me. I do know that he had always been amazed that I, among all his nephews and nieces, had never asked him for money — Uncle was wealthy, you see, though he never flaunted it. That hadn't stopped him from continuing to try to bribe me, and it was the same on that evening I went to see him. Alone.

Uncle's house was on a narrow street which wound down like a bandage into Oriental Bay. I had friends further down the street, James and Ilse, and I was almost tempted to drive past Uncle's and talk Russian literature with the wondrous Ilse. But I stopped the car and stepped out. The house was olive green and there were no lights shining in the diamond windows. Then I saw my Aunt Roha, looking through the curtains at me. I ran through the rain, past the tall slapping shrubs, to the front entrance. The glass panels shimmered with a woman's shadow.

"Well look what the wind blew in," my aunt said when she opened the door. Roha was an attractive woman, very slim and elegant. Tonight she looked sallow and waspish.

"I've come to see Uncle," I said.

She kissed me. As her cheek brushed mine I felt the velvet of her skin. "It took you long enough," she answered.

She ushered me in and shut the door against the wind and the rain. The house was warm. Some of my cousins were home watching television. I saw one of them drifting past in a dream, a renaissance beauty with a bee sting for a mouth.

"Say hello to your cousin," Roha said.

She turned to look at me. "Oh, hello, cousin," she whispered vaguely. She was like a somnambulist, a fairy princess sleepwalking her way down the dark corridor.

Roha took me to the main bedroom. It was dark. After all, what did a blind man need with the light? Uncle was sitting up in bed looking at nothing and listening to the wind and the patterning of rain against the window. "Alex," my aunt said to him. "Your nephew's here to see you. Te Ariki's son."

Uncle's face swivelled around in my direction, searching upward to where I might be. He looked bloated, with a greyness beneath the skin. His eyes were concealed behind large dark glasses, but the glasses could not completely hide the infectiousness of the welcome which spread across his face. I had always thought that Uncle Alex was devilishly handsome, a 1940s film star, a cross between Tyrone Power and Cesar Romero. When he and Roha were married they had been the most glamorous couple I had ever seen. I was supposed to be the pageboy at the wedding but at the last minute I decided I looked too ridiculous for words, and I wouldn't go ahead with it. Roha tried to get me into the velvet outfit but I made my body heavy and lumpy and she gave up in despair. Uncle laughed and ruffled my hair. "If he doesn't want to, he doesn't want to. Too stubborn. Anyway, there are enough stars at this wedding as it is," he said as he kissed her, "you and me." He led her out to the wedding car. He looked like Escamillo and she, in beautiful white lace and satin, like Carmen, in the last act of Bizet's opera. Later, at the church, they ran out smiling in a shower of white rose petals.

Thirty years later here they were, Uncle Alex and Roha. The white petals had long browned, shrivelled and dried in my aunt's memory book.

"You'd better stay for tea," Aunt Roha said.

"No," I answered. "Thank you, though, for the invitation."

"You can't expect to come here and then just leave," she said. "Your uncle's got a lot to talk to you about. You'll stay. You should have brought Regan with you."

I walked over to my uncle. He was still grinning, and the grin kept growing larger and wider, the skin stretching and breaking over his teeth. "I hope you brought a rifle with you, Tama," he said pleasantly. "I may as well be shot right here and now in this bed. I'd rather be dead than blind."

I looked at Roha. Her eyes were shaded from me. "Don't talk like that, Alex," she said. "What's the use of talking like that?" Her voice was tight.

"I'm no good to anybody now, girl," he told her. "I shot a bull once. It had gone blind. I put the bullet right here," he continued, jabbing his fingers insistently at his forehead. "Here. Here. Here. It was a kindness. The bull kept on blundering into trees and fences. Couldn't even find the cows. So Dad told me to take the rifle and go out into the paddock and shoot it." Then his mood changed. "Hey, have those kids said hello to their cousin yet?"

"Yes, Uncle," I said.

He pierced me with his voice. "Don't you do it to me too, boy. I may have lost my sight but my ears are as good as they ever were." He turned to my aunt. "Don't think I don't know what's going on in this house."

Roha retreated, a sad smile on her lips.

I gripped Uncle's hands together in mine. The palms were so soft. "I'm sorry I couldn't come earlier," I said.

His hair was greasy and shot through with grey. "Nobody likes to visit a blind man," he said. He began to laugh again, a shocking sound. "I think I must be going mad. I can't even sleep because the dark is all the same to me; I don't know what the time is unless the radio is on. I spend my time just listening. Listening. To what's going on. Only I don't know what's going on. Someone could be in the room and I wouldn't know. Your aunt has been trying to get me to go out, but I've seen blind people out on the street. Being helped across intersections. Onto buses. Friends come to see me, but what's the use? Someone's put a hoodoo on me, Tama. They stuck pins in my eyes."

"It's good to be here, Uncle," I said. "Nobody has put anything on you. All your family love you."

"Love?" He answered. He pulled my head to his and put his lips to my ear. "Tell you what, though. If you love me, I'll make it worth your while. A thousand bucks, boy. If you shoot me."

"Not enough," I joked. I knew he wasn't serious.

"Make it ten thousand. And I'll throw in a new car."

Uncle was one of the last of the big-time gamblers. Cards, horses, billiards, you name it and Uncle Alexis had at least $500 on it. And there'd be a new car in the street if the loser could not pay any debt to Uncle in cash.

I pushed him away. "Hey, there," I said. "Don't tempt me. You know I'll never take your money now or ever. I'm proud of that, Uncle. It's a thing with me. I'll make my own way. My own money."

He grew silent. Then he nodded his head. "You were always too proud. I could never do anything with you." His face grew gentle. "Move closer to me, Tama, I want to know you're here and that you won't make a fool of a blind man by sneaking out while I'm talking." He seemed to be enjoying an inner joke.

Outside the rain was lashing at the landscape.

"You won't remember this," he said, "but once I made a bet with Mum about you. You were eleven at the time and you were to receive an award from your school for being the top student in your class. Well, you know your grandmother — she said I had to drive her into Gisborne in the Lagonda to your graduation ceremony. It was such a nuisance. As usual, she got dressed up to the nines in a long black dress and grey fur coat, and she threaded pearls through her hair. "My grandson likes the pearls," she said. She looked really stunning and she winked at me and said, "Not bad for an old lady." So I took her in, and of course she was always good at making entrances with that walking stick banging on the floor. Everything stopped until she sat down. Well, it was so bloody boring, the whole thing. But when you came on to receive your prize, Mum seemed to glow and she changed the whole atmosphere of the place. It was almost as if she willed everybody, forced them to acknowledge your achievement. I was sick of it. She was always making you into something special. Somebody great. So I told her, I bet her, that I could bring you down, make you fall. Like the angel Lucifer, I would cast you out of heaven. She turned to me in the darkness and she said something I'll never forget. She replied in biblical language, "No, Alex, you will never be able to do that because I have made him into a likeness as unto me." Uncle laughed again. "I'm still not sure what she meant by that. But she can't say that I haven't tried."

3.

In *The Matriarch* Tamatea Mahana is promised a kingdom and a succession by his grandmother, Riripeti, the ruler of his iwi. However, when she dies the succession is taken by Tamatea's grandfather, Ihaka. A curse — otherwise known as the mate — is said to have been placed on the House of Mahana. As a consequence, the kingdom becomes, in mythic terms, a wasteland with other factions fighting over it.

Enter Tamatea as a young man. He embarks on a quest that has all the hallmarks of the hero's journey, facing down many challenges as he works through the dynastic interplay and intrigue that flow through the narrative. For instance, unbeknownst to him, his own grandfather has established a rival for the succession.

Throughout the timeframe of *The Matriarch* (and *The Dream Swimmer*) Tamatea's every attempt to win the kingdom is foiled, not just on a temporal plane but, it seems, on the spiritual plane too. However, not until he regains his rightful inheritance will destiny be made right, the mate overturned and, to reference TS Eliot's *The Waste Land*, the dead land bloom again.

You can see how closely the configuration matches my own life! But I am not Tamatea and he is not me. I like to think of him as my hologram. Indeed, the Māori historian Rawiri Taonui once observed, correctly as it turned out, that "Witi Ihimaera does not exist, he is a construct." Yes, Rawiri, I've been a chimera ever since I was fifteen and used the surname, for the very first time in a professional sense, in the School Certificate examination.

And in *The Matriarch* I deployed Tamatea as my "persona". To invoke a Greek comparison, he became an *eidolon* Ihimaera, an image-self. He was the effigy the reader could follow through the narrative and I think his evolution pretty much conformed to Carl Jung's definition in his essay "Images of the Unconscious" (1950): "the persona ... is that system of adjustment or that manner through which we deal with the world ... One could with some exaggeration say: the persona is that which a person essentially is not, but rather what he and other people want him to be."

Jung was the founder of analytical psychology and, actually, the character of Tamatea Mahana was prefigured by him when he uses the term "*mana*-personality."

Jung claimed in his book *Zwei Schriften über Analytische Psychologie (Two Essays on Analytical Psychology)* (1964) that the mana-personality was an archetype of the collective unconscious, "a being filled with an occult, conjuring capacity, or mana, and endowed with magical skills or powers". He went on to remark that "the mana-personality manifests itself historically in hero figures and divine images".

Jung must have been acquainted either with Māori or with Polynesia. Perhaps he was even familiar with Tāwhaki.

Chapter Thirty

She is Whaitiri

1.

While I'm at it, perhaps I should talk about the Whaitiri figure in *The Matriarch*.

My very real grandmother became the fictional Riripeti. (Yes, Maaka, the air around me fizzes with your nuclear fission thing, you were an inspiration also.) I've not been able to find a fictional figure quite like her in the 1980s, a woman warrior leader, but do let me know if there is.

And I guess it was inevitable that at some point I would want to write about Teria. After all, she had been, up until her death when I was eleven, the senior woman in our clan. She operated at the highest levels of tribal and intertribal politics, and it didn't matter that she was a woman. Along with other leaders of the Waituhi Valley, she travelled locally, regionally and nationally, to one hui or another to prosecute Te Whānau-a-Kai's land claims as well as to show her support for any Māori kaupapa.

Teria realised I was an imaginative child. As grandmothers do, I think she fed my imagination in ways she would not have realised. For instance, it was through her that I developed a keen sense of how the natural and spiritual worlds interacted with the human and the ways in which the past was intertwined with the present. Thus my childhood memories were charged with the possibilities of fantastic meaning.

My grandmother might have simply been saying a poroporoaki to the sun at twilight but I thought she was talking to Te Rā. Whenever we walked along the Waipaoa River all she might have been doing was greeting the eels, but when they brought their mouths up to the top of the water and opened and closed them I thought they were talking to her.

We went up to the urupā to clean the graves one afternoon, and on our way back, she said sharply to me, "E tū", which meant stop. She began to sing a song.

I asked, "Who are you singing to, Grandma?"

She got me to look down at the blades of grass and all I could see, as the afternoon light was coming across, were these threads spun by spiders from one leaf stalk to another. The spiders were springing into the air. She was telling them, "You should forgive a clumsy boy who is making his way through your kingdom." She showed me a way of looking at the world which was Māori. It was fantastic, but it was Māori fantastic.

And as you know from *Māori Boy*, Teria also gave me political epiphanies into Pākehā thinking. For instance when I came back from school she asked me, "So, e Wit*sh*, what great new wisdom did the Pākehā teach you today?" I told her about Jack and Jill and Little Miss Muffet and she commented, "What a stupid place to put a well, and what a silly little girl to run away from a spider, she should have said kia ora to it." I learnt from Teria in word and deed that the values of the Pākehā world were anathema to ours.

I suspect I got my curious nature from her too. She taught me how to reach for something . . . even if it would hurt. Like putting your hand into a fire. To reach for an object in the flames, and to keep on trying to grasp it, no matter that it might be burning, if it was important.

Metaphorically, Teria was like Whaitiri, ambushing me at the foot of the aka matua, and every time she did that . . . she threw me a sweet potato. So would begin our game with the kūmara.

"What does this potato *mean*, e Wit*sh*? And this one? What is the *purpose*? And this one? Where is the *intellect*? Use your head, mokopuna! Look with your heart . . ."

And just as my grandmother Teria was able to invoke the dawn, Whaitiri's doppelgänger — Riripeti in the novel — in the following episode, has commanded the sun to go out.

2.
from *The Matriarch*

Wellington, 1949
La luce langue, il faro spegnesi
Ch'eterno corre per gli ampi cieli!
Notte desiata, provvida veli
La man colpevole che ferirà.

Light weakens, and the beacon
That eternally courses the far-flung heavens is spent.
O desired night, you providentially veil
The guilty hand which is going to strike the blow.

"So be it," Riripeti said.

She pulled her dark veil down and over her face.

On the forecourt of Parliament, the prime minister, chiefs of Māoridom and all who were gathered there looked up into the sky, crying out in alarm. The clouds were joining across what had once been a brief space of sunlit sky, like viscous liquid poured, spreading and streaming into the blue gap of air. It was as if Ranginui, the Sky Father, so long separated from Papatūānuku, had finally wrenched free of his heavenly imprisonment and wished to embrace the Earth Mother again. With relentless power he descended, blotting out the sun in his inevitable embrace of earth.

"Grandmother," the child cried out.

Like everyone else he was afraid. He felt the warmth withdrawing, and the light being sucked away, as the moon slowly began to bite into the edge of the sun. He looked up and saw the black cutting edge across the sun's glowing face, and tears sprang to his eyes because the light was still blinding in its intensity. He averted his gaze a moment. He heard people screaming, even members of the ope, the group that had come with Riripeti. Through his blurring vision he looked at the group.

They were all staring into the sky. Only Tiana's face was averted from the sun and, for a brief moment, the child saw his mother looking across at him. Her face was expressionless, immobile, yet it had intensity in the gaze. Then the child saw his mother's eyes shift, almost imperceptibly, to the matriarch. Her responding glance was autocratic and triumphant.

The light lessening, lessening. The black disc of the moon closed like a gate on the sun. The pearls in Riripeti's hair began to change colour. The lustrous pale of the pearls became drenched with blood.

The child looked up into the sky again. The sun was almost out now, but around the black hole where its light had been was a bright circlet and, from it, there erupted bursts of flame, spectacular, wondrous, curling into the black universe.

The clouds were completely joined, and the upstaring faces and the marae itself were bathed in a wan light. The sun seemed to stand in blackness for eternity. There it shone, a beacon smothered by the clouds, still, forbidding, angry, with its corona of fire. It was like looking through a piece of smoked glass. The effect was powerful and brooding.

Riripeti looked across at the elders where they sat on the paepae. She nodded at them. She inclined her head to the Prime Minister.

"So it is done," she said. The crowd on the marae was still in a state of alarm. Some were crying out to her.

Then the child saw that the pearls in her hair were changing again, assuming their usual sheen. Whatever was happening would soon be over. Alert, he listened as Riripeti called to the ope and pulled them together with her presence.

"It will soon be time for us to reply to the speeches of welcome," she said. "When the sun comes, I want us to be ready. As soon as the fullness of the light returns, I will give the sign, and our first speaker will begin."

The sun, black and awesome. Then, gradually, the moon moved away from the sun's face and the intensity of the light increased, ever increased, and, as it did so, Riripeti lifted the black veil from her face. The clouds opened. The sun hurled its light like a hammer to the earth. Ranginui, the Sky Father, returned to the heavens. Riripeti seemed to blaze on the marae.

("Well," the journalist said, "the sun going out like that was a brilliant coup de théâtre, and Artemis's sense of timing was absolutely impeccable. What a flamboyant trickster she was, such a charlatan, such a sorceress! I'm sorry if you object to my using those terms but, after all, you can't believe that it was she who made the sun go out. It was a total eclipse, of course, and it lasted about seven and a half minutes, maybe less. I'd read that it was going to occur but I had forgotten the timing of the event. So had most other people. Your grandmother, clever woman as she was, must have known about it all the time. There is no other explanation. She certainly used it to her advantage, my oath she did.

"Oh, the pandemonium when it happened. I've not been one to believe in witchcraft and all that, but when that sun started to go out I was struck with fear. Of course it didn't take me long to realise what was happening. Artemis knew all along. Later, after the welcomes were over, Timoti and some other elders in the paepae refused to have anything to do with her. They were apoplectic with rage. But one of them, I think his name was Whai, roared with laughter and complimented her. 'Legends will be woven of this day when the Matua made the sun go out.'

She had beaten them all, you see. But more was to follow —")

With the return of the sun, the mood on the forecourt to Parliament turned to elation. Smiling, Riripeti turned to Grandfather Ihaka. "Come, let us start our replies to the speeches of welcome which have been given to us. Let us be the best that anyone has seen or heard."

She motioned him forward.

"Kia hiwa rā! Kia hiwa rā!" Grandfather Ihaka began. "Be careful. Be wakeful. Ka moe ararara ki te matahī tuna . . . You have to stay awake to catch eels. You have to stay awake to catch a war party—"

His speech was taunting. It brought images of sentries patrolling the stepped terraces of an ancient hill fort in the red light of dawn.

"Ka tiritiria, ka reareaia a tama tū ki tona hiwa rā. Scatter, rise up, stand in your places. Kia hiwa rā. Be watchful. Be wakeful. Be alert on this terrace. Be alert on that terrace, or someone will wound you and make you bleed—"

He patterned the ground like a sentry, springing back and forth, swaying, probing, seeking out the enemy on the horizon.

"Papaki tū ana te tai ki Te Reinga. The tide is beating to Te Reinga. Eke panuku. Eke Tangaroa. Hui ē! Tāiki e!"

On the last words, the ope and the people gathered on Parliament Grounds joined in a huge shout of acclamation. "Tāiki ē!"

("Your speakers were superb," the journalist said. "I understand that your grandfather was the first speaker. The second was Tamatea Kota, the priest who was known as Artemis's Left Hand of God. The third was your father, Te Ariki. From all accounts, they were so proficient that everyone kept on roaring with the pleasure of their imagery and wit. As you know, I can't fully understand your language, but I can gauge when a good show is put on. Your speakers had the crowd with them all the way. Oh, they were so glorious to listen to, and to watch. They made references to genealogy and land and everything they said was appropriate and correct. The old man near me, well, his eyes were gleaming with the pleasure of it all. 'I haven't seen or heard such a fine display of oratory for years,' he said. One after another, your speakers followed upon each other, representatives from Te Whānau-a-Kai, Rongowhakaata and Te Aitanga-a-Mahaki. It was just brilliant. Then it appeared as if the last speaker had spoken.")

The excitement on Parliament Grounds had reached fever pitch.

"You have all done well," Riripeti said. "Our mana has been sustained. Kei te pai. Ka nui te hōnore kua homai ki a au. You have given me a great honour."

But the iwi knew that the Matua was still angry at the slight done to her.

"Now it is my turn," she said.

Instantly, there was a murmur in the ope.

"No, don't do it," Grandfather Ihaka said. "The Prime Minister, chiefs of Māoridom and the tangata whenua await us."

"Haere mai koutou ki te rūrū," came the call.

("Well, you know," the journalist said, "we thought it was all over. Everything seemed to be calm enough. People started to chatter among themselves again and to talk over the events of the welcome. You know, to relax.")

"Don't do it, no, don't," Grandfather Ihaka said again.

("The elders on the paepae called Artemis and your people over to meet in the hongi. But your grandmother didn't move. And Timoti began to get angry again. 'No, she wouldn't do it, she's a woman, she wouldn't dare.' Everywhere, conversation began to fade, and silence fell. It was quite uncanny.")

Riripeti turned swiftly to the child. "Listen, mokopuna, listen to me. This is a very dangerous and difficult course that I am embarked upon, but it must be done. Do you think the chiefs of Māoridom will let me say what our iwi has come here to say when this is the last day of the hui? No, I have to speak now, while our people still hold the ground."

("You know your customs better than I do," the journalist said. "Oh yes, the role of women must be difficult in your society. I must say that I felt an immense respect for Artemis.")

"Mokopuna, you must pray for me. For while I have done what I am going to do in my own land, I have not done it outside the home ground. There may well be a price to pay."

"Haere mai, haere mai," the call from the tangata whenua echoed across the iwi again. One second, then another went past.

The child heard his grandmother's bracelets tinkling like Oriental wind chimes as she gripped her walking stick.

"No, don't," Grandfather Ihaka said for the third time.

Her knuckles went white as she pressed on the walking stick. Her long black gown rustled and swept into the wind. The pearls in her hair were shivering like drops of water on a web.

"Te Whānau-a-Kai hei panapana maro," she said. "Our people never retreat, whether they be men or women."

There was a roar of anger, like a whirlwind, as Riripeti levered herself to stand on the marae, her body climbing higher and higher against the backdrop of the sky.

3.

The Matriarch belongs to a new personal era of empowerment. My belief is that in at least one of your books you should shoot for something epochal, even if you don't reach it. Therefore I also decided that in *The Matriarch* I would write the book as a contemporary myth, not comfortably recessed in ancient Māori times but impossibly, jarringly, being worked out *now*. As a consequence when I was writing the novel I was thinking at a different level of consciousness and subconsciousness, and in a more ambitious way. I saw the possibilities of utilising international postcolonial and postmodern strategies, which is why the book became so long — two books in fact.

Therefore, while the book was based on a Māori urtext, I saw the possibilities of deploying *intertext* (kōrero o te ao whānui). The intertextual mythology I chose was from Ancient Greek culture, primarily *The Iliad*. If you're into the cinematic Marvel Universe — you know, Taika's *Thor: Ragnarok*, and *Wonder Woman, Wolverine, Iron Man, The Hulk* and *Black Panther* — welcome to the Original

Greek Universe of gods, mortals and monsters. Written in the eighth century BC but describing events some four centuries earlier, *The Iliad* covers only a few weeks during the Trojan War. However, like the Marvel Universe, the saga expands to cover the entire ten-year siege and the terrific ebb and flow of battle and of cause and consequences.

And the characters! Agamemnon, Achilles and his companion Patroclus, Helen, Diomedes (described as the most insane, over-the-top ass-kicker of the war), wow.

So as well as the Polynesian Tāwhaki multigenerational framework I also framed *The Matriarch* against Greek mythology. In particular, against the trilogy by Aeschylus, *The Oresteia* (458 BC).

Somebody shouldn't have let me out of the shed.

However, before anyone thinks that my leap from Māori mythology sideways into Greek pūrākau was entirely self-motivated, I have to point out the very clear interest in Greek myth that my forebears had — in particular, two tribal rangatira, Te Kani Te Ua and Rongowhakaata Halbert. Although they had both died by the time I came to write *The Matriarch,* Te Kani in 1966 and Pāpā Rongo in 1973, I had come across their life stories and the work they had written, while researching the book. Both had attended Nelson College where they studied classics. Rongo became a prefect, was in the rugby first fifteen, and had an extensive music training — he played the cello, viola and piano. Te Kani, as well as another relative Turuki (one of my grandmother Teria's brothers), joined him. Te Kani had a similar music education, specialising in Chopin.

I wish I had known Te Kani and Pāpā Rongo better. They never wore their academic training in any conspicuous manner, and I would have loved to have spent some time with Rongo particularly. He wrote an astonishing book, *Horouta: The History of the Horouta Canoe, Gisborne and East Coast*, which was published posthumously in 1999.

Early in my career I came across the Tairawhiti Historical Association and its biennial journal which had been published in the 1950s. In it, Te Kani Te Ua observed that there were strong parallels between Māori myths and the Greek inventory. He considered Māori might be regarded as barbaric and savage, but our knowledge, philosophy and view of the spirit world demonstrated a high plane of thought reminiscent of the earliest Greek philosophers, such as Empedocles and Anaximander. Te Kani's observation simply blew me away and I decided to try to affirm his view in *The Matriarch* and *The Dream Swimmer*, hence their framing within *The Oresteia*.

There's no doubt that the exaggerated emotional turbulence of *The Matriarch* came from my decision to create an analogue reading. Tamatea became Orestes and Riripeti became Artemis. *The Oresteia* concerned in part the curse on the House of Atreus and how Orestes negotiated its removal. Uncle Alexis became the blind man, Tiresias, waiting at the sphinx to direct Orestes to his duty.

Why did I do this? Well, Katherine Mansfield said of her own work, "Oh, I want for one moment to make our undiscovered country leap into the eyes of the Old World. It must be mysterious, as though floating." This was my moment. I took the leap.

The reviews were mixed. My colleague Atareta Poananga took three articles in *Broadsheet* to spell out the book's innumerable failings, particularly the failure of Artemis as a representative Māori character. And Karl Stead called it a "war book" and castigated me for "picking over old wounds and ancient evils".

The Matriarch won the Wattie Book of the Year Award in 1986 and was runner-up for the inaugural Commonwealth Writers Prize in 1987. Margaret Atwood was also up for the Prize for *The Handmaid's Tale* (1985), as was Ben Okri for *Incidents at the Shrine* (1986). The winner was Olive Senior's *Summer Lightning* (1986).

With *The Matriarch* I established the wero in my work. I trained myself as a toa kaituhituhi, the literary equivalent of the warrior trained in mau rākau. The training brought me to this point of anarchy, of challenging any sanction of the Treaty process.

I felt I had good technique and good posture. My three ceremonial rākau (darts) were rākau whakaara, rākau takoto and rākau whakawaha. They announced, "I guard this domain (I stalk it), I lay claim to the sovereignty of this domain and, if I regard you with sympathy, I will allow you entrance."

I saw the field ahead and discerned all the worlds seen and the unseen, worlds from time beginning, worlds unending.

Began to paw the dirt with my feet. Spittle spraying from my mouth. The veins of my eyes red.

Placed the first dart down.

Chapter Thirty-One

The Third Poutama

1.

Back to 1967.

Can you see what was happening? There was no Māori poutama for you to climb.

And you failed to ascend the Pākehā stairway. Perhaps, if you had succeeded, your life would have been entirely different.

But you didn't. Therefore, if you were to become a writer, you had to find another way upward.

Ascend the poutama of the *imagination*.

This was how it all began.

I was twenty-three when I returned to Gisborne after four years at the University of Auckland.

Beaten. My tail between my legs. But nobody made any comment about my failure, as if it had been expected. All that Nani Mini and the whānau said out at Waituhi was, "It's good to have you home, moko."

Dad was fifty-two and Mum was forty-five and, clearly, life had impelled them on. During the time I had been away Dad had decided that while we still farmed Maera Station, the family should move back permanently to the house in Haig Street. "I can keep the farm going by working it during the week," he told us.

It was a puzzling move and even today my sisters and I can't understand it. He had already let Bulla go and, although Uncle Puku was still with him, were there continuing financial problems? Or was he falling out with his brother? Dad was such a proud man, he never spoke about the matter.

Having loved the farm so much, Mum grieved.

2.

Sometimes you think that life only goes by where you are and stops everywhere else. But life had clearly moved on — for all of us.

While Kararaina, Tāwhi and Viki were still, as Iris Whaanga called them, "Witi's sisters", Kararaina was twenty-two and, returned from teacher's college, began her career at Te Karaka Primary School. She was also being romanced by Gan Haapu, a military boy back from Malaysia.

Tāwhi had gone to Wellington. After high school (and a year at the Church College), she hadn't been able to find a job in Gisborne.

As for Viki, she was shearing and had met shearer Hore Lewis.

A consequence of my sisters' maturity was that they all began to have issues with Mum, mainly to do with her absolutist views. So I don't want you to get the idea that my mother was without blemish. There were times when she could not escape the way life had treated her as a young girl. Loving, she was also a disciplinarian. For instance, like other women of her generation she had certain expectations of my sisters. They had to remain virgins until marriage (nobody asked that of boys, of course, we were expected to sow wild oats). The question was, therefore, how many daughters of that generation managed to maintain that status, given the number of shotgun weddings; do the maths.

Another assumption was that daughters could not marry and (or) leave home until they had turned twenty-one. In Tāwhi's case, Mum's refusal to allow her to marry a boy who actually came to Haig Street to ask for her hand in marriage, was one of the reasons why she went to Wellington.

I assumed yet again I'd join Dad, helping him and Uncle Puku with the farm. "I can't afford you, son," Dad said.

What I didn't know was that the property wasn't paying its way and, instead of farming, Dad was scrubcutting and shearing; he had formed a new gang with Robbie Cooper. Soon he let Uncle Puku go.

Broke from my Auckland years I was therefore desperate for a job and found one short-term with Mrs Holdsworth, the matriarch of the Holdsworth family. I lived in a small whare on the property getting £10 a week plus board and food. I admired Mrs Holdsworth's grandeur — she could have come straight out of *Downton Abbey* — but she could never remember my proper name and called me Riki.

Yet another identity to add to the list.

Jim Holdsworth, her son, managed their estate, keeping his mother in the manner to which she was accustomed. He liked to look at the death notices to see if the poems that people wrote scanned properly. I didn't know until many years later how erudite Jim was, truly a "gentleman farmer" of impeccable intellectual mien. He had been a friend of my two koroua, Rongowhakaata Halbert and Te Kani Te Ua, and a stalwart of the local historical association.

Hiria came to stay with me on the Holdsworths' farm. I like to think that we were still very much in love. Or, at least, I was in love with *her*. We had begun to talk about marriage and our relationship deepened.

My temporary job with Mrs Holdsworth over, on the off chance I went in to see Ted Dumbleton, the chief editor of the *Gisborne Herald*. The newspaper from time to time employed a cadet reporter, but they already had someone filling that position.

Disappointed, I tried the Gisborne City Council, the Gisborne Harbour Board and Gisborne's local radio station broadcasting from Peel Street. I would have loved to join station manager Keith Bracey, senior announcer Leo Jervis and Māori announcer (and famed waiata composer) Bill Kerekere; my cousin Hēnare Te Ua had already left to take up a position with head office in Wellington — but 2XG had just appointed Derek Fox as their Māori recruit for the year. I suspect that Derek was more naturally suited than me to radio, and he proved it by going on to ascend the poutama of broadcasting to national acclaim.

At a loose end, I had a good friend in Ben Milner, an up-and-coming rugby star working as a farm agent for Dalgetys; he was a more appropriate friend than Jackson, less of a hell raiser. I was just about ready to try Army Headquarters again (I had tried first before I went to university) when I got a call from the *Herald*. The position as cadet reporter was now vacant. Would I like it? Would I what.

3.

Fifty years later. *Bien joué, Witi,* read the headline of the *Gisborne Herald,* 20 July, 2017, *Well played!* The occasion was my induction into the French Order of Arts and Letters as a chevalier and, because

I had always been something of a favourite son, the *Herald* liked to celebrate with me. I have never been anybody else to them but Witi.

And I owe them big time. In lieu of the kinds of programmes in creative writing that university students are able to do these days, my stint at the *Herald* allowed the next best thing — a career in journalism.

I spoke with John Jones, now in his seventies, who had been chief reporter at the *Herald*. Now mostly retired, John still kept his hand in by writing car reviews and covering the occasional local body meeting.

Not having kept a diary, I wanted to establish with John that I had, in fact, been on staff in 1967; all we could gauge was that it was definitely after 1965. I may therefore be out with the chronology, I could have started as a reporter in 1966 — so much was happening in that chaotic descent of mine — but I *was* there.

"You couldn't have chosen a better place than the *Herald* to start climbing again," John chuckled. "Did you know that way back then, it was regarded as one of the best, if not *the* best, newspapers in the country?" That was such a great reputation for a provincial newspaper during the heydays of print media. Geoff Muir, managing director, was one of the astonishing "*Herald* Muirs". They were a pioneering family of publishers whose story warrants a television history series. Among them was Robin, who ventured further afield to co-found the Canterbury Pegasus Press. The chief editor, Ted (Dumbleton), had been an army man. He favoured tweed jackets, smoked a pipe, and was a Jack Hawkins type who could have made movies for J Arthur Rank.

"They were real newspapermen in those days," John continued.

I grew up with Michael Muir, whose wife Ann established Muirs Bookshop on Gladstone Road, which, like the newspaper, became one of the best bookshops in the country. Their son Jeremy is now the *Herald*'s editor, exploring ways to keep the independent newspaper — one of the few left in the country — in business, including on-line publication.

"Do you remember your mates?" John continued.

I had told him I was writing about the office and asked how he would like to be described. He wrote back, "Adjectives that can be attached to my name include impressive, sagacious and even strikingly handsome if you are feeling generous." His sense of humour was still intact.

Jack Jones — John's father — was chief reporter at the time, and John and Iain Gillies were his deputies. Jack gave me what was known as "The Morning Calls", which required me to get to the office earlier than the others. I entered the building from the back doors where, in the afternoons, as a paperboy, I had waited for the newspapers for delivery.

Up the stairs to my desk I'd start telephoning. The fire station (to see if there had been any fires during the night). The hospital (any car crashes or other medical emergencies?). The police station (any major criminal activity). The airport (to check flight times and delays). The meteorological office (to get a weather update; from memory the office was at the airport) and the harbour board (to see what coastal vessels were expected).

My desk was hard on the left as you entered one of the two reporters' rooms. Mr (Jack) Jones would come bustling in and then Iain, John and my Gisborne Intermediate school friend "Spud" Arthur, already a reporter. When Spud left the *Herald* he became senior journalist for the Financial Times Group in London.

Percy Muir was the chief sub, the man who checked our stories. Percy was punctilious and seemed to know the initials of every person in Gisborne — he'd send misspelt names back to reporters for correction. Jenny Bain covered women's news (the activities of such as the Country Women's Institute). Alan Peake and Bev Davy operated the photographic section, and Bev was the first woman ever employed in that role. She was given a scooter, but kept falling off it so the bosses decided that a car would be safer — and gave her one.

Following my reports to Jack, my main activities were focused on the machine which spat out the New Zealand Press Association news (incorporating Reuters). The NZPA reports came clattering out of the the teleprinter and I sped them by hand to Ted or Jack. But mostly, in the first months, I was assigned to Percy and his fellow subeditor Jim Murdoch. They were the ones who taught me to write.

"You were taught by the best," John chuckled.

I certainly was. Apart from verifying correct grammar, spelling and house style, Percy and Jim edited for precision, brevity and concision. According to John, Jim Murdoch was "priceless", creating good tight copy, the best sub he had ever worked with.

I was then given over to the two copyholders who checked the printed copy before the go-ahead was given to print. They were elderly ladies (well, they looked old to me in those days) and I wasn't keen on spending most of the day with, well, women.

I sat on one side of a slanted board reading from the various takes that the reporters had sent in and which had been column printed. The ladies and I read for any errors the printer may have made and, because we were like weavers shuttling words back and forth, I called them "The Ladies of the Loom".

"Speak up, lad," May Gillies would say, "I canna hear what you're sayin', och, your accent is atroh-shus." She could talk.

And I had to articulate in a special way. For example: "Mr capital M, Charles Adams cap C cap A, Adams with an s, of 62 Number 6 Number 2 Henley cap H, Crescent cap C, Kaiti cap K, was yesterday found lying in Gladstone cap G, Road cap R the victim of a hit and run no hyphens accident estimated by Police cap P to have occurred at 3 am number 3, last evening full stop."

May's colleague, Jean Colebrook, was not as peremptory. Although not Scottish, she would ask, "Do roll your Rs a bit . . . for May's benefit, there's a dear boy."

After a while I simply melted in their presence. They were like Whaitiri come to life in two (young) Pākehā women. From Jean I learnt to ask the five Ws and the one H: who, what, where, when, why and how. May showed me how to craft the purr-fect sentence of the Scottish kind, to ensure that there was always a subject and a vurr-b and to aim always for clarr-ity on the page as well as in the intention.

Sadly, irony had no place in their armoury, and the consequence is that, ever since, my writing is direct and unambiguous. What you read is what you get. And, sorry May, sentences don't need to have vurr-bs now.

Jean absolutely loved copyediting Ted Dumbleton's editorials. They seemed to have a special relationship going, concerning not only what he was writing in his editorials but also how he wrote it. Usually, the editorial was the last to be subbed before being okayed for print. The whole universe stopped while Jean checked the text — not only for grammar and spelling but, more importantly, for whether the subject was worthy or not of a highly respected editor and newspaper.

And if the subject was *not* worthy, woe betide Mr Dumbleton. Into his office Jean would go to upbraid him. "Mr Dumbleton, you cannot release this! You would bring disgrace to your profession! What are you thinking, man?"

We worked 7.30 am to 4.30 pm most days and then went to have a drink at the Coronation Hotel. Most of the talk was about sport — rugby or football. Iain Gillies, for instance, had been brought over to New Zealand by Ron Johnson to play centre half for Gisborne City. Eventually his whole family joined him, mother, father, two brothers and sister. I went along with them to the local Caledonian Club, dancing my tiny feet off, and there discovered my own Scottish blood — after all, I was a Babbington. Whenever I hear the rallying cry "Scotland Forever!" I raise my fist with pride along with everybody else.

Very soon I was given small stories to write: a report on a bring-and-buy, a gymkhana, a cat rescued from a tree, a swimming carnival, a prize pig at a local agricultural show.

"I remember you filing a story," John said, "and saying you felt like a real writer now. However, anybody could see that you were not a fire-engine chaser."

I felt a little disappointed by his assessment. But after thinking his opinion through, I realised he was right. The short, swift storytelling of reportage was not my métier. I needed the long story form. And so I did what most reporters dream of: although I began my publishing career as a reporter I made the crossover to novelist.

I like to think that I realised many a reporter's dream for them.

4.

And now the tika.

Recently, in 2017, I told Kararaina that I had discovered Dad's notes about Maera Station and the perilous situation which had developed over its finances from the 1950s — and especially around 1967.

Here's how Dad himself described those minatory years. His account is written in clear handwriting in one of the exercise books that he wrote his memories in. It's a précis which doesn't make sense unless you follow the spiral of memory from 1956, and I include it in this memoir because it exemplifies the huge difficulties that farmers were facing during the 1960s and 1970s. The punctuation is Dad's own, I haven't altered it — and he must have written it after 1967 because he uses decimal currency:

> After 5 years my flock [in 1956] had increased to 500 sheep. My firm was Dalgety's. I was operating on cash somehow. Dalgety's were paying my rent & supplying me with the necessities like sheep drenches etc. My first two years I bought a crutching plant & shore my sheep on the property packed the wool down a steep gully across the Waikohu river onto my six wheeler truck baled it at Tangihanga Station & then to Dalgety's. I built a little hut on the property. I packed all the timber a mile & 1/2 onto the block. I was lucky. I am a bush carpenter. So this was the story of my life. Mum used to come & camp with me & the kids do the wool work and back to Haig St for the kids school.
>
> By 1956 I had worked a good relationship with Dalgety's. They said I needed cattle I said I have no money. They bought 100 cows for me. My a/c pumped up to about £20,000 pounds at that time. No mortgages or anything between me & Dalgety's. We operated on trust alone. Nothing signed. I guess they trusted me. I sent all my wool in to them. Sheep cattle sold by them. From 1951 — 1980 [the figure could be 1986, as Dad has gone over the 0 or 6 so that I can't tell]. All these years we operated on trust & goodwill. Boundary fences were repaired and internal one's a little scrub cut etc.
>
> Then Rural Bank came in [this must have been in the late 1950s or early 1960s] to help develop the land. Dalgety's all for it. A loan of $280,000 Dollars was allocated. Dalgety's decided to buy sheep etc. I said no, nothing has been signed. My A/c at this time was down to $14,000 dollars.
>
> Dalgety's said it's O.K. we'll buy & start the operation. I had 1,000 breeding ewes & 500 replacement stock, 50 cows, stock enough assets to cover my debt of 14,000 dollars.
>
> Dalgety's bought over 2500 ewes @$32 Dollars ea. Cut 500 acres scrub. Did it ourselves. I protested about too many sheep. Fences needed to be done. They said it's O.K. we'll supply materials. I see the a/c going up & up & up.
>
> They sent carpenters up to repair roof of the home. They the carpenters worked over the weekend. I was living in town [so we are now around 1968 or 1969]. My daughter Carol [Kararaina] &

Geo [George] were on the farm. I arrived Monday on the farm to do some work. I saw the carpenters finishing off the roof. Jobs done. Then the carpenters moved to the woolshed.

I said what are you doing. They said build a $3000 dollar night pen onto the woolshed. I said no. They said firm authorise them to do it, I said no if you go ahead I won't be responsible for the debt. The Rural Bank paying for it. I said find out but if you build it I won't be responsible. Nothing signed. They rung & came back packed their gear & went home.

To cut long story off I held the lease myself. John Kinder the lawyer said for me to transfer the lease to Dalgety's as they were wanting to give me fencing materials for fencing. I signed it over to them in 1978 and a year later they sold me up. The a/c had risen to $120,000 dollars. I guess they couldn't see how they were going to get their money. Stock had decreased in value the sheep they sold fetched $18 dollars a drop from $32-00. Big sheep losses no fences too many mixed maybes [?] They sold the freehold, I was lucky my home in 11 Haig was freehold no mortgage on it. The rural bank reneged on the deal. After everything was sold I found I was still owing about $50,000 to Dalgety's with no income no land to service the debt.

I went to Maori Affairs to borrow $50,000 dollars money to repurchase the Freehold block on this side of the river. They loaned me $38,000 dollars I had to find the rest. Thank you Maori Affairs for your help.

"Why didn't Dad tell me?" I asked Kararaina. "Why didn't he tell us? We could have all helped out." I had always been inordinately proud of Dad for having been one of the very few mid-twentieth-century Māori to have had his own sheep and beef cattle farm.

"You know our father," Kara answered. "He always thought he could manage his own affairs. And he had his neighbours, especially old man Devine, who gave Dad a hand in fattening the stock so that they would get a better price at the saleyards."

"I would have come back from Wellington to help out," I said.

"Don't you understand anything?" she answered. "We were *all right*, and then Gan and I began to manage the farm. Your coming back would have been the last thing Dad wanted."

Chapter Thirty-Two

My Grandfather's Successor

1.

And then the business of Toroa comes up and out of nowhere.

You turned from me, Grandad had said to me in Auckland.

A fist to your face. A punch to your guts. A slam to your heart. A chop at your throat.

You are told there's a new fella in town. He walks around with your grandad and uncles. The whānau at Waituhi slap him on the back, Hey boy, good to see you.

Fuck, you already have the physical presence of the rapist to contend with.

And then you hear that Pera Punahāmoa has adopted him. Made Toroa his whāngai, his grandson. Brought him into the family. Toroa is his successor now.

People are saying, "Not Witi or Puke but the *other* son."

You can smell Toroa on the air. You can't understand why your father is letting it happen. To all appearances, despite his earlier promise, he has not dealt with it. Why is he hurting your mother in this way?

You picture yourself at the carved portal of Poho-o-Rāwiri meeting house, looking in. It is the early 1940s and the meeting house is crowded with young men, both Pākehā and Māori. They are looking across the huge divide of the dance floor at the pretty girls. Alas, to reach the object of their desire they must get past the stern old women, chaperones sitting around the perimeter or on guard to stop the girls sneaking out with a dangerous boy. There is an orchestra playing on the flower-decked stage, some Glen Miller tune — you make it "Moonlight Serenade". A group of young men are smoking near the band and a few daring girls join them, and the haze of the smoke gives the scene a romantic golden glow.

Suddenly there's a break in the crowd and, on the dance floor, two couples are dancing. As they waltz past each other, one of the girls whispers to the other girl — and they swap partners. The other girl is your mother. She sees you watching and her eyes twinkle with humour. "So you've come to spy on me and your father, have you?"

She is slim and attractive in a shimmering sequinned dress. Whenever she moves the sequins flash like tiny mirrors. Her high heels make her stand straight; she wears a necklace of greenstone shards. Her hair is thick, full and a bit untamed because the sparkling butterfly comb she usually wears has a broken clasp. She has made herself up very lightly, a dash of lipstick and that is all. She used to say that Pākehā makeup slid off Māori faces.

As for your father he looks dangerous, with somewhat slanted eyes and shining black hair. He wears a shirt, tie and double-breasted suit with the hint of a handkerchief in the top pocket. No doubt about it, this boy's dressed to kill. He holds your mother easily.

You love your father so much, but you stop the music and stop the dancing. The band puts down its instruments. The haze drifts between the couples. Everyone is watching you.

"Take your hands off my mother."

2.

Rightly or wrongly you feel that they — at Waituhi — are messing you around. Your mana is being usurped. Although you are Dad's legitimate eldest son, Pera's machinations are looking awfully like the testing of that legitimacy and, by extension, your rights by whakapapa, implicit and explicit, of succession.

You remember the day you and Dad had come across a grieving ewe and its dead lamb. In metaphorical terms you feel that Grandad has found an orphan and put the dead lamb's coat on it and the flock has accepted it. But you aren't dead.

Yes, you may have been self-destructive but, in this serious matter involving whakapapa, ironically, Pera becomes the agent by which you begin to fight for yourself.

You have the matter out with Te Haa.

"I thought you had dealt with Grandad," you say to him. "But now he has adopted Toroa."

"Are you questioning me, Witi? You owe me more respect."

"Dad," you persist. "Pera has acknowledged him, do I need to spell it out? It might be a whāngai arrangement, a customary adoption, but whatever it is, Toroa's a Smiler now."

"You're taking this too seriously," Dad answers. "I have talked to Pera and told him how much his actions are hurting us. You know your grandad, he's a law unto himself."

"What about Toroa? Have you told *him*?"

"There hasn't been the chance."

"If you're my father—"

"*If*?"

"—and if you love me and my mother, prove it. Tell Toroa before all this gets worse."

Whatever Dad does — or says — doesn't work. People are asking, "Why hasn't Tom accepted Toroa? Pera does."

The following weekend you hear Toroa is with Uncle Puku preparing for a hui at Pākōwhai marae in the Waituhi Valley.

Dad is there too. Perhaps he has gone to "fix it".

You don't know what the hui is about, but you are recklessly determined, hell-bent for leather. You take an extended break from the *Herald* for lunch and drive out to Waituhi. Sometimes you are decisive to the point of stupidity.

You park the car on the road and stride in. The last time you were at Pākōwhai marae was some years ago when you had to kill a piglet, a rite of passage into manhood. *Please stop squealing. Stop squealing. Stop. Please stop. The sooner you stop the sooner it will be all over.*

The marae is crowded with villagers. Good. If you're going to take any action about Toroa, let it be as publicly as possible to all within listening range. Nothing can stop you from acting on your opportunities, can it?

As soon as the people of Waituhi see you, they begin to smile and greet you. They are puzzled when you push through them towards Dad.

"Hello, son," he says. "We've just finished lunch. Are you staying?"

"Which one is Toroa?" you ask him. "Have you told him yet?" Your eyes are already searching the crowd.

Immediately Dad stiffens. "If you've come to make trouble, son, this is the wrong time to do it."

"When will there ever be a right time, Dad?" you ask him.

"Toroa is my business, son. I'll tell him my way. Stay out of it."

"Sorry, Dad, but it *is* my business. If you can't handle it, I will. My mana is at stake. And after all, what have you got to lose by telling the truth. Is Toroa my brother?"

"I have already told you, no."

"That's all I need to know. Now which one is he? And why don't I tell everyone now, while they're all here?" You don't wait for an answer. "Good."

"Witi, no."

But you have already seen Toroa, you would have recognised him anywhere. And you can't be stopped. You thread your way towards him. There is no doubt that he is striking in the old Māori way. His bearing is regal and his neck and ear ornaments are redolent of the classical Māori.

No wonder Pera has adopted him. He is everything that you aren't.

But something's wrong. Toroa's happiness in seeing you — this is the first time you have ever met personally — is so unguarded, that you falter. All this time you have fabricated an enemy in the abstract. In the reality he appears softer, kinder, somebody who under different circumstances you might have been friends with.

You mustn't think of him in this way. If you do, you might start to sympathise with him and, perhaps, to like him enough to think he *could* be your brother.

"Tēnā koe," you say to him.

You can hear a pin drop as you press your nose to his. *Oh, isn't this lovely, isn't it nice, two siblings acknowledging each other.* Tears begin to run down his cheeks. He tries to embrace you. Instead you push him away.

"This is the first and last time I will greet you," you tell him. "Stay away from my family."

Somewhere in the universe you hear a snapping sound as if a thread has broken.

And it is at this point that Pera arrives.

"You dare to intervene between me and my whāngai," Pera says to you. "You know nothing of my relationship with his family—"

Pera has support. Uncle Puku and your cousins come to shove you away. "Pokokōhua, Witi," you hear somebody shout. "We'll boil your head."

Let them curse you. What the fuck do you care? And where's Dad? "Pera may have adopted you, I can't stop that," you say to Toroa. "But I know what he's up to—"

"You know nothing," Pera says.

You turn on your grandfather. "Are you trying to put him in my place? Is this how you punish me, Pera? Don't think that bringing Toroa here to Waituhi will legitimise him." Oh, you are the smart-aleck boy who has learnt too much up at that Pākehā university, eh.

"Using your fancy talk doesn't cut it here," someone yells at you.

And Grandad has staked the ground; he holds it. "Toroa will be my heir."

You challenge him. "But why now? You've had all your life to do this, why choose this moment?"

"I gave you your chance when I was in Auckland," Grandad answers. "You didn't want it. You didn't take it."

Had you misunderstood that meeting? You thought it was only to do with helping him find longjohns. Was it more than that? Was there something he asked you, and you hadn't heard or didn't want to hear? You were always talking past each other. Or not saying what you thought you were saying.

Your head is whirling. And when you answer, your voice is guttural and spittle sprays. "Do what you like," you answer. "Appoint any heir you like, I am Teria's."

And then your father, shocked, separates you both. "Whakahīhī, Witi, you are out of place here." He pushes Pera back, "Dad, enough." And then he pleads with you: "Witi, go home. This is for me to sort out with Pera, Toroa, my brothers and sisters."

"Then do it, Dad." Your lips curl with disgust. "Please clean up your fucking mess."

But you can't help having the last vicious word. "You wouldn't have had the guts to do this," you say to your grandfather, "if my grandmother was alive."

Shouldn't you take some of the blame too?

Your father married your mother in 1943, and you know they were faithful to each other all their lives. Only after they were married did your mother discover that he was father to Puke, and there must have been the rumours of another boy even then. Whether Dad told her or she found out because somebody told her, you don't know; you suspect the latter. When you confronted your father he said, "I loved your mother." He was panicking. "If I had told her about me she would never have married me, don't you understand?"

Yes, you understood. Life had caused Turiteretimana Keelan to adopt a position of absolute moral certainty. And so, if Tom Smiler had told her before they were married that he had fathered another child, possibly two, she would have said, "No, I can't marry you."

She would have lifted her face to the light and, no matter that she loved him, defended herself.

Indeed, she made that absolutely clear when, upon arriving in Gisborne from Hastings after their wedding, and being confronted with the fact that your dad had fathered another son, she left him at the railway station. She returned home to her parents in Uawa. Despite your father's pleading she would not return to him. Your mother always lived in the light, in absolute clarity and acuity. She was so proud, and the fact of your dad having children out of wedlock diminished her. She was strong in maintaining her certainties. Christian, you have always been convinced that if she had lived in Roman times she would have gone gladly to the lions.

And then she discovered she was pregnant with you. So did your grandmother Teria, who made the decision to take your side in all things, even if it meant going against Pera.

Admit it. Your grandfather and you were pitched against each other from the day you were born.

Chapter Thirty-Three

Decision at Rongopai

1.

The record will show I gave my notice at the *Gisborne Herald*.

I became a postie, picking up mail from the city mailboxes and taking them back to the Central Post Office for sorting. Somebody there found out that I had six units of a degree and suggested that I take a management course at Trentham, near Wellington.

I had already planned to leave Gisborne anyway. Lick my wounds. Reinvent myself. Or maybe I was just trying to keep myself together sexually.

Dit *der* dit *der* dit *der* dit *der*
Der dit *der* dit *der* dit *der* dit
All of these things.

The evening before I left, I told Mum and Dad that I was going out to Waituhi.

My family knew that I wanted to say goodbye to Rongopai meeting house. All my life, whenever I was in Gisborne, the first thing I did was to go out to the whare; and when I left the city, I always said goodbye. Rongopai was my lodestone, my compass point at Waituhi.

"I'll come with you," Dad said. "You're not exactly flavour of the month out there."

"I can look after myself," I answered.

These days one or two or all of my sisters come out with me and, while I am at Rongopai, they go up to the graveyard to do some weeding around the graves and to say hello to all our tūpuna.

"I have to fill the troughs for the cattle," Dad said. "The water's low."

Good. I wanted to talk to him anyway.

2.

I've always said that if you want to know what my heart looks like, look to Rongopai.

Dad dropped me off at the gate and away he went to do his mahi. The sun was just going down, but the meeting house was still inviting in the falling light. I stepped onto the porch, opened the door and walked through.

Greeted all the ancestors. Closed my eyes. Breathed in and out. Surrendered.

"I've come to tell you all something," I told them.

Ever since I was a child, Teria had encouraged me to talk to the whare. I never grew out of the habit of kōrero, of sitting in the dark having a conversation with the ancestors on the panels along the walls.

"I have decided to leave Waituhi, to go away from Gisborne altogether."

There, I had made my admission and now I had to explain.

"Too many things have happened to me lately and . . . I have reached a point of understanding. What I have come to is this: I will never be the kind of tribal person who can rise to leadership in the valley."

I paused, trying to collect my thoughts.

"All my life I had thought that this was what Teria wanted. And maybe, if she were still here, she would have supported me to become a leader — her successor. But she died. And that pathway has become closed. Even if the pathway was open, I just don't have the qualifications. My reo is ratshit. I don't know how to whaikōrero. I've never had the same skills as other boys. You've all seen how hopeless I am at the haka. I go left when the men go right, or go forward when they retreat. And I'm not going to get any better."

Talking to the panels, unburdening myself.

"And now the events of the past few months have shown I can never be *anybody*'s successor," I continued. "Not Teria's, not Pera's, not Waituhi's. I don't have anyone to champion me. To raise me up. In a strange way, I even understand Grandad's search for such a boy. And if I look at myself and Toroa, and his great skills, I can understand and sympathise with Pera. I am of no worth to Grandad."

The light falling. The shadows deepening.

"I've also tried to climb the Pākehā poutama but I am not equipped for that either! However... I have found a way, te ara auaha. But it does not lie here, in the valley."

I had said my piece. Me and Rongopai were never melodramatic with each other. I told the house everything — well, not quite, because there was one thing the ancestors would *never* know.

"Please don't worry about me. I will be all right."

It was time to leave. I went out the door. Shut it. Looked across the landscape. Shivered, though the twilight wasn't cold, because what I had just done felt like I had put myself into exile and banished myself to te whakarau.

And the clouds swirled across the sky, casting strange patterns like fleeting kōwhaiwhai designs across the earth. My heart was thundering with longing for Teria. I wanted her to be there with me again, taking my hand and filling my life with splendour.

"Grandmother, you said you would live forever."

It had been so difficult to live without her.

And suddenly, the clouds changed. I was walking on a long-ago day with Teria. We were looking across the greenstone land. The kōwhaiwhai in the sky swirled a pattern of calm, such calm.

"Kia kaha," Teria whispered. "Kia manawanui."

Her voice struck the reverberating drum of the land. Her face, veiled, was mysterious. Her beauty shone out of her with a gleaming light that you could almost touch and feel. It vibrated and electrified the air.

"E Witsh, haven't you understood anything?' Teria asked. "Life carries on, all the mana and the tapu of it does not wax and wane at birth and death and birth again. They are passed from generation to generation through whakapapa and I have already passed them to you. Open your eyes, grandson. Nothing can take them away. Nothing."

That was when it happened, and I felt it happen. One moment I was looking at the hills and bush, and then I blinked and looked again and the world had undergone a transformation. I saw into the essence of things. I saw the gleaming sap of the trees and I saw the blood coursing through my veins, and both were one and the same. I saw the geological formations of the earth, and the interlocking structures were one and the same with the gleaming cellular composition of my body. The movement of the light and wind and cloud were the same as my own life forces. The heartbeat of the earth was no different from the rhythm of my own beating heart.

Then I looked up into the heavens and saw worlds being created beyond this earth, and the creation of new suns and nebulae were the same as the worlds in my blood. I was in the universe and the universe was in me.

Suddenly, I felt myself being lifted into the universe and I began to be afraid and wanted to cry out. I was spiralling back through the many changes of day, into Te Pō and the many changes of night. The light began to diminish, ever diminish, until all was utter and complete blackness. So black it was that I felt as if I had no form or shape at all. The blackness was me and I was the blackness. With the blackness came ice, cold and the sense of dread, and I knew that I had reached Te Kore, The Void. The Nothingness.

Then, "Kia kaha, kia manawanui," a voice said.

I heard a karanga and I saw that it was Teria. She was calling me to return. From one generation of the tribes of man to the next, generation upon generation. The light grew brighter and brighter as I spiralled through the many changes of day.

And then Teria spoke to me again. The clouds were swirling in the sky, casting strange patterns across the hills.

"E Witsh, listen," Teria said. Her voice was not unkind. "The mana and the tapu remain. They are not something that can be seen with the eye but with the heart, soul and intellect. It doesn't matter whether you stay or go, whether you are here or there, they are always yours."

I heard Dad returning on his truck, the dogs barking. When I went out to join him, he said, "Rongopai will be here when you get back." His eyes were twinkling.

My father didn't realise that right at that moment our relationship was at the lowest ebb it had ever been in our lives. I could have smashed him, I was so angry. Instead, helpless with love, I managed only enough strength to square off with him.

"I'm not coming back Dad," I said. "Not until you have sorted out this business with Grandad."

He was shocked at the force of the words, and stepped back as if I had hit him.

I loved my father and he loved me, but he was a careless man, and I felt I was fighting for my life. I would not take any further equivocation from him.

"You don't mean it," he said.

Would he never understand?

"The trouble is, I do," I answered.

The next morning, though, your mother, oh, the mother you loved more than anybody in the world, didn't understand.

She lifted her face to the light. Her cheekbones were prominent, her eyes deep and staring. "Do you really have to go?" she asked, challenging you. "Why can't you stay at home where I can see you? You're running away from me . . . or something. What is it, son? What is it?"

You couldn't look her in the face. "This has nothing to do with you," you whispered.

But, really, it had everything to do with her. How were you to know that when you were born you had given her no choice? You had forced her to compromise everything she believed in. She who would otherwise have said to your father, "No, I will not stay with you," had to say, "Yes."

You had to get away because you were ashamed you had done this to her.

She was looking at you as if some malevolent hobgoblin had taken charge of her boy.

"Nothing?" She stepped forward and stared into your eyes and you couldn't avoid her gaze. "I see, nothing, eh," she said in a contemptuous way. "Well then, do what you want."

And then she took Dad's side. "This is the way our son rewards his loving parents."

She went into the bathroom. When she came back with water, she literally threw handfuls at you, the water stinging. Oh Mum, I'm so sorry.

She was in her usual way blessing you, but you knew she didn't mean it. Instead of flaying you with love she may as well have used acid.

"Go then," she said.

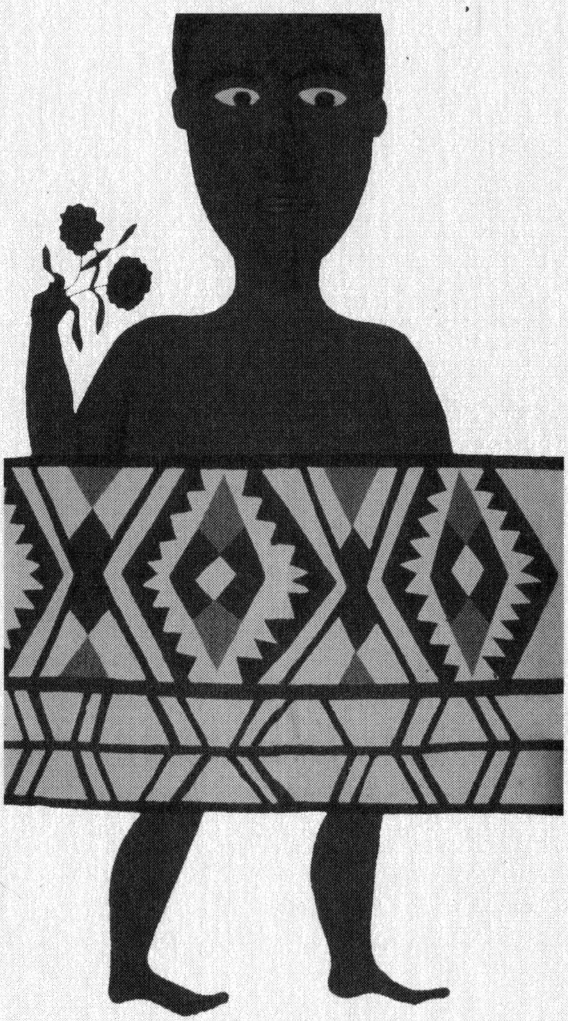

PART FOUR

TE ARA AUAHA
THE CREATIVE WAY

Chapter Thirty-Four

The Time When Blood Began to Flow

1.

You will recall my telling you about Tāwhaki. It was he who brought the sacred baskets of knowledge down from the heavens — though some other tribal traditions attributed this feat to Tāne, god of man, which he achieved in a previous epoch.

In the baskets was all the wisdom handed down by the gods so that humankind could flourish, generation upon generation in Te Ao Tūroa, the atua-created lands made for them. Once so actively involved in the creation of the world, the gods now began, more or less, to leave the Māori race to its own devices. I say more or less because the gods bequeathed to us the regulations — practices of tapu, protocols and other laws — by which we, their creation, could balance the relationships with our own kind and, especially, all our environments. Their regulations enabled proper iwitanga and kaitiakitanga.

The atua remained in Hawaiki, the Māori Valhalla, looking over their race of playthings, their great creation, their worlds without end — and they didn't mess with us as much. Anyhow, the Māori race was already battling between themselves in much the same way as their makers did. I suspect the gods delighted in this, as if they were watching themselves on a huge chessboard.

2.

It is Tāne who is credited with creating the first man. This is the same Tāne, you will remember, who makes the first woman, Hineahuone, mates with her, and fathers the daughter Hinetītama, who becomes Hinenuitepō, the great lady of Te Pō.

Clearly, our Lord needs to establish a second line, one that will lead to generations upon generations of men and women, and thus he creates a certain being he names Tiki. Tāne presses noses with his invention and says, "Kia ora, come alive." When he sees that Tiki has started to breathe and has opened his eyes, Tāne says, "Tēnā koe, there you are."

These are the original meanings of the kupu, kia ora and tēnā koe. Today they are generally translated as hello and . . . hello. In such ways are the mythical meanings submerged.

Now clearly Tiki requires a mate, and some versions say that her name is Iwi or Kōiwi. The latter name translates as "the living self" and relates to the assumption that she is made from Tiki's left rib. Sound familiar? It may be *too* familiar. So let us just say that Tāne makes her as an equal to her husband. It is only later (male) scholarship that relegates her role to the secondary position. However, two other versions give Tiki his own agency and either one is much to be preferred.

In the first version, Tiki mixes his own blood with clay to create a woman. The second, having a narcissistic subtext, is intriguing to say the least. In this version, Tiki lives a lonely life without a partner. We are not told how long he lives like this, but he begins to crave companionship. He is overjoyed when he sees his reflection in a pool of water, but his joy quickly fades when he dives in . . . and (the comparison with the story of Narcissus cannot be missed) the image shatters.

What are we to make of this? That man has, from the very beginning, sought man as his companion? All we are told is that in his anguish, Tiki covers the pool with earth — soil or loam being associated with the Earth Mother and, therefore the "bed" from which life can spring. It is the earth which gives birth to a female companion (though some translations say "dirt" which gives a negative connotation).

Whatever the story, the union is consummated. And Tiki and Kōiwi's son is named Kapiri. One of the meanings of his name, To Weave, points to his purpose as one of the progenitors of humankind.

Māori have a stunning image to accompany this transition. Our elders may very well have pinpointed with deadly accuracy the difference between gods and men. With astounding aptness they define the period of changing from one state to another — the metamorphosis — as Te Oho Hemorere. It's the time when Blood Began to Flow.

Chapter Thirty-Five

First, a New Iwi

1.

This may sound an odd thing to say but I think, when I was twenty-three in 1967, the needle on the gauge of my life was moving out of the red. I was no longer as much a danger to myself as I had been. It was the age when I was able to embrace my dangerous compulsions, understand them and move past them into the clear.

I finally came to terms with the person I was or, rather, the *persona* I would adopt.

And so, that year, I went to Wellington. Over the rainbow, if you like, arriving to an unbelievable halcyon summer. Straight off the NZR bus, I headed out to Island Bay. I wanted to go for a swim and, in the process, say a karakia while standing in the water. The day was absolutely stunning. Teal-blue ocean surmounted by an impossibly blue sky. Taputeranga, the island, was picture-perfect, and bobbing in the waves were picturesque fishing boats.

Why, I wondered, was the beach deserted! Only me and a couple of Greek fishermen mending nets.

"You go for swim?" they asked.

I nodded my head, shucked off my clothes and dived in ... and my balls froze and fell off.

Tangaroa, do you want me to freeze to death today?

The water was the evil spawn of icebergs, straight from Antarctica. Quickly I offered up the required prayer of thanksgiving and hope for the future, and got out fast. Back on the beach I hoped the Greek fishermen would have pickaxes to chip me out of the ice.

They nodded to each other, laconically accepting the fact that I had returned. "He go in," one said.

"But he come out," the other added, disappointed.

2.

Down to business. I telephoned Hiria in Hastings to come to Wellington. In *The Arabian Nights* aka *One Thousand and One Nights* (first English-language edition 1706) comes the advice: "Do what your manhood bids you do. From none but self expect applause. He best lives and noblest dies, who makes and keeps his self-made laws."

Many years later, at some moment in the 1990s, I was in Canada with my friend, writer and academic Ngāhuia Te Awekōtuku. We had been invited to an indigenous peoples conference in Ottawa and had just successfully stage-managed a remit to acknowledge the cultural contribution of men and women of two spirits. Now, with a great sense of release, we were walking beside the St Lawrence River.

It was autumn, and the leaves were all shades of red and yellow. The wind was chill, and I was totally unprepared when, out of nowhere, Ngāhuia asked a question.

"When did you come out to yourself as a boy?"

Ngāhuia was one of the strongest and most political people I knew. She was a woman who was totally tūturu Māori. Protesting a Pākehā world which persisted in reinscribing its own hegemony was her — and my — obsession.

"I didn't," I answered. "My cultural registration was more important to me at the time than my sexual registration."

She looked at me, surprised at my answer. Ngāhuia had announced her lesbianism as a very young woman. In 1972 she had been refused a visa to enter the United States, an act that sparked the gay liberation movement in New Zealand. As we walked beside that dark, swirling river, she threaded an arm in mine.

"And now?"

"I've come out publicly," I answered. "Isn't that enough?"

Yes, even when I did come out — and openly — with the publication of *Nights in the Gardens of Spain* (1995), I still did not admit it to *myself*.

I'll be traversing this in my next memoir. Meantime, as *The Arabian Nights* recommended, I created a self-made law and committed myself to Hiria. To not do so before talking to her about becoming my wife would have been immoral. I would not do that to her.

But was it "best" and "noblest"? At the time, I believed so.

Hiria arrived in Wellington and she had become — I'm trying to think of a word to describe what she looked like — womanly. She was beautiful, curvaceous, and her warmth and sweetness made me believe that we could make a go of it.

For the first week we stayed with Uncle Mafeking, otherwise known as Maf, and Auntie Girlie in their big house in Hataitai. Auntie Girlie didn't seem to mind, and Uncle Maf asked me, "Is this serious?"

"Yes," I told him.

Uncle Maf was Hermes in the family pantheon, and he took to Hiria. He may have been one of the few family members who met her. There was something "Teria-like" about Hiria, he told me, noting her strong will and imperious nature.

One of the benefits of that visit was that I got to know my uncle better. Well known in Wellington as a billiards player, he also happened to be a bookie — but I didn't know that. I did wonder, however, about the reinforced doors and telephones in his office. One morning he had to go out for something and asked me to, as they say, look after the store.

"When any of the phones ring," he instructed, "answer them and take down the numbers that the callers will give you." He showed me the small slips of paper I was to write the amounts on.

I presumed the figures included the punter's ID, the race, the horse and the amount placed by the bettor. You know, 73/42/7/5000, or something like that.

"If the cops show up," he continued, "they'll take some time to get through the doors. Every piece of paper you have written on, eat it."

It was while I was staying with Uncle Maf that he tried to bribe me. He pretended he was paying me for my job, but I knew his tricks. When I refused his money he laughed, saying, "Maybe next time."

I never took money from anybody, and there would never be a next time.

As for Hiria, after three days of exploring what we really meant to each other and whether we were compatible, I asked her, "Will you marry me?"

She didn't answer straight away. It wasn't until I took her to the railway station to return to Hastings that she said, "I need more time."

When the train departed the station I wondered if there was something going on in her life — or someone else — but I never asked her.

After she left, I set off to find my sister Tāwhi. She had been staying with another uncle — Sid — who had told her to "Go to an employment agency."

The agency asked Tāwhi what job attracted her. "I'd like to work for a bank," she said.

"Oh, you mean the Post Office?"

"Too many Māori work there," she said. "I want to go to a Pākehā bank and find out what makes Pākehā tick."

Given that I had just arrived to continue my employment in the Post Office, her comment made me feel a bit awkward.

The agency must have been amused at Tāwhi's forthright opinion. They arranged an interview for her with the ANZ and then the Bank of New South Wales (now Westpac). One of her two references was ineligible as the small Four Square grocery store in Te Hapara which had supplied it had closed down. She rang Dad to get her a new reference, which he did, from accountant Henare Ngata; in *Māori Boy*, I mistakenly implied he was a lawyer.

Henare wrote, "I don't know Polly (my sister's Pākehā name) but I do know her father, Tom."

Typical, but it worked, and Tāwhi got a job with the Bank of New South Wales. The first thing my mother said to her was: "Don't you steal, eh Pol, because you're representing the Māori nation."

When I found her, Tāwhi had moved from Uncle Sid's place and was flatting around the corner. She was an effervescent girl and was taken up by our Keelan cuzzies from the East Coast.

They used to call me a townie. "So who's the townie now!" I said to my cousin Richard when we met at his flat in Wilson Street, Newtown.

Richard and my cousins were "dusties". Among them were Percy, Turi Kirikiri, Rangi, Joe, Jerry, Tai, Harvey Walker, Haua and Tommy. They were such a strong team of Coasties they kept other tribes out of the council's domestic rubbish collection biz. Whenever a new cuzzie showed up in town they would take him to the council and sign him on. Clambering up Wellington's steep hills and bringing the bins down to the trucks made them as fit as.

"All that running from the cops at Uawa," Richard winked.

And could they party? Could they what. Come payday Thursday, the bash began at Wilson Street and didn't finish until Monday when they went back to work.

A girl sat on my knee at one of them, and my cousin Rangi, drunk, wanted to punch my lights out.

I spent six weeks at Trentham to train for higher things in the Post Office. I joined savings bank trainees, telegraph operators-under-instruction, linesmen-in-training, telephone operators and would-be Post Office tellers and managers. Although we weren't there at the same time, my friend and colleague, Tony Watson from Whitianga in the Coromandel, was one of them. "I think the Post Office needed people to staff Wellington so they inveigled all us young men and women down to the capital," he laughed. "Compared to Whitianga and Waituhi, Wellington was much bigger."

On Fridays, one of the guys would ring any of the girls at the Telephone Exchange to find out where the best parties were. We crowded onto the suburban train to go into the city.

I successfully passed the management course and was interviewed about what jobs I might be interested in, if I stayed in Wellington. There were plenty of opportunities either at Central Post Office on Featherston Street, the Telephone Exchange not far along, or at the Regional Engineers Office and Accounts over in Herd Street. Post Office Headquarters on Waterloo Quay was added to the real estate later in the decade.

Two jobs as registry clerks were available in Savings Bank Division at Herd Street, and I scored the first of them. Tom Martindale was one of my peers, and among the bosses was a certain gentleman, Charlie Jelley, who, way before Wellington city pavements became crowded with joggers of all competencies and kinds, would be out at lunchtime running into the wind. In 1981 Charlie was veteran M60 athlete champion.

3.

My life expanded in other ways that surprised me. I moved from Uncle Maf's place to board in the Aro Valley at 6 Essex Street with my beloved Auntie Joey and her young son, Anthony. Auntie Joey was Aphrodite in the family pantheon, the beauty among the Smiler women. She, Uncle Win and Uncle Maf were the three of Dad's siblings who had made their lives in Wellington — and the reason why I had initially gone to university in Auckland, away from prying family eyes.

This was the same Auntie Joey who had appeared on the cover of the *New Zealand Listener* with The Beatles during their New Zealand tour in 1964, and she was soon on my case. She was managing Pendennis, a hostel for Māori girls (one of the girls who worked there, Rongo, runs the hostel now), and Auntie would find some way of inveigling me to meet her after work. Change the lightbulbs, carry heavy furniture, do some painting.

Although I had told her about Hiria, Auntie would conjure up a nice princess from Te Arawa. "You need a girlfriend in Wellington," she would say. "A bird in the hand, not one in the bush."

A number of candidates presented themselves, including Iwa, a laughing girl with stunning skin and bright sparkling eyes, except she turned out to be a cousin. No matter that she was three or four times removed, Iwa was still too close for Auntie's comfort.

As it was for many other young Māori of the time, Ngati Poneke Young Maori Club became my whare and my marae. Formed way back in 1937 when Wellington only had 336 Māori living in it, the club was an offshoot of a church mission society. During the war years it became the place where American GIs could come to haka boogie their tiny tits off.

The club's kapa haka group became Ngāti Pōneke's visible face. "The object of Ngati Poneke was not just dancing Maori dances and singing Maori songs," Kingi Tahiwi told the *Evening Post* in 1944. "It set out to make the best Maori there was for the good of New Zealand. It aimed to retain the best of Maori culture and to bring the Maori and pakeha closer together."

Ngāti Pōneke became famous in Māori lore because when the Maori Battalion went to war and sailed from Wellington, only their members were allowed through the locked gates to farewell the troops.

During the 1950s the rural-to-urban migration kept on booming, and so did Ngāti Pōneke. Other urban marae were established in Christchurch, Auckland and Dunedin. They became the first places that any homesick young Māori man or woman, looking for a brown face, could go to find one. In White Wellington it was a brown oasis. By the time I came along in the 1960s, the club was a Wellington institution.

Uncle Fred Katene was the resident kaumātua, and there was a range of kuia like Auntie Millie, Auntie Harata and Auntie Dovey ready with love, advice and — if there was a nice boy, whether or not he was looking for a girlfriend — matchmaker services.

One of those boys, my cousin Kani Horsfall from Waituhi, had witnessed the time I brought the village haka team down with my inept skills. He saw me auditioning (at Auntie Joey's insistence) and yanked his finger at me, "Oh no you don't. You, *out*." However, Ngati Poneke had a hockey team with some mean players, such as Bill Nathan (he became an equerry for the governor-general and his wife Donas was one of the best poi exponents ever) and George Parekōwhai, the father of sculptor Michael Parekōwhai and his equally talented sister Cushla. In boyhood, George had been raised with Dad for a time by Pani Tūrangi, a well-known Gisborne kuia.

I soon found myself playing on the left wing in Wellington's weather. The wind was far more efficient in turning me into an iceblock than the water at Island Bay.

4.

I have to say that I loved working for the Post Office.

In the mid-twentieth century it was an iwi, and the local post office in every city, town and village was the local marae. One of the government's principles was social responsibility, and the New Zealand Post Office, a government department with its own minister, took that principle seriously by keeping communities together and caring for one another. In its heyday, it distributed huge volumes of national and international mail; and if you want to know why New Zealanders are addicted to cellphones, in the 1960s we had one of the largest populations of telephone owners in the world.

Post offices were also places where, apart from registering births, marriages, deaths and cars, or paying your television and fishing licence fees, or enrolling to vote and collect your pension, or getting married (the postmaster could perform marriage ceremonies), you could also meet to have a bit of a natter.

And, according to Tony Watson, you could breastfeed your baby on the premises apparently. When a young Northland mother was doing that, and the baby was slow on taking the offer, the mother scolded, "Take my breast or I'll give it to the postmaster."

Yes, the Post Office was certainly a family.

And then Charlie Jelley discovered my work as a cadet reporter in the *Gisborne Herald*. He suggested that I would do better in Public Relations Division. "What do they do?" I asked him.

"Write speeches for the postmaster-general, press releases about new post and telegraph offices, put out a monthly magazine for the rest of us. They've had some poets and writers working for them. If you're interested . . . we'll put your name down."

A bunch of wankers, yep.

Whaitiri must have started to move some pieces around on a Māori chessboard.

You hear that Fred Leighton, one of the bosses in the Post Office's executive suite — he's an assistant director-general — is interested in the Māori boy who has fetched up in the firm. Very soon you are interviewed by Pete Smith, in charge of all the reporters. Public Relations has a large staff, and you come across Tom Martindale and your colleague and friend Tony Watson again.

The boys from Whitianga and Waituhi, yeah.

Whaddya know, Paul Katene, another Māori (and Mormon) is in the art section. The other journalists are a mix of colourful characters like Angela Griffin, the extraordinary John Berry, Jan and Ashley Conlon, Canadian Lorraine Hart, Nigel Fitzgerald and Cameron Scott.

"Make yourself at home," Pete says on your first day. You get the desk by the door, natch, regulation public-service size, not new but recycled. You fantasise that this was where James K Baxter or Marilyn Duckworth once sat. There's a typewriter on the desk, and Pete gives you your first assignment.

"Five hundred words," he instructs, "to go with the photograph of the stamp. We'll send it out tonight to all media, if Murray Hill at the Philatelic Bureau gives the release a tick. Nothing fancy, the stamp will sell the story."

You are taking off your jacket to drape over the back of your chair when you hear the young woman approaching before you see her. There's the sound of a door slamming and in she storms. She's late, not by much, but regulations are regulations and late is late.

Everybody looks at her, *Oh, it's Jane.* The interesting thing is that they leave her ay-*lone.* Even Pete.

The girl reminds you of the flower known as the amaryllis. (You make the mistake, some months later, of telling her this and she fair bites your head off.) The variety of hippeastrum that you are thinking of is the spectacular red pearl, with the blooms firm-standing atop tall, sturdy stems. She's a good-looking girl with long dark-brown hair, brown eyes, cheekbones, and she is wearing a red-purple dress, cerise maybe or merlot. Her complexion is what you think of as "colonial Pākehā". Not English rose, but sandier and sprinkled with freckles. She wears a brooch studded with purple garnets, hard, durable and brilliant.

Her desk is on the other side of the room, against the wall, and she seats herself at it or, rather, claims it. She's not yet ready to face the world, obviously, and you wonder about her weekend. Out of her bag she takes a small compact with a mirror and starts to blink into it. Although you later discover that she doesn't often use makeup, she is not averse to a bit of mascara.

While applying eyeliner, pushing back a wing of long brown hair, she suddenly cries out, "Fuck." She quickly goes down on her knees, showing a nice bit of leg, looking for something on the floor.

Nobody goes to see what the problem is. What should you do?

You're trying to make a good impression on everyone. So you walk across to her and you are just about to open your mouth to ask her, "Can I help?" when she looks up at you and says, "Stop, don't come any further."

She glares at you or, rather, you *think* she's glaring but, as you realise later, she is as blind as a bat. "You might step on it," she says.

You are puzzled, retreat carefully and leave her to her search. Step on what?

As you return to your desk you hear her say, "Found it."

When you look back you see she has her head upturned and is trying to put back into her left eye the contact lens that has popped out. Finally the mission is accomplished and she looks across the room at her would-have-been helper. You.

Oh, the new guy.

Chapter Thirty-Six

Empire City

1.

Do you know the European artist Gustav Doré's engraving *The New Zealander*?

It's a somewhat surreal dystopian illustration from *London: A Pilgrimage* (1872) by Blanchard Jerrold, and it shows a black-caped man looking upon that great city in the future, a London in decay, rotting and dying.

Author Christopher Woodward (in *In Ruins*, 2010) has an interesting interpretation of Doré's engraving. "The wizard-like figure ... is a traveller from New Zealand, for to many Victorians this young colony seemed to represent the dominant civilisation of the future. He sits on a broken arch of London Bridge to sketch the ruins of St Paul's, exactly as Victorian Englishmen sketched those of Ancient Rome."

Indeed, from the comfort of their armchairs, the English middle and upper classes looked with particular pride to Wellington. Because it appeared to epitomise all that they hoped for themselves, they called it Empire City.

2.

Of course Wellington was from the beginning a "company town". By that I mean that its company was Albion (Great Britain) and its business was colonialism. The New Zealand Company under Colonel William Wakefield had chosen the location for the first British settlement of the new colony, and the first settlers arrived on the *Aurora* on 22 January 1840.

Cut to 1967 and, while Wellington was not the largest New Zealand city, it had become the capital of the country. The usual accoutrements came with that rank. The Parliament, Te Paremata o te Pākehā. The world's embassies, consulates and legations. The city was to the nation what Ottawa was to Canada and Canberra to Australia. It had a larger status as a capital of the Commonwealth and, although the country repealed the statutes of Westminster in 1947, it still conducted its business to the letter and in the same spirit.

All the principal government departments were in Wellington. The headquarters of the major banks, finance and law companies. The Post Office, if not the largest of the "company's" enterprises, was certainly the company's largest employer. All this, before the country was SOE-ed, when government departments were turned into corporations. Nobody will be able to convince me that New Zealand today is better.

As for the Public Relations Division, well, it wasn't a bunch of wankers.

The reporters, however, were a strange-looking crew, having, as it were, not risen in the ranks — from the typing pool, for instance, or the telephone exchange — but employed via situations vacant for our writing skills.

Thank God, Pete Smith was a bona fide journalist, but even he must have wondered how to weld us all together as a team. Whenever we walked into the Post Office Headquarters café at lunchtime, joining all the suits and lowerlings in white shirts and ties, you could have heard a pin drop.

Sixty-year-old Irishman Nigel Fitzgerald, affectionately known by us as "The Colonel", was the historian among us. Tall, silvery-haired, distinguished in tweed coat and pinpointing his steps with a swagger stick, Nigel knew how to make an entrance. Back in the UK he had been an actor and writer of detective stories. "The sort reviewed in the *Times Literary Supplement*," he would say, "not *Boys' Own*."

John Berry would turn up for work in hotpants, often pink. The bed he slept in was not a four-poster but it did have huge wooden angels at each corner. Indeed, in later life John became a Catholic priest for the Archdiocese of Wellington.

Angie-Baby — Angela Griffin — would be next, in her miniskirt and with her sense of cute. Angie would blush at any remark. She's much more sophisticated today, having been one of Auckland's media power brokers.

Among the straggle of others from the journalist, art and photographic sections was Jane. *Oh what the fuck am I doing here?* She most often hung out with fellow agent provocateur Jan Conlon, muttering imprecations against the "Po" and investing that word with every negative filthy nuance you might think of.

Having recently graduated with an MA in English, Jane had initially been employed to write articles for the centenary of the Post Office Savings Bank, 1967, speeches for the Postmaster-General and official press releases. I was attracted to her style, her "I don't care what you think" attitude. And I secretly admired the fact that she had been part of the editing team for Alistair Te Ariki Campbell's poetry collection, *Blue Rain* (Wai-te-ata Press, 1967).

There was also the way in which Jane would argue the point with the Post Office establishment. Well, actually, any establishment.

Asthmatic, sometimes her passionate protests had her diving for her inhaler.

My job was to edit the monthly staff magazine, *The Post Office News*. No offence to Pete, but he preferred mentoring young women and pretty much left me to it. Using my skills from the *Gisborne Herald*, I put the Postmaster-General on the front page (Jack Scott and later Allan McCready, always a good political move to keep them happy). Pages two and three featured lead articles on recent developments (progress on cabling, a new post office opening), and page four was a personal profile (a smiling postie who had won a local award). I chose my own captions, including one which had Jane and Jan in hysterics: "Neville Coop and his Swell Organ". The photograph showed a very proud Mr Coop playing the Baldwin he had recently bought for his sitting room.

So, yes, Jane also had a wonderful sense of humour and I didn't mind that she laughed at me. At least Neville's you-know-what at last brought me to her attention.

And then Gill Shadbolt arrived.

She became one of my strictest mentors. The first wife of author Maurice Shadbolt, she improved my skills not just with writing, but also with respect to layout, choice of fonts and, well, my titles improved.

And why did the latter talents matter? Because I later transferred my editorial skills to my literary armoury when I became a writer. What my books looked like in terms of cover, page arrangement and print layout became as important as their content. This was the concept of the book as an artistic as well as literary object. I do judge my own books by their covers.

Actually, Gill had her own life before and after Maurice. Tall, tawny tousled hair, gypsy skirts, beads and sandals, she was a free-wheeling, free-speaking, independent and spirited lady, unforgettable for her down-to-earth views. She brought a hippie vibe to the division, and with her Māori partner, Johnny, livened up the hills of Kaiwharawhara with their parties.

At the same time Gill joined us, so did Rosie McLeod. Rosie later became a popular columnist for *The Dominion;* she and I always credit Gill as one of our greatest teachers. Another journalist who turned up around the same time was Cameron Scott, who went on to become Public Relations Officer for the Premier of the Cook Islands.

Gill was a hard taskmaster. When I admitted to her that I wanted to be a writer and showed her some of my work, Gill became even firmer. "I can't see *you*," she said when I showed her some work. "Where's the blood on your fingernails?"

She was the mother of Sean, Brendan and Tui, and had shared the earliest years with Maurice, travelling the world with him and keeping the family in tow. One morning, she stormed into the office having just read a recent novel by one of Maurice's amours. "This is the third time I have been killed off in either Maurice's or someone else's fiction," she said. "And this time I die in a car crash, and I'm pissed about it."

Gill had a huge circle of friends, including James K Baxter. One Friday afternoon when work was over she said to me, "Come to Jerusalem with me and Johnny, we're going to see Jim." For some reason I couldn't go. "Next time," she laughed.

Next time? There is never, ever, such a thing.

3.

My sister Tāwhi and I decided that we would flat together in a house in Island Bay. In the mornings she would go off to the bank and I caught the bus to the Post Office. Tāwhi had realised that her cousins, partying all the time at Wilson Street, were not saving money. One day she turned up there and got them to sign up for bank accounts. Next, she started to arrive on payday to take dollars and deposit their money before everything was spent.

It only takes one person to show the way.

I began to notice that at our flat a door had been unexpectedly unlocked or a window opened. I said to Tāwhi, "Someone has been breaking into the house." Nothing was stolen though, so maybe it was my imagination.

Meanwhile, Hiria and I were writing and telephoning each other. She was so much in my head that, while I was constantly "dating", I wasn't serious. I can't find the letters to illustrate how deeply we appeared to be committed to each other. Nothing appeared to be amiss.

However, the following January, I was back on military service at Waiouru when I was told that I had an urgent phone call. I didn't recognise the telephone number but I was given permission to ring back.

The caller was Naumai, Hiria's eldest sister. She had always been the supportive go-between in our relationship, but this time she had bad news.

"Hiria is leaving for London on Friday."

London? Friday? "Is she there? Can I talk to her?" I asked Naumai.

Hiria came to the phone and we were soon both pleading with one another. She told me she had to go to figure out what she really wanted — and I had the sense that there was somebody else in her life. I asked her to delay until we could talk the matter through. She said there was nothing I could do to stop her. I asked her to cancel her ticket.

I was panicking. I sought leave to go to Auckland to stop Hiria from getting on her flight. However, my story was an old one to the army — a young man having trouble with his girlfriend — and my request was declined.

On the day that Hiria's plane was due to fly out, I had become bitter. I pointed my rifle at the sky and pressed the trigger. "Go then," I said. "See if I care."

The truth was that I cared very much.

People in your life have their own lives. Hiria and I corresponded and our letters were still filled with love for each other. She sent me a photograph of herself in Trafalgar Square, smiling, feeding the pigeons. When I received the photograph I kept wondering *why*.

The birds were flocking everywhere around her.

Whether or not it was Hiria's departure, I don't know, but I began to feel listless. Motionless. In the doldrums. Was this what life was all about?

The preconditions began to appear to prepare me for the final push to becoming a writer and emerging out of my environment. Indeed, in my case, the French novelist Gustave Flaubert signalled the way.

"Be regular and orderly in your life," he wrote, "so that you can be violent and original in your work."

And then those ancestors of mine, sitting in the room behind my eyes, took over.

"Look up, Witi," they said. "See the steps ascending into infinity? The correct poutama, the one that only you can climb, is before you. Pick yourself up, dust yourself off, and start all over again." They liked popular songs from the 1930s, did my forebears.

When they began to scrape my skull, I was forced to take hold of the aka matua, firmly, firmly. The bone dust was falling around me and the universe above was ablaze with stars.

Now, once again, I began to climb.

4.

And now the tika. How were Māori faring in Empire City?

The governmental focus of Wellington gave race relations an interesting aspect. After all, the relationship between Māori and Pākehā was part of the company's business. And because the kōrero was constant, it kept me alive to the politics of difference. The ways in which policies and attitudes maintained the Pākehā in power.

At the same time, the same focus on Māori also, ironically, worked positively and to my benefit — Wellington was, for instance, much more egalitarian than Auckland. There were more compatible spaces for me to inhabit — to make friends among like-minded Māori and Pākehā and to meet at film, music and literary gatherings — and at late-night coffee bars. To discover what made Pākehā tick. To start rocking the boat.

On top of this there was a kind of Māori generation attracted to Wellington — to work in government or the university — who were mainly pro-Western, educated and upwardly mobile. They were vigorous young educated men and women from Whitianga, Waituhi, Waipukurau or any other whistle-stop collection of whare, who, on closer engagement with the company, could also start working inside it to confront its core racism.

On the company level, the racism was institutionalised; it still is, there's a few years to go yet. And personally, whether you were upwardly mobile or not, a Māori was still a fucking hori — or became one when White guys got pissed.

For instance, one weekend, our hockey team was having a good time at one of the beer barns in Stokes Valley when taunts began to be thrown at us from the White side of the pub and, next moment, bottles too. Would it surprise you to know that the ones the Police charged when they arrived were the Māori?

On another occasion my friend Francis Hemopo and I were at the railway station seeing our Pākeha girlfriends off and were attacked by Porirua hooligans. Francis ended up spitting blood and a broken tooth.

And again, Jane and I were in a hotel and the owner objected to the fact that a White girl was holding hands with a brown boy so ordered us to leave.

My sister Tāwhi had a great story to tell. She was working at the bank when she saw that the line of customers waiting to be served was getting rather long. She opened up her till and called to the next person in line. However, when the woman saw that Tāwhi would be serving her she went "Oh", clutched her purse, and returned to the queue she had been in.

But here's the thing. When the woman eventually reached the (Pākehā) teller — who had seen what had occurred with Tāwhi — the cashier slammed down her *Closed* sign.

"If Tāwhi is not good enough to serve the bitch," she said, "neither am I."

Both Tāwhi and her friend were reprimanded — among other things, for bad language — but the woman's account was closed and she was directed to take her business elsewhere.

Every now and then, the relationship was redeemed.

However, in the shadows of Empire City darker stuff was happening.

And it was happening not to Pākehā, but to Māori. Overcrowding. Alcohol. Soon, drugs. The urban environment for Māori was to become so *Once Were Warriors* as streets became divided into patches.

The young man I have mentioned as spitting blood and a broken tooth was my best friend Francis Hemopo, a Taumarunui boy. I had met him at the Downtown Club and we teamed up. Very soon we were spending a lot of time together, either at a city club or at the flat in Berhampore that he shared with his brother Richard and his wife. It was through Francis that I met his sister Anne and friend Vapi Kupenga, both managing to beat the system.

One night I told Francis to come to Wilson Street with me. Cars were arriving, the front door was open and music was blaring into the street. Francis took one look at the cuzzie bros and their girls going in and said, "I'm not going in there."

I was surprised and told him, "My cousins live here."

He answered, "I'm still not going in. I've heard of this place." Partygoers spilling into the streets, fights, cops called to close parties down. Yes, that was part of the Wilson Street reality, part of the fun. And then one morning, around three o'clock, I was ready to go home and I saw a girl in one of the bedrooms. She was unconscious and some of the guys, drunk to the gills, were pulling her clothes off. They held her down as one mounted her.

I saw red. My mother always intervened in moments when women were being smashed about or used sexually by men. "You have to help me stop this," I said to my cousin Tommy, who was standing nearby.

He was in a drunken stupor and, panicking, began to fight *me*, anything to stop me from going in. My cousin Richard turned up, two against one, and soon had me down for the count.

When I recovered, Richard said to me, "Sorry, cuz, but you should know better. Those guys are not our gang. They would have killed you."

Another partygoer, leaving, added, "The girl was just a pig anyway. She was asking for it."

The comment shocked me so much then, and I was glad that my two cousins had the boy up against a wall to apologise.

And what of my own rape? Had I been asking for it?

Recently, I spoke to Te Whānau Pani Matemate Crawford (Barney, or Pani), my brother-in-law, who had lived in the house. I wanted to verify what I had seen. Married to my sister Tāwhi, he admitted, "Yes, all that went on."

"Is that why you locked the door whenever I was there?" Tāwhi asked.

In 2018 my friend, academic and writer Reina Whaitiri told me that she did not know of one woman, not one, who had not been sexually abused in some way. The #MeToo movement hasn't come soon enough.

And that word, *pig*.

No woman should be called that.

But my cousins were very good to me and protective of Tāwhi.

They were hardcase, hard drinking, hard fighters and hard working. You crossed one of them, you crossed all of them.

I was waiting at a bus stop with early morning commuters. It was raining heavily. The bus was late. All of a sudden a big council truck went past, screeched to a halt, backed up, and my cousin Richard yelled out from underneath his yellow hoodie, "Is that you, Witi? Hop on, we'll give you a lift."

At the back of the truck was a platform and there were another couple of cuzzies standing on it. They made room for me — in my nice suit and tie — threw a council parka over my shoulders, and off we went. Zooming down Courtenay Place, down Manners Street, into Lambton Quay and then they let me off in front of my office.

Just at the same time the Postmaster-General was arriving in his government limousine for an early morning meeting. We eyed each other up and down — and then we nodded to one another.

I know I certainly made the better entrance.

And I reckon I had the better ride.

Chapter Thirty-Seven

Taonga Tuku Iho
Gifts from the Sea

1.

Not all the wisdom to enable humankind to construct a future came from the heavens.

Following Tāwhaki, other Māori heroes embarked on epic quests to enlargen our world.

Two such champions were Ruatepupuke and Mataora, and their narratives are among the greatest search and rescue stories in all of our pūrākau, mythology. Ruatepupuke journeyed from Te Ao Tūroa to the kingdom of Tangaroa in search of his son taken captive in a city beneath the sea. And Mataora travelled to the underworld, Rarohenga, to seek his wife, Niwareka.

Their separate journeys are of great importance to contemporary Māori artists and writers because the whakapapa of our artforms can be traced to the gifts they brought back. They are taonga tuku iho — treasures that have come down to us — that inspired and determined my practice as a writer.

Ruatepupuke was in the third generation from the gods, being the grandson of Tangaroa, monarch of the sea. He was also the father of a beloved son, Te Manuhauturuki (though some versions say that Manu was a daughter).

One day Te Manu was sailing on the sea.

He went missing.

This was because Ruatepupuke had made an error which angered Tangaroa. He had fashioned a stone into an exquisite fishing lure, which he named after his grandfather without his permission. Despite the beauty of the hook, the problem was that Ruatepupuke took for granted — gave the name of a god to a common thing — and one should never assume any god's assent.

And when he gave the lure to Te Manu to take on his canoe, he turned his son into a target.

Not knowing any of this, Ruatepupuke set forth to find Te Manu. He searched everywhere on land and along the coast. He saw, to his dismay, the place where someone had launched a waka. But there was no sign of the boat.

Thinking that the waka had sunk he swam downward, ever downward. And he came across Tangaroa's underwater kāinga.

Right in the middle of the submarine kingdom, Ruatepupuke saw Tangaroa's house, Huiteananui. Maybe somebody there might know what happened to his son?

He spied something familiar secured to the roof gable at the peak of the house, but he swam by and into the interior. The carvings on the porch had been silent and, with gleaming pāua eyes, had watched mutely as he entered. But to Ruatepupuke's amazement, the interior carvings were speaking and singing to each other.

Startled but still wanting to find his son, he asked them, "Have you seen a boy?"

One by one the panels replied, "Ask the tekoteko. Ask the tekoteko."

And Ruatepupuke realised that the "something familiar" he had glimpsed as he was swimming downward was his son Te Manu.

Auē, Tangaroa had punished Te Manu by pulling him down to the depths.

Now, there are variant stories, one of which says that Tangaroa had killed Te Manu, but I find it difficult to believe that a grandfather would do that to a great-grandson, no matter the crime of the boy. And for Te Manu to be dead does not allow for any transformation scene that would give the story its beauty as a trope of forgiveness. Another variant tells that Te Manu had been punished by being changed into a talking tekoteko, just like the carvings inside Huiteananui.

I conjecture a third variant. Tangaroa had punished Te Manu by affixing him as a living ornament atop Huiteananui. There he was, hair swirling in the currents, eyes wide with fear, nailed to the gable. Air dribbled from his lips as he asked, terrorised, "Father! Why have you taken so long to get me?"

2.

Ruatepupuke greeted his son with mournful tangi.

"This is my own fault, son," he said. "I should never have given you the fishing lure. Nor should I have named it Te Whatukura-o-Tangaroa. No wonder you were so successful catching fish with Tangaroa's name on the hook."

"Yes, Dad," Te Manu answered. "One haul of fish after the other."

"Tangaroa must have been watching, son."

"Mine is the fault too," Te Manu acknowledged. "I should have remembered to offer the first fish back to him."

Ruatepupuke started to release his son from his bonds. Very soon Te Manu would be freed and they could swim upward from the domain of the sea to the kingdom of the land.

However, he paused, becoming angry at the terrible revenge his own grandfather had exacted on his son. Why couldn't Tangaroa have forgiven him and Te Manu for such small transgressions? Instead, his grandfather had enacted a punishment that was surely too large for the crimes.

Ruatepupuke therefore decided to confront Tangaroa and exact his own payback. It was a brave thing to do. Who could challenge a god, even if a tupuna, and win? But Ruatepupuke had an advantage, having arrived at Huiteananui at a propitious moment. The hordes of Tangaroa were away, hunting for food. There was time to put a plan into action.

At this point you'll notice similarities with the story of Tāwhaki's attempt to uplift the bones of his father, Hema, from a different beach domain of the seagod.

In that story, Tāwhaki's mother Urutonga functioned as the slave woman who served the ponaturi. In the Ruatepupuke narrative, there was a similar caretaker, Hinematikotai, who like Urutonga agreed to help the brave father.

She must have had her own grievances with Tangaroa because she advised Ruatepupuke: "The ponaturi have an aversion to sunlight," she told him, "and the brightening sea can destroy them. Do you see that there are gaps between the wall posts of the whare? When the ponaturi are sleeping, close them. That way, Tangaroa's horde will not know when daylight comes. They will sleep on, still thinking it is nighttime and not realise they need to seek the lower depths."

Immediately, Ruatepupuke confirmed his plan. He swam up to his son to explain the strategy.

"But I must leave you here otherwise Tangaroa will notice you are gone and suspect something. Everything must appear normal to him."

Te Manu was stressed and kept crying out, "The bonds are so tight around me and I feel like I am dying. Must you do this? Can't we escape now?"

"Kia kaha," Ruatepupuke said. "Be brave. Once I have taken utu, revenge against your great-grandfather, we will return home."

Suddenly, throughout the ocean, came the sound of strange and eerie karanga.

"Oh, quickly," Hinematikotai called out. "My devilish lords are returning."

Chapter Thirty-Eight

Pākehā Girl

1.

In 1968 there were waves of international and national protests. From anti-war demonstrations to demands for indigenous rights, from burgeoning Black consciousness to the formation of women's rights movements. The years became hard-edged with a mess of violence which can be traced from the Detroit riots in July of the previous year and encompassing the My Lai massacre in March 1968. Martin Luther King Jnr was assassinated in April. In May, French students began rioting in Paris. Robert Kennedy was assassinated in June, and the Soviet Army invaded Czechoslovakia in August, putting an end to the Prague Spring.

People remember Black Power and the landmark Civil Rights Act of 1968, but we should also commemorate the Indian Civil Rights Act of the same year, which extended many of the guarantees of the Bill of Rights to First Nations peoples.

In sum, the civil rights revolution, as it came to be known, the Vietnam War, the urban riots — coupled with the rise of rock music and TV culture — all signalled cracks in the old façade of what had been predominantly a male and White world. And while Woodstock in 1969 seems to signal a peaceful flower-filled world, in the same year Charles Manson hit the headlines with what became known as the Sharon Tate murders in Los Angeles.

People sometimes forget that Manson intended the killings to incite racial hatred against Black people.

2.

I'm mentioning this as context because when Jane and I first met and got to know each other the state of the world was something we constantly talked about. At the time we weren't serious about each other. I was still dating, most often girls I met when I was with Francis Hemopo at the Downtown Club.

Sometimes, though, I felt I was dancing, dancing, dancing on the same spot. Things might have been connecting in some ways but not in others.

For instance, there was a postie who bicycled her way into my life. Her name was Tui Walker and did she create havoc for a while. At nights she swapped grey post office shirt and shorts for a red dress, and became one of the most vivacious girls in the world. When my thoughts about Jane began to elevate her, Tui got a bit cross — until she met Jane.

"She's better for you," Tui said in acknowledgement. "She strikes sparks off you of the right and the wrong kind, whereas I kindle fire of only one kind."

Tui later married one of the most important young lawyers in the city and, man oh man, did the other ladies of Wellington ever bewail his loss to a Māori *woman* — I'm being polite here — but it is difficult to use the word *bitch* for the glorious Tui.

Of course Jane didn't know that I was starting to look at her in a romantic way. She had her own boyfriend — or boyfriends, for all I know — and one of them, Neil, was a pretty cool character. Sometimes at office parties she looked immensely desirable sitting on his lap.

I grew to admire Jane for her independent ways. She was so interesting and was one of those people who kept her circle. Most of the girls she went to school with at Wellington East were loyal to each other — they still are. I called them "The Group", after Mary McCarthy's novel.

In many ways, I was both right and wrong about looking Jane's way; hindsight has given me that perspective. But at the time wanting her impelled my heart not my head.

There was another compulsion. I think that the restraints that held me to Mormonism were broken when Hiria went to England. That released me in all sorts of ways. I was already drinking a lot, often to the point of chucking. Laddish behaviour was the same in New Zealand as anywhere else. And I was smoking a pack a day; I liked the taste and smell of Gauloises, which were associated with French Resistance soldiers.

A lot of marijuana freely circulated among the hotel, nightclub and coffee-bar circuit.

Sexually, well, me and monkdom had never been a good fit. And Jane was such a babe with a tiny waist and beautiful hips and, whereas many New Zealand girls had thick ankles — the colonial inheritance maybe? — Jane's were slim.

Her occasional asthma attacks, which made her dive into her handbag for her inhaler, brought out my protective instinct too.

There came a night, after some party or other, when I walked home with her. She had lost the key to her flat and needed somebody to help her break in. We were talking volubly, it may have been about French nuclear testing in the Pacific. Having not signed the international limited test ban treaty, France had begun a programme of nuclear weapon trials on Moruroa atoll in French Polynesia. I'm fairly sure we had just heard the news on radio that a thermonuclear device had been detonated over nearby Fangataufa.

At the time Jane shared a two-storey flat with three other girls — I was to discover they were as politically minded as Jane was — but they weren't at home or, if they were, Jane didn't want to disturb them. And so I climbed the rickety fire ladder to an open window, let myself in, tiptoed down the stairs and opened the front door.

I went in for the kiss but, "Good night," Jane said. And then she added, "I will never bring children into the world, not while the threat of bloody fucking France exploding its bombs hangs over us."

Slam went the door.

The possibility of kicking for touch with Jane wasn't actually sealed for me until the evening we went to a candlelight vigil at Parliament. Her boyfriend Neil was not quite out of the picture, but things were cooling between them.

Wellingtonians converged on Parliament Buildings to protest the Vietnam War and to try to convince our lawmakers to bring back our troops. I watched Jane put a match to her candle in that sea of flickering lights, and then she transferred the flame from her wick to mine. Then she turned away from me, Witi forgotten, to concentrate on the speeches and proceedings. There was an intensity about her gaze and a stubborn jut to her chin.

"We the people hereby petition the Prime Minister of New Zealand and the Members of Parliament to withdraw our troops and to call upon the United States of America to end this war."

And then all was silent as we meditated on the horrors of young men and women on both sides, civilian as well as military, suffering the murderous consequences of a conflict not far from Aotearoa itself.

From memory, I think Jane and I sat there on the parliament lawn until midnight. A tremendous sense of aroha bound us together with the several thousand people at the gathering.

That evening, when I walked home with Jane, we held hands. All the way, not a word. The cumulative sense of unity at the protest had been powerful and overwhelming and affected both of us.

This time, when I kissed her, she kissed me back.

"I have a girlfriend," I told her. "When Hiria gets back from England, I hope to marry her."

Jane just looked straight at me. Whether the look in her eyes was shortsightedness or anger I don't know.

"Fine," she said. "I'm going on my OE soon, anyway."

This was the Age of Aquarius, no need to look too far into the future.

And so we took it from there and for the second time in my life the innermost chambers of my heart unclenched.

Jane liked plays and orchestral concerts, right up my own alley, and one of our early dates was to see Bruce Mason's *Awatea* at the Wellington Town Hall. I had been a fan of Mason's work for years. Inia Te Wiata had returned from England to play Werihe Paku, the old blind man waiting for the visit by his son, Matt. Werihe thinks the boy has been a success in Pākehā society but, when Matt arrives on stage, he is accompanied by a "friend" who happens to be his jailer. It is up to Gilhooly, the postmistress, making her entrance by bicycle along the aisle, to act as the agent of truth.

Gilhooly was played by Davina Whitehouse in a part written for Pat Evison. As for Matt, he was played by cuzzie bro George Henare who, in the 2012 Auckland production, graduated to the part of Werihe Paku.

After the play Jane and I walked the streets arguing its merits. I had liked the play but felt that the very real story had not been able to realise itself, due to the artificiality of theatre. Or was the problem a Pākehā writer writing a Māori play? Metamorphoses were happening at the margin of theatre which would lead to Māori playwrights writing Māori plays. And there was a distinction between them. It's a difference I will come back to when I talk later of Mataora and tā moko.

When we arrived back at Jane's place we went to bed together.

As simple, comfortable and as easy as that.

3.

I think it helped that our growing relationship was leavened by humour. We were both pranksters. I've always been good at playing the fool. I'd turn the hose on Jane while she was gardening. Or get her to move left when I took a photograph, where there was a cow ready to give her a lick. She had the best line of outraged expletives of anybody, inventive and colourful. More to the point, I've always fallen in love with the whole person, and it helped that Jane just happened to be the smartest girl I knew.

And so, as in the usual way of things our intimacy deepened. The love was surprised out of me, I wasn't looking for it or expecting it; I doubt Jane was looking for it either. Sometimes I stayed over at her flat on The Terrace, meeting the other boyfriends — by this I mean Jillyflower's Roger, Tat's Bob and Margie's Greg — as we stumbled out in the mornings, "Uh, hi."

There was a strong core to the relationship and enough helices whirling around, some in opposite directions, for the double spiral of us to be combative as well as cooperative. We didn't always agree and — Tui Walker was right, the sparks could certainly fly.

"But we'll always be friends, won't we?" Tui asked.

Jane sometimes stayed over at the house in Newtown that I shared with my sister Tāwhi and her husband Barney. They now had a small child, Carol, and the mystery of the person who had been breaking into the flat in Island Bay was solved; bloody Barney! There, she sometimes had to help me with babysitting Little Caroline, who was a beautiful baby and so easy to look after. One of the reasons was that she was toilet-trained very early by my mother who came through Wellington with Dad on the way back from shearing in the South Island. At the same time that Carol was drinking from the bottle, Mum had her sitting on the potty.

Although Carol must have been approaching a year old — maybe she was a little older — Jane was always uneasy about my habit of bringing her into bed to sleep with us. In the mornings Carol and I would have had a great moe, but there was Jane, as rigid as a board, not having slept at all. Because of the now-publicised dangers of rolling onto them, I wouldn't bring a baby to bed with adults today, but in those days it was a Māori practice and we didn't know any better.

Today, Māori have invented the wahakura, or Pēpi-Pod, a small flax basket for baby; paediatricians realise that sleeping close to parents soothes the child. Now the child can be safe.

And Jane didn't always need to be taken out or entertained. One night, when I suggested we go to a movie she said, "Why don't we stay home tonight, and read a book? Or you go, I want to finish the book I'm reading." Jane was a great reader of nineteenth-century literature. She loved George Eliot and read *Middlemarch* (1871–72) at least once a year. Jane Austen was a special favourite, as was Charles Dickens. She had a guilty secret in being a fan of Georgette Heyer.

Without another word she sat in one chair and left me to choose a book from her bookcase. Because I was having trouble making a selection she chose volume one of her precious hardback trilogy by JRR Tolkien, *The Lord of the Rings* (1937–1949). Our relationship was almost terminated when I became so engrossed that I spilt a glass of water down the spine of *The Fellowship of the Ring*.

The moral is that if you want to be a writer it helps to have a reader in the family to keep a weather eye on the literature and your place in it.

Looking back, I like to think that Jane and I knew what we loved each other for — and for what we didn't. Before you think that an admission that I didn't love her fully, or that somehow I loved her less, it isn't. Nor is it a confession that I already knew, because of my sexuality, that our love couldn't be as complete; it was.

We decided to start living together along with some of our friends, Anthea and Bob, Jonesy and Dixie, who was English and looked like he played with a Pommie rock band.

When you start living together life either gets better or worse. In my case, life got much, much better.

And then Dad came seeking me, as I knew eventually he would.

4.

There you are, Te Haa.

My father knocks at the door of memory and I open to him.

"The light wasn't on," he laughs, "but I knew you would be home."

He looks handsome in white shirt and grey slacks, and I'm really happy to see him, but I pretend I'm not. "It's after midnight," I answer, "my flatmates and I are asleep."

My father is in the prime of manhood and breathtakingly comfortable in his skin. The farmer's life has kept him strong and without stoop, and, except for the glint of steel in his hair, he bears none of the woes that age visits on other men. He has a mate, Jim Leach, with him. They organise shearing schools for the Wool Board along with the Bowen brothers, Claude Waite and Jim Tawhai, and must be in Wellington on business.

"I suppose you want to come in," I say to my father, crossing my arms.

He thinks I am joking. "Jim and I haven't got a hotel room and we need a bed, but first we want to have a feed, we're starving, eh Jim. No problem, just show us the way to the kitchen."

They have brought tripe, pork bones, pūhā and potatoes with them. As soon as they open the plastic bag with the tripe in it, the smell rises and it's a wonder that all the people sleeping in Wellington aren't instantly asphyxiated. Waituhi has come to the capital, folks.

Very soon, Dad and Jim are settled in the kitchen, giggling and cooking up a storm and filling the air with steam and stink. Fortunately, the stove is along the hallway and away from the bedrooms, but, even so, one by one Jane, Dixie, Anthea and Bob and Jonesy come to investigate the terrible stench.

"Oh, is this your father?" Jane asks before opening every kitchen window.

"And you must be the lovely girl who was stupid enough to let my son into her life," Dad roars. He kisses her affectionately.

"Would you like a hot chocolate?" Jane asks. She was going to say coffee until she remembers he's Mormon.

"We'll have a cup with our kai," Dad tells her. "You go back to bed, we'll talk in the morning."

Chocolate and tripe, ugh. Jane makes a lucky escape.

I settle down with Dad and Jim and listen as they talk, in between slurping the tripe and pūhā down their throats, about Wool Board business. Afterwards I offer Jim a beer and Dad surprises me by saying, "I might try one of those."

"I have to work in the morning," I tell Dad. That's my hint that we should all go to sleep. I show Dad and Jim into the big living room where Jane has already made the sofas into two separate beds.

Half an hour later, I am lying in bed with Jane when Dad comes in.

"Jane, shift over," I say to her. "It's Dad."

Although it's still a bit of a shock to her, she has become reconciled to the fact that Māori sleep together. And I have told her previously that when Dad visits any of his children he likes to curl up beside them in bed — no matter who else is in it.

Dad holds me close, puts his fingers to my nose and starts stroking the bridge of it. And then he starts to talk about Maera Station, about Mum and my sisters, about Waituhi and all his aunties and uncles who live along Lavenham Road.

"I must speak first of your mother.

"She is grieving, son. Her sisters and brothers have decided that her mother Hoana must go into a home. Hoana has dementia now. Naturally your mother is deeply upset. Even I am barely able to console her. Perhaps you already know of the depth of her sadness. She always turned to you, son."

(Mum? What is it, Mum? You come in my dreams, your feet paddling, your white gown floating around you, please, Mum, tell me.)

"Now to the people. They are well, the people are strong. The meeting house, Rongopai, still holds up the sky, I visit it when I can to cut the grass and clean the grounds, so that it is always ready to welcome those who come to visit us in the lands of Te Whānau-a-Kai. We still fight on, and I have been to a few land meetings at Poho-o-Rāwiri, we must get the confiscated land at Patutahi back. I have also been up the Coast to Uawa to support your mother's land rights and over to Whakatōhea with Pera Punahāmoa to help him with Hine Te Ariki's claims. You would be proud to see how well your grandad is respected there as a rangatira, a chief.

"Son, one of the main topics of all the rangatira Māori now is about who will look after the hau kāinga, the home places, when we are gone?

Even in Waituhi, we are becoming a village of old people, but for us age is of no moment, we still have our physical strength and as long as that holds, we hold. And what better gift can we have than to see our young getting educated and finding good jobs, even though that means that they leave us, like you have done?

"Let me now speak to you of an important matter. It concerns the future of the Wī Pere Trust, established by my great-grandfather Wī Pere Halbert for the benefit of the family. My Uncle Rongowhakaata came to ask my support to a proposal: at the moment the trust benefits the children of Wī Pere's two sons, Te Kani and Moanaroa. Uncle Rongo asked me if the time had not come for us to split the Trust in two so that Te Kani's heirs — mainly the Pere side of the family — could begin to administer their own affairs separate from the Moanaroa heirs — mainly us, the Smiler side of the family. I can understand the request and I have great love for my uncle. At the same time I am concerned that the kaupapa, the purpose of the Trust, which was to keep the families together, will be ended. What should I do?

"Meantime, my tasks as a provider for the whānau continues, and will ever be so regardless of what might happen. Every week I kill a fine beast and I take meat to my aunties and uncles along Lavenham Road, only the best sheep or steer because our people are royalty. I go out and harvest some of the maize, kamokamo and pumpkins that I grew for the whānau, you know how your Nani Mini loves her maize. She pretends she is in good health, your kuia, but she knows that life is shortening for her, and she asks constantly after you, 'Where is Witi! Tell him to come home and play me a tune on the piano.' You must visit her soon. And, of course, she is anxious that the Māori hockey tournaments continue in Waituhi. I am thinking of getting the committee together to organise the Hana Konewa tournament next Easter. Can you come back for it? Bring some of your mates with you, they may be better than Nani Skipper who is on crutches now.

"I must turn to your grandmother Teria's will. As you know, she charged me and your Uncle Winiata with the responsibility to keep her own land, separate from the Wī Pere Trust, safe for the Smiler family. Now that Win has gone, I am the sole trustee. I've been paying the rates all my life, the burden of it lies heavily on me, son, but I honour my mother and carry it lovingly. At the moment, I am grazing some of my cattle and sheep on the land and, when I sell them, the profit on the fattened beasts helps to cover the annual bill. Perhaps when you are next home, you can come out to Waituhi with me and we might think of alternative ways in which we can bring income in? Your Auntie Alice and Uncle Puku, for instance, would like to have a carving school in Waituhi, what do you think of that idea?

"Have you been to see your Auntie Joey lately? You have a responsibility to keep her well, as you must also your Auntie Margaret, Uncle Win's widow and, after all, she has their children to raise by herself now. Your Uncle Mafeking here in Wellington is not well, you must see him soon and offer him support. Although they are far away from Waituhi, I am the eldest of the Smiler whānau and, while I can't visit Wellington often, you must act as my agent and on my behalf.

"Your grandfather has been doing a bit of carving, and he and Moni Taumaunu have been repairing Rongopai so that it still holds up the sky. Your grandad has also received a great honour: he is the genealogist for the Māori pou that will be erected in front of Gisborne's Public Relations Office. Why can't you get on with him? He told me he offered you a blessing, he has the Melchizedek priesthood. Did you refuse it?

"I must speak now, on an environmental matter. Ever since the council changed the course of the Waipaoa River, Waituhi has suffered from floods. During winter the water comes rushing off the mountains inland and, by the time it hits Waituhi, nothing can stop the water from overflowing the banks. Do you know any ministers of the Crown? If you do, please tell them of our huge dilemma, I do not want our people of Te Whānau-a-Kai to be flooded out of our homes as I see happens frequently in India.

"I return to the rates. They are too high for tribal land. My aunties and uncles cannot afford such rates, the council should be ashamed of itself. Whenever they see me coming into the office to complain they start ducking for cover.

"Speaking of land, your Uncle Puku wants to build a house on one of the paddocks, what do you think? I am considering giving over the reins of the Smiler shearing gang to Puku. I know you and your uncle have had your differences, but he still admires you for arguing that the women and children get the same amount of pay as the adults, even though you were wrong. If he takes over the shearing, I can concentrate on the farm with your mother, she is worth two men; so as long as we are fit and healthy we can keep the farm going.

"The gorse on some of the land at Waituhi has come back. I have your axe ready for when you are next at home so that we can go up there and attack it. Also the fence is broken up at the village graveyard, it's a two-man job. I know you like the view from up there, Witi, you can see all the way across Waituhi and the lands of Te Whānau-a-Kai to the sea.

"We abide, son. The past is not behind us, it is before us and, as long as we listen to the tūpuna, we will prevail."

At 6 am, your father gets up from your side and goes to wake up Jim. There's the rattle of dishes as they have breakfast and wash and clean up the kitchen. Then Dad returns to you and says, "Jim's already gone, he has a moko to catch up with. I'll say a prayer for us before I leave, eh?"

Oh, if only your Dad's skein of karakia had been able to save his mate Jim. Soon after that visit to Wellington, Jim was murdered by his daughter's ex-boyfriend who had come knocking on the door with a shotgun in his hand. "Quick," Jim said to the children, "go and hide in the kitchen cupboard." He tried to save his daughter and, in the process, was shot.

After the prayer, "I love you, son," Dad says.

You go out to his car with him. The battery has gone flat and he needs a push to start it. Jane comes to help and, much to your Dad's alarm, ends up collapsing on the pavement gasping on her inhaler.

Meanwhile, Dad finally gets the courage to tell you about Grandad. "I've told him to stop all this business about Toroa," he says. "And the boy himself, I have told him he is not my son. Pera and the boy are both upset, but your grandfather has agreed to acknowledge you."

His lips are trembling.

"Will you come home now?"

Chapter Thirty-Nine

A Tekoteko Cradled in Loving Arms

1.

Shrilling, the hordes of Tangaroa descended from the sky of the sea.

The sound was so deafening that Ruatepupuke, hiding in nearby kelp forest, became dizzy and disoriented. And it came to him that this was the way the ponaturi hunted. Surrounding their prey, whether squid shoal or battery of barracuda, they would open their jagged mouths and *scream*. The welter of sonics stunned their prey sufficient for the ponaturi to go in for the kill.

Ruatepupuke saw that the hordes of Tangaroa had secured a fabulous catch. Having already eaten their fill, they had captured a female humpback whale which they would consume for parakuihi, at breakfast. A distressed calf, unwilling to leave its mother, followed her.

Some ponaturi guided the bellowing whale down by biting her with their razoring teeth and, by degrees, manoeuvring and tethering her in an underwater corral. Others swarmed to the meeting house to rest, oh, they were so unpredictable, they could well kill Te Manuhauturuki now. No, rather, they toyed with him, circling around him and taunting the boy with rude songs and antics.

"Oh, be brave," Ruatepupuke whispered.

And then the ponaturi entered Huiteananui.

Quickly, Ruatepupuke swam to an outside wall and, with thundering heart, peered through a crevice. The hordes of Tangaroa were amusing themselves with singing, dancing and hand-clapping contests. They recited genealogies, charms and folk tales, and regaled themselves with stories of grim fighting.

Eventually, after some hours, they went to sleep.

Ruatepupuke sprang into action. Auē, he realised he would never complete his plan before dawn.

But he heard a voice. *Waiho mā mātou koe e awhina. Let us help you.* He thought the instruction came from Hinematikotai.

Ki te ora koe ka ora hoki. Your salvation will be our salvation. No, it was the mother whale who was talking to him! *Loosen the tether restraining my flukes,* she told him.

Ruatepupuke swam to her and untied the bonds.

Like you, the mother whale said, *I wish to save my child. I am not the ponaturi's kai, he is. Let us work together.*

She began to create a strong current and, magically, coral and kelp from the forest swirled towards the meeting house. Working as fast as he could, Ruatepupuke cemented the material in the cracks of the walls.

Just in time. The dawn arose, seeping through the sea and, lo, the interior of the house was still in darkness. Inside, Ruatepupuke heard some sleepers stirring.

But the sea hadn't brightened sufficiently. "Not now," he panicked.

Voices started to call out, "Hey, Hinematikotai, surely the daylight is here — and we should seek the darker recesses of the sea."

She replied, "Sleep on, masters, it is a long night." Her tone was mysterious; verily she must have had her own motives for siding with Ruatepupuke.

Finally, the sea was blazing as if the sun had fallen into it.

Ruatepupuke sprang into action. He unplugged the gaps of the walls and the sunlight poured in.

"Auē, we shall be killed," the ponaturi screamed.

They were trying to escape the sunlight as it poured into the meeting house but it lanced them all and their bodies caught fire and exploded. Some tried to escape through the door, and the very first of them managed to get out. They were the forefathers of the fish we find in lakes. However, Ruatepupuke soon took a position outside the door and kept the rest inside. He brought out his fighting weapon, and began to slice at the ponaturi.

"Hei runga, hei raro," he cried as he swung his mere up and down.

The stingray was hit on the nose, which explains its flat, squashed face. The octopus was assaulted so hard that its backbone was broken. The leatherjacket and snapper, burnt badly in their rush from the light, bore the red scars for the rest of their lives.

Very soon the thousands of ponaturi trapped inside Huiteananui had perished from the sunlight. And bodies lay slain or dying at Ruatepupuke's feet.

He swam to Te Manu and released him from his bonds. "Me haere māua," he said.

Before leaving the scene of his great victory, he released the mother whale and her calf.

Thank you, the humpback said as she shepherded her calf away swiftly through the sea.

Te Manu's salvation had, indeed, been theirs.

And then Ruatepupuke quickly moved towards the porch, snatching four ornate poupou from the mahau. Oh, if only he had taken the speaking ones!

The poupou, being wood, began to float towards the surface of the ocean. Ruatepupuke took hold of one and Te Manu of another. They rose together through the brightness, and the sea was singing. But something began to happen to Te Manu. Because there's always a price. So that when the skin of the sea was before him, Te Manu was only able to say one word.

"Father . . ."

And when, with an elated cry, Ruatepupuke reached the surface, he turned to see not just four poupou floating in the calmness, but a fifth.

His son, changed into a wooden tekoteko.

2.

The carved slabs that Ruatepupuke brought back served as the blueprints for whakairo rākau. In particular, they performed as models for the art of carving as taught at Te Rāwheoro, the famous school of learning established at Uawa. From there the new art of building and decorating our meeting houses in the new style spread across the land.

In my lifetime, I have been privileged to meet or know Pine Taiapa, Moni Taumaunu, Bill Mou on the East Coast and in Gisborne — and Pera Punahāmoa could be counted among them. Then there was the formidable but always generous Pakariki Harrison with whom I sat one afternoon comparing the carver's art with that of the contemporary writer.

I learnt from Paki that to be a student of carving required training in the necessary draughting processes — and that only a certain type of applicant was selected as a tauira, apprentice. The selection began from birth where the process of adapting him into the rua i te whakairo, the knowledge, began in earnest.

As a writer, I have tried to apply the same thought processes as the carver does. From rua i te mahara, I have exercised the power of thinking and memory. I have risen up, pupuke, and I have learnt how to construct something out of the thought, te whaihanga. Somehow I have managed to translate the thought into a concept, te mahina, and from there, begun to construct a narrative, kōrero. My work has become a repository, te pukenga, and I have felt the desire, te hiringa, to expand, te horahora, the body of knowledge, te whanaunga, as I continue to write the narrative into existence.

The writing becomes richer as my understanding grows, te wanawana, of all the possibilities inherent in the work. Always, the aim is to achieve beauty, rua i te akamai, without chips, te kukakore, or dust, te parakore.

My books are my carved meeting houses, my whakairo rākau.

And now the tika.

The story of Ruatepupuke and, especially, the ponaturi are prefigured in one of the most significant worlds that I possess — my dream world. The narrative convinces me, without any shadow of doubt, that dreams, too, have a whakapapa, a genealogy.

This is why. I am a direct descendant of Ruatepupuke, I may even be a descendant of his son Manuruhi, whose great-grandfather was Tangaroa. In the nineteenth century it was my ancestor Mokena Romio Babbington who directed the building of a famous meeting house known as Ruatepupuke II, which was opened with great ceremony in September 1881. My descent from Tangaroa through Ruatepupuke comes down to me through the Babbington line and cannot be disputed.

Until I discovered the story of Ruatepupuke, some time in my thirties, I had no idea that the sea of my dreams originated from personal whakapapa. Not until then did I know the moemoeā were not randomly derived but, rather, came out of ancestral memory. And it is no wonder that the emotional upheaval of the conflict between myself and my grandfather should have triggered, in my subconscious, an attempt to work out a resolution in myth.

Here are some possible readings. My grandfather was prefigured as Tangaroa, and there's no question that Tangaroa had reason for punishing both his grandson and great-grandson, as Ruatepupuke and Te Manu had transgressed his ancient rule and domain.

Could my father be the saviour figure, Ruatepupuke? However, in rescuing Te Manu, he forever consigned his descendants to the revenge of the ponaturi. Still angry at the killings in their meeting house, and their subsequent dispossession, do they still spill into our nightmares to take their utu?

Some part of me remembers the rush of water as I rise. Alas, I am no longer the human boy that my father rescued — *Will you come home now?* — but a construct, a tekoteko, cradled in a father's loving arms. Is this the moment of my emergence, my transformation, shivering and penitent, into an imaginative life?

On the other hand, am I still there at the bottom of the sea? If I am, I must be the boy forever lashed to Tangaroa's meeting house. My dreams are like seaweed drifting. Seahorses keep me company, nibbling at the coral garlands that flower over and around me.

In the distance, whale herds forever sound. Diving deep, they thread the sea with whalesong.

Chapter Forty

Joining of Two Whakapapa

1.

One weekend, Jane took me to meet her maternal grandmother, Freda Bridge.

Freda lived in Sutherland Road, Lyall Bay, where her family, the Kilfoys, had owned land since 1910 — certainly since trams had begun running from Wellington. Apart from enabling the city's population to expand outward — to Seatoun and Island Bay as well — the trams turned Lyall Bay into a popular beach destination. Ordinary working people flocked with armchairs and umbrellas on day excursions to sunbathe and swim throughout summer.

> *Oh I do like to be beside the seaside . . .*
> *I do like to stroll upon the Prom, Prom, Prom!*
> *Where the brass bands play, "Tiddely-om-pom-pom!"*

Today, the bay in bright sunlight wears its early twenty-first century seaside personality well. There's a mix of gracious dwellings, some renovated as posh cafés, but still retaining the feel of good old Sussex by the Sea. The perfect place, in fact, to host Prince Harry and our Meghan when the royal couple stopped off at the Maranui Café during the royal tour in 2018.

It was on such a bright day that I met Freda. She was a widow in her mid-seventies — her husband was Jane's maternal grandfather Lionel Septimus Bridge — and Jane and I were coming for morning tea. While waiting, she was doing a spot of gardening. She was wearing a perky straw hat and gardening gloves and, as I approached her with Jane, she peered through her glasses to take a closer look.

Then, "Ooh, Jane, a Māori!" she chortled. "What would Cyp have said!"

With those words — I'll explain soon who "Cyp" was — Freda proclaimed the astounding likelihood that my Māori whakapapa was about to merge into colonial Pākehā history in a surprising and startling way.

Mum's Māori-driven genealogy, whether it liked it or not, was about to be disrupted.

2.

Although romantic relationships between Māori and Pākehā had been going on ever since whaling days, even by the 1960s it still took guts for Pākehā to go out with Māori and vice versa. On the world stage, it was only in 1968 that the United States Supreme Court ruled (unanimously) that state laws prohibiting miscegenation — marriage, cohabitation or sexual intercourse between a White person and a member of another race — were unconstitutional. And of course in South Africa, the Prohibition of Mixed Marriages Act had been in operation since 1949. New Zealand led the way in terms of enlightened policies even if the reasoning for supporting sex and intermarriage was sometimes suspect: for instance, as providing a means of "civilising" Māori.

There's no doubt that Jane was gutsy. But some of my whānau, when they heard I was going out with a Pākehā, were very unsettled. My grandfather Pera, for instance, viewed the situation from his position as a full-blooded Māori; he had previously tried to negotiate an arranged marriage for me to a Tūhoe girl which I refused.

Not all attitudes went down this way — and there were nuances. Ngāi Tahu MP Tahu Pōtiki related that when his Pākehā mother decided to marry a Māori her parents were accepting, but his father's sister was not only prohibited from marrying a Pākehā but also any Māori from another tribe; Tahu himself had deliberately married within his tribe. As recently as 2010, Māori Party MP Hone Harawira made headlines when he said that he would not feel comfortable if one of his children came home with a Pākehā partner.

But what did Māori and Pākehā expect! By the 1960s half of all Māori were living in built-up areas, and by the mid-1970s some three-quarters of us were urban dwellers. Were the Māori boys expected to keep their hands off Pākehā girls (or boys) and vice versa?

And talk about insidious racial and sexual profiling. If you were a Pākehā girl going out with a Māori boy you might be considered a slut, and if you married him everybody started to count the months. Conversely if you were a Pākehā boy dating a Māori girl she was your bit of brown sugar — and, if she got pregnant, there was no need to marry her. You sowed your wild oats, boy, wise up and settle down with an appropriate (Pākehā) girlfriend.

The times were not lacking in literary and film representations of the "problem". In New Zealand, *Maori Girl* (1960) by Noel Hilliard looked graphically at the issue. Rudall and Ramai Hayward's film *To Love a Maori* (1972), with Val Irwin and Marie Searell, showed that the subject was still controversial. The following year Albert Wendt's novel *Sons for the Return Home* (1973) narrated a Samoan parallel as a New Zealand-raised Samoan boy romanced a middle-class palagi girl.

American cinema was more histrionic, but *One Potato, Two Potato* (1964), *A Patch of Blue* (1965) and *Guess Who's Coming to Dinner* (1967) had synchronicity with Jane's and my experience.

During the following decade, Jane was often on the sidelines of political discussions at our house. The kōrero sometimes became overheated, and somebody would start chucking off about White this and White that and White trash but, suddenly seeing Jane making the kai, would yell, "Sorry, Jane, we're not talking about you."

And Jane as White trash? With her master's in English literature? Get off the fucking grass.

All Pākehā girls going out with Māori boys had their own stories of racism — and vice versa. Jane's ultimate word on the matter came when she was interviewed by French journalist Gabriel Lingé. He asked her, "What's it like to be married to a Māori?" The interview was published in Lingé's book, *Nouvelle-Zélande: Terre des Maoris* (1972). I don't have the exact words, but Jane responded along the following lines: "As I have not been married to an Eskimo, a Chinese man or an Indian, let alone an African or a tribesman living in the Gobi Desert . . ." pause ". . . I have no basis for comparison."

However, there was one extra dimension to our relationship and it had to do with that business of who "Cyp" was.

In Jane's case I was very much sleeping with the enemy.

3.

Let me explain.

The first New Zealand Bridge family member was Colonel Cyprian Bridge (1808–1883) who had arrived from Australia as a major in command of the 58th (Rutland) Regiment of Foot to take part in the war in the north. He was at the action at Kapotai Pā (May 1845) and the battles of Puketutu (also May 1845), Ōhaeawai (July 1845) and Ruapekapeka (January 1846).

As well as commanding the 58th, Colonel Bridge was also a war artist. His most well-known painting is probably his rendition of the fall of Ruapekapeka Pā — "the bat's nest" — when 1300 British troops and four hundred auxiliaries took the fort. His mess dress uniform, regimental colour of the 58th Regiment, mess dress jacket, tunic, regimental badge, original diary and watercolours are held by the Auckland War Memorial Museum. And Jane still has his swagger stick.

Colonel Bridge married a woman called Louisa Bowen, and they had two sons, Cyprian Wynyard and Herbert Bowen. When Colonel Bridge and Louise returned to England in 1858 the boys went with them, and Herbert Bowen was educated at Cheltenham College.

Now, I have always found the next part of Jane's whakapapa fascinating.

New Zealand's history is filled with families moving back and forth across the globe. Then, as now, we have always been great travellers. Even though there were waters wide, in 1869, eleven years after being taken back to the Home Country, Herbert Bowen returned to Aotearoa, where he became a journalist. His elder brother Cyprian Wynyard followed him soon after.

Once smitten by New Zealand, you were in her thrall forever.

Both brothers married in 1874. Herbert Bowen's wife was Adele Lenore (sometimes Lenore Adele) St John Greaves (sometimes spelt Graves), the daughter of a Captain Greaves who ran the office of Customs at Akaroa, Banks Peninsula. They had ten children, all boys, my goodness, makes you faint to think of it — Māori weren't the only ones to produce big families! The boys' names, which are so delicious they are worth listing, were Herbert, Cyprian Everard, Percy de Bohun, Cecil Dare, Gerald, Reginald, Lionel Septimus (named so his dad could keep track that he was the seventh son), Charles, Lance and Hugh

Decimus (known as "Deci" or tenth.) Percy de Bohun and Charles died in infancy. Herbert died when he was thirty-four.

Back to Freda now. She married Lionel Septimus, who was one of five brothers who volunteered for World War I. As you can gauge, she loved the whole idea of Jane, a descendant of Colonel Bridge, having a Māori boyfriend. Not until she raised it, however, had I really thought about the transgressive nature of our relationship. After all, wasn't I a descendant of the rebel leader Te Kooti?

4.

As well as Freda, Jane also introduced me to her Aunt Peg Smythe, who was as welcoming as her grandmother. I like to think of Aucklander Alan Smythe, actor John Smythe, designer Michael Smythe — all the Smythe family — as whānau.

But one meeting was still to be scheduled. At some point in 1969, Jane and I decided it was time I met her mother, Nancy, and her father, Tony Cleghorn.

We flew up to Auckland where Tony was at the airport. He greeted his daughter fondly, shook my hand, and from that moment we treated each other with wary politeness. I think Tony wasn't quite sure what to make of this development — his daughter bringing home a Māori *friend*, the degree of friendship unknown. But he must have decided that it was better not to ask because he didn't. I don't know how familiar he was with Māori, but there must have been Māori among his acquaintances.

On my part I didn't know what to expect. Tony was in his midfifties, fit and lean. What I noted most on first glance was an upright frame and a certain personal style — jacket and well pressed trousers — the New Zealander south of Balmoral. Despite thinning hair, his head was beautifully shaped and he had a profile that belonged in movies. He was wearing the shiniest shoes I had ever seen.

When we arrived at the house, Nancy had prepared herself — she was a fashionable lady, thin, smoking determinedly on a cigarette — and she came onto the patio to meet us. She favoured discreet colours, dove blue, mauve and pink, and — when it was getting cold of an evening — a pretty pullover. She looked as if she had just returned from having a perm at the local hairdresser.

"Hello, dear," she said to Jane. "And this is Witi?"

She had decided it was better not to ask either. Discretion being the better part of valour and all that.

Tony and Nancy lived in Kohimaramara. Their house was a lovely modern bungalow, down a drive shaded among trees, two blocks from the beach. At the time the suburb was in a state of nervousness over what the Melanesian Mission, who owned the land, might do in terms of the Kohimaramara property leases, which were expiring soon.

Every seaside Aucklander's appurtenance — a small single-sail dinghy — was parked off the drive. Just around the corner lived old lady McNeish, author James McNeish's mother, and further up Sage Road was the local celebrity, broadcaster Angela D'Audney.

Kohimaramara was very middle to upper class, a desired suburb to live in, but there seemed nothing much to gossip about except Angela's latest carryings-on and James's infrequent visits to see "poor old" Mrs McNeish. Incidentally, James's father was part Māori — perhaps they also gossiped about *that*.

From the very beginning Jane and I were trying to please — and so were Tony and Nancy. The tension of their not knowing that we were living together, and our not saying we were, meant we all went around walking on eggshells. Cohabiting without a wedding ring was not that commonplace, and so I and the girl I was living in "sin" with agreed to keep that cat in the bag for now. Accordingly, when Tony showed me where I was to bed down — in the small shed off the carport — I bleated "Thank you." Jane's bedroom was opposite her parents' in the house, so every evening I would wish her goodnight and retreat to my little old home in the West.

Any tensions were eased by having Jane's sister Sarah around. She was going to university, and her doings meant that she became a welcome diversion in any conversation. Better that than to ask how Jane and I knew each other and what we were up to in Wellington. I must have been, at that time, just a colleague of their daughter's who worked in the same office.

The only people who seemed to "know" what Tony and Nancy didn't were Bob Cleghorn and his wife Jill, who came in from their farm at Waiuku with son Richard to look me over.

They guessed, we blushed and the cat was out of the bag.

I liked Nancy Joyce Cleghorn née Bridge a lot. The black-and-white photographs of her are misleading and don't do justice to this formidable but fair woman. Despite her slight frame and small heart-shaped face, both Jane and Sarah declared her backbone was made of iron and her disposition was firm. She held strong opinions, was forthright in voicing them and found a favourite outlet in writing letters to the editor of the *New Zealand Herald* where her views on council matters were sometimes adamantine. Nancy ruled the Cleghorn roost and, while she was proud of her daughters and would never have interfered in their lives, I recall how in a fit of pique she felt that going to university had ruined them both.

I don't think she included me as an example of the ruin, but the subtext was clear.

Tony Cleghorn, an Aucklander, had met the young and pretty Nancy Bridge while in Wellington prior to World War II. He saw action in Greece, Crete, El Alamein and Monte Cassino.

On the basis of his soldier's record and education, Tony was sent to Cambridge for officer training. From there he was seconded to Military Intelligence, 8th Army General Headquarters, Cairo, Egypt. This was a famous unit, involving Paddy Costello, who was General Freyberg's main intelligence officer, and Dan Davin, New Zealand Rhodes Scholar, author and publisher.

Perhaps this explains Tony's shiny shoes.

Out of this connection sprang an interesting literary spiral because, when I became a published writer in 1972, I had a brief correspondence with Dan Davin.

He was one of New Zealand's most important academic exports and then living in Oxford. I had very much admired his early novels *For the Rest of Our Lives* (1947) and *Roads from Home* (1949) and, in 1972, had just finished reading his latest novel *Brides of Price* (1972). Irish Catholics in Southland were as much tribal beings as Māori and, in *Roads* particularly, I found a strong correlation between the story of an Irish Catholic family making their way in Otago during the 1930s and Māori families like mine traversing New Zealand in the 1950s.

To close the gap between two writers who were strangers, I casually mentioned Tony to him in a letter; Davin was totally astonished. We arranged to get together if ever the circumstances allowed it — he and his wife Winnie's hospitality to New Zealanders was legendary — and he was particularly taken with the idea of meeting "Tony Cleghorn's daughter".

Davin was featured in a splendid book by his friend and fellow writer James McNeish, *Dance of the Peacocks* (2003), about five New Zealanders who went to Oxford in the 1930s; the others were James Bertram, Geoffrey Cox, Ian Milner and John Mulgan. McNeish also referenced the charismatic Paddy Costello, linguist, soldier and later one of New Zealand's most brilliant diplomats — and slipped in mention of Tony Cleghorn, who was Costello's No. 2. Tony was further featured in James's companion volume, *The Sixth Man: The Extraordinary Life of Paddy Costello* (2013).

Tony ended his war service as a captain in 22 Infantry Battalion, 2NZEF.

Both Tony and Nancy moved with certainty within their marriage and society. Up to this point in their lives and in the expectations they had of their two daughters, everything was going according to plan.

I tried to compose my short story "Masques & Roses" around the way in which Jane's parents conducted themselves. I had in mind the masque — a popular entertainment in sixteenth- and seventeenth-century England which involved a slow processional dance. My Pākehā couple, their daughter and her Māori boyfriend all circle each other observing the niceties of the dance. I tried to capture Nancy's grit, her love for her two daughters and her sense of fairness, and Tony's innate decency.

They became, in my work, representative of the mid-twentieth-century New Zealander, at the cusp of extraordinary change in the country.

5.

And then Hiria telephoned from England to say that she was coming back from England.

She asked me, "Do you still want to marry me?" Her question brought all the old emotions I had for her back to the surface. I had to face a choice between the girl I loved and the girl I was living with.

I could never hide anything from Jane, and when, in her usual forthright style, she asked me point blank what the problem was, I told her.

"Oh well," she said, "maybe you should go back to her and anyway, as you know, I was always planning to go overseas."

We agreed to split up, and I started moving my things out of our flat at Ranfurly Terrace and over to Berhampore where my sister Tāwhi and Barney were renting.

When Hiria landed in Auckland, we spoke again on the telephone. "I'll drop my bags in Hastings," she said, "and come on down to Wellington."

The final afternoon of my move coincided with Hiria's arrival at the railway station. I don't know why people do these things to each other, but my and Jane's final farewells were said at the terminus. The light was fading and the day was cold. Jane was wearing a scarf against the wind.

"Good luck," she said.

The train arrives. There is a squeal of brakes and a hiss of steam. And then one by one the doors of the carriages begin to open and passengers begin to alight. You start to walk along the platform looking for Hiria. You see her in the distance, stepping off the train. She is wearing a long coat trimmed with fur. She smiles and waves at you.

You turn to look at Jane. She is still there, but she usually never waits. For a second you catch a glimpse of her face before, inevitably, she disappears into the crowd. And then Hiria is walking towards you. There's no doubt in your mind that you have come to the station to take her into your arms to love her forever.

But you realise that your love for Hiria has gone and that the person you now love is the girl who has actually brought you to the railway station. Your first words to Hiria are, "I can't go ahead with it. I can't marry you."

Of course it wasn't as easy as that.

I took Hiria to Tāwhi and Barney's place, and then I raced around to Ranfurly Terrace. Anthea met me at the door. "You've got a cheek," she said.

I went in to see Jane. "I'm still going on my overseas trip," she said.

It took a while, but I finally managed to get her to forgive me. I asked her to marry me, and we decided that we would go to England together.

As for Hiria, she returned to Hastings.

There's a line from Wordsworth that is quoted in one of my favourite films, Elia Kazan's film *Splendour in the Grass* (1961), which comes closest to paralleling the extraordinary intensity of the story I share with her.

> Though nothing can bring back the hour Of splendour in the grass, of glory in the flower, We will grieve not, rather find strength in what remains behind.

I saw her briefly over the following years. I met her again when she married a good man, worthy of her. We are still closely in touch.

Jane and I flew up to see Nancy and Tony to tell them that we planned to marry. Tony was silent and then he left the room. Nancy followed after him, but returned alone. She sat down, lit a cigarette and said to Jane, without looking at me, "Well, you're over twenty-one, dear, and you can do what you like, but your father and I will never approve of it."

Although I was disappointed in her reaction, I could recognise it. Nancy and my mother shared the same sense of absolutes — and, from the very beginning, one look into her steely blue eyes and I understood where we stood with each other. We could both be polite with each other, we would observe the niceties; better that kind of relationship than one with someone who would pretend they liked what was going on and was prepared to accept it. With Nancy I wouldn't have to stand around playing Happy Families.

And then I took Jane home to Gisborne to meet Mum and Dad and the whānau.

"Will you come home now?" Te Haa had asked when he'd turned up in Wellington. This was my first time back since my self-imposed exile, and I didn't know what to expect. Was Toroa still in Gisborne?

I prepared myself for another fight but, on my arrival, it appeared that while Grandad had not backed down — he still claimed Toroa as grandson — he had backed *off*. And the rest of the passionate family had put my volatile outburst against their beloved father at Pakowhai marae behind them; it was just Witi being Witi.

Everyone had moved on. Lightning on a summer day. Therefore, when I took Jane around to see Pera, it was on the expectation that we could be civil with each other. He surprised me by greeting us both warmly. And like everyone else he bowed to the inevitable: this was the girl I had chosen, and I would marry her.

Dad, having met Jane earlier, was over the moon, but the person whose approval I really wanted was Mum. Our love for each other was so close, I wondered how she would respond to Jane. I guess she took the measure of Jane's own strength and that she would be good for me. Or maybe she was so preoccupied with bringing up her other son, Derek, my brother who was fifteen, and the young ones Gay and Neil. And perhaps she was still battling her family about what to do with Hoana, her mother.

Whatever it was, all Mum said was, "Well, I should now think of putting Jane's name next to yours on the whakapapa."

As for my sisters, they were overjoyed at the prospect of a sister-in-law. They had all married in the same year, 1968. Viki was first, marrying Hore Lewis in February. Then came Kararaina, who had returned from Ardmore to teach at Te Karaka Primary School and Te Karaka District High; she married George (Gan) Haapu. This was an important union because, as you know, Kararaina and Gan moved up to Maera Station where Gan took over working the farm on a permanent basis. And I've already told you about Tāwhi and Barney.

As for Gay, later on she was to marry Kani Waititi, and they now live in Haig Street, making it as beautiful as Mum and Dad had. My brother Derek married and now lives in Australia. Neil Lamarr was a bachelor in Wellington.

When my sisters met Jane, they asked her, "What lies did our brother tell you about himself?"

Then Jane and I went to the Gisborne hockey ground to meet Nani Mini. She was sitting in a chair on the sideline, and I should have realised that she was not well. But I was so glad to see her that I didn't notice.

"A young man should never bring a rival to meet the woman who has always loved him," she reproved. Then she grinned at Jane and said, "You're just in time to help us out. Our women's team is short a few players."

Jane wanted to go onto the field, but Dad, remembering her asthma, stopped her. "Not you, dear."

And so your life and its fictions become infused with the forces of another colliding spiral, and the helices begin to work in strange and transformative ways.

If Māori history is a continuum, Pākehā are part of it. Maybe Te Kooti sits down with Cyprian Bridge to kōrero. Teria with Nancy. That doesn't mean they are happy about it, but they have to get along because there are tearaway mokopuna now in the picture.

The kids run around creating havoc. They've been playing with "toys", and at the end of a happy afternoon there's a taiaha next to an umbrella, a swagger stick leaning against a tekoteko and a deckchair has been shifted closer to the whare.

All litter my — and your — real landscape now, creating new imaginative realities.

Cut to 2017.

28 October is chosen as the day, nationally, when the New Zealand Wars will be commemorated. All eyes look to Ruapekapeka, the site selected for the inaugural event.

Many Northland Māori are reported as hastening to witness the place where their ancestors had fought the British.

You hide a smile and think that your two children — Jane's daughters — and your three Māori–Pākehā grandchildren should join the thronging crowd.

They could whakapapa back to the pā . . . the kauri and the oak . . . but they would do so not through your ancestry but Jane's too.

In so doing, you like to think of Sir Tīpene O'Regan's words on the subject. The son of a Pākehā father and Ngāi Tahu mother, he said, "I learnt very early that coming from two cultural streams doubled your cultural potential, it doubled your sense of identity and didn't divide it in half."

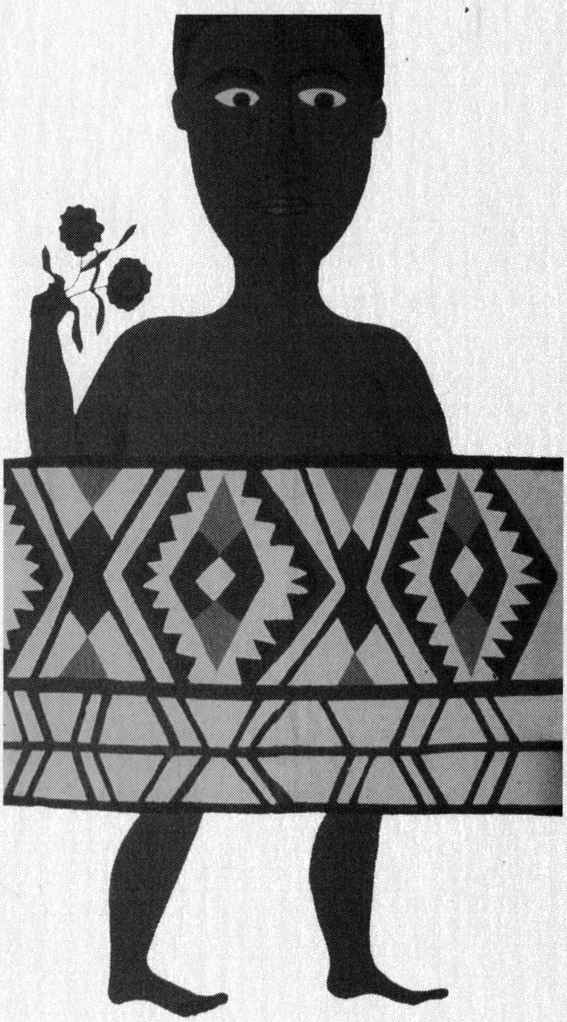

PART FIVE

PUĀWAITANGA
BREAKTHROUGH

Chapter Forty-One

A Book to Press Noses With

1.

I like to think that my books are objects you can hongi, press noses with.

You see Māori do this all the time when they are greeting carvings in a meeting house. They cry over a painting of an ancestor in an art gallery as if the representation is the ancestor himself or herself. And memoirist Diana Wichtel, in an interview with Anne Salmond in the *New Zealand Listener* on Anne's work for the television series *Taonga* (2018), writes the following.

> Salmond accompanies whanau from Uawa (Tolaga Bay) as they are reunited with a carving of their ancestor, Paikea, whale rider, at the American Museum of Natural History in New York.
> Paikea is wheeled out of storage, shrouded in plastic, an object of historical interest. The interaction between descendants and their tipuna indicates that he is much more. "We talk at home and think of you being lonely in a foreign land," Paikea is told. "That last scene with Paikea, everyone was crying, the camera guys . . ." says Salmond. "The curator from America was crying."

And there it is, a photograph of Lance Ngata pressing noses with Paikea.

2.

Like the Paikea that my Uawa relatives went to greet, there was a time when I lived in New York, at West 67th and Broadway, just ten blocks away from him.

I was the New Zealand Consul for three years 1986–1989, and I wrote my novel *The Whale Rider* (1987) while living in the city. I've talked about the book in *Māori Boy: a memoir of childhood* (2014) — and why whales are special to me — and I will cover those New York years in my next memoir.

From the thirty-third floor of the apartment there was a view down the Hudson River to the Statue of Liberty and the harbour. By then my two daughters, Jessica and Olivia, had been born, and were now aged nine and seven. They stayed home in New Zealand with Jane, but came to visit me during the holidays.

It must have been shortly after they returned to New Zealand in 1986, and spring arrived in the Big Apple, that an astounding event occurred. A whale came swimming up the Hudson River to Pier 86 at 12th Avenue and West 46th Street. I can recall watching the event on local television and, today, it has become part of the city's folklore.

"Yeah, that whale, what a thing to do, right?"

If you're sceptical about what I am writing, look at YouTube where you will see that humpback whales have subsequently made frequent returns to the city.

I am telling you this because a huge part of my practice comes from the spontaneous inspiration of the moment, of inaianei. The two events — my daughters' recent visit and the whale's arrival — compelled me to rise up, pupuke, and, as the desire, te hiringa, expanded, I began to steal time at the office to write the novel. The consul-general's secretary, Vivienne Troy, was in on the venture, and she also purloined moments to type up the manuscript. We were a great, conniving couple of thieves! As my understanding grew, te wanawana, the story became an example of the hero*ine*'s journey — and it put down two roots.

The pito, the umbilical, took the novel to Whangarā where the story was to be set. When, at the beginning of the book, the original Paikea throws his last rākau, the place where it lands is where the pito is.

Then the story put down te more, the taproot. The tuber took me to kōrero pūrākau, the mythos surrounding the original whale rider — the novel's urtext.

As for the kōrero o te ao whānui (intertext), the inspiration took me to a very interesting other world. Not the Greek and Italian realms of *The Matriarch* (1986), for instance, but to the very fascinating society of the paikea balaena — the whale domain.

Here is a section from *The Whale Rider* which takes you into that world. It follows the moment in the journey of the heroine where Kahu, my main character, undergoes her greatest ordeal — the descent into the abyss where she faces death. Perilously riding the whale, she has been taken down by the ancient bull whale as it has sounded.

The section was in italics originally to indicate that the reader would be entering a different world. I have slightly altered the extract for sense.

3.
from *The Whale Rider*

Apotheosis. In the sunless sea sixty whales were sounding slowly, steeply diving. An ancient bull whale, twenty metres long and bearing a sacred sign, was in the middle of the herd. Flanking him were seven females, half his size, like black-gowned kuia, shepherding him gently downward.

"Haramai, haramai e koro," the women sibilantly sang. "Tomo mai i waenganui i ō tātou iwi. Come, old one. Join us, your whale tribe in the sea."

The sea hissed and sparkled with love for the ancient bull whale and, every now and then, the old mother whale among the female whales would close in on him, gently, to nuzzle him, caress him, and kiss him just to let him know how much he had been missed. But in her heart of hearts she knew that he was badly wounded and near to exhaustion.

From the corner of her eye, the old mother whale noticed a small shape clasping her husband just behind his tattooed head. She rose to observe the figure and then drifted back beside him.

"Ko wai te tekoteko kei runga?" she sang, her voice musically pulsing. "Who are you carrying?"

"Ko Paikea, ko Paikea," the bull whale responded, and the bass notes boomed like an organ through the subterranean cathedral of the sea. "I am carrying my lord, Paikea."

The sea was a giant liquid sky and the whales were descending, plummeting downward like ancient dreams. On either side of the bull whale and his female entourage were warrior whales, te hokowhitu-a-Tū, swift and sturdy, always alert, a phalanx of fierceness.

"Keep close ranks," the warrior whales warned. "Nekeneke."

The leader signalled to some of the warriors to fall back to the rear and close up and tighten the remaining herd of women, men and children.

Meanwhile, the old mother whale was processing the information that the bull whale had given her. "Ko Paikea? Ko Paikea?" The other women caught flashes of her puzzlement and, curious themselves, rose to look at the motionless rider. One of them nudged the tiny shape and saw a white face, a human girl. The female whales hummed their considerations among themselves, trying to figure it all out. Then they shrugged. If the koroua said it was Paikea, it was Paikea. After all, the bull whale was the boss, the chief, and they knew how crotchety he became if they did not respect his words. But . . . e hika, he must be getting blind if he could not see that this was a girl and not a grown human male.

"Keep close ranks," the warrior whales whistled reprovingly.

The whales shifted closer together, to support one another, as they fell through the sea.

"Ko Paikea? Ko Paikea?" the old mother whale wondered anxiously. Although she loved her husband, and had done so for many whaleyears, she was not blind to his faults. Over the last few decades, for instance, he had become more and more depressed, considering that death was upon him and revisiting the places of his memory. The Valdes Peninsula. Tonga. The Galapagos. Tokelau. Easter Island. Rarotonga. Hawaiki, the Island of the Ancients. Antarctica. Now, Whangarā, where he had almost been lost to the herd.

Then she realised. "E tū," the old mother whale called. "Halt." In her memory's eye she saw Paikea himself and he was flinging small spears seaward and landward.

Instantly the herd ceased its sounding and became poised in mid-flight between the glassy surface of the sea and the glittering ocean abyss.

The warrior whales glided up to the old mother whale. "He aha te mate? What is the matter?" they trumpeted belligerency. She was always calling for a halt.

The old mother whale's heart was pounding. "Kei te kōrero ahau ki te koroua," she said sweetly. "I wish to speak to my husband."

So saying, she descended gently towards the ancient bull whale, to talk with him.

The sea scintillated with the sweetness of the old mother whale as she hovered near her ancient mate. She noted that the tekoteko had opened its eyes and had known that the whale herd had stopped descending further. Oh, what was happening!

Below, illuminated jellyfish exploded silvered starburst through the dark depths. Further down, a river of phosphorescence lent lambent light to the abyss like a moonlit tide. The ocean was alive with noises: dolphin chatter, krill hiss, squid thresh, shark swirl, shrimp click and, ever present, the strong swelling chords of the sea's constant rise and fall.

The tekoteko took air that was leaking from the koroua's blowhole.

The old mother whale realised that she had to hurry. "E koro, my lord," she began in a three-tone sequence drenched with love. "E taku tāne, my man," she continued, adding a string of harmonics. And then she breathed with slyness, threading her words with sensuous major arpeggios. "Kaore āhau te tekoteko a Paikea. The rider that you carry isn't Paikea."

The other female whales edged away carefully, but they secretly admired the courage of the old mother whale in questioning the identity of the whale rider.

"Āe rā, ko Paikea," the bull whale said, grumpy and insistent. "It's Paikea."

The old mother whale cast her eyes downward, hoping that the bull whale would take this as a sign of female submission but, trust me, she knew exactly what she up to. "No, no my sweet lord," she belled sweetly.

The female whales gasped at the old mother whale's stubbornness. The warrior whales waited for the word from their leader to teach her a lesson.

The bull whale responded in a testy manner. "Of course it is Paikea! When my lord mounted me, he said his name was Kahutia Te Rangi." Surely the old mother whale should know this was another name for Paikea. "Ko Kahutia Te Rangi, ko Paikea."

The old mother whale allowed herself to drift just below her husband. "Perhaps, perhaps," she trilled in soprano tones of innocent guile.

The other female whales now decided to give her a wide berth. She had a lot of gumption all right. Fancy saying "Perhaps" to their leader.

The old mother whale saw the warrior whales preparing to give her a sharp nip in the bum. She moved quickly towards the ancient bull whale and let a fin accidentally on purpose caress the place of his deepest pleasure. "Nō te mea," she told him, "ka kite au te tekoteko, e hika mā! But when I look at the tekoteko, I don't see Paikea at all."

"Then who is it?" the ancient bull whale asked grumpily.

"He rite tonu te tekoteko ki tētahi rākau," the old mother whale answered. "The tekoteko looks like a spear. Think back, husband." Her song inflected her kōrero with graceful ornamentation.

The other female whales nodded to each other. They too had heard about Paikea, in the old time, and how he had thrown rākau seaward and landward. The old mother whale was clever, that one. They were dumb by comparison. By asking questions she was enabling their leader to come to the decision she had already reached. No wonder she was the queen and they were the ladies in waiting.

The ancient bull whale waved the warrior whales away. He was getting irritated with them and their fancy drills.

"Think back?" he repeated to himself. And through the mists of time he saw his master, Paikea, flinging wooden spears into the sky. Some in mid-flight became birds. And others on reaching the sea turned into flounder. And he, Paikea himself, was a spear populating the land and sea so that it was no longer barren.

And occasionally, yes, the ancient bull whale on previous visits to Whangarā had seen the spear. It had taken the form of a young human female calf.

The ancient bull whale began to assess the weight of the rider and, hmmm, it was light all right, and the legs were shorter than he remembered and—

"Āe," the old mother whale crooned, pushing him in the direction of the right decision. "He uri o Paikea, tēnei. This is the last spear, the one which was to flower in the future." She let the words sink in, because she knew that it always took the males longer than the females to understand. She wanted to make sure that the bull whale really understood that the rider was Paikea's descendant and it had a task to fulfil. "It is a mokopuna of Paikea," she said, "and we must return it to the land."

In her voice was ageless wisdom.

The ancient bull whale swayed in the silken tides of the stirring sea. Though tired from his travail at Whangarā beach, he sensed the truth in his consort's words. For he remembered that Paikea had hesitated before throwing the last of his wooden rākau and, when he did this, he had said, "Let this one be planted in the years to come when the people are troubled and it is most needed." And the spear, soaring through the sky, came to rest in the earth where the afterbirth of a female child would be placed.

And as he remembered, the ancient bull whale began to lose his nostalgia for the past and to put his thoughts to the present and future. Surely, in the tidal waves of Fate, there must have been a reason for his living so long? It could not have been coincidence that he should return to Whangarā and be ridden by a descendant of his beloved golden master. Perhaps the fate of the whale iwi and that of the rider on top of him were inextricably intertwined? She might be the one to remind her world of the love and relationship between tohorā and tangata, whale and humankind.

The herd as they waited for the ancient bull whale's judgement began to add the colour of their opinion. The female whales chattered that they knew all along the old mother whale was right, and the warrior whales, seeing the way things were going, added their two cents' worth also.

The ancient bull whale gave a swift gesture. The tekoteko could not sustain itself on the air from his blowhole alone. She must be getting frightened down here in the dark.

"Me piki mai tātou ki te rangi," he commanded. "We must return to the surface." He steadied himself for a quick ascent. "Do we all agree?"

The herd sang a song of agreement to their ancient leader's decision. "Uia mai koia whakahuatia ake, ko wai te whare nei ē? Ko Te Kani! Ko wai te tekoteko kei runga? Ko Paikea, ko Paikea!"

The ancient bull whale tensed his muscles, making ready to power to the surface. "Then it shall be done?" he asked.

"Āe, āe, āe!" the whale herd chorused with benign and burnished tenderness. "Yes, yes, yes!"

Slowly the phalanx of whales began their steady procession to the surface of the sea, broadcasting their orchestral affirmation to the universe.

Haumi ē, hui ē, tāiki ē.

Let it be done.

4.

Of all my books, the one that most people hongi is *The Whale Rider* (1987). It was published the year after *The Matriarch* (1986) and it represents the culmination of the first phase of my career as a writer.

The urtext (kōrero pūrākau) is the original myth of Paikea. The intertext (kōrero o te ao whānui) is the world of the whales. The pretext (kōrero pūtake) acknowledges the whales as deus ex machina, powerfully moving a myth forward and, out of it, creating a new myth for the present. The context (kōrero horopaki) is the voyaging motif as the whale herd travels from the Valdes Peninsula to Rapa Nui to Tahiti to Hawai'i and past New Zealand to the icy regions of Antarctica.

There are two subtexts (kōrero mātāpono). The first has to do with "interlock" and the environment as the whale herd negotiates a Pacific Ocean that is enduring pollution, declining fish stocks and nuclear testing. The second concerns their human counterparts, the villagers of Whangarā, as they seek a new leader to take them through troubled times. Other themes add to the novel's *textuality* (kōrero matarau), like those set in Australia and Papua New Guinea.

With the book I began to use what I considered to be the indigenous structure: *kōrero tāhuhu o te huringa o te ao*. This was the seasonal framework that begins with summer and then goes to autumn, then winter, and ends with spring. With very few exceptions I still apply this structure, either overtly or as "various states of mind" in all my work. It is the beam to my whare whakairo and, by taking me to the state of rebirth, enables me to give radiance to the endings of my books.

And the text itself is dually English and Māori. When the old mother whale asks, "Ko wai te tekoteko kei runga?" this is actually the first line of the contemporary Paikea haka; and when the ancient bull whale replies, "Ko Paikea, ko Paikea!" that is the second. I've always maintained from boyhood the conceit that if Paikea was able to speak to whales, the language of the paikea balaena must be the reo.

In all my books, therefore, the endgame could be to produce what literary theorist Roland Barthes characterised as "the ideal text" — the text as a "galaxy of signifiers" and as an absolutely plural creation based on the infinity of language — in the case of Māori, based on the infinity of kupu.

Or, Barthes might say of my work that it is an attempt to create a "hypertext" composed of lexia — blocks of signification.

Whatever the case, there's a scene in *Whale Rider* (2002), the film adaptation of the book, which captures all that I have wanted to do as a writer. It is the scene where Pai, just before she mounts the whale, puts her nose to the whale in hongi.

In that moment, it all comes together, ihi, wehi, mana, aroha, all those things I have talked about so far. Mokopuna with tūpuna. Past with present. Tinana with wairua. Human world with natural world. Aotearoa with te ao hurihuri. And young woman with future.

When Pai presses noses with the ancient bull whale she makes her hongi with history.

Haumi ē, hui ē, tāiki ē.

Finally, I like to think that *The Whale Rider* is the book where I tried my best, for my daughters' sakes, to affirm them as young women and to create an indigenous heroine who could stand alongside the champions that were inspiring them at the time, like Dorothy from the film *The Wizard of Oz* (1939). Olivia had a passion for Helen Keller, and Jessica for the female companions of television's *Doctor Who*.

Cut to the Golden Globes, January 2018, and Oprah Winfrey takes the stage to remind all young girls that times are changing. "There is a new world waiting on the horizon," she tells them. And I recall the final scene of Pai in *Whale Rider* (2002) paddling the waka. The canoe is filled with hopeful young women and men, being piloted by a young woman.

Yes, they *will* get to that new world, together, with all of their strength.

Chapter Forty-Two

Back to University

1.

I return to 1969, before I had even published a novel, and I begin with a reminder.

Sometimes I think that my position as first Māori novelist was not a relevant statistic. At the time there were a lot of contenders and, even though they didn't make it, their work is being discovered today.

Among them was Rowley Habib who was mentored by Bruce Mason. At the time, Mason was editor of *Te Ao Hou* and he had predicted the appearance of a novelist. Although I had met Mason as a schoolboy, Rowley must have surely been Mason's pick. He made himself into a playwright rather than a fiction writer, and was the first Māori writer to gain an award from the New Zealand Literature Fund in 1972. In 2018, actor Nancy Brunning created a stage show around his work that was shown at the Auckland Writers Festival.

Then there was Jacquie Sturm, one of the the first Māori women to obtain a university degree, the first Māori librarian and also the first Māori writer to publish stories in English. Her breakout appearance occurred in *World Classics: New Zealand Short Stories* (CK Stead, 1966). Later I discovered that she, like Rowley, had a manuscript of short stories under her bed. *House of the Talking Cat* (1983) was finally brought out by the Spiral Collective, who also published Keri Hulme's *the bone people* (1984). I launched the book in Wellington and told the audience to consider the irony that her book had already existed, albeit in manuscript, long before *Pounamu, Pounamu.* Just because you came first doesn't mean you are the best — or that you deserved it.

Another *Te Ao Hou* editor, Margaret Orbell, who succeeded Bruce Mason, favoured Riki Erihi or Mason Durie. I never met Erihi but I was impressed that he could write long rather than short, and I thought he could naturally stretch to the novel if he wished to. Durie, like most of the writers — and they included Hirini Moko Mead — had other primary aspirations to achieve for the people. Durie's was in Māori health, and Mead was already renowned as a professor of Māori Studies. I think this was the main reason why the generation of writers before mine did not make the breakthrough.

When I turned up on the scene, the editor at *Te Ao Hou* was Joy Stevenson, and she had bets on Patricia Grace, Arapera Blank and Kāterina Te Heikōkō Mataira. Mataira was one of our most innovative educationalists and writers for children. Arapera Blank had won a special prize in the Katherine Mansfield Memorial Award 1959, and her story "One Two Three Four Five" is one of the best in the Māori canon. Her son, Anton Blank, published a book of his mother's work in 2016.

Patricia Grace of course became the first Māori woman to publish a book when *Waiariki*, her collection of short stories, came out in 1975. In 1978 her novel *Mutuwhenua* was published; that was a good year for Māori women writers, as June Mitchell's *Amokura* also saw release.

Then there was Pat Heretaunga Baker, published by Christine Cole Catley off her fishing boat in the Marlborough Sounds. His book, *Behind the Tattooed Face* (1975), was the first Māori historical fiction.

Other writers of that generation included Rora Paki, Ani Bosch, Atihana Johns, Renee, and Bub Bridger. Some Pacific writers joined us: Albert Wendt, Alistair Te Ariki Campbell, Florence "Johnny" Frisbie, Vincent Eri and other writers in Papua New Guinea nurtured by Ulli Beier.

Most of them were writing while I — as Rowley Habib used to like saying — was still shitting in my nappies.

2.

Because neither memory nor the Māori way of thinking work in strictly linear, chronological tracks, I am writing *Native Son* without the aid of a diary and I am, rather, letting the events of my life spiral around my narrative. At this point my recollections have become a bit of a Gordian knot, so, in the attempt to disentangle them, do forgive me if I get anything sequentially wrong or assign incorrect emphases.

Jane and I set a date for the wedding — in 1970, a year and a bit away — and we got on with the business of saving for it.

My boss Fred Leighton and Jane made my life more complicated when they ganged up on me to go back to university. "You've only got three more units to complete your bachelor's degree," Jane said. "I'll help you."

As a sweetener, Fred proposed that I could take a year off with pay, conditional on returning to the Post Office. Well, I wasn't planning on going anywhere else, so I said yes.

So off you go, Witi, heigh ho back to university, riding the red clanging cable car from Lambton Quay or huffing and puffing your way up the hill from Willis Street — St Mary's of the Angels on your right — and ascending the Allenby Terrace steps. Stop to catch your breath when you reach the Terrace but what a view, looking back, across the harbour. The city through sunlight or mist, and the clouds captured in the black mirrors of the capital's highrise buildings.

And you have a mate! Tāwhi and Barney's daughter, little Carol. To enable Tāwhi to go to work, you take Carol to 'varsity, she enjoys the ride up the hill, eh. You sit in the last row of the lecture theatre just in case she cries, hush-a-bye now, or you have to change her nappies in the boys toilets.

"Oh *gross,*" they moan, averting their eyes and making a mental note to wear a condom the next time they sleep with Susie.

Through Carol I met lovely English student Jan Rivers, just married to Lou. She went all dewy-eyed and protective when she saw my niece. We became best diaper-changing friends and began a funny, warm relationship that later extended to poet and, later, publisher, Tim Chamberlain. A memento of those days was a clay sculpture that Lou decided to make of my head; almost fifty years later I still have it in my downstairs library. It was never "fired" and should have crumbled into dust years ago, but there it is, like the picture of Dorian Gray — except that it keeps young as *I* get older.

My academic transcript, obtained in 2017, shows that Witi Tame Ihimaera Smiler, Student No. 196001790 in 1969 enrolled in Medieval English II, Maori Studies I, Italian and History.

History appeared to be going through a somewhat bipolar period at the time. Following along with Keith Sinclair's *The Origins of the*

Maori Wars (1957) and *The New Zealand Wars* (1959), historians like John Beaglehole, Emeritus Professor at Victoria, were engaging with New Zealand history. In Beaglehole's case, his pursuit of New Zealand's story was lifelong. There's a lovely letter that he wrote to a lady named Ida Leeson on 18 November 1946 saying, "I don't know how to put this without a terrific lot of explanation, but I think I am becoming a New Zealander." (*"I Think I Am Becoming a New Zealander": Letters of J.B. Beaglehole* (2013)). His magnum opus was considered to be the four 1000-page volumes, *The Journals of Captain Cook on his Voyages of Discovery,* and he had completed the series only two years earlier in 1967. Bill Oliver had just departed the faculty for Massey University, but Mary Boyd was still pursuing her interest there in Pacific history.

None of this was evident, however, in the course on offer: a traversal of early Modern Europe from the Renaissance to around 1603. Or was it the history of England in the seventeenth and eighteenth centuries? My tutor was a lady by the name of Dorothy Crozier, and two of my colleagues were the twins Malcolm and John McKinnon. Malcolm became a historian and John an ambassador in the New Zealand diplomatic service. Miss Crozier was determined and valiant. I was the first Māori she had ever taught, and she may have had impossible dreams.

3.

The head of history, Peter Munz, was the glamour star of the department. He was already wildly popular, having just given his inaugural lecture as professor. His specialty was European history and, like other students, I would sneak into his classes simply to hear and watch one of the most brilliant minds in New Zealand. Russell Price writes of him, "Easily distracted by latecomers, or the sound of a motorcycle, he would go to the window to observe the offender; then, returning to the rostrum, he would ask, 'Where was I?' 'In Constantinople. The Fourth Crusade,' might come the reply. 'Ah! Yes,' he would say, and resume."

Sometimes I wondered what he thought of the New Zealand student as a species. He would stop regularly and ask us, "Why do you all laugh when I am being serious and you don't laugh when I am telling a joke?"

Munz was a German Jewish intellectual who arrived in New Zealand in the 1940s. Fleeing Nazi Germany and fascist Italy he and other refugees pursued new lives in less perilous countries, where their different philosophical, scientific, mathematic, political and philological skills transformed the thinking of their hosts — as Munz did of New Zealand. "His intellectual energy was manifested in his extra-curricular enthusiasm for philosophy," Russell Price writes, "in sessions with Karl Popper in Christchurch, Ludwig Wittgenstein at Cambridge, and in his writing on philosophical and scientific topics."

Karl Popper! One of the twentieth century's greatest philosophers of science, here in New Zealand? He was the most famous of the Jewish academics, having arrived with his wife, Henni, in 1937 to teach at Canterbury University College — she referred to New Zealand as "halfway to the moon". For almost ten years, Popper lived among us where he wrote *The Open Society and its Enemies* (1945) and *The Poverty of Historicism* (1957). He spent his later career in the United Kingdom.

I wouldn't have agreed with the proposition in *Open Society* that national, religious, ethnic and racial identities and differences are malign utopian fantasies, but the opportunity to debate such questions would have been fascinating. On the other hands, the thesis's ideas on the installation of a cosmopolitan community sound like something the world is coming to via the internet.

Now for the tika.

We still don't have in New Zealand a cosmopolitan or intellectual culture — what passes for it today is popular talkback on radio, there's certainly nothing on television. In the 1950s and 1960s, however, we almost achieved a culture of mana. The arrival of intellectuals like Munz and Popper meant the infusion of new ways of thinking. Paul Morris in *Jewish Lives in New Zealand: A History* (2012) credits Popper with "the start of the Copernican revolution in our universities", a paradigm shift in what was taught.

We almost *made* it. Why didn't we? Well, working in isolation or in silos didn't help. Most of all, New Zealand had a long tradition of anti-intellectualism. Prime Minister Robert Muldoon, for instance, around 1975 or 1976 began to say that here in New Zealand "the ordinary bloke is king". We were Rob's Mob. Our hero was the cow cocky like Fred Dagg in the black T-shirt, floppy hat and gumboots. Or the young man in the black shirt with a football under his arm. Or the rock musician or singer with purple hair. Not the boy or girl in university cape and gown. Even among Māori, intellectuals were distrusted. Intellectualism equated to Europeanism, and we liked our brainboxes dressed up with bandana'd afro and T-shirt with appropriate slogan to show they hadn't sold out.

In my mind's eye I still see Professor Munz walking in the sunlight, smoking a pipe, sports coat, hair unruly. He was always surrounded by a bevy of eager, excited students. Sometimes I would catch glimpses of him with other, presumably, Europeans at Suzy's or the Monde Marie, run by Mary Seddon. They were two of the coffee bars that were such a haven for European émigrés in provincial Wellington. I suspect the émigrés were as exotic a culture to most New Zealanders as Māori were.

I would have forgiven Professor Munz anything, even the fact that he was a committed Europhile, but — and it's a big *but* — he could not engage the possibility that Māori thought could be at a similar level of discourse as European. In retirement he embarked on a series of studies developing a critical history of knowledge itself. Within this evolutionary context he wrote a review of my friend and colleague Anne Salmond's book *Two Worlds* (1991); he said my tūpuna had "early minds", a limited capacity for intellectual inquiry. I presume, though I am not sure, not being a student of the discipline, that this was in line with his studies and in accordance with Karl Popper's distinction between open and closed cultures. He may have believed, using Popper's distinction, that Māori had a closed culture. For instance, he considered that the marae disallowed open debate and inquiry.

Munz liked to be provocative and perhaps this was one of those times. That notwithstanding, one of the aims of this memoir is to show that, far from having early minds, Māori intellectual practice showed a high degree of sophisticated thought. Professor Munz, too European, never knew that.

Today, I would not stand back, Professor Munz, as you passed by with your bevy of acolytes. I would tug you on the sleeve and perhaps we would talk and debate the subject — after all, we were both minorities in New Zealand and, in that respect, had more in common than both of us might have expected. I would have said to you, "Come to the marae, Professor Munz." I am sure that you would have enjoyed the cut and thrust of kōrero, leavened by wit and humour, I grin to think about the possibility. You would certainly have discovered that Māori culture was not a closed one.

What might you then have thought of the possibilities available of expanding your thesis by exploring Māori empirical thought?

Or would that have been a step too far for you, as it still is for us today?

Chapter Forty-Three

Story Singer

1.

On 20 July 1969, I can remember walking up the hill to university.

It was a sunlit day. I looked up at the sky and thought to myself, "Two men have landed on the moon, Neil Armstrong and Buzz Aldrin, how amazing is that?"

This was the time of my breakthrough, and my next quantum leap was when Jane saw an advert for a weekly Workers' Educational Association (WEA) writing class run by writer Barry Mitcalfe.

"Why don't you enrol?" she asked.

As if I wasn't already busy with university studies and, well, other stuff. In the mornings I still babysat Carol, collecting her while Tāwhi folded sheets at the hospital, and took her to university with me. In the afternoons I took her back to Tāwhi — once she had finished her shift for the day — and wrote my essay assignments.

But nothing ventured nothing won.

The class was restricted to twelve students who met once a week in the early evenings, and Barry was a highly regarded poet, editor and educator. He had a great interest in Māori culture; a few years later he would write a book called *Maori Poetry: The Singing Word* (1974). He clearly heard the beauty of kupu, and his definition of our poetry as the word that sings is still the most apt of any description of waiata. Barry's mother was Barbara, and it was at her place on the Whangaroa Harbour that Robin Hyde wrote *The Godwits Fly* (1938). There had always been in the Mitcalfe family, as there was in Barry, a huge advocacy for te reo Māori, conservation and, of course, peace activism. Although he looked like an aging cherub, you undervalued Barry as a man and activist at your peril.

Barry's class performed the function of helping me to get my juvenilia out of my system. You know, the stories you write on the way to the stories you are supposed to write. I think most apprentices in all artforms do this. We are the masters before we emerge as ourselves; another way of looking at our earlier stories is that they are the work done in the chrysalis.

My juvenilia were mostly Pākehā stories and their contents can be gauged from their titles: "Khachaturian", "Porcelain Pig", which Barry thought was "excellent", and "Revolution", about which he commented, "the puppet clown could be the means by which the boy, the outsider, gains recognition — after all, the tragic clown is a figure of comment and ridicule, but, with an all-too full insight into human frailty. Otherwise *why* did the witch woman give him the puppet. And the clown could dance while the boy weeps."

Puppet clown? Witch woman? I have no idea what Barry was referring to, as most of these stories have disappeared into the mist of time. But Jane does remember one opus called "The Cornfield" where the maize must have been higher than an elephant's eye because reference to it always makes her guffaw so much her eyes stream with tears and she has to find a handkerchief to stuff in her mouth.

However, partway through the course, I submitted two stories to Barry, including two very Mansfieldian character studies, called "Flame" — substitute Katherine Mansfield's nasty old man drowning a fly in an ink spot with a horrible old lady seducing a moth to fly into a candle, and you will get the idea — and the other called "Springtime and the Spinster", and I literally outed myself. I actually sent the latter to the Katherine Mansfield Short Story Competition where it wasn't placed.

You can't blame me for trying to write Literature that was High Art, as opposed to fiction. The whole idea of high and low art, does anybody care about that anymore? Those distinctions seem to be collapsing around us. Actually any kind of art would have been good.

But after noting the quality in the two stories, and that I was Māori, Barry kept telling me, "Write what you know." It became a mantra with him. But what he really meant was, "You're Māori, so when the bloody hell are you going to write what Māori know!"

I was enjoying his classes so much that very soon I spent more time writing creatively than on my university studies. And I heard Barry, because I abandoned notions of high, low or even middle art altogether to try to create something different. An artisan approach that had to do with the modalities called Māori writing: cyclic patterns and the rhythmic cells more akin to my culture. In my mind's eye I had the image of myself as following in the traditions of the traditional carver or tattoo artist.

I made a deal with Jane, though it was clearly to my own advantage, to help me out with my university work to give me the time for my creative explorations — but I only cashed my chips in with her once. In English I was down to present a seminar for forty-five minutes on Joseph Conrad's *Nostromo* (1904), which I never read. Instead, I asked Jane, "Could you write the seminar? It has to last for exactly forty-five minutes, no, let's make that fifty minutes, so that nobody will have any time to ask any questions and find me out."

This was just the kind of exercise that my clever Jane liked to do — but the problem was she didn't like the book. And, the night before I was due to give the seminar, we had a lovers' spat.

The consequence was that I appeared at the seminar, began to read my (sorry, Jane's) paper, hey, I was sounding excellent! There were some nodding heads from the tutor at valid points I was making about the incorruptibility of the eponymous anti-hero. All was going well until I arrived at the 30-minute mark. I realised that, still irritated with Jane that morning, I hadn't been concentrating — and I'd left the remaining pages of Jane's paper at home.

I feigned a sudden illness, burst into a coughing fit, and asked to be excused from class. Some of my classmates later told me that mine was the best seminar given that year.

Jane, however, was cross that she had done half the work for nothing.

2.

I wrote my first Māori story in Barry's class. Like all initial attempts my hands were shaky, the pattern not thought out sufficiently, the penetration should have been deeper.

I called the story "The Faraway Side of the Hour" for some reason I can't remember; I think I was still trying to be clever. The story was the precursor to "Tangi" the short story and then *Tangi* (1973) the novel. I went from being one of the class to the Great Brown Hope.

Barry must have thought, "About bloody time."

Up until then I had mostly arrived late, running from varsity and quietly slipping in the back. There I could pretend to be deaf whenever he vaulted a question in my direction. Anyway the ladies in the class always took the front seats. There was only one other guy in class, Len, and he was writing in the Sargesonian mode. Class members were invited to present their work, but I would say, "No, thank you."

"The Faraway Side of the Hour" changed all that. Barry played a trick on me and told everyone else to take the rear seats first.

"Ah, Mister Ihimaera Smiler," he said when I arrived. "There's a seat down here in the front."

I was forced to walk all the way to the only empty chair, right in front of him. And then I had to read the story. I was so nervous I started to chain-smoke using my matchbox as the ash tray. And Mahuika played a trick on me too. Next moment, hot ash ignited all the matches and the box caught fire.

Barry was the person who helped me to define myself as a Māori writer — *to* myself. People call me a storyteller.

But I am not a storyteller. I am a story singer.

Meantime, I was still heading up the hill to do my university work. There, in Maori Studies, I was fortunate to begin my lifelong friendship with Joan Metge and Bill Parker, and to be taught by Koro Dewes and Bernie Kernot. Bill, who had a stellar career in Māori broadcasting, liked to call me Tāwhaki (or was it Tāwhirimātea?), because you could never tell what I might accomplish next. He took me through the study of waiata using Sir Apirana Ngata's *Nga Moteatea* (original two-volume edition, 1929). This volume, together with the subsequent volumes, translated variously by Pei Te Hurinui Jones and edited by Jeny Curnow, are at the source of my own spring of inspiration. Whenever I think myself into writing new work, I read the *Moteatea* because within them pulse the rhythms, the beauty, the passion and intellect — the lifeblood — of traditional Māori song poetry.

The kupu which revives the English words and makes them sing.

What's interesting is that Tā Api changed the course of waiata as a practice. Until he came along, Māori literature had been chanted. Tā Api is credited with being "The Father of the Action Song", alluding to the appearance of waiata ā-ringa around 1924 or 1925. The "new" genre was so melodious, no wonder that the songs of Tuini Ngawai, Pine Taiapa, Pararaire Tomoana, Henare Waitoa, Hirini Wikiriwhi, and then Dovey Katene-Horvath, Kingi Ihaka, Bill Kerekere, Napi Waaka and many others, are still sung today.

Sometimes I like to think that all I've ever done is follow in Tā Api's and Pei Te Hurinui's footsteps by moving the action song — waiata ā-ringa — into literature — waiata ā-tuhituhi. And just as waiata ā-ringa transformed itself into kapa haka, it has always been my belief that the next transformation of Māori literature will come from that corps of story singers.

From the transcript I see that I also took Italian, translating at sight the likes of Pirandello and Italo Calvino, and indulging in free composition into Italian. I relished the opportunity of resting from the white bread of English literature and biting into the pungent, rich texture of *pani* Italian.

I was loving Victoria University in a way that I hadn't loved Auckland. I talked about this with Helene Wong, when we met up at the Tauranga Festival in 2017 and were both on the same panel on writing the memoir; she was with husband Colin Knox. Helene's own book, *Being Chinese: A New Zealander's Story*, is equivalent to my *Māori Boy*.

At Auckland Helene had been the Chinese chick appearing in Roger Hall's university revues. She had been brought up in a small country town, Taihape. Highly intelligent, she later worked for Prime Minister Rob Muldoon, where she became the "Think Tank Lady"; at the same time I was working for Foreign Affairs.

"We were just *us*," she said. "We thought anything was possible."

3.

My main subject of course was English.

Professor Ian Gordon was the nuggety head of English and a language expert with a double degree from Edinburgh. He was popular for his "My Word" column in the *New Zealand Listener*.

James Bertram was the literature exponent of the department. I knew nothing of his astonishing history when I was taught by him. He was just this tall, austere, somewhat dapper, suave-looking man with beautiful silver wavy hair and always a pocket square in his jacket. He had been one of those brilliant academic expatriates who made their careers under the "dreaming spires", contributing to the "New Zealand mafia" at Oxford and giving the Poms a bloody good run for their money.

I wonder why the amnesia? Referring to the times, writer James McNeish offers one reason: "We boast of our infantry going to fight abroad but not our artists and intellectuals whose fight for recognition, out of the great loneliness of being a New Zealander, may be rather more difficult." Was it loneliness? In my novel *The Rope of Man* (2005) I express that same condition of, simultaneously, being both approved of and disapproved of, not as one of loneliness but as *un dilemme exquis*.

Professor Bertram was simply a shambling haphazard presence who gave lectures in an offhand way, but sometimes he would stop and smile as if having a private joke with himself; maybe the joke had to do with some self-reflection about having to lecture such fidgety students. He wasn't quite what I expected, not quite New Zealand, which is a terrible thing to say about such a man, committed as he was to defining the New Zealander. But it was hard to associate the slow-speaking academic with the young spunk in winter greatcoat and hat posing like "Lawrence of China" for the camera in northwest China, 1938. Nor, as he spoke to us across that wide divide between teacher and student, was there any sign of the fearless spirit which had driven him as a Rhodes Scholar to Oxford. Following his education there he had become an old China hand, and the Sleeping Dragon had been his obsession; he interviewed Mao Zedong, the first Westerner to do so. Then, captured by the Japanese after the fall of Hong Kong, Bertram was imprisoned in Ōmori Camp.

His later memoir, *Capes of China Slide Away* (1993), was a prophetic title for this man, returned to live among Belmont neighbours and ignorant students. Back in New Zealand he was one of Charles Brasch's closest friends and actively supported him in establishing *Landfall*.

I took Medieval English II and came across my old friends "The Wanderer" and "The Dream of the Rood". I would not have been surprised if they had exclaimed *What? Not you again! Who let you in!* And because I was repeating the same texts from the University of Auckland, I sometimes think that my final degree accomplishment was illegal, but don't tell anybody that. English III Additional, however, brought me new friends with Joseph Conrad, James Joyce — I totally devoured his first novel *Portrait of the Artist as a Young Man* (1916) — TS Eliot, Ezra Pound, Robert Graves and Robert Frost.

TS Eliot's *The Waste Land* (1922) haunts me still. And so, too, does the visit by renowned English novelist Anthony Burgess, author of *A Clockwork Orange* (1961). I managed to find a rafter to hang from in the packed lecture theatre and almost fell off it when he said that all literature conforms to the dictates of music; he was both a writer and a composer.

As for my English student compatriots, among them was Lydia Wevers.

I may have first glimpsed Lyd when she was working part-time at Smith's bookshop on Mercer Street. You could bump into everybody from Count Grotowski to James K Baxter to Denis Glover, all in animated discussion with Dick Reynolds, the bookshop's owner. He once told Lyd, "Marriage is more than four naked legs in bed" — the things we remember.

Lyd tells me we first met when we were both slogging up Allenby Terrace to our 8 am English lecture. She was such a pre-Raphaelite beauty, I was taken aback that she'd talk to me (a Māori boy), but with baby Carol on my back I must have looked safe — and, after all, she was a girl from Masterton who wouldn't have known any better.

Lyd sometimes borrowed my notes, even though she surely had no need of them. A fledgling poet, she was adored by our lecturer, Frank McKay, who was dedicated to the work of James K Baxter. Lyd also happened to be infuriating as, just before most of our tests, she would appear drawn — like the illustration by John William Waterhouse of "The Lady of Shalott" (1888) — and declaim, "I am going to fail, I am never going to pass."

She always came top of the class. Ended up at Oxford, actually.

We *all* adored Lyd. Through her I got to know her charismatic boyfriend, lawyer Hamish Tristram, Margot Kennedy, Roy van Panhuys, John Morrison and lifelong friends Peter and Annabelle Rodger — they are my younger daughter Olivia's godparents. In later years, referring to Hamish, Lyd once introduced me as "The boy who fell in love with my boyfriend." The truth is that because we all fell in love with Lyd, we naturally fell in love with everyone around her. She has only recently retired from being head of the Victoria University Stout Research Centre.

Not from thinking about literature, however.

Over lunch at Victoria University recently we were talking about the need for New Zealand literary theory to start thinking for itself — and she did a riff on one particular notion.

> There is no equivalent in the reo to the verb 'to be'. There is no equivalent in Māori for "Who am I?" In Māori one doesn't express identity this way but, rather laterally throughout layers of spectra, for instance, geographically through mountain, river and iwi. What has always struck me about Māori thought is that Māori never say "My name is so and so." Your sense of who you are is always positioned spatially to past, to landscape, to whakapapa. European philosophy is based on the subjectivity of the individual. Pākehā say, "I think, therefore I am, je pense donc je suis." Māori would not say that but, rather, "I am not because of who I am but where I am." And *where* can refer to time as well as space or, rather, times as well as spaces. And spaces, well, they can be mythological as well as contemporary. You're *in* all these . . . realities.

Phew, go Lyd.

Glyn Woodbury, another close friend, married vivacious Eva Rizko, a friend of Jane's, when Eva returned from a trip overseas. Larry Mitchell, too, was a good mate, whose parents, at the time, farmed close to Waituhi in nearby Manutuke; now a finance and policy analyst (local government) Larry and other Pākehā boys like Richard Parker worked with the Cooper-Smiler shearing gang when they were home; indiscernible under suntans, grime and lanolin, you couldn't tell them from the rest of us.

Then there were Simon Morris, Rick Bryant ("Remember *Mammal?*" Lyd asked) and Dennis O'Brien, all rock musos. They traded in Literature for Music, and Dennis, the one I still keep in touch with, was the pianist–vocalist for Triangle. In 1975 he was in London and played at rock's most hallowed turf, the Marquee Club on Wardour Street, where the Rolling Stones first performed live in 1962. Dennis now owns Slowboat Records in Cuba Street, selling secondhand music to nostalgia buffs remembering the good old days of the real rockers.

Taunoa Kohere was a *rara avis* negotiating the higher stratospheres of Pākehā knowledge. Taken up by the academic literati, he was the only other Māori I ever encountered at Stage III. He was a beautiful young man whom James Bertram considered one of his most gifted students and someone likely to have become a writer of distinction.

Peter Walker, author of *The Fox Boy: The Story of an Abducted Child* (2001), refers to Taunoa as having a "clever and curious long-lost gaze".

He was actually a cousin of mine, although I didn't know it. When he died, while still a student, and I discovered our whānaungatanga, I was deeply remorseful.

Why hadn't I known?

Chapter Forty-Four

Gifts from Rarohenga

1.

A sideshow machine at Wellington Trades Fair gave me a character analysis.

Maybe there was a ghost in the machine, perhaps Mahuika or Whaitiri, just waiting to let me have it between the eyes. Just so you know, Witi.

> Your attractions are many. Both practical and idealistic, you usually dominate your environment and make a profound impression on those around you. You are drawn to anyone with literary or artistic gifts, yet you do not want to do without the bread of life. So love in a cottage is not really your scene. Curiosity about life drives you to wish to feel many emotions.
>
> You grasp at straws of experience, stuff them away in your memory box. You are capable of more joyousness than many of your contemporaries, but can also hand out more unhappiness than most . . .

2.

With the above prophetic warnings in mind, let's bring in the final of all the myths which most contributed to my thinking and theorising as a Māori writer.

It's the thrilling "search and rescue" narrative of the hero, Mataora, into the Underworld. What he brought back from Rarohenga was as important as what Ruatepupuke had returned with from Tangaroa's domain. This was the art of tā moko (tattoo). Indeed, a case can be made for tattoo as our first writing. It was our first inscription of meaning, albeit on skin.

As we shall see, however, Mataora brought back much more than that.

The story initially posits Mataora's quest within the classic male trope. Nobly born, he is a chieftain and, from the beginning, destined to become a hero. Late one night while sleeping he hears sounds outside his sleeping house. They are different from the usual rustle of flax in the midnight wind or cry of an owl navigating the face of the moon.

He reaches for his fighting staff and cries out, "Who's there?"

His enquiry brings forth a group of shimmering visitors, the like of which he has never seen before. They are just as surprised at his powerful, dark appearance. He looks as if he could dominate the universe.

"Are you a man or a god?" they ask.

The question is not surprising as humankind and atua are the main inhabitants of the World Above, and Mataora is clearly not a monster.

The travelling party has ascended from Rarohenga. The World Below would be a better description than the Underworld, which has unfortunate European connotations.

It's the realm of Hinenuitepō, the great Mother of The Night, as well as the domain of spirit tribes who serve her. And it begs a question: If Hinenuitepō rules both Rarohenga and Te Pō, are they the same world? Regarding the latter, Te Pō has always been positioned as a period during the creation of the Māori universe: first there was Te Kore, The Void; after Te Kore came Te Pō, The Night; and following Te Pō arrived Te Ao Mārama, The Dawn of Light. By comparison, Rarohenga has a more specific location.

Bearing in mind Māori physics, perhaps we could posit the great mother as the axis around which both realms revolve, double helixes spiralling so fast that the distinctions resolve themselves — time and space — into the one singularity. Is Hinenuitepō therefore the agent by whom the universe is able to expand and contract and connect with fluid time? Through her, do ora (life) and mate (death) find balance and harmony?

Mataora's visitors emerge out of the darkness. Their appearance takes his breath away. They are not quite human. On the other hand, they are not inhuman.

"What are you?" he asks in a hoarse voice.

They are extraordinary beings, and they have crossed the border into Te Ao Tūroa at a place solely located at Poutererangi — a location in time as well as space — where Te Kūwatawata, its guardian, regulates the entrance.

You will recall that the god Tāne sought ingress at this same crossing when pursuing Hinetītama, girl of the dawn. And Māui, also, negotiated at the gateway with Te Kūwatawata when seeking to defeat Hinenuitepō and thereby bring immortality to humankind.

Māui's father, Makeatūtara, had earlier made the crossing to become, like Hinenuitepō, a guardian of the underworld. He was fortuitously positioned, wasn't he, to mourn over his son when Māui failed his task? Indeed some people put the blame for the non-fulfilment entirely on Makeatūtara because, when Māui had been born, Makeatūtara incorrectly recited the correct prayers at his baptism.

Imagine the gateway as a busy thoroughfare. Human tohunga and priests, wishing to visit the sacred sites of instruction and learning within Rarohenga, gather eagerly on the Te Ao Tūroa side of the tollgate. Meanwhile on the Rarohenga side, multicoloured subjects of that world, curious, wide-eyed tourists in rich, scintillating gowns, wait to rush into our world to visit its fabled sites.

And to Mataora's question his visitors reply, musically, "We are tūrehu."

They are a fabulous and stunningly beautiful tour group which has come through the gateway to pass among the tāngata of the human world. Maybe their itinerary includes visiting the Waitomo Caves or the hot pools at Whakarewarewa, for these locations are much talked about in Rarohenga as being among the wonders of the World Above.

Pākehā chroniclers equate tūrehu with "fairies", ugh. While it might be true that the visitors are ethereal, fair-haired and fair-skinned, they are not elven or gnomic. Imagining them as such, diminutive with red hair, is probably some wish fulfilment by those searching for the Celtic in indigenous histories. I like to think of them, rather, as Ngā Tūrehu, an earlier form of humankind, serving the great mother. Perhaps they are an interspecies, close enough to the DNA of Māori to be able to couple with humans and to bear children.

Mataora's tūrehu are distinctive in another way.

They are all aristocratic young women and are probably looking for a good night out on the town with some lowly lucky likely local lads. The beauty among them is Niwareka, who holds a very high rank in Rarohenga. In fact, although Mataora is human, Niwareka's tūrehu lineage is higher than his. Her father is Uetonga and she is fourth-generation direct descendant from Rūaumoko, the youngest of the god brothers.

She is also second-generation mokopuna of the great mother herself.

You can see, can't you, that the Mataora–Niwareka story is rich in detail and meaning. It's a story that has multiple strands and ambiguities, some caused by terrible interpretations of what Rarohenga is, and who tūrehu were — oh, so many acts of wilful interpretation have been perpetrated which rob the story of its original insights. And information freely available on the internet still maintains the totally disgusting, damaging, colonised readings of the contexts as well as the text itself.

Suffice to say that Niwareka and her entourage dance. The dancing is stately and unlike any that Mataora has ever seen. Not like the haka boogie kapa haka of modern performance, which completely robs Māori women of all desirability. Rather, the dancing is slow, sensual and scorching to the senses. During the dance, Mataora falls in love with Niwareka as she shimmers in the moonlight, tantalising him with her beauty. She is a being of glittering light, and moonbeams swirl around her.

And she is drawn closer and closer to the warrior chief. Indeed there is one part of his body that absolutely fascinates her.

The tattoo on Mataora's face.

Entranced, she touches the moko . . . and, impermanent, it smears.

Mataora begins to romance Niwareka and, after a time, he asks her to marry him. She accepts his proposal. They are happy for a while, and Mataora's kinsmen are entranced by Niwareka's strange beauty.

One day, however, Mataora notices that his older brother Tautoru is paying too much attention to his wife. Jealous, you might expect him to fight Tautoru.

Instead, he beats Niwareka. Savagely. Perhaps because she is too beautiful and he wishes to destroy that element of her that makes her so desirable to other men. Such is the way of the male who, rather than fight his brother, takes it out on the female spouse.

The beating shocks Niwareka. Is Mataora really the hero that the texts make him?

"Surely, I have not deserved this," Niwareka says to herself.

She has probably seen enough of humankind to know that an upraised hand is the way all men reprimand their women. And it is not in her nature to wait around for another backhander. Accordingly she wraps a cloak around her and, fleeing from Mataora, makes her way to the gateway. Gaining entrance from Te Kūwatawata, she descends swiftly into Rarohenga.

At least Mataora redeems himself by being penitent. Remorseful and distressed, he dresses in his finest cloak, kilt and ornaments. He paints on his tattoo, applying the colours and lines carefully, and tracks Niwareka to Poutererangi.

"Has a woman passed this way?" he asks the gatekeeper when he reaches the border crossing.

"What is she like?"

"She is beautiful and pale, with long transparent hair, like īnanga, and fair skin, and a straight nose."

"A woman of that description passed this way many days ago, weeping as she went."

"May I follow her?"

"Only if you have the courage."

"I do."

Will Te Kūwatawata let Mataora cross the border?

Well, this all depends on Mataora abiding by the rules of entry. And the regulations appear to be of a similar kind to those any traveller must declare when going through modern-day Customs. No food, no currency that might be used for commercial purposes and, above all, Mataora must, when leaving, acknowledge possession of taxable income or dutifiable goods — and, of course he will not be allowed to take tapu or sacred taonga out of Rarohenga. All countries these days have such rules to stop the thieving that has occurred in the past of one country's artefacts by another.

Mataora makes his inward Customs declaration, and Te Kūwatawata steps aside. "Enquire of Tīwaiwaka for further directions," he tells the chieftain.

Tīwaiwaka is the very same fantail that accompanied Māui in his own journey through Rarohenga — and which laughed when the demigod tried to conquer Hinenuitepō. The bird's account of Niwareka's appearance is graphic.

"Her eyes were red with weeping," he tells Mataora. "She has passed on with swollen eyes and hanging lips."

All our assumptions of what the story is going to be about are overturned.

The quest motif widens to become a complex narrative exploring domestic violence, marital love and forgiveness. It makes the story one of the most rewarding and nuanced in our literature.

Hints at Niwareka's constancy.

And Mataora's disturbing psyche.

Chapter Forty-Five

Double Helix Play

1.

Jane left the Post Office and began a career in teaching. Because she had a master's degree, she wasn't required to go to training college. She quickly obtained a job at Wellington High School and then at her old school, Wellington East Girls' College.

Our life expanded with new friendships via the education link, such as novelist Anne Holden, who was the writer of the highly influential book *Rata* (1965); she was a Pākehā writing about Māori. Anne's one of the very few New Zealand writers to have had a Hollywood movie made of her work, *The Witnesses* (1971).

Photographer Warwick Teague breezed into our lives. Laconic and lanky, he gave me the photograph which inspired me to write "Big Brother, Little Sister", as I have earlier related. Then there were Angela Sears and, through her, Mike Nicolaidi, lovely Marie and John Bullock, Margaret and Ian Hindmarsh, and Max Broadbent and Coral Atkinson. Max was a librarian and bibliographer at the time. Coral, later in life, became a publisher and wrote the novels, *The Love Apple* (2005) and *The Paua Orchard* (2006).

Meanwhile, Jane also kept a weather eye out on my progress as a writer. Halfway through 1969, she realised that I had enough short stories to put together in a collection.

"I think you're ready," she said one evening.

I agreed, "I have to get serious about this," and I called the manuscript *Exercises for the Left Hand*. I did the hardest thing for all writers to do, and let the manuscript go. In so doing I was buoyed by a letter from George Webby, then principal lecturer in drama at teachers' college, to whom my writing tutor Barry had sent some of my work. George wrote, "I think, every writer writes for an audience in the long term (even if it is for himself in the short term). He also cries out for that spark of recognition where the reader says 'Yes, that is what it is like, why could I not have said that?' And, of course, the more it *is* like it is, the less likely it is for us ordinary folk to be able to say it."

Yes, I was yearning for recognition. I wrapped *Exercises* in brown paper, looked up the address of Albion Wright, Janet Frame's publisher at Pegasus Press and, with all the bravado of youth, sent it to him. May as well aim for the top, eh.

I returned to the Post Office after sitting my exams in October, and, not long after, Mr Wright returned *Exercises* with a rejection letter. He was very kind to a writer too stupid to know that a volume of short stories was normally the collection of the very best pieces of an established author of reputation, selected over a number of years, and sometimes curated by an authoritative figure. And who was I? Some hick town hori from Waituhi.

However, "Did you know the publisher of *Landfall*, Robin Dudding, works out of the Caxton Press here?" he asked. "Why don't you send him some of your stories?"

By that time, I had already begun to write my novel *Tangi*. I caught those ancestors in the room behind my eyes asleep on the job. They sat up, wiped the pīkare out of their eyes, watched up and listened up.

How do I start writing a novel? *You start from the beginning.* Where is the beginning? *Don't ask us! Just start is the main thing and see where you end up.* What do you mean, end up? *Maybe if you write the end first your novel will have a destination to head for.* That's a good idea. My hero is a boy named Tama Mahana and, after the tangi, he is at the Gisborne railway station saying goodbye to his mother and sisters. *So Tama will tell his own story?* Yes, in first-person present though, maybe, I could tell it as a narrator in third-person past. *What's the difference?* If I as narrator tell the story, I can observe everything from above, as if I were God. *And we know you like to play God, don't we? No, tell it as Tama experiences the story, that will enable him rather than you to express his emotions in a more intimate and personal way.* But he will only see what he sees, whereas the narrator can observe everything. *What's wrong with that? You're not convinced?* No. Okay . . . what style do you reckon? *Waiata tangi of course. Oh, ka nui tō pātai, if you keep on asking these questions you'll never get started! And we have been waiting like, for-everrrr.* But what if things get difficult? *You know how to sculpt an elephant out of stone, don't you?* What do you guys know about elephants? *If you can't sculpt the elephant, carve away everything that isn't the elephant.*

All of a sudden the room behind my eyes began to swirl with stars. I felt many hands pushing me around and around, and I had the sense of becoming a Māori mevlevi, a whirling dervish twirling around and around in the same spot.

One last question. What happens if I get writer's block? *You won't.* How can you guys be so sure? *You know the reason yourself. Now sing your song, e* Witsh, *open your throat, waiata atu tō waiata ki te ao, so that all the world may hear.*

All that spinning. Before I knew it I had written ninety-seven pages of the novel. I flicked them off to Robin Dudding, along with short stories with titles like "Do You Like Khachaturian?" and "Liebestod", and some poems. Yes, I was trying poetry too.

2.

Nothing could slow me down. Undaunted by one rejection, I sent *Exercises* to Wellington firm AH & AW Reed where Tom Kennedy and Ray Richards were bringing new energy to the firm's New Zealand list. Their great literary seller was Barry Crump, whose first novel, *A Good Keen Man* (1960), was followed by other runaway bestsellers.

Maybe they might be interested in a good keen Māori man.

On 4 December 1969, I received from Reed my second rejection letter. However, editor Tim Curnow telephoned to ask me to meet with him at their offices on the corner of Taranaki Street. With him was a very austere-looking woman, Margaret Orbell, who had followed Erik Schwimmer and Bruce Mason as editor of *Te Ao Hou*.

"As it happens," Tim said, "Reed next year is publishing an anthology of Māori writing, the first ever. There's one story from your collection that we'd like in it."

The story was "The Faraway Side of the Hour". Margaret suggested "Tangi" as a better title.

"Your style weakens some sections of your story and it needs work," she said, "but Tim and I like the idea of an unpublished contribution in the book by someone new."

The anthology was *Contemporary Maori Writing* (1970) and my story had just made it into the collection. The writers included *Te Ao Hou* alumni such as Rora Paki, Rowley Habib, Rose Denness, Hirini Moko Mead, Hirone Wikiriwhi, Riki Erihi, Harry Dansey, Hone Tuwhare, Katerina Mataira, Arapera Blank and Patricia Grace. I closed the anthology and, as with all writers who are given that honour, indicated the arrival of the literature at a new point of departure.

I've always been impatient. Fortuitously, Pete Smith sent me to Christchurch to cover the opening of a new post office, it may have been at Riccarton.

Mr Wright and Mr Dudding, I'm coming at ya.

Albion Wright was very kind. He told me that although Pegasus was a literary press, it also had to be commercial in its decision-making. "And you are a young writer with no reputation as well as being a Māori."

So? What of it?

"Get some work published so that people will begin to know who you are and, when you do publish a book, they will connect your name to it so that it will sell."

But as I was leaving, he asked another question. "Who will buy your books?"

"Māori will," I answered, surprised.

"Māori don't buy books," he said.

I felt somebody had knocked me to the floor, I know Mr Wright wasn't aware of the huge psychic impact of his opinion. I was already halfway through the door, no time to turn back. And then I thought, Well, fuck you Mr Wright, this is Christchurch after all, hardly a Māori in sight.

You can understand why, therefore, when I turned up to see Robin Dudding, I wasn't exactly in a good mood. His son Adam Dudding has written a memoir of his dad, *My Father's Island* (2016), in which he reports on my encounter with his father.

> In 1970, the young Maori writer Witi Ihimaera arrived at Robin's office in Christchurch to ask why he hadn't received a response to stories he'd submitted to *Landfall,* and made his point clearer by

pulling out a taiaha and performing a warrior's challenge on the steps of the Caxton Press. Robin waited patiently, then Witi said "Kia ora" and they went inside to talk. A chapter of what would become Witi's first (and award-winning) novel *Tangi* appeared in *Landfall* later that year.

By 1972 Witi was becoming a literary celebrity with the success of his collection *Pounamu, Pounamu,* but his 1973 story "Clenched Fist" which was published in *Islands,* marked his turn towards darker, more political themes.

When I meet Witi for coffee in Ponsonby he tells me about his dramatic first meeting with Robin, and how he was always grateful to him for making him visible "at the highest level". Even though Robin was supportive, he didn't mince words when rejecting weaker material, chiding Witi when he thought he was overdoing things, or being melodramatic, or boring, or superficial. They hatched a plan to work together on a book of modern retelling of Māori myths, but it never quite happened.

I didn't have a taiaha but I wish I had because I would have welcomed the chance to release my anger in a symbolic manner. I did, however, do a haka on the steps of Caxton Press.

"Are you going to accept one of my stories or not?" I asked Robin.

He took it all in his stride and, after my temper had cooled, we began to hit it off with each other ("Yes there's always a Pākehā bed in Christchurch for you and yours when you're here or passing through. Just turn up.")

When Robin finally read the stories he was, indeed, trenchant in his criticism of my dreck. I had a tendency to overdo, to push, to be melodramatic, to be boring, to treat writing as an exercise in style, to be superficial, to be too copyist. For instance, about "Do You Like Khachaturian?" he wrote, "Shades of *Last Exit to Brooklyn* eh?" Robin was the master of subtext. Read between the lines to discover what he really felt.

The extract from *Tangi* — that, however, showed an advance. Not long after I returned to Wellington, Robin wrote that he would hold it for a while longer to decide on possibly publishing a piece of it in *Landfall*.

And yes, we did "hatch a plan" to work together on a book of modern retelling of Māori myths. It was a huge project to think about then; it was still huge in 2005 when I tried to get it off the ground, without success, with Geoff Walker and Brad Haami.

3.

Back in the capital, I began my deep and grateful friendship with Joy Stevenson at *Te Ao Hou*.

When she opened her door to me, I couldn't help thinking of Katherine Hepburn in *The African Queen*.

Joy's office was always full of people, both Māori and Pākehā, it was a kind of informal salon. On one visit I might meet Māori Council President Graham Latimer. On a next visit, playwright Adele Schafer, poet Rowley Habib or writer Elsie Locke might be talking to Joy. Or the Mother of Kōhanga Reo, Iritana Tāwhiwhirangi, might have decided to wait to say hello.

Energetic as ever, Joy might be interviewing Nganeko Minhinnick, Hiwi Tauroa or Rose Pere. Then, with energy unabated, she would give me a grin and ask, "So, Witi, where are we?"

In a letter to the *Listener*, Sheila Natusch quite rightly wrote of Joy's mentorship of Māori writers. There she was pulling me, at least, upstream. She took over from Barry Mitcalfe, not by teaching me more stuff, but by making sure I had better trim. And when she asked the question, "So, Witi, where are we?" she was really asking, "What are you writing now?" She kept pushing me to pen more, new stories, like "The Halcyon Summer", trying to help me to lose my juvenile feathers and exercise my wings so that I could achieve better thrust and lift.

Meanwhile, mindful of Albion Wright's comment on making a reputation for myself, I had decided to aim to have one story or essay or article or letter to the editor — *anything* — published anywhere per month. Write, let go, write, let go, write, let go.

Even a letter to the editor counted. For instance, in February 1970, a letter to *Records and Recording* on the subject of the great Italian soprano, Renata Tebaldi.

Well, it got published, didn't it?

At one of her "salons" Joy introduced me to Patricia Grace, recently arrived with her husband Dick, in Wellington.

I invited Pat to meet me at Post Office Headquarters for lunch. I was very nervous as Pat was, and still is, regarded as one of New Zealand's finest writers. At that stage she had established a strong reputation from her short stories in *Te Ao Hou*, although her first book, *Waiariki,* was a few years away. Very soon we were meeting regularly to talk about Māori literature and how to write it into existence.

One weekend, Jane and I went out to Hongoeka Bay, the site of Patricia's marae. To get there you drove from Wellington out to Plimmerton, took a left turn over the railway line and followed the road along the coastline to the sickle of sand and sea. There, sheltering against the hills, was the marae, small surrounding settlement and urupā. When you read Pat's prescient novel *Potiki* (1986), Hongoeka leapt before your eyes.

The bay was an extraordinary place — an encounter really. One of its ancestors, Wīremu Te Kākākura Parata, was a politician in the 1890s at Parliament at the same time as my own tipuna Wī Pere Halbert. A staunch fighter for Māori, Parata donated the land that the township of Waikanae now sits on. But his generosity there was thrown back into his face when he fought a legal case to retain Ngāti Toa land at Porirua. He invoked the Treaty of Waitangi as precedent, only to hear Chief Justice James Prendergast dismiss the treaty as "a simple nullity".

Terra nullius thinking was not restricted to Australia.

In 2014 Pat followed in Parata's footsteps by challenging the Public Works Act to prevent the new Kāpiti expressway from barrelling through a graveyard. She appeared before a Māori Affairs Select Committee at Parliament to do it. Fiona Kidman, Anne Salmond, James McNeish, Paul Moon, Dale Husband and I signed an open letter to government supporting her. It was typical of Pat that, although she won her case for Hongoeka, she was more concerned with those of her relatives who lost theirs.

Incidentally, Pat didn't do it for herself. Once her case was won she gifted the land to the generations to come. In our kaupapa, I like to think that she and I are representatives of both spirals of the spinning helix.

And our axis is constant.

Chapter Forty-Six

Hoa Wahine, Wife

1.

All this, and Jane and I were arranging our wedding in Wellington.

I asked Francis Hemopo to be my best man. And Jane and I went over to the local Anglican church in Lyall Bay to talk to the wonderfully named Cyril Cooze, a New Age hippie kind of minister, to ask if we could be married in his parish. We set a date, and Jane rang Tony and Nancy to let them know.

They were both generous. "Your father and I will pay for the wedding," Nancy said. "Why don't we say a catered affair for fifty guests, twenty-five from our side of the family and twenty-five from Witi's?" The happier news that they would come to it did not dispel my foreboding about two aspects. Fifty guests in total. Catered.

With that information in hand, Jane and I trotted off to look at venues for the reception, and once we had made our choice, Jane started to talk over menus. I didn't want to look a gift horse in the mouth, and while fifty might be large by Pākehā standards it was small by Māori standards.

"Twenty-five will just cover my immediate family," I explained to Jane, counting them on my fingers. "Mum and Dad, Carol and Gan and kids, Polly and Barney and kids, Viki and Hore and kids, Derek, Gay and Neil, Nani Mini and Uncle George . . . oh my, what about the rest of the whānau? Not to mention our Wellington relatives."

Jane was on her mother's side and quite reasonably said, "You can't expect us to cater for the whole tribe. And we must have some of our friends there."

"Jane, dear, think tribes, plural," I smiled with my teeth. "You know that Mum was one of thirteen and Dad was one of fifteen. Both the

Smilers and the Keelans have huge kin associations. I don't know how I'll be able to choose."

She tried to be helpful. "Why don't you ask just the ones in Wellington? Uncle Sid, Uncle Maf, Auntie Joey and Uncle Win's widow Auntie Margaret?"

"If I ask some, the others will find out and ask where their invitations are. And catered . . . that won't allow for any extras just in case . . ."

"Just in case *what*? And you're not planning to have children there are you? This is your problem, dear, you sort it."

We were using the word *dear* in an extremely not-dear way, if you get what I mean.

2.

A wedding takes a lot of organising, and I began to have an awful feeling. One night in bed I told Jane, "I think we should sneak off to a registry office."

By this point we were both tetchy with the other, trading *dear* more regularly than any relationship could stand.

"No, dear, the invitations have already been printed. Now be a good boy and choose who on your side they should go to. And good *night.*"

The next day I did the deed, posted off the twenty-five invitations, and that evening I pulled the quilt over my head. But nothing could prevent the sun from coming up the following morning, the day after, and the day after that. And then the telephone rang. "Did you run out of invitations?" Mum asked.

"No."

"Then how come Auntie Hiro and Auntie Polly didn't get an invitation? And Dad is asking where Auntie Mary and Uncle Hape's invitation is."

"The wedding is small," I answered. "Immediate family." I was speaking softly because even from this distance my relatives up the Coast were bound to hear.

"Speak up, Witi," Mum said dangerously. "How can you expect to keep the wedding small? You know what we're like. Those people who have got invitations tell those people who haven't and, next minute, they're all asking me questions! And Dad had a hui at Waituhi, and you know how proud he is of you, he told everybody there, about seven hundred, and some of them have asked if they can come."

"Oh no," I said. "There are caterers involved, they won't be prepared to provide food for everyone. Can't you explain to the whānau?"

"Oh no you don't," Mum said. "You can come back home and do your dirty work yourself."

Things got so stressful that Jane and I were soon not speaking to each other. One morning, trying for the umpteenth time to explain to her that we had a disaster in the making, she said, "For goodness' sake, go away and do something that will take your mind off the wedding. Write a story."

I wrote "The Liar" and let it go, popping it into the mail to the *New Zealand Listener*.

Later, Jane joined me. "Everything will be all right," she said.

"No it won't," I answered.

Actually a wedding is always a great situation around which to write comedy.

I later used Jane's and my experience as the basis for a short story called, you guessed it, "The Wedding". The crosscultural madcap madness is enacted in the story as a wedding march.

In 2006, I turned again to the situation comedy, writing of a wedding in *The Wedding* (2006) as a ballet for the Royal New Zealand Ballet. It was a Kiwi effort involving New Zealand talent. Composer Gareth Farr was on board for it, as well as choreographer Mark Baldwin. On opening night Beryl Te Wiata was in attendance and overheard someone say at the after-reception, "It wasn't a real ballet."

She answered, "And I am so glad it wasn't. When was the last time you ever heard an audience laugh at the ballet?"

3.

On the morning of our wedding day, 9 May 1970, a letter came from Alexander MacLeod, Editor, *New Zealand Listener*, to say that "The Liar" would be published.

Noel Hilliard, one of the literary editors, had been alerted by Joy Stevenson that I really was Māori, and had urged Mr MacLeod to accept it.

But how could I get excited about the letter? I spent most of the morning trying to get my best man Francis in condition for the ceremony. I had been staying over at his place with his brother Richard, and we were all suffering from having drunk too much.

Around 11, Cyril Cooze telephoned me urgently from the church to say, "Your ... er ... tribe has arrived." I hadn't even had time to shave but I hastened down to the church to find Mum and Dad at the head of a caravan of cars ... there may have been a bus; some elements of the affair I have tried to forget. My whānau hadn't had time to stop off and change for the wedding – they must have left Gisborne around midnight and come straight through to Wellington – and were using the small bathroom at the back of the church. Māori are very good at ... crowd control ... and the washing at two handbasins was going along swimmingly.

Everybody was calling out to me, grinning and laughing. "Kia ora, Witi, we made it."

My sisters Tāwhi and Viki recall driving down together in a car with their babies in the back seat. The car broke down in the Manawatū Gorge and they expected to spend the night there. Some time in the dark a van went past, backed up and stopped, and Tāwhi saw that there were some boys in it. She had a small hammer in the car and got out.

"Lock the door," she told Viki.

I can just see my sister standing there ready to defend Viki and the babies.

As it happened the boys were on their way to a camp, they may even have been Boy Scouts. They got the car working for my sisters, who were then able to complete the trip to Wellington.

I telephoned Nancy and Tony at their motel to tell them the great news about the arrival of the Waituhi whānau. Uncle Hape was beside me when I made the call.

"Tell your in-laws not to worry about the catering," he said. "We've brought our own kai with us and some pork, chicken and beef. The boys are ready to go on in advance and dig the hāngi at the place where the party is."

So I then rang the caterers to advise them that the hāngi party was arriving any minute.

"With Māori you either roll with it or get run over," I said in my most diplomatic but firm voice. "It's your option, but if I was you I would go with the flow, okay?"

It was time to get ready and dash over to the church. Goodness me, it was full to the gills and didn't the whānau look absolutely smashing? Francis was looking better dressed than I was, which made me cross as I had thrown myself together and looked a bit tragic.

I wasn't feeling very good, and my feelings got a whole lot worse when Nancy arrived. She came straight down the aisle, looking neither left nor right, and took her seat in the front pew.

And then Jane arrived on Tony's arm with Anthea, her maid of honour. She discovered a beautiful sight, all those lovely brown faces, and my aunties gave her a karanga, a soaring welcome into the church which, I hoped, would mollify her feelings. Tony walked her down the aisle and then joined Nancy. Late arrivals among the cuzzies had squeezed in either side of her.

"You look lovely, Jane," I smiled at my bride.

"Don't you dare speak to me," she answered.

Cyril Cooze was splendid, I don't think he had ever seen his church so, well, over*flowing*. I said my vows in Māori, Jane said hers in English, and I may have got a few of the words wrong. I used to tease Jane, whenever she was cross with me, that I had not said "I do" but "Maybe". Tui Walker arrived, in red dress and picture hat, and sobbed all the way through the ceremony. She certainly added to my reputation.

After the ceremony Dad asked, "Man oh man, your accent. What language were you speaking?"

I knew what he meant. I could have been a Mongolian farmer in the Gobi Desert calling to his herd of yaks.

4.

On to the reception.

You know, Māori are really good at crisis management. By the time Jane and I, Tony and Nancy and the bridal party had arrived, you wouldn't have known at all that the reception wasn't supposed to be anything other than big.

The people organising the occasion had been arm wrestled into submission, and their kitchen taken over by new cooks and helpers. To be fair, they were very helpful and accommodating. My uncles had already gone ahead to dig the hāngi and put the stones they had brought on the bus in the earth.

The pork was delicious. I felt that perhaps Tony would have liked to have put an apple in my mouth and spit roasted me, but by that stage everybody was getting into the swing of things. The caterers told me later that the wedding reception was the most extraordinary they had ever had. I think that was supposed to be a compliment.

Afterwards there were many speeches, and then my whānau got back into their travelling clothes, cleaned up, said goodbye and off they went back to Waituhi.

And that's when it hit me. They had come from Waituhi to Wellington for my wedding and now were returning to Waituhi again. All in one day. Not long ago a few of them had called me "Pokokōhua". Yet they had come, willing to forgive and forget, and aware of the ties that bind.

"You can't get away from us that easily," Uncle Hape laughed.

The next day Tony and Nancy returned to Auckland. They had given us, as a wedding present, the rental of Jane's grandmother's house in Sutherland Road, Lyall Bay. And actually, I think that Nancy had really enjoyed herself. But when Jane rang them that evening to ask if they had returned safely, they answered, "Yes, and it was a lovely wedding, and we are now sitting down to a nice cup of tea."

We spent our honeymoon at Lou and Jan River's place in Featherston. What Lou and Jan didn't tell us was that they had also invited about ten others who had not been at the wedding to stay over with us — the first inkling we got of the extended group was when we saw them all on the same train.

It was a riotous weekend, full of hilarity, but with so many people around I wondered whether we would ever be alone.

One person had been missing at the wedding. My beloved Nani Mini Tupara had died on 14 July 1970. I knew she was frail, but I refused to recognise her physical diminution. It was her voice that gave everything away, being what the French call *une voix blanche*, a "white" voice lacking in body and tone.

Nani Mini was very young, she was only sixty-six. Writing "A Game of Cards" was a way of remembering her and, in remembering, of continuing to love her. She will always be my "old" Incan princess, petite, ageless eyes, her skin polished dark by the sun.

And now the tika.

You are able to write about the wedding in a humorous manner, yes, but as with all things, you and Jane will have a lot to work through. Among other things there are few Māori–Pākehā couples you can call on for advice or support whenever things turn shitty. When you are shouted down on a marae for marrying a White girl. Or when Jane is facing crap because her husband is a hori. Among your biracial friends are Noel and Kiriwai Hilliard, Rowley and Dee Habib, Fiona and Ian Kidman and, later, Albert and Jenny Wendt. But most of the time, you will have to deal with the racism yourselves.

You have always wanted to be a father. It is part of your cultural makeup, it has always been a driving cultural force as well as a personal imperative. You cannot think of a life without having your own family and, at the time, the construct of family is of wife, husband and children.

You wish with all your heart for a good marriage. Oh, you could have had children without marriage, but you had your father's example to dissuade you from that course. Whenever you think of it now, you consider that generation lacked responsibility. They led messy lives. They left hundreds of children looking for fathers or mothers. Looking for a home, a tribe, people to belong to. Looking for whānau, looking for whakapapa.

Finally, you also wanted a wife who would be a mother to your children. Oh, you didn't care about having a helpmate or someone who would support your career — or you, hers. What you wanted was someone who would be strong for your children when or if you weren't. Constant when or if you weren't. There, when or if you weren't.

You found that woman in Jane.

She was your hoa wahine.

Chapter Forty-Seven

The Forgiveness of Niwareka

1.

When Mataora strikes Niwareka, she is horrified.

Overturned are conceptions of violence, what is permissible and where it is practised. What is startling, for instance, is that while cruelty, brutality and sadism are a way of life in Te Ao Tūroa, it is unknown in Rarohenga. Niwareka feels the pain of the blow, the shock of experiencing a barbarous act, and the confusion that sometimes inflicts the victim with doubt — perhaps the punishment was condign. This is what most women have been brainwashed to think when a man hits her. And, like them, Niwareka seeks sanctuary in the house of her parents, there to recuperate from her wounds and try to decide what next to do for herself.

Meanwhile Mataora, in pursuit of her, makes a remarkable discovery.

Rarohenga is clearly not "Hell" or "Hades" as conceived within Pākehā thinking. On the contrary, the Māori underworld is a place ... of *light* ... and so another human presumption is overturned. It is Te Ao Tūroa which claims to be a world of daytime light but is in fact dark — with all the connotations of the word.

Not only that, but, unlike his own warring world, Rarohenga is a place where the people sing and dance and play, and they live together in harmony. It is as much an escape from the harsh realities of life as listening to a story, or as writing one.

Indeed, no obstacles confront Mataora as he searches for Niwareka, no demons, no dragons, no undead of the sort that the underworld is supposed to be peopled with. Darkness, evil and fear have no place there. Nobody tries to rob or murder him as he makes his way through the various kingdoms. Evil of the kind that visited itself in Christchurch on 15 March 2019 would find no purchase here. The court of the great mother is associated with peace and the inspirational arts.

And so Mataora mingles freely among the citizens of Rarohenga until, one day, he comes across a whare where people are watching a tattooist at work. A young man is stretched full length on the ground and the tattooist is cutting lines into his face with a bone chisel and hammer; the blood flows freely. Mataora is dishevelled and exhausted and he can't help but comment on the procedure he sees taking place before him.

"Your way of tattooing is wrong," he says. "In Te Ao Tūroa there is no spilling of blood."

What an upstart Mataora is to think the human way is the right way! As cocky as a young writer can be. Everyone laughs at him. And the tattooist corrects Mataora's thinking.

"Bend down your head," he says. He looks at Mataora's tattoo — painted red, blue and white. "Oh, the upper world!" he says. "Ever is its adornment a farce. Behold how the moko can be effaced as it is merely a marking."

And he reaches forward and, as Niwareka had done, wipes at the tattoo.

In so doing, not only does Uetonga belittle human moko, he also discredits Mataora's mana. If Mataora had been wearing a crown, the act of despoiling the tattoo would have been similar to knocking the crown off his head.

The plot pivots in another of those ironies which make the Niwareka–Mataora story so fascinating.

The tattooist is Uetonga, Niwareka's father, a rangatira of Rarohenga. He doesn't know that the stranger is his son-in-law. If he had known that this was the husband who had mistreated his daughter, do you think he would have welcomed Mataora? No.

And Mataora must be recompensed. "You have spoilt my tattoo," he says. "You must now return it. Or I will seek justice by killing you."

Remember . . . violence is unknown in Rarohenga. Therefore, Uetonga undercuts Mataora's mounting anger by mediating in a friendly manner. "Oh," he smiles, "let me gift you a better moko."

He invites Mataora to take the place of the young man whose own moko has just been completed. "Prepare the visitor," he tells his assistants, watching as they mark the pattern with charcoal that he proposes to etch on Mataora's face.

Mataora observes with keen and curious interest as Uetonga lays out the uhi matarau, which are the finely crafted instruments used in tā moko: the range of bone chisel blades which will produce the deep grooved lines of the tattoo; the various combs, tapers, handles, mallets and hammers that will assist in the intricate patterning; the pigments that will be tapped into the scarification of the skin.

"I shall begin," Uetonga says.

To the sound of karakia, and using the design known as hōpara makaurangi, Uetonga follows the marked lines with his chisels and taps the colour into the wounds with his tools. While he does so, an assistant stretches Mataora's skin so that the surface is always taut.

And Mataora is taken to the threshold of human pain.

Waves of agony sweep his body. They emanate from the point of the chisel. No matter how fine the instruments are, the gouging and channelling of the grooves and insertion of dark pigment soon makes him feel that his face is on fire.

Mataora must be forcibly restrained as Uetonga continues the work. Spiral shapes curve over his nose, cheek and lower jaws. Rays radiate down his forehead and from his nose to mouth. Using his own artistic eye, Uetonga adds other design elements to accentuate and enhance Mataora's own personal beauty.

Can we think of the process as a symbolic punishment as well as embellishment?

Indeed, as he is being tattooed Mataora tries to mitigate his pain by chanting a song, pleading for Niwareka to come to him.

And when the work is complete, Uetonga is immensely proud.

"You have a living face now," he says to Mataora.

Ironically, Uetonga inevitably seals the fate of all.

Unwittingly, he endows Mataora with a moko that irrevocably joins Mataora to Uetonga's whakapapa. It is a bold visual expression, not only of Mataora's authority but also his own.

Unintentionally he also reveals the uhi matarau, the satchel of instruments which will be credited to Mataora when he becomes the "discoverer" of the art of tā moko. They belong in fact to Niwareka's father.

2.

Mataora's song reaches Niwareka where, during her recovery, she has been spending her time weaving cloaks; in creativity she is attempting to find self-respect and worth again.

Can we imagine her receiving care from the women of Rarohenga? In particular from one of her grandmothers, Hinenuitepō, surely the most important kuia in the entire world? Or Rohe, another goddess of the spirit world?

Let us picture Niwareka, therefore, on first reaching sanctuary, seeking an immediate audience with the great mother of the pō. She runs into her arms just like any child to her kuia.

There, there, Hinenuitepō soothes. *Stop weeping now.*

What kind of emotions must register in the older woman as she reflects on her own abuse? After all, it was her own father, Tāne, who slept with her. Multiple times he committed incest, and from each act children were born.

How else could humankind be propagated?

Nor was Hinenuitepō a free agent. The choice was never hers. Her father enslaved her, keeping her a prisoner in a house with talking posts.

Until at long last she was able to gain the personal strength and will to escape him. To mitigate her shame as a victim by taking the guilt of the children upon herself.

And then Niwareka hears the waiata of Mataora resounding through the halls of Rarohenga. Regardless of advice from Hinenuitepō to give Mataora the heave-ho, her heart opens to him.

Isn't that always the way? Mataora has erred, but don't we all make such human mistakes? And Niwareka, isn't she only showing her divinity by forgiving him? Aren't women always doing this, forgiving men?

Niwareka follows the song to the source but, on first meeting Mataora, she does not recognise him. His face is swollen and purple from the tattooing procedure. But he recognises her and, when he begs for forgiveness, she pities his suffering and greets him with tears.

And what are Uetonga's feelings in this matter? After all, by giving Mataora the family moko he has unwittingly acknowledged the man who beat his daughter.

We don't know how the various reconciliations are effected.

But we do know that once the wounds of his carved moko have healed, Mataora wishes to return to his own world. Indeed, he is forceful in making his intention clear. When men command, all must obey.

However, Rarohenga is not his kingdom. He is the foreigner here. Therefore, try as he might to impose his human rangatiratanga, he has to face the humiliation of not having his wishes listened to.

"The matter must be left with me and my kin group to decide," Niwareka tells him. "In particular, my elders will make the decision."

Niwareka invokes the practice of having a third party making the judgement. Uetonga is of the opinion that Mataora should return home alone. "Leave my daughter here," he says. "While the practice of wife-beating might be acceptable in Te Ao Tūroa, it is not condoned in our realm."

Niwareka's brother Tauwehe, however, takes a different tack. He endeavours to persuade Mataora to remain in Rarohenga. "Your world is a place of darkness and warring clans, whereas there is no crime and no darkness here. Why not make a clean break from Te Ao Tūroa?"

Mataora is adamant. He must return to Te Ao Tūroa — and with Niwareka.

Let's not leave Hinenuitepō out of the debate. She must surely weigh the balance, and I like to think that it is she, ultimately, who has the final say.

Let us see if a male child of Tāne is able to learn to alter his ways. Yes, humanity must have one more chance.

And Mataora achieves a personal transcendence. As a tribal chief in Te Ao Tūroa, he has not been accustomed to any decision-making process of the consensual kind.

He makes a promise before Niwareka's family that he will adopt the customs of Rarohenga.

Indeed, when he begins the return journey with Niwareka to Te Ao Tūroa, he has been transformed and retrained by the Rarohenga paradigm. Physically, he now has a living face, the magnificent legacy of his stay in the world below. And the citizens of Rarohenga adorn him with a stunning cloak of blinding, shimmering colours. Named Te Rangihaupapa, "Sky of Peace", the kākahu is a symbol of all the hopes they have that a prince of Te Ao Tūroa will change not only his own personal savagery but also the brutality of his world itself.

"My three pet birds will guide you back," Uetonga tells his daughter and son-in-law. And the birds — the ruru, the moho pererū and the pekapeka (more correctly a bat) — are freely given.

But what about the other "gifts" in Mataora's possession? The satchel of instruments known as the uhi matarau. And the rangihoua papa, which becomes the blueprint for tāniko, weaving.

On the arrival of Mataora and Niwareka at the gateway — if I might make a border patrol analogy — Mataora fails to make an appropriate outward Customs declaration.

"Are you sure you have nothing to declare?" Te Kūwatawata asks.

"Nothing."

Whether consciously or unconsciously, Mataora is literally enacting theft — will humanity ever learn? On the other hand, perhaps we should give the prince of Te Ao Tūroa the benefit of the doubt.

Be that as it may, the instruments must have been of great tapu and mana, priceless and irreplaceable and of great worth and significance to Rarohenga.

Their removal, once discovered, leads to pandemonium — and an immediate closing of the border.

From that moment, only the dead can enter.

Chapter Forty-Eight

His Name was Hilliard

1.

Following the wedding, Jane and I started to save money again, this time for a delayed honeymoon to Europe.

I thought I would keep the momentum up and make extra cash from writing. And seeing as the *Listener* had accepted one story, they might accept another, right? On 4 June 1970 they went for "Queen Bee", and then on 4 August 1970 they accepted "The Child".

Noel Hilliard, whom I had not yet met, wrote me a lovely letter about "The Child".

> It is one of the very best stories I've read in my life by *anyone*.
> The tenderness, the compassion that you convey so movingly are found only rarely in literature today — and are rare enough in the works of past times too, and are found with such sincerity as you convey only in the greatest writers. You have a unique and splendid talent and — to me *most* important — your human values are right.
> . . . it's as if you've been writing for years and years and have worked through the arithmetic and algebra and the geometry of the game and are now in the rarified atmosphere of pure maths . . .

Nicholas Zisserman, Professor and Head of the Department of Russian Language and Literature, University of Otago, also wrote to me. "Not only did the story touch chords of personal memory," he said, "but I admire your story as a work of art — its language, its manner of representation in its seeming simplicity! They reveal a great writer's talent."

Nicholas was a friend of Vladimir Nabokov, so I was more than happy to bask in the association. Nicholas told me that his mother,

Hilde, a poet and also a countess, was an invalid in hospital where he read her the story. James K Baxter's *The Man on the Horse* (1967) was dedicated to Nicholas. Hilde Zisserman's poetry collection was published as *Gedichte aus Neuseeland* (1970, English version by Charles Brasch), and there are a couple of lines from one poem that I find terribly affecting. They speak of the exile's feelings when one comes to a new, strange place. And also of the hope that waiting there might be those whom one can come to love.

The third person to comment about "The Child" was Professor Bertram, who clicked onto my name. At the end of the English class after the story was published, he stopped us as we were leaving. "By the way," he began, "one of the students in this class is being published in our distinguished weekly journal."

I blushed red and was relieved that he didn't mention my name.

He had a faint smile on his lips, "Congratulations are therefore in order."

2.

Finally I met Noel Hilliard. He invited me to come to lunch, and I turned up at his office at the *Listener*.

"You're Ihimaera?" he asked. He came bounding from his desk. He was slightly taller than me, his eyes lively in a big, open face, and he shook my hand.

After having admired Noel for his novel *Maori Girl* (1960) it was exciting to meet him. "When your story 'The Liar' crossed our desks here," Noel said, "nobody was sure if you were a Māori writer or not. Some thought you might be a Pākehā writer masquerading under a Māori name, so I asked around my mates, Hone Tuwhare, Bill Pearson, Harry Dansey up at the *Star* and Alistair Te Ariki Campbell over at School Publications, but nobody had heard of you! Then I called Joy Stevenson and, bingo, she sent me a couple of stories . . ."

("'Halcyon' marvellous. 'Tangi' even better. You say his name is Ihimaera?")

"A couple of weeks later you send in 'Queen Bee' and it's so bloody good everyone wanted to take a look at you!"

Noel was forty, appeared to have won a bet, and was chortling with glee. He looked like a cow cocky, not a journalist or writer. "Come on, we're going to have a beer and lunch."

A few weeks later, Jane and I drove out to Titahi Bay for the day. Noel lived with his wife, Kiriwai, in Richard Street overlooking the sea. I can never think of Kiriwai without getting a huge grin on my face.

"Noel's in his writer's shed," she said, rolling her eyes.

"Don't disturb him," I answered. "We're in no hurry."

She introduced us to the kids, Moana, Harvey, Hinemoa and young Howard, the apple of the family's eye. "Do you want to see the crocodile's tail?" Howard asked.

Out on the sea was a low rock formation which indeed looked like a scaly amphibian lashing the waves. A few fearless skindivers were tickling its underbelly for shellfish.

While waiting for Noel, we played cards in the sitting room. Kiriwai could have been one of my card-playing Waituhi aunties, and she had a laugh that was worth a million dollars. After a while, though, she yelled out to Noel, "Hey, Hilliard, get your arse in here." When he didn't respond, she told me to go and get him.

Noel's typewriter looked like a relic from World War I. He was crashing out words on the keys. The most prominent sight in the hut was a clothesline strung back and forth across the ceiling of the shed. Along it were pegged pages of the novel he was working on — with gaps signifying there were pages still to be written.

"Once the line is full," Noel told me, "I know I have a book."

"What will you call this one?"

He whistled through his teeth. "I'm thinking *A Night at Green River*."

Later, on our walk, he saw the skindivers, still there, and began to shout at them to fuck off. He feared the area would soon be denuded of kaimoana.

Very soon we all joined in. "Fuck off! Fuck off! Fuck off!"

Following that first visit, my relationship with Noel became another in the line of older man–younger man relationships in my life. By now, however, I wasn't as interested in "the meaning of life" but, rather, how to realise my life's ambition: a career in literature. And when I discovered that as a boy he boarded at Gisborne Boys' High School while his father worked on the Railways, my hopes lifted.

If one Gizzy boy could crack the literary business, so could another.

From schooldays Noel managed to begin a career in journalism with a left-wing reputation, earlier writing for papers like the *Southern Cross,* a "down-table" reporter. "Now," he roared with glee, puffing a cigarette, "at the *Listener* I've made the high table!"

There was some deeper empathy driving our friendship. I think one of the reasons why Jane and I got so close to him and Kiriwai was that they had had a hard row to hoe as an interracial couple in the 1940s; they wanted to be there for Jane and me in the 1970s. When they arrived in Wellington, Noel had been shocked to see advertisements seeking people for jobs and accommodation which said "No Maori".

Had things changed since then? Maybe. Possibly. Better look after Witi and Jane, just in case.

Noel's entire life, public and personal, was in socialist and left-wing politics; his last book, *Mahitahi: Work Together: Impressions of the USSR* (1989) was published in Russia. He stood up for the common man, and detested capitalism and racism.

His house at Richard Street was always busy with people coming and going. Hone Tuwhare, who introduced Kiriwai to Noel, and whom Noel helped in establishing his reputation as a poet, was a frequent visitor (and his wife, Jean, was Pākehā). Among many others, I glimpsed Jack Goodwin, editor of *New Zealand Education* (and also Secretary, Homosexual Law Reform Society of New Zealand) and ethereal Jean Watson. The conversation was always political and inflammatory, and Jane and I often found ourselves still there for breakfast.

In argument Noel became a raging bull, and at the height of his fury the veins on his neck stood out. It didn't matter that he only had one lung, he couldn't help punctuating his words with a damn cigarette — one day smoking will kill him. I learnt later that, as flatmates, Noel and Alexander Fry, his *Listener* colleague, became tubercular when sharing an unheated flat.

I never knew anybody as gleeful as Noel. One afternoon, after I had spent a joyous weekend with Noel and Kiriwai, Noel asked my help.

There was a building being demolished in Wellington and he, Alex Fry and a few friends were working on a plan to save a mural. Noel showed me a photograph of it; a large, highly coloured socialist mural of workers, iconic and emblematic that would not have looked out of place in Russia. Trouble was, Noel didn't drive and, apparently, neither did any of the others.

I quite liked the idea of being the baby driver of the getaway car. But for one reason or another the heist fell through. All my life I wondered what happened to the mural. I don't think it would have fitted in the car anyway — and it may have been painted on plaster.

We began the kind of correspondence that every young writer hopes to have with an older writer. In one exchange we must have been discussing nationalism in literature. Someone had told me I was Māori to my fingertips. It may have been Nicholas Zisserman, whom I finally met when he arrived in Wellington to assess Russian exam papers. Or it may have been Mrs Heinegg, with whom Nicholas was staying, or Prof Lopyrev, who told me that good writers must have a political bias.

About the comment Noel writes:

> Tolstoy *was* Russian to his fingertips, and it is the very Russianness of his writing — and of Dostoevsky's which enhances its great technical power and facility. No Frenchman, not even Napoleon, was as French to his fingertips as Balzac; he didn't happen to be French, no, his Frenchness is the very bone and blood and marrow and sinew of his work.
>
> Only a fool or worse would try to make out that Richard Wright's or James Baldwin's Negroness has nothing to do with their accomplishments as writers. It's surely obvious to the whole world that it is the very Negro component of their work which gives it the special strength and depth and relevance that it has.
>
> If you write from the deepest well-springs of your spirit (and that's the way I think the greatest writing is produced) then your Maori nature will be implicit in what you write — not added on, not grafted on, but there, root-and-branch.

There's a photograph of Noel and me sitting together at Richard Street. In my opinion, it's the most relaxed shot you'll ever see of me. With Noel I didn't need to be anybody else except myself.

I truly loved the man. Still do.

3.

I was also loving Wellington for the great literary capital that it was. Most of the writers I met were friendly, like Ian Cross, Sam Hunt, Marilyn Duckworth and Graham Billing. But Alistair Te Ariki Campbell in those days was something of a mandarin, difficult to get to know, and he took a while to like.

Selwyn Muru, working at Radio New Zealand, was not about to make friends of any upstart who hadn't proved himself . . . yet. He had just made a radio programme on Parihaka and I telephoned him to ask for a copy of the broadcast. "Who are you?" he asked. "What right do you have to write about Te Whiti?" Then he slammed down the phone. Having no connection to Taranaki, I wanted to go where angels feared to tread.

I was being published regularly. "My First Ball" appeared in *Te Maori* in August 1970. So did "Pakeha, I Wish You'd Been Swinging Too at the Town Hall" in the *Evening Post* on 31 August, an article on the Māori kapa haka competitions at the otherwise staid and dignified Wellington Town Hall. The day after, Robin Dudding wrote to say he would publish an extract from *Tangi* in *Landfall*. I told Sheila Natusch of my successes in a letter and she responded: "3 Witis in one go — a letter, *Listener* & *Evening Post*."

I met Bruce Mason again, together with his extraordinary wife and supporter, Diana. Mason was performing his stunning one-man play *The End of the Golden Weather: A Voyage Into a New Zealand Childhood* at Downstage, I think; it must have been for the four hundredth time or thereabouts, a huge triumph. Yes, many New Zealand writers have engaged with the exquisite dilemma of being of this beloved country.

Bruce and Diana were part of the upper Wellington social set, and Jane and I always found a welcome from them both. The last I saw him was sometime in the early 1980s when he had been diagnosed with cancer. It was some PEN function or another; he may have had a stroke. We sat together in the afternoon, hardly speaking, watching the sun go down. We were two men, one old one young, sharing the sunlight together.

More writing opportunities came my way. On the weekend of 19–20 September, Douglas Drury, Michael Noonan and John Hinton invited me to a seminar on writing for television. During the morning break I found myself sitting outside on the pavement with a sassy chick dressed like Mary Quant who had just arrived from Rotorua with her husband, Ian, to pursue a career as a writer. Her name was Fiona Kidman and, of our first meeting, she writes:

> Ours was an instant friendship. Witi has frequently reminded me of the way I dressed that day: white knee-high boots, a miniskirt and a leather cap. Although there are only four years' difference in our ages, he looked to me like a merry teenager and I kept telling him he should be in school. By the end of that day, we had laughed at a great number of things, and at each other. The day didn't stop after the door shut behind us, and we found ourselves sitting on the edge of the street [Witi: again], still talking. None of this — or the conversation where we came from — seemed in any way forced or artificial. I had grown up in the North, immersed for periods of my schooling in classes that were predominantly Māori. We felt like a couple of country kids who had hit the Big Smoke. I hadn't felt so alive or joyful since I arrived in the city earlier that year.
>
> What else did we talk about that afternoon? Well, we shared dreams of becoming "real" writers, we both felt we had many things to talk about. Witi loved the movies. He wanted to "follow the yellow brick road". When at last we parted company, he said, "I reckon we're hitched to the same star, you and me."

Fiona and her husband, Ian, had bought a house in Hataitai, an eyrie from which Ian could watch the planes arriving and departing from Wellington Airport. Ian was a teacher and affiliated to Ngāti Maniapoto, and Jane and I were their oldest Wellington friends. Ian and I often talked about being Māori and looking after our wives. To keep this real, Ian and Jane often talked about being teachers and putting up with writers.

Mine and Fiona's novels seem to have coincided pretty regularly, and my autograph to her has always been "Still hitched to the same star." Sometimes we have added variations to each other like "for better or worse" or "whether you like it or not".

4.

Following that television seminar in 1970, Fiona managed to find some work as a television writer; she is one of the creators of *Close to Home*, the soap opera that ran from 1975 to 1983. I wasn't similarly successful, and found better chances in radio when Fiona introduced me to a splendid old BBC character, script editor Arthur Jones. I had never thought of radio as being a destination for stories, but he said that he would give me thirty dollars a story. The cash would come in handy in London. "They have to be no longer than ten minutes," Arthur warned, "and able to be read by a narrator."

"A Game of Cards" and "In Search of the Emerald City" were originally radio stories and they bear all the hallmarks of their radio genesis, being swift, economic storytelling. When Arthur asked me for four more, I was only too willing to oblige. They were read by my cousin, actor George Henare — a Shakespearean actor, whom I proudly watched and listened to during the recording session — and, when another six were ordered up, George read those too.

People began to notice my name. Dennis McEldowney wrote in *Outlook*: "Witi Ihimaera, who shows more signs of going places than any other young New Zealand writer with whose work I am acquainted." A couple of years later, as editor of Auckland University Press, he wrote me a letter saying that several members of the AUP committee had been impressed by stories of mine and wondered if I had a sufficient body of work for consideration of a publication in book form.

And then I thought to myself, "Hey, Witi, why not apply for a writing grant from the Arts Council?" On 15 November 1970 I applied to complete a short-story collection and a novel while I was in London. The application was passed to the New Zealand Literary Fund, with references from Joy Stevenson, Robin Dudding and Noel Hilliard, who, at that time, was preparing to take up the Robert Burns Fellow at Otago University.

I quote from Noel's reference — I can just imagine him writing with his usual great gusto and glee:

> When Witi Ihimaera asked me to be a referee in his application to
> the Council for a grant, I little thought I would be approached to fill

in a dossier on him more comprehensive I suspect than anything in Brigadier Gilbert's files.

Surely details of his educational and general background and professional training would be better obtained from him than from me; similarly details of his work to date.

I consider it an affront to be asked to classify a creative writer — especially one who is a personal friend — as A, B, C or D. This should surely be confined to primary-school annual reports.

You urge me to take into account "public interest" when making this appraisal. Frankly I don't give a good god-damn for public interest where creative writing is concerned and I don't believe anyone connected with the arts should do so.

The application was declined. But I've never assumed entitlement. The world doesn't owe me anything.

5.

At the end of 1970, I passed my final undergraduate paper and completed my Bachelor of Arts degree. Time to celebrate at parties and the pub with friends.

My ever-patient father sent me a telegram reading CONGRATULATIONS STOP ABOUT TIME STOP. I imagined him being stopped on the street, "You did well, Tom."

And so it came to pass that I graduated from Victoria University with my very bad BA. Bill Pearson, recently returned to Auckland after three years in Australia, wrote to congratulate me and to reflect:

> I know you did English to Stage III with us, but although I remember marking a W.T. Smiler in 1963, I was away the following year and don't remember ever knowing you personally. Apparently you did not take part in Maori Club affairs and I somehow escaped getting to know you. (You must have kept away from the pub.) . . . I read that you are going to Europe in March. I do not know how you are travelling, but if you can possibly travel by way of Western Samoa, you will find a fellow writer, a Samoan, who has a B.A. and has recently become headmaster of Apia College, aged about 28 or 30, Albert Wendt, who has written

stories and verse and one novel (as yet unpublished) and has been working on another.

It was good to be reminded by Bill of my long climb up the Pākehā poutama. However, if you adjudged my consequent career as a Māori writer writing in English, by the poutama's standards it is suspect. My academic transcript shows that my highest mark at the University of Auckland for English was C+ and for Māori there are two DNS in a row. At Victoria University of Wellington I had improved, my passes had moved upward and I was now King of the Bs.

But I still wouldn't trust me if I were you.

And then without telling you, Noel writes to his publisher, managing director Maurice Dowthwaite, at William Heinemann New Zealand.

If he had not done that, your life might have been entirely different.

He recommends that they take a look at your work. Maurice passes the letter on to David Heap, their rising star, to investigate Noel's recommendation.

You never were patient. Not for you, sitting around and waiting. And, after all, you and Jane were leaving for Europe in a month's time. On 18 January 1971 you follow up on Noel's letter by writing to David yourself.

Then, nothing ventured, nothing won, you fly to Auckland to see David with the battered copy of *Exercises for the Left Hand* in your carry-on bag.

Chapter Forty-Nine

The Writer's Duty

1.

Mataora became famed throughout Te Ao Tūroa as the exponent of tattoo by puncture. His first attempt at tā moko is not successful, as must be the case with all artists starting out. However, his story is one of perseverance, and he recreates the many designs taught to him in Rarohenga.

Niwareka, also, does not return without a gift for humankind. Hers is the shimmering art of tāniko, Māori embroidery, weaving.

Some people say that you may lose your most valuable physical possession — your home, your personal jewellery and worldly wealth — through theft, robbery or some other adversity but, through life, your moko will always be your companion. So it has become with my writing.

Your tattoo will also be your passport when you die. It comes from Rarohenga and, therefore, you will be recognised for it.

Ah, this is the moko gifted by whakapapa from Uetonga.

My writing is my moko. The rhythmic tapping of a sharpened bone chisel lashed to a wooden haft echoes my tapping the virtual keys of an iPad. But the difference between writing and *Māori* writing is that without the inspiration of tā moko, the inscriptions of our stories would only be superficial and easily wiped away. Unlike other writing, Māori writing is the act of creating incised patterns from our own flesh. From one line on the page springs the second, third and fourth as acts of creativity which are also acts against oblivion. The geometric designs of moko, the balance and beauty of them, and the flat incisions into which pigment is inserted, take me to kupu — to my genealogy, not any other — which is at the source of my work. And of course it is a methodology that you must have the techniques for, the skill and concentration.

Only with practice and application can you ever hope to tattoo onto the page the same complex interplay that exists in tā moko. The aesthetic language that gives expression to our own living face as writers. But there's more. As I tap tap tap away, I get the extraordinary sense of Māori writing as an act of recovery.

The superimpositions of European moko are, thankfully, only superficial after all. And it is possible to retrieve our world, our identity, our politics — our past, present but, most of all, our future — by rewriting back. When we do, the patterns shift and motifs we previously only sensed beneath the surface return to their natural alignment. Just a small correction or additional incision and the pus seeps out. With the careful placing of the chisel and opening up of a new channel, the stories are unpoisoned and the red blood rightly flows.

Now, put into place the beautiful pigment. Restore the pūrākau.

Redeem ourselves. Return kupu to its origin.

I've said before that sometimes when you shift the universe a little — by a single thought or sentence or understanding — you actually shift it a lot; you open up the future to an alternative that was never there before. But the commitment as a creative writer is something that you have to keep honing and improving and developing, even fifty years later. Only now, for instance, am I beginning to understand such things as the spaces between the tattooed designs. They are not empty. Within them are representations of te kore which balance the seen with the unseen, time with space, past with present and future — and they are as important as the designs themselves.

There's another matter. The threshold of human pain is involved in the practice of tā moko, and so it must also be with writing. Just as the blood flows freely in the tā moko process, so must the toto flow through our words.

The pain authorises us to proceed without fear. To go to those places where evil dwells or explore those depravities that men do. To write about those profound iniquities and atrocities so that those who inflict them are aware they are being watched; that we know.

To write *A Karakia for Christchurch*.

There's more. When the blood flows freely, it allows us to *tell the truth*. In my case I have always felt that I can counter the pain of truth-telling with creativity. Indeed, the moko of writing sometimes takes me to almost unendurable agony — for instance, my conscience often bothers me terribly that when I write I disclose not just myself but others too — and I can only hope for their understanding.

Dad once said about a decision I made, "Look, you made it. Now you *own* it. And *you* take full responsibility for it." Do you think it is easy to know that what I write is permanent, is there forever?

The kaupapa must remain constant.

I trust to the truth and the pain.

2.

Mataora's journey was heroic, but there were severe outcomes.

One, as you know now, was that the gateway between Te Ao Tūroa and Rarohenga was immediately closed. No longer would humankind be able to journey to the fabled world of light.

That didn't stop some from trying ... and in some cases succeeding. Among later visitors was Hutu, who sent his soul from Te Ao Tūroa after his beloved, Pare, to find her wairua and return with it. Another was Rangirua and his brother Kaeo, who sought Rangirua's wife, Hinemārama, after she had died; because she had not eaten food, they were able to bring her spirit back and revivify her body. Then there was Ririkoko who, on the death of his daughter, went to Te Reinga to reclaim her.

While we might therefore praise Mataora for bringing back the gifts that he did, what other undreamed of taonga could we have possessed?

Undreamed of? Ah! But when we dream, as all artists do, our unconscious can take us back there. As a writer, I therefore owe much of my inspiration to Rarohenga. It comes from the court of Hinenuitepō, the patron goddess of all our creative arts.

The second consequence of the gateway's closure was a more intimate one. Niwareka was forever denied the sanctuary of Rarohenga and, from that moment, should she suffer again by the hand of her husband or any human, she would have to turn to the judicial systems that exist in the overworld for redress.

Indeed, it is interesting that the party, guilty of violence towards his wife, goes to Rarohenga, to the spirit world, to obtain his forgiveness. In a sense both husband and wife approach death, but through the intervention of the wife's father and family they achieve resurrection. And by crossing back to Te Ao Tūroa, they are returned to life.

However, there was a twist. The gatekeeper, Te Kūwatawata, had not seen — or perhaps he did — the "hidden" gift of Uetonga that both husband and wife carried across the border.

And this unseen benefaction was as powerful a present to us as the arts of tā moko and tāniko because it offered the wisdom that would forever alter the way that Māori conducted their affairs with one another.

I call it the "Rarohenga" system of conflict resolution.

Up until Mataora's time, Māoridom was in a state of constant warfare. Any argument over land, food, boundary — women — was immediately answered by a declaration of war.

Settlement by sitting down and having peaceful kōrero was unheard of or, at least, not the first option in conflict resolution. Such an innovative iwi-to-iwi way of arbitration changed intertribal dealings by offering an example of harmonious existence to strive for.

At the whānau level, both Mataora and Niwareka must also have realised that they needed to establish a method by which men and women could acknowledge the existence of domestic violence and violation; Niwareka's life and the life of all women and children depended on it.

I like to believe that what they put in place led, eventually, to the development of the family court as we know it today.

3.

While I can say that my moko is my writing, and I honour Mataora and Niwareka for bequeathing it to me, it has a greater obligation.

It takes me to a memory of childhood when my grandmother Teria and I are walking in the small flax plantation at the side of the homestead.

The flax bushes attract the korimako, and Teria takes advantage of the fact that we are there with the bellbirds to remind me of a larger truth.

"Listen," she says. "What do you hear, e Wits*h*?"

There is sunlight all around but, in the breeze, the tall fluted blades are clicking together.

"The flax is asking us, what is the greatest thing in the world?" *The greatest thing, the greatest thing, the greatest . . .*

"E Wit*sh*? What is the answer? He aha?"

Although two important art traditions, tā moko and tāniko, were brought back to Te Ao Tūroa to fill a savage world with the possibility of redemption through art and beauty, one of the important aspects that we must recognise is that our work is not only creative.

It also has to do with being humanitarian. With having aroha ki te iwi.

Kāterina Te Heikōkō Mataira, in *The Maori People in the Nineteen-Sixties*, referring to the writer's purpose, writes: "it becomes clear, that if the Maori artist, on the stage, in the graphic and plastic arts, in his music, and in his poetry and writing can imbue society with this quality of *aroha,* then he will have made his greatest contribution to society and mankind".

Through art, we can and must establish governmental and judicial practices that provide safety for the iwi within a world where the messages are mixed and often extremely violent. Where the powerless require voices. Where those facing death need rescue. Where people need to be fed and have access to clean drinking water. Where the planet needs saving.

Our voice must have moral urgency. In Niwareka's sacrifice of her father's world for her husband's, we are given a duty to repay her, through creativity, for forcing her to live forever with human irrationality.

Her return to her own world was certainly closed to her. But for her mokopuna, there is another gateway — to the future — that we must ensure, through every means within our power, will always remain open.

The flax clicks in the wind, the bellbirds await our retreat so that they can return and continue to sip at the honey inside the flax shoot . . .

E Wit*s*h, my grandmother whispers in my ear, *he aha te mea nui o te ao?* What is the greatest thing in the world?

I am able to answer her now. *It is men, women and children, grandmother.*

She nods her head. *Then, e* Wit*s*h, *serve them.*

Chapter Fifty

Shimmer of Sunlight

1.

I went to see my friend David Heap and his wife, Sue, in 2015 in their lovely cliff-face apartment in Devonport, overlooking the sun-flecked sea. Describing Sue as "his wife" is an insufficient description for a vital woman who has made her own career in life, so I hope she will forgive me.

We had lunch together and talked about those early days. By 1971, Heinemann Educational had over 150 books on their list. David's enthusiasm for publishing was shared by his secretary Hilly Wilson. Although they published strictly for schools, they hoped to expand their base into the general market.

"How ambitious you were," David laughed.

I thought nothing of going into the arena and goading the bull with a few passes of the cape. Ever since I have kept provoking the taurus and sometimes been gored.

Not in this case, for I owe David for the careful crafting of a career which has lasted a lifetime. It's a story which I think worthwhile for young writers to know.

In reply to my letter, David had written:

> I mentioned my interest in New Zealand literature to Noel Hilliard when he was last in Auckland as there is an increasing interest in local writing at something more than the superficial level now. In my position as an educational publisher, my particular interest is in anything which will find a place in courses on New Zealand literature. The fact that you are a Maori writer and have an ambition to make

your mark in the world appeals to me. However, I will be quite honest with you and state that I see no point in anyone writing unless the material they produce is first-class and for your material to be accepted, be you Maori or Pakeha doesn't really matter providing the writing is impressive.

David did not pussyfoot around:

I do not mean to be pugnacious in this respect, but from the tone of your letter I think you will appreciate honesty. I don't care whether you have established a reputation or not, my ambition is to publish first-class material and to sell it. I am not necessarily interested in that which is an easy proposition; I am more interested in the future than the present.

As you can see my main interest is in literature which we will be able to keep in print for many years and which will contribute something to society but which, of course, will sell. In other words, that this literature carries out what I regard as my purpose as an educational publisher — to increase people's awareness of their own society and to help them understand it.

It appears that we both have fairly definite ideas of what we are prepared to do or not to do — I hope they coincide. I look forward to your reply.

2.

I enjoyed my first meeting, in 1971, in Auckland with David. I was only there for the day, and we discussed what definite ideas he had about publishing and what definite ideas I had about writing. I think we were — yes, that word — "goading" each other to ascertain whether we could, as they say, waltz together.

I've always liked my partners in dance to be able to swap the lead, flow, adjust, keep the tempo, add a bit of glam and sass. I thought that I had found, in David, the publisher who would join me in a dance that would be fun for us both, even if matadorial.

Hard work, yes, and we would have to learn each other's steps. And play with the cape as we ran at each other. But fun. In many ways, my negotiation with him that day set the process for me — to work with the publisher at least by the halfway mark, and to achieve a publishable text by final delivery.

In those early days, New Zealand's decolonisation was David's too. It sounds easy now, but one of the things Māori had to do was to put ourselves in the middle of the publishing landscape. Previously world fiction, let alone New Zealand fiction, was not about us; that was not the story White writers knew or their publishers wished to sell. One of the great triumphs of Māori literature was staking a claim to being published. When we did that, we were able to come in from the margins, to finally etch our black marks onto a page that had mainly been white. And the publishers joined us.

However, our work was published mainly in English. Recently, Auckland University Press publisher Sam Elworthy, after launching a book in te reo only, observed that once upon a time publishers would have required the Māori authors to provide a parallel text in English. Not any more.

And I am the kaitiaki of a new project to publish one hundred books in te reo.

In the beginning was the Word and now the word truly *is* kupu.

In the afternoon I flew back to Wellington, leaving David to look at *Exercises*. Would third-time submission to a publisher be lucky? As you will recall, in the title I had a cack-handed God in mind. I had the wish to affirm the deviant practice of the literary art. And, as you know, I thought of the book as a New Zealand version of Janet Frame's first collection *The Lagoon* (1958). Go flatter yourself, Ihimaera.

Jane and I were counting down to departure from Aotearoa. Would Heinemann give me a contract before we left?

During the month until we sailed letters went back and forth, and I must have mentioned in one that I was writing longer stories and a novel, because David subsequently wrote, "I would first like to read the three longer stories which you are preparing. We can then study the two ideas together — a collection of Maori short stories or a volume of your three longer stories. We could then look at the proposition of a novel when the time comes.

"This may not be very satisfying to you. To a certain extent we are still hedging our bets as there has got to be a lot of selection made yet before we can see what type of market we could cater for."

A few weeks later, David confirmed that Heinemann would consider a Māori-only short-story collection. "Comments seem to indicate that your Maori-setting stories are the best," he wrote, "and also that the longer stories are better than the short ones." And, "I have a feeling that it may be worthwhile publishing a set of your Maori stories with this as the only criterion."

Everything in me said *yes*. Oh, I had been going round and round the world and David directed me back home.

With that correction made to my GPS, I got myself on track.

And then about a week before we were due to leave, a further letter arrived from David to say that contracts were under consideration but . . . he preferred to see two completed manuscripts.

"Are you willing to leave the manuscripts with us under these conditions," he asked, "and will you send us your longer stories when they are completed (and probably after you have left the country I suppose)?"

I was on my way — to more destinations than just Europe.

3.

Jane and I left Wellington on the *MV Akaroa* on 13 March 1971. A year later my first book would be published. My childhood years had informed the content. My juvenescence honed the writer in me, and all that was needed was a bit of distance — and that day had come.

Thirteen is a good number for me. I don't know if you will understand this, but just as in music the diminished seventh needs to be resolved to the major eighth, the number thirteen similarly needs to find concord by going to fourteen. It is the number *in anticipation*.

The ship left the quay on a cold, windswept afternoon. Joy Stevenson came to see us off. She had a long white scarf and waved it very slowly, you could see it for miles, fluttering back and forth, back and forth. Jane and I stayed at the stern, wrapping ourselves in each other. The other passengers melted away, shivering, to find warmth and cosiness inside the staterooms.

"It's just us now," Jane said.

The water in the inner harbour was grey and calm. As we approached the Wellington Heads, however, the waves were choppy and then, when the *Akaroa* went through, the swell of the open sea set up a sublime rhythmic lifting and falling — and the colour of the water turned a startling deep blue. By the time the ship turned northward out of the Cook Strait into the open sea, the light was fading.

Where's Hikurangi? I turned northeast. In my mind's eye I saw the sun sparkle on the summit, shooting rays back across the universe.

There and mark.

Then, "Look!" Jane said.

Three dolphins came leaping, speeding after us through the waves. The moment was magical as they skimmed through the phosphorescence of the ship's wake. They wrapped themselves in it and, leaping, tossed the glowing spray with their tails to each other.

And now the tika.

I knew that Jane and I were on honeymoon, yes.

I also knew that I would be completing both *Tangi* and the short-story collection that would eventually become *Pounamu, Pounamu*. I realised that the ancestors in the room behind my eyes were confident that I would do it. They had entreated me to sing my song, open my throat, so that all the world may hear. Nevertheless, I had to repeat a question to them.

What happens if I get writer's block?

You won't, e mokopuna.

How can you guys be so sure?

E Witsh, you already know the reason yourself. Don't you remember?

Oh yes, I remembered.

My parents, family and I were out shearing and I was sleeping with my cousins in one of the quarters. How old was I? Eleven. Halfway through the night a relative woke me up and, putting a finger to my lips, beckoned me to go to another, empty, hut with him. Trusting, I followed him.

It was dark. He entered me. Soon I was bleeding. I felt like I had been ripped to pieces.

I don't think the rape was born out of desire. No, it was more sinister than that, premeditated, deliberate, an attempt to take away my tapu, my sacredness.

And yes, you do know the reason.

All your life you have battled yourself, your sense of worthiness and unworthiness. Take a bow, for you have been an exemplary opponent.

You have oscillated between unweening ambition and self-destruction. Brought up in two cultures with their own firm views of masculinity and sexuality, you have willingly and wilfully transgressed. Still wrestling with angels, you have paid the price.

You have, for instance, found great difficulty celebrating yourself. Your relationships have all been affected by your rape by a relative. Beloved of Teria though you have been, you have felt unworthy as a grandson. You have been undeserving of your iwi and whānau.

Only the intervention of loving parents and mentors has brought you through it.

In particular, your father. He reached into Te Kore, The Void, and pulled you out; every time, you never told him why you were there and he never asked. You can say the same of your mother. She always came to you in your world of moemoeā, *What is it, son, what ails you?* She was the dream swimmer; every time you never told her, either, and she never asked.

Like all parents, they came without being asked. After all, this is what loving parents do.

Your relative turned your world to chaos. Jane had said, "It's just us now," and you have to believe you are leaving him, and what he did to you, behind. The young man, aged 28, kicking up his heels on the cover of this book still lies just ahead. The photograph, taken in 1972, the same year that your first book, *Pounamu, Pounamu*, was published, shows you confident and smiling. But behind the smile you are still wary.

You must not admit the tohu, the shame of the rape, the imprint of it on your life. You must write, write, write. You have to transcend yourself, you just have to. For the sake of *everything*.

If you don't, he will win.

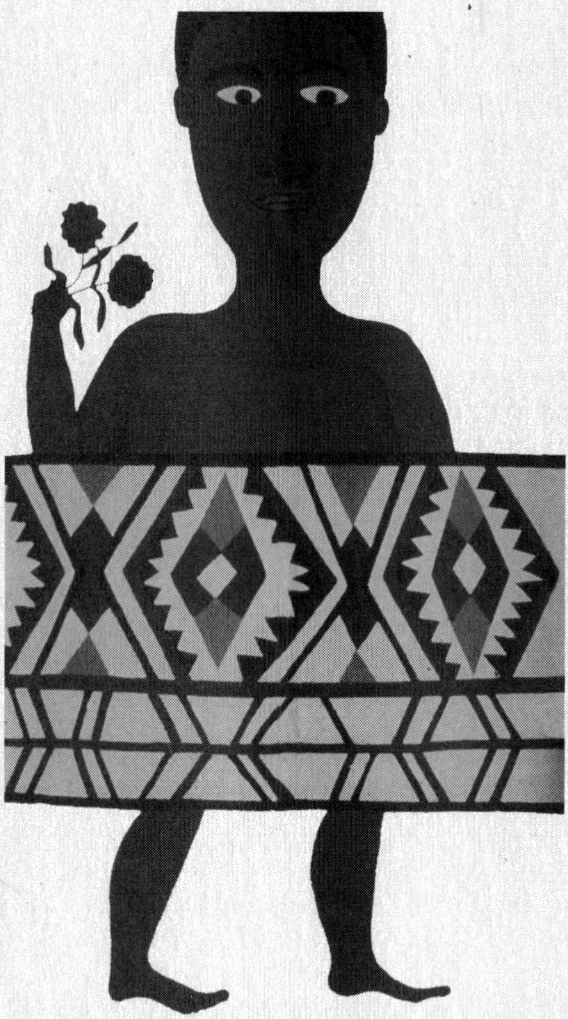

EPILOGUE

AHAU
I AM

Chapter Fifty-One

2018

1.

April, Berlin.
 And I think of my grandfather, Pera Punahāmoa.
 Many years have passed since the time in 1960 that I travelled with Pera to Te Whāiti. I was supposed to enrol at the Church College of New Zealand at Hamilton the next day. Instead, he kidnapped me for almost a week and took me on "whakapapa business".
 On the final morning of the trip, I can remember pretending to be asleep in the car — but I was really furious.
 Pera started the engine. Thank goodness, we were finally on our way.

Fifty-eight years later here I am in Berlin. It's Easter and cold on this annual festival when the Christian world, celebrating Jesus Christ's resurrection from the dead, reflects on its humanity. A good time to think about Pera as I walk along Unter den Linden and visit the Brandenburg Gate and Jewish War Memorial.
 Actually, while I walk among the gay chattering holiday throng, I have a good time with my memories. Pera died in 1972, the same year my first book was published. Did he ever understand the route I had chosen?
 Maybe what really matters was whether I had understood his.
 A few nights ago, I began to comprehend him. I saw a performance of *Adam's Passion*, a new production by Robert Wilson based on Arvo Pärt's music. After being expelled from the Garden of Eden, Adam anticipates all of mankind's catastrophes, blaming himself for them. I surprised myself by thinking, *Grandad, I wish you were with me. In your bandana and waistcoat, you would have been the most fashionably dressed gentleman here.*

Yesterday, on a tour to Potsdam, the old city of kings and kaisers, flakes of snow had started to fall. I thought again of Grandad, *Tell them I just want the old-style longjohns, the pink ones, the flannel kind.*

And then, last evening, at Richard Wagner's *Parsifal* at the Staatsoper Berlin, I was finally able to let go of my grief over him. Of what he had tried to do when he took Toroa's side — I couldn't keep holding that grudge. Of my arguments with him, head to head, about what he wanted me to be — those, too, I can't hold against him. After all, hadn't I always been disobedient?

Pera was not to blame for pressing upon me a plan of succession and, then, of attempting to resolve it in his own Māori manner. In a world changing rapidly — when rural-to-urban migration was taking the young generation from the marae — he was simply trying to secure his world the autocratic way, as the patriarch anticipating all of mankind's catastrophes perhaps, through one successor who would stay at home in the wā kāinga. Did he know even then that *I* wouldn't?

Neither of us was to know that Māoridom would find another procedure. At the tribal level, the rūnanga model of governance, providing for democratic decision-making. And at the extended family level, the whānau trust model which enables the Ihimaera Smiler family to unite behind collective leadership.

Surely, I am man enough now to call a halt to our old enmities?

I sit in the Staatsoper, and I begin to honour Pera and ask his forgiveness.

I remember that Wagner had characterised the challenge of composing *Parsifal* as, "The agonising labour of calling a non-existent world into being." That so reminds me of what Pera had been endeavouring to do by gathering the whakapapa! Of course the genealogies had not been "non-existent" — the tūpuna lived within our memories, minds and hearts, but gathering them had certainly required labour.

As the opera proceeds, I realise that the kaupapa of the Grail knights, the brotherhood living in the sacred forest, was so like Pera's as a Māori — but also as a Mormon Melchizedek — priest. Under the first King of the Grail, Titurel, the knights guard two relics which promise salvation and eternal life. They are the Holy Spear which was thrust into Christ's side when he was on the cross, and the Holy Grail which caught his blood when it spilled from his body. Wasn't Pera's guardianship of whakapapa similar?

Is there, anywhere in the world, music more heartbreaking than this? I wonder.

After the first, rising phrase of the melody, the second phrase contains an incredible haunting falling fifth, relating to the guilt of Amfortas, Titurel's son. The kingdom has been plunged into chaos by the apostate knight, Klingsor, and in fighting him Amfortas has lost the Holy Spear.

Erbarmen! Amfortas cries. *Erbarmen! Du Allerbarmer... Mercy! You, All-Merciful, mercy...*

Oh, Tolo, blood should have mattered. Kin should have mattered.

You should have mattered.

You realise that the wound that needs healing is not in Pera's side but in your own.

You have to acknowledge some cosmic pattern of reconciliation with yourself because, in the end, Pera did matter.

"I know you're awake," he said. "All my whakapapa work is for us, grandson, and that includes you. Maybe, one day, some of it will go in."

"In where?" you snarled.

"That stubborn head of yours."

Yes, my head was thick but, see, Tolo? All *I* have ever been doing has been to call a similar nonexistent world into being. Albeit fiction, my work similarly chronicles the stories of iwi and of whānau, paralleling the magnificent genealogies that link our Ihimaera Smiler family by blood, generation by generation to each other, to other tribal archives and, ultimately, to our mythic origins.

Surely, my work is not too dissimilar, also, to the magnificent carved pou, commissioned by the Gisborne City Council, unveiled just before you died? You were the genealogist on the project which traced the whakapapa of Māori and Pākehā from the coming of the Māori to man's first landing on the moon.

Oh, Grandad, hasn't your work and mine only ever been about the making of a genealogy?

Wagner's music swells. Here it comes again, that incredible falling fifth.

You have had the last laugh, old man.

Something did go in.

2.

A month later, Aotearoa.

I am the Writer of Honour at the Auckland Writers Festival. My friend, colleague and fellow Māori writer Paula Morris, is in the chair, interviewing me and I have hearing problems. When I explain to the audience that I am blind in one ear, they laugh.

The session has gone well, and I have been telling people about some of the issues I have faced in my career, its triumphs and its failures. They think I have shown great bravery, but they need to know something.

I never went back for my younger self.

The young boy I had locked away — until four years ago, I did not go back for him.

I turned the key on him when I was twenty, and at the University of Auckland, because I wanted to forget what had happened to him.

Until I was seventy-two, I left him sleeping.

And now you stand at the gate and look at the house.

Walls of towering pōhutukawa have blossomed all around, but you have found your way through.

You salute the fortress and sacred mountain that have protected the house. The sun is sparkling on the river and the valley glows like pounamu.

The curtains are still closed.

On this one matter — that I was grievously raped as a young boy — I had never been able to speak. I never disclosed that night in a small hut near the Waiapu River to anyone. Not to Mum and Dad. My sisters and brothers. To Jane or my daughters.

I wanted to get on with my life. It was easier that way.

And then in 2015 my publisher Harriet Allan suggested I write *Māori Boy*. Up to that moment I had created my life anew. I wrote another person, the older self I have become, into existence.

I created a new mythology out of an old history.

The house has three bedrooms. A back door and a front door. Windows.

You go quickly up the path to the front door. It is still locked. You unlock it.

Your heart is beating fast as you go through the house, drawing the curtains and letting the sun in. The light floods every room.

Oh quickly, go to the bedroom where your younger self is sleeping.

He still lies in darkness.

When I left my younger self in the house, all those years before, he asked, "When will you be back?"

I answered, "Soon."

He asked me, "When is soon?"

I replied, "Soon is soon."

I should never have left him to hope that I would come back *soon*. A child who hears you say that thinks you will return in an hour, by the afternoon or in the evening. I told him, "Go byebyes now," as if I would be back the next morning.

The curtains in the bedroom have been closed for too long already, open them.

And the sleeping boy floats in blinding radiance.

The box of treasures is opened, so he has been having fun with the boyhood delights and mysteries you left him. The floor is glowing with the scattering of sky-blue marbles; how they gleam.

You sit there on the bed, looking at him. He breathes evenly, in, out, in, out.

Before I left I had cradled him in my arms and told him that I loved him, not to be afraid.

Then, "I've forgotten to do something," I gasped.

I dashed into the bathroom and, as soon as I did that, he began to giggle. He knew Mum always blessed us whenever we were saying goodbye. I turned the taps on at the basin, the water flowing into my cupped hands. Laughing he ran away and I chased after him.

"I'm coming to get you!" I told him.

The water was spilling through my fingers but, when I caught up with him, there was still enough left to sprinkle him with.

They glistened with rainbows.

Let him not sleep another minute. He has been dreaming for much too long.

And so you stroke his hair. Witi, time to wake up now. *Have good dreams attended him?*

In. Out. In. Out. Then a deep inward gasp of breath. And the boy yawns. Opens his eyes. Blinks against the sun. Recognises you, and smiles.

Puts his arms up and around you, oh, how tender his embrace.

You're back already? *he asks. Then he looks at you, puzzled.* Why are you crying?

He wags a finger at you.

You and me, we never cry.

No, we never cry.

And ever since I woke him up, I have been honouring the boy. Many people contacted me after I had published *Māori Boy* to say they, too, had undergone similar experiences, and I pay tribute to them as well. And three years on another opportunity to honour him — and them — is about to happen, now that my session at the Writers Festival is over.

"I think we should sing 'Pōkarekare Ana'," Paula tells everyone.

Immediately there's a murmur of excitement. The audience loves this traditional waiata aroha, this song of two sweethearts. Although most of them know the words — after all, they are all New Zealanders — the kupu appear on a screen. With great gusto they begin singing the waiata — move over Kiri.

The song opens, flowers, and fills the Aotea Centre with beauty.

Pōkarekare ana, ngā wai o Waiapu,
Whiti atu koe e hine, marino ana e

And I join in.

But whenever *I* sing the waiata now I alter the words a little, and sing the song to my younger self. *The waters of the mighty Waiapu were restless, they separated me from the boy and kept him far from me.* The song has become my waiata to him. Whenever I sing it, I do so proudly.

And it has become an anthem now. To honour him. But also, to honour *you*. For you must never let sexual abuse of any kind define you — whether it is long-term molestation, rape or incest. It is trite to say that words are easy and actions are harder, and God knows I have spent all my life getting over what happened to me. But *you* must fight hard not to blame yourself or to let what happened blight your life and all your relationships.

Like Niwareka, you must not let abuse prevail.

Go on with life.

E tama e, hoki mai rā
Ka mate ahau, i te aroha e

The waiata soars, the song lifts, a swelling karakia shimmering in the air. *But now I'll face the raging tide for I die of love for you.*

My heart is beating, dit *der* dit *der* dit *der*.

It took me so long to go and get you, Witi. I am so sorry for leaving you there for all that time. Will you forgive me?

I can look at you now.

And I therefore place you in my whakapapa where you have always belonged.

I tell your story.

Acknowledgements

Apart from the mentors, without whom there would never have been a writing life or career, there are some special people and organisations to thank.

Anyone who has seen the film *The Wife* (2017) will know that the writer does not work alone and that, in fact, the family write the book too. Jane, Jessica and Olivia went through four years of *Māori Boy: a memoir of childhood* and propped me up for the four years I took writing *Native Son: the writer's memoir*; I'm taking a break now but I know they are keenly awaiting the four years that it will take (us) to write the third memoir, *Indigenous Envoy: a memoir of maturity*, yeah right. I am grateful to Jane in particular for her constant rigour and for reading and checking the manuscript for fact.

Harriet Allan, my publisher at Penguin Random House, kept faith with me and was patient with my delay tactics. They are her own fault, really, as both memoirs have not come out as I originally intended, disclosing matters I had not thought about since my twenties. Anyone who has been raped as a child can never carry life lightly; therefore, I have had to take deep breaths in between writing to rethink, reshape, redirect and eventually trust in and let go of the narrative of the long trauma that attended it.

Jenny Gibbs took my absences (writing) and lack of concentration (writing) with great aroha. Among other things she took me to Berlin for a break during Easter 2018, but, even there, though enjoying ourselves, I also wrote two speculative fictions, an essay on the Pacific Ocean and, most importantly, came to terms with my relationship with my grandad.

Friends Jenny Te Paa Daniels, Robin Scholes, Albert Wendt and Reina Whaitiri, cousin Haare Williams, Deborah Walker and cousin Leo Koziol, Robert Oliver, Robin and Erica Congreve, Simone Oettli (my biographer) and Hēmi Kelly and many others didn't appear to mind when I was out of whack.

I ran away from *Native Son: the writer's memoir* by travelling constantly but discovered that no matter where I went the world wouldn't let me forget it. Conversations with old friends like Maarten Van Dijk in Toronto, Judy Corbalis and her husband, sculptor Phillip King, and Russ Ladwa in London, Edwin Thumboo in Thimphu, Dewe Gorode in Noumea; with new friends like Debarshi Dasgupta in New Delhi, John Kier in Singapore-UK-Israel-Tunisia-Turkey (we were filming a documentary); and with fellow literary travellers like Paula Morris, Tina Makereti, David Eggleton and Karlo Mila at the *Oceania Exhibition* in London, or Whiti Hereaka, Selina Tusitala Marsh, Brian Morris, Judith White, Eboni Waitere, Eleanor Catton and Adam Dudding at the Taiwan Book Fair, kept me constantly inspired to chip away at the text and create the elephant.

Most of the research material comes from archives in the JC Beaglehole Room, University of Wellington. When I focused on the work, I was greatly assisted by interviews and kōrero with family, friends and colleagues who could fill in any gaps. They are quoted in the text or from their work, and I thank them all: among them Jane Ihimaera Smiler, Kararaina Haapu, Tāwhi Crawford, Ken Williams, Norman Maclean, John Jones, Tony Watson, Fiona Kidman, Lydia Wevers and John Huria.

I sought help in securing photographs (I don't take photographs myself) from my ever-patient family: Kararaina, Tāwhi, Viki, Derek, Gay and our youngest sibling, Neil, the darling of the whānau. Cousin Mona supplied some valuable iwi photos, Ken Williams lent CCNZ yearbooks, and Dudley Meadows looked through the *Gisborne Photo News*; I thank Paullee Jones for the photo of Maaka, Janet Hunt for the photo of Pat and Hone, Olivia Dawkins for the photos of Tony and Nancy and Jane, and Tāwhi for the one of only two photos that exist of my and Jane's wedding day.

The photograph inside Rongopai was taken by my dear friend Peter Coates while filming the documentary *Roimata Toroa* (1987), and the stunning panorama of the interior of Rongopai meeting house by Macduff Everton during an editorial assignment in the 1990s. When seeking permission from Mr Everton I mentioned that if anybody wanted to know what my heart looked like, all they needed to do was look at Rongopai. In allowing me to use the photograph, he wrote, "There won't be a licensing fee for a scan of your heart."

My first memoir, *Māori Boy: a memoir of childhood*, won the Ockham Book Award (for non-fiction) in 2015, and I was the recipient of one of the Prime Minister's Awards (for fiction) in 2017. Both awards straddled the research and writing of *Native Son: the writer's memoir*, and I am most grateful to have had this financial support. Thanks also to Creative New Zealand for administering the New Zealand Public Lending Right for New Zealand Authors scheme, which was my third main source of income.

John Huria edited *Native Son: the writer's memoir*. The edited draft was passed through a program that picks up inadvertent research duplication. I take full responsibility for any that may have been missed. Gillian Tewsley and Kate Stone proofread *Native Son*, and Katrina Duncan and Laura Sarsfield managed design and production. Thank you all.

As well as a family, I am fortunate to have an extended whānau and iwi. No matter that you are a writer, life happens to you, and I am grateful that Mum and Dad taught me how to work and, in particular, gave me the skills to write *through* life.

To the dream swimmer, I thought you had gone forever.

My beautiful brother, Neil Lamarr Gillen Ihimaera Smiler, twenty years younger than me and the youngest of the siblings, died in October 2018. I remember, also, my cousin, Tiopira Rauna, who died in December 2018. Ngā mate, haere, haere, haere ki Paerau, ki te huinga o te kahurangi.

Nā reira, te hunga ora, tēnā tātou.

Auckland,
September 2019

Photo credits

Inside-cover photo courtesy of Macduff Everton. Photograph section: page 1, page 2 top group photo and portrait of Witi Teka, page 3 photo of Mini Tupara, page 4 top left photo and bottom photo of Mini Tupara all courtesy of Witi's cousin Mona Tupara (McKenzie); page 6 and 7 photos courtesy of Ken Williams, Mormon Research Centre, Hamilton; page 8 group photo of Mr and Mrs Grono and friends at the Head Teachers' Annual Dinner, *Gisborne Photo News*, 3 November 1971, page 9 Shearing School instructors, *Gisborne Photo News*, 27 March 1968, page 17, *Gisborne Photo News*, 9 August 1962, page 18 *Post Office News* photos, page 28 "Pole Presented", *Gisborne Photo News*, 6 September 1972, all with permission of Tairāwhiti Museum and Art Gallery/Te Whare Taonga o Te Tairāwhiti; page 10, *Te Ao Hou*, No. 48, 1964, and page 11 bottom photograph, *Te Ao Hou*, No. 55, June 1966, with permission from Te Puni Kōkiri; page 11 photo of Maaka Jones courtesy of Mereana, Con and Pauletta Jones, page 12 "A Gathering of Maori Linguists", thanks to Alan Haronga and *Te Ara, The Encyclopedia of New Zealand*; pages 14–15 photo of Witi Ihimaera courtesy of Peter Coates; page 16 Warwick Teague photo Witi Ihimaera collection, scan of the *New Zealand Listener*, issue June 23–29, 1964, thanks to *New Zealand Listener*; page 24 photo of Maaka Jones courtesy of Gillian Chaplin (the photo appears in Gillian's and Judith Binney's book, *Ngā Mōrehu: The Survivors: The Life Histories of Eight Maori Women*, BWB Books, 1986); page 27 photo of Fiona Kidman, Penguin Random House New Zealand; page 29 top photograph and pages 30–31 group photograph by Reg Graham, courtesy of Janet Hunt, both published in her book *Hone Tuwhare: A Biography* (Godwit, 1998).